Investment Intelligence from Insider Trading

D0940603

Investment Intelligence from Insider Trading

H. Nejat Seyhun

The MIT Press
Cambridge, Massachusetts
London, England

First MIT Press paperback edition, 2000

© 1998 Massachusetts Institute of Technology

This book was set in Stone Sans and Stone Serif by Achorn Graphic Services, Inc.

Printed and bound in the United States of America.

Seyhun, Hasan Nejat, 1954–
  Investment intelligence from insider trading / H. Nejat Seyhun.
    p.   cm.
  Includes bibliographical references and index.
  ISBN 0-262-19411-2 (hardcover : alk. paper), 0-262-69234-1 (pb)
  1. Insider trading in securities—United States.   I. Title.
HG4910.S416   1998
364.16′8—dc21   98-24347
                                                    CIP

To the loving memory of my parents

Contents

Preface

This book deals with investment implications of reported insider trading. The objective of the book is to determine whether outside investors can improve the performance of their stock portfolios by using publicly available information about insider trading. This book can be used as a supplementary textbook in an undergraduate or graduate level finance course or a security analysis course. This book can also be used in a course on personal investing. Investors who personally manage their own stock portfolios should find the book beneficial, and to improve the readability of the book, statistical issues are de-emphasized and often relegated to footnotes.

The book is organized in three parts. The first part, comprising the introduction and the first five chapters, analyzes the predictive ability of insider-trading variables. The second part, containing chapters 6 through 13, compares the predictive ability of insider trading with other variables typically used in evaluating stocks. The last part (chapter 14) describes an implementaton strategy and provides recommendations to outside investors.

The introductory chapter provides background information about insider trading, discusses the investment strategies investors typically use, and explains how this book can be helpful to outside investors. It defines insider trading and also provides background information on regulation of insider trading.

Chapter 1 describes the data base used in the book in analyzing the information content of insider trading, the construction of the insider-trading variable, and its historical statistical properties and provides a brief overview of insider-trading regulations. The objective of this chapter is to familiarize the reader with some important characteristics of insider-trading activity.

The predictive ability of insider trading for future stock price movements is provided in chapter 2. Year-to-year profitability of insider trading, the effect of stock price movements before the insider-trading month, and duration of stock price reaction to insider trading are examined. Statistical properties of insider trading are used to determine if insiders sometimes manipulate stock prices. Manipulation refers to selling stock based on good news and buying stock based on bad news.

Chapter 3 constructs a stock-picking strategy based on insider trading. Additional predictors of future stock returns such as the identity of insiders, volume of trade, firm size, and consensus among insiders are analyzed. Together with chapter 2, this chapter provides a detailed analysis of using insider information to predict firm-specific future stock returns.

Chapter 4 examines the ability of insider trading to predict overall market movements. This type of information is particularly useful to market timers. Aggregate insider-trading signals can be constructed that predict future stock market returns. The ability of insider trading to predict sector and industry returns is also discussed.

Chapter 5 provides an application of the predictive ability of aggregate insider trading uncovered in chapter 4 to the stock market crash of 1987. Aggregate insider-trading signals are used to determine whether the crash of October 1987 represents a fundamental shock or an overreaction. Lessons provided in this chapter are also expected to help with market-timing strategies.

The second part of the book contains chapters 6 through 13. Here are compared the predictive ability of insider trading with other signals that investors typically use in evaluating stocks. A typical valuation signal used by investors is the dividend yield. High dividend yield is usually taken as a signal for above-average future stock returns. Chapter 6 takes the predictive ability of the dividend yield and runs a horse race between insider trading and the dividend yield.

Another signal of valuation is the dividend initiation. Firms that initiate a dividend usually experience stock price increases on announcement. Chapter 7 examines the stock returns around dividend initiations and includes insider buying and selling activity as an additional predictive variable. Insider trading is used to see if one can predict which firms will initiate dividends. Insider trading is also used to forecast postannouncement performance of firms initiating dividends.

Firms that announce better-than-expected earnings experience prolonged stock price increases. Firms that announce worse-than-expected earnings experience prolonged stock price declines. Chapter 8 examines the earnings' surprise to investigate the postearnings-announcement stock price drifts. Insider trading is included as an additional predictive variable around earnings announcements. The objective here is to test if insider trading can be used to improve the earnings-drift strategies.

Chapters 9 and 10 examine the predictive ability of price-earnings ratio (P/E) and the book-to-market ratio (B/M). These ratios are typically used in practice to determine whether a stock is fairly priced. Chapter 9 introduces insider trading as another forecasting variable that can affect the predictive ability of the P/E ratio and the B/M ratio. An issue of interest is why the B/M ratio or the P/E ratio can predict future stock returns. One possibility is that these variables capture differences in risk. Another possibility is that these variables capture mispricing. The insider-trading variable is introduced to sort out these two explanations.

Chapters 11 and 12 look at corporate takeovers and insider trading around corporate takeovers. In particular, they examine whether it is possible to predict the takeover status of bidder and target firms using pre-announcement insider trading. These two chapters also examine whether the postannouncement performance of bidder and target firms can be better predicted using the pre-announcement insider trading.

Chapter 13 examines the performance of momentum and mean-reversion investment strategies and whether insider trading can be used to improve these strategies. Momentum strategy refers to buying past winners and selling past losers. Mean-reversion strategy refers to selling past winners and buying past losers. Usually momentum strategy is practiced over short horizons up to one year while the mean-reversion strategy is practiced over longer horizons between one and five years.

The last part of the book contains chaper 14. This chapter considers the results of implementing insider-trading strategies based on a careful account of reported delays of insider trades, transaction costs, and risks of imitation. The objective here is to take a realistic approach by replicating the information available to outsiders and including the trading costs. The chapter also shows how to measure the risks to outsiders from mimicking insider trades. The chapter concludes with recommendations to outside investors.

Acknowledgments

This book has benefited from the support and encouragement of my colleagues and associates at the University of Michigan and elsewhere and comments and constructive criticism I received from many colleagues who read numerous earlier drafts. I am indebted to Bill Schwert, Jerry Warner and Cliff Smith (all at the University of Rochester) who supported my early work on insider trading. My current and former colleagues at the University of Michigan, including Kaushik Amin, Michael Bradley, Susan Chaplinsky, Kathleen Hanley, Stanley Kon, Gautam Kaul, E. Han Kim, M. P. Narayanan and Jay Ritter provided support and constructive criticism over the years.

I am especially grateful to my friends Linda Gross and Dick Gross who read the very first draft of the book and made numerous, important, substantive and editorial contributions to the book. I am also grateful to Sugato Bhattacharyya (University of Michigan), Aadil Ebrahim (University of Michigan), David Hirshleifer (University of Michigan) and Bill Robinson (Purdue University) who commented on the book and to Patti Lamberter and Brenda Falkowski who provided timely and expert help with figures.

Finally special thanks go to my wife Zeynep for her unwaivering support and encouragement for the duration of this project.

Introduction

Why is there a need for a book on insider trading?

The term *insider trading* refers to the stock transactions of the officers, directors, and large shareholders of the firm. Most investors believe that the corporate insiders are informed about the prospects of their firms and that they buy and sell their own firm's stock at the most favorable times and reap significant profits. Whether insiders are just lucky or good at predicting future stock price changes is the subject of this book.

A related and more interesting question for the rest of us is whether it makes sense for us to monitor insiders' transactions? Further, is it possible for us to successfully imitate insiders? If so, how do we imitate insiders' success? Should we simply mimic on all insider trading, or can we develop some strategy that can help us do even better? Does insider trading add new insights to the usual rules of thumb investors use to judge the valuation of firms, such as past stock price performance, book-to-market ratios, or the price-earnings ratios? Does insider buying coupled with a high book-to-market ratio provide us with any additional information than a high book-to-market ratio alone? Can we look at current insider-trading patterns and improve our understanding of recent stock price changes or dividend yields? For instance, if stock prices have increased recently and insiders are selling, is this a good time for us to sell as well? Finally, does insider-trading activity help us evaluate the long-term impact of important corporate changes such as acquiring another firm or being acquired by another firm? These are some of the central questions that this book will address. If you are interested in exploring these issues, this book will show you that investing guided by insiders will help you perform significantly better than you can by investing in a passive index fund.[1]

This book's thesis is that insider-trading signals can provide valuable investment advice. This book will demonstrate that insider trading is more informative than most other valuation yardsticks used in practice, such as the book-to-market ratio, price-earnings ratio, or dividend yield. Insider trading in fact has important interactive effects with these other measures of stock price valuation. Knowing what insiders are doing changes the interpretation of a price-earnings ratio or a book-to-market ratio.

Fortunately there is no shortage of insider trading or insider-trading information. Insiders' transactions are reported on a regular basis in the financial press.

- The *Wall Street Journal* now has a weekly column on Wednesdays entitled "Insider Trading Spotlight" which reports large insider transactions over the past week.

- The *Financial Times* also provides a weekly coverage of insider-trading information in the United Kingdom.

- *Value Line Investment Survey* regularly reports and uses insider-trading activity in their valuation estimates.

- Electronic on-line services such as Insider Trading Monitor provide continuous real time insider-trading information as soon as insiders report their transactions.

- Other newsletters such as the *Official Summary*, the *Insiders' Chronicle*, the *Insiders*, and the *Market Logic* also provide timely insider-trading information.

Why are all these financial publications concerned with insider trading? Clearly demand exists for insider-trading information. A significant number of investors are willing to pay to find out insiders' activity. These financial publications provide a service demanded by the marketplace.

Given the easy and timely access to information regarding insiders' transactions, do we really need a book on insider trading? Why not simply subscribe to a financial newsletter and simply imitate whatever insiders are doing? Buy if insiders are buying and sell if insiders are selling. What can be easier or more straightforward?

The simple answer to this question is that there is too much of a good thing. During the late 1990s there are more than 100,000 open market stock purchases and sales by insiders per year, not to mention even a greater number of private transactions, exercises of stock options, and a whole host of other stock acquisitions and dispositions. A typical small investor cannot begin to cope with the sheer volume of insider-trading information. Imitating every insider transaction is clearly out of the question. What investors need is a proven strategy to guide them to a subset of insider transactions that is likely to provide successful results.

The second reason we should not attempt to imitate every insider transaction is that a percentage of these transactions are related to liquidity concerns rather than confidential corporate information. Insiders often sell the stock because they need the cash, or buy the stock because they have excess savings. Consequently, trying to imitate every insider transaction even if we have the capability to do so would not be warranted.

Third, because it takes time to disseminate insider-trading information, as more outsiders pay attention to insider trading, corporate insiders would be tempted to manipulate stock prices.[2] If everyone expects insider buying to be good news, insiders can buy a small number of shares when they receive *bad* news, disclose their purchases, drive up the stock price, and then sell an even larger number of shares.

Hence insiders can trade to deceive uninformed traders and thereby hide their true information.[3] Similarly, if everyone expects insider selling to be bad news, insiders can sell a small number of shares when they receive *good* news, disclose their sales, drive down the stock price, and then buy an even larger number of shares. Security laws are designed to mitigate these games, but insiders also have ways of getting around the regulations. This book will not only examine whether insiders play these games but also alert outsiders to detect these games.

Finally, imitating every insider transaction is undesirable because of the costs related to collecting and acting on insider information. The time costs of such an undertaking make imitating every insider trade impossible for most individual and institutional investors. In addition the investor would have to pay commission fees, bid-ask spreads, and additional taxes on realized capital gains. To avoid these costs, we need a market-tested strategy to help the investor know when to trade and when not to trade.[4]

It is instructive to note that even market professionals have a hard time distinguishing between information motivated and liquidity motivated insider trading. Mark Hulbert, editor of the *Hulbert Financial Digest*, reports that most investment newsletters making recommendations based on analysis of insider-trading activity are beaten resoundingly by a passive market index. For instance, Hulbert reports that the portfolio of stocks recommended by the *Insiders*, an insider-trading newsletter, gained 118.9% from January 1, 1985, to June 30, 1992. During the same time period the Wilshire 5000 index, a broad market index comprising 5,000 stocks, gained 197.6%. This comparison reveals an almost an 80 percentage-point underperformance for the insider-trading newsletter. Moreover the insider-trading portfolio had 1.9 times the market risk; therefore the underperformance is even more pronounced on a risk-adjusted basis.

According to Hulbert, another insider-trading newsletter, *Market Logic*, did even worse. The stocks recommended by *Market Logic* gained 339.2% from June 30, 1980 to June 30, 1992. During the same time period Wilshire 5000 gained 432.7%.[5] This underperformance of almost 100 percentage-point once again ignores the fact that the insider-trading portfolio had greater volatility. This evidence suggests that even the professional market newsletters misinterpret insider-trading signals.

Understanding the motivation for a particular series of insider transactions is no simple task. A given insider transaction could be due to information, liquidity, or manipulation. This book uncovers when insiders' transactions are likely to signal future stock price movements, which type of insiders have access to important corporate information, in what of types of firms insiders are likely to exploit important private information, and what motivates a given pattern of insider transactions. To successfully replicate profitable insider transactions, the average stock market investor must understand the signals given by insiders' transactions. This book should provide such a comprehensive guide.

This book utilizes all reported insider trading in all publicly held firms over the past twenty-one years, containing over one million insider transactions. Hence the findings reported in this book are drawn from the universe of all available insider-trading information in the United States from 1975 to 1996. In contrast, many academic insider-trading studies use a limited sample of firms over a short time period. The shortcoming in this latter approach is that the results may not generalize to other firms or other time periods. For instance, if a sample only includes large firms, then the findings from this analysis may not generalize to mid-cap firms or small firms. Alternatively, if we analyze only large shareholders' transactions, this may not generalize to top executives' experience. Hence, to provide the most complete picture, we analyze all types of insiders' transactions.

Two Investment Styles and Insider Trading

Most investors in the stock market are aware of the two investment styles, the value-based approach and the growth-based approach. Value-based investment approach uses the book-to-market ratio (B/M) or the price-earnings ratio (P/E) to uncover undervalued firms and identify above-average future stock returns. This approach attempts to uncover undervalued stocks by focusing on firms with high B/M ratios and/or low P/E ratios, with the expectation that market participants will eventually raise the current market prices to catch up with the higher book asset values or higher earnings.

An alternative investment approach is the growth-based technique, which tries to identify firms with earnings momentum or price momentum. The logic of this approach is to take advantage of those firms that are in favor with investors. By buying firms with recent earnings growth or stock price gains, investors hope to get onto a bandwagon. In practice, the growth-based investing technique identifies firms with low book-to-market (B/M) and high price-earnings (P/E) ratios. To ensure that the high-growth firms are not too pricey, the earnings growth rate is sometimes compared with P/E ratios. Some followers of the growth-based approach select high-growth firms that are not already too pricey. For instance, Magellan Fund's former manager, Peter Lynch, selects high B/M firms or high-growth firms with an earnings growth rate that is greater than its P/E ratio.[6]

How does insider trading fit in with these investment styles? How does the information content of insider trading compare with the information contained in earnings' growth rates, book-to-market ratios, price-earnings ratios, and dividend yields? Does the availability of insider trading change the way we interpret value and growth styles? This book will provide answers to these interesting investment questions.

First, this book will demonstrate that using insider-trading information can augment and strengthen other signals, since insider trading contains an independent signal of firm value and is forward-looking. In contrast, measures such as P/E ratios, B/M ratios, and dividend yields are linked to the current stock price by construction. For instance, the P/E ratio is computed as the current stock price divided by the earnings per share over the past year. Similarly the B/M ratio is computed as the book value of equity divided by the current stock price, and it therefore contains the current stock price in the denominator. The dividend yield is computed as the dollar dividends per share divided by the current stock price.

All three indicators of value are constructed using the current stock price. Consequently the historical changes in stock price can affect these ratios mechanically. When the stock price falls, the P/E ratio will be low while the B/M ratio and dividend yield will be high by construction. A low P/E ratio, a high B/M ratio, and a high dividend yield may all signal greater future returns. If low stock prices also signal greater risk, then it is quite possible that all three of these predictor variables are simply capturing a risk premium and not necessarily identifying profit opportunities. It is difficult to distinguish whether these variables predict abnormal profit opportunities or simply a compensation for bearing additional risk. In contrast with the value or growth-based approaches, insider-trading activity (e.g., defined as number of shares bought or sold) does not depend on the current stock price by construction. Therefore obtaining corroborating signals from insider-trading activity is likely to increase our chances of success.

A second important distinction is that other stock market indicators provide only historical, statistical relations. In contrast, insider trading is the only indicator that may be based on expectations of *future* developments. Corporate insiders combine their knowledge about developments in their own firm, their own industry, and the economy in general and put their *own* money on the line. If they guess right, they stand to make money. If they guess wrong, they stand to lose money. The other statistical predictor variables do not have the wealth consequences that insider trading involves.

What exactly is insider trading?

The term insider trading is poorly understood. To understand the economic implications of insider trading, we first need a working definition of insiders and insider trading. The terms insiders and insider trading conjure up different images to different people, which causes confusion and miscommunication. A clear understanding of who insiders are, and what insider trading is and is not, should dispel confusion and erroneous beliefs about the subject.

The two most common misperceptions about insider trading are the following: First, many investors erroneously believe that *all* insider trading is illegal. This confusion arises because some transactions by insiders are illegal while others are perfectly legal. To someone who is convinced of the illegality of all insider trading, the idea of imitating insiders is similar to committing an illegal activity. As we will see later in this book, this is a misconception. The law only prohibits certain specific kinds of transactions by insiders, while the overwhelming majority of insider trading falls within legal bounds.

A second common misconception has to do with the usefulness of insider-trading information. Some observers erroneously believe that if insiders make money, then it must be illegal. These people also believe that to avoid prosecution, insiders only report their unprofitable transactions and that they camouflage any transactions motivated by exploiting nonpublic information. To these people, reported legal insider trading cannot contain any important information. Consequently reported insider trading cannot be useful as an investment guide.

While this second line of reasoning sounds plausible as a theoretical argument, it is easily testable. We have constructed a data base that contains all reported transactions by all insiders in all publicly held firms. This data base allows us to investigate whether reported insider trading does or does not contain useful information. In this book we will demonstrate that insider trading does contain economically material information, yet it may not satisfy the definition of legally material information.[7] We hope to convince the reader that reported insider trading provides useful information about future stock returns.

Let's start first with the definition of insiders. The securities laws define insiders as officers, directors, and owners of more than 10% of any equity class of securities and impose certain restrictions on this group. Our data set is confined to this legally mandated group. For a given officer to be legally considered an insider, decision-making authority rather than title is the important factor. For instance, most commercial banks contain hundreds of individuals with the title of vice president. Clearly not all of these individuals have decision-making authority that affects the entire bank, and consequently they would not be considered insiders as far as the securities laws are concerned. Another guide in deciding whether an individual is considered an officer for the purpose of insider-trading laws is membership in the executive committee of the bank or the corporation. Such individuals are almost always considered insiders. Hence, to be considered an insider for the purpose of insider-trading regulations, the officer must have decision-making authority that affects the entire organization.

There is less ambiguity for directors and large shareholders. All members of the board of directors are considered insiders. Large shareholders can be individuals or other corporations. For a large shareholder to be considered an insider, once again the law is clear. The large shareholder must own more than 10% of any equity class of securities. This ownership can be direct or indirect. Direct owners are entitled to all the benefits of share ownership. Indirect owners do not receive the dividend checks but can vote the stock for the beneficial owner. An individual, who owns 9.9% of the equity or 90% of the straight debt is not considered an insider regardless of how much influence he/she has over the corporate affairs. In addition insider status must apply at the time a particular action is taken. For instance, suppose that a large shareholder who owns 11% of the equity, sells one-fifth of her holdings on January 2, 1996. She is no longer considered an insider after January 2, 1996.[8]

The insider trading covered in this book is limited to officers, directors, and large shareholders of the firm. It does not cover commercial bankers, investment bankers, lawyers, speculators, raiders, or arbitrageurs. Hence this book does not have any transactions by people like

Dennis Levine or Ivan Boesky who were convicted of engaging in illegal insider trading in the 1980s in takeover targets. Levine and Boesky illegally bought and sold material, nonpublic information about firms that were takeover targets for the purpose of profiting on the basis of such information. Since they knew they were engaged in an illegal activity, they did not report any of their transactions, and therefore they are not represented in the insider-trading sample analyzed in this book.

A central feature of the insider-trading regulations involves disclosure. The securities laws require all insiders to report all their stock transactions in their own firms to the Securities and Exchange Commission (SEC) and the stock exchange where the transaction took place in a timely fashion.[9] Failure to report their transactions on a timely fashion is a violation of securities laws which currently involves fines of up to $2.5 million as well as ten years in prison. Insiders must report all transactions within 10 days of the calendar month following the month in which the trade took place. All insider-trading activity used in this book is obtained from these public sources.

In addition to stocks, trading in convertible securities (e.g., preferred stock or debentures that are convertible into common stock) and equity derivatives (e.g., options and warrants) are also included in the definition of insider trading. Hence insiders have to report in a timely fashion all transactions involving convertible debt and convertible preferred stock. Insiders must also report the awarding, exercise, or expiration of executive stock options. In addition insiders must report all purchase, sale, exercise, or expiration of call and put options and warrants. What is not covered is trading in straight debt. Insiders do not have to report any of their transactions in straight debt (this is nonconvertible debt), nor are they subject to other restrictions on insider trading as far as straight debt is concerned.[10]

Now what exactly is illegal insider information? Contrary to what many believe, profitable trading by insiders is not per se illegal. What is illegal is trading by insiders *while in possession of material, nonpublic* information. Hence the law is intended to prevent insiders from trading on the basis of important information not available to the public at large. Unfortunately, the definition of what is material, nonpublic information has never been made clear by the U.S. Congress or the SEC.[11] While the U.S. Congress has had two separate opportunities to clearly define illegal insider trading with the passage of Insider-Trading Sanctions Act of 1984 and Insider-Trading and Securities Fraud Enforcement Act of 1988, it chose not to do so at the urging of the Securities and Exchange Commission (SEC), which considers some ambiguity desirable. Consequently the term "material, nonpublic information" is subject to interpretation both by the SEC and the U.S. Courts. Currently there is no clear, unambiguous definition of illegal insider information. Given the criminal penalties, only a court of law can decide if a particular transaction by a particular insider was made in possession of material, nonpublic information. Consequently everyday buying and selling of stocks by insiders is not presumed illegal in the absence of a ruling to the contrary by a court of law. In this book we assume that all insider trading reported by insiders falls within legal bounds.

In most large firms there are very clear, *private* guidelines that govern the timing of insiders' transactions. First, all insiders have to obtain permission from the compliance officer of the firm to execute contemplated buy or sell transactions to ensure that no rules or regulations are transgressed. In some firms insiders must not only clear all potential transactions in their own firms but also *all* transactions for their portfolio. Hence many companies impose a higher standard of ethical conduct on their employees than the legal requirements. The logic behind these more strict, company-specific rules is to prevent the insiders from exploiting a given piece of information by buying or selling competitors' stocks. For instance, suppose that insiders in an airplane manufacturer find out that they just won a major contract. One way to exploit this information is to buy their own firm's stock. Given the current restrictions, this would be quite difficult. Alternatively, insiders can exploit this information by selling their major competitor's stock. (There are really two major airplane manufacturers in the world.) If insiders are required to obtain a clearance for all their transactions, they also will not be able to exploit this information by selling competitors' stocks.

Second, most firms have explicitly defined blocks of time when buying and selling can be done safely. These time periods usually follow quarterly earnings announcement dates by about one to two weeks. This particular restriction ensures that stock prices fully reflect the most recent earnings announcement. In addition insiders are literally precluded from trading on the basis of upcoming earnings announcements. Taken together, these guidelines ensure that insiders can carry on the task of managing their portfolios without having to worry about whether they are violating the law.

Given all these restrictions, what sort of information can insiders trade on? Suppose that the firm is about to announce a big increase in dividends. A given insider may want to buy stock to exploit this information. Clearly the compliance officer of the firm will not permit such a transaction to occur. Alternatively, assume that the firm is the target of an acquisition attempt. Once again, the compliance officer would not clear a buy transaction under these circumstances. In fact the restrictions we have just discussed pretty much prevent insiders from exploiting any upcoming, important corporate announcements. These include but are not limited to such events as dividend announcements, earnings announcements, major initiatives by the corporation, and takeover attempts. These announcements which represent low-risk, high-profit trading opportunities for insiders are off-limits.

If insiders cannot trade on corporate announcements, what sort of information can they trade on? Insiders can clearly trade on the basis of their understanding and interpretation of public information outside the moratorium periods. For instance, assume that the stock price of the firm goes down sharply. The decline of stock price is, after all, public information. Now suppose that insiders do not know anything about their firm that would justify such a price decline. Insiders in this case can comfortably buy stock of their firm (and support the market) without worrying about insider-trading regulations.

Second, insiders can and do trade on the basis of their long-term outlook for their firm, usually one to two years ahead. By their everyday involvement in the firm, insiders have a very good appreciation for the demand and supply of their product, impact of new technological developments for their own industry, and competitive developments around the world. For instance, the significant drop in the prices of personal computers completely eliminated the demand for new type-writers (though some old timers still prefer typewriters to computers). Insiders in a typewriter manufacturer can sell the stock of their firm on the basis of this public information without having to worry about violating any laws, because there is nothing illegal about these transactions. What gives insiders an edge with this type of trading is not a particular piece of confidential information, but rather their expertise that comes with experience in a particular sector of the economy.

As the discussion above suggests, legally defined insiders have to re-port all of their transactions in their own firms to the Securities and Exchange Commission (SEC) and the stock exchange where the trade took place. Very small transactions are exempted from reporting re-quirements. In addition, shares received as part of preapproved com-pensation plan are also exempted from reporting requirements. The reports filed by insiders, known as Forms 3, 4, and 5 form the bases for all publicly known insider-trading activity. These insider-trading reports are published by Securities and Exchange Commission (Official Summary) as well as by various private newsletters.

We have already discussed the restrictions on insiders relating to nonpublic information. There are still additional restrictions on insider trading. In particular, insiders cannot profit from short-term price movements in their own firms by buying and selling shares within six months. Any such profits are called short-swing profits and are recover-able by the corporation. Such a recovery can occur at the insistence of the corporation, any shareholder, or the SEC. Moreover there is no requirement of fraud (i.e., acting on the basis of material, nonpublic information) in order for the corporation to recover such profits. All that is necessary is that a profit was made from two offsetting trades within six months.

The purpose of the short-swing profit restriction is to remove any temptation on the part of insiders to manipulate upcoming corporate announcements to benefit themselves. Imagine a situation where insiders have made significant additions to their stockholdings. Without the short-swing profits rule, insiders would have incentives to accentuate the positive developments and defer or postpone any negative announcements. They would have incentives to increase the stock prices first, then sell their excess stockholdings, and then announce any negative information. With the short-swing profit rule, insiders are effectively prohibited from selling over the next six months for the purpose of realizing a profit. In this case insiders must keep any negative developments from becoming public for at least six months, which is a much more difficult task since the firm will announce two quarterly earnings during this time period. Therefore the six-month short-swing profit rule makes it difficult for insiders to benefit from short-term stock price movements. As a consequence it removes incentives to manipulate stock prices, and it aligns the incentives of corporate insiders more closely with those of the long-term shareholders.[12]

Finally, insiders are prohibited from short-selling their own stocks. Short-selling refers to borrowing some shares from a broker and selling them. The short-seller does not actually own the shares but instead borrows them, sells them, and hopes to return these shares by buying them at a lower price later on. Short-sellers therefore hope to make money from price declines by selling high first and then buying low later on.[13] Short-sellers profit when stock prices decline and shareholders lose. Since it is difficult to imagine situations where short-selling can serve the interests of the firms' shareholders, securities laws prohibit short-selling by insiders.[14]

What can we learn from insider trading?

Insider trading is of special interest to stock market investors, security firm analysts, as well as policy-makers, regulators, and the academic community. Each group views insider trading from a different perspective. The focus of this book is on the investment implications of insider trading; specifically, how investors can benefit from this source of information, although we will discuss the legal and policy implications of insider trading to the extent they help clarify insiders' motivations.

In sum, insider trading can serve as a valuable guide in stock market investing. Potential stock market investors mostly worry about two issues: Is this a good time to go into the stock market? And, if yes, which stocks should I buy? This book will demonstrate that insider trading will help answer both questions.

The decision to invest a portion of the overall portfolio to the stock market rather than to government or corporate bonds or to real estate is called *market allocation*. Some investors will decide on their stock market allocation based on their risk preferences and will stick with a more or less constant allocation. Others will continually change the market allocation based on their expectations of future market returns.

Actively changing market allocation is also referred to as *market timing*. Active investors' first concern is whether this is a good time to go into the market or increase the proportion of the portfolio allocated to stocks. The answer to this question depends on whether these investors expect stock prices to increase more or less than the average return on bonds or real estate. If investors believe that stock prices will increase, then (1) they would want to get into the stock market, (2) increase their equity position if they are already in the market, (3) borrow to buy stocks, or (4) choose stocks that perform even better than market averages in a bull market. All of these actions are part of market-timing strategy. On the other hand, if investors believe that stock prices will stagnate, then (1) they can reduce their margin borrowing, (2) decrease their stock market exposure by selling some of their stockholdings, (3) sell all their stocks and leave the market altogether, or (4) choose the safety of corporate bonds, the municipal bonds, or cash (because of their extreme safety, Treasury securities are often referred to as cash).

The second concern for all investors is which stocks to buy. This is also called *security selection* or stock picking. The alternative is not to pick individual stocks but simply invest in an indexed fund. Stock pickers do not worry about how the overall market is going to perform but rather how individual stocks will perform relative to the market averages. They analyze hundreds of individual stocks and determine whether the stock price performance is likely to be better than or worse than the market average. Hence active stock pickers would like to know which stocks or sectors of the economy have a better expectation of outperforming or underperforming the market averages. They buy those sectors or individual stocks that are expected to do as well or better than the market averages and sell those securities not expected to do as well.

Understanding the predictive ability of insider trading can help with both investment styles. This book will demonstrate that insider trading can be a useful tool for those investors who choose to time the market. Knowledge about insider trading can be used to get into the stock market, increase one's exposure, or to take even a more aggressive posture in the market. After all, most investors do not own individual stocks but rather mutual funds that hold large portfolios of stocks. Hence insider trading can help with market investing. For those readers who are unfamiliar with insider trading, this assertion may seem odd and counterintuitive. It is nevertheless true. In chapter 4 we will discuss in detail the market-timing ability of insider trading.

Insider trading can also benefit stock pickers. Potential stock pickers would benefit from knowing how large stock price movements tend to be following insider trading and how long these price adjustments are expected to last. Indeed, if history shows that insiders earn 20% from certain transactions, then outsiders stand a better chance of stock picking by imitating these insiders, than if insiders have only earned 2% in the past. Potential stock pickers would like to know whether stock price movements are completed by the time insider-trading information becomes "public" or do the stock price reactions continue after the publication of the information? If the stock price reaction to insider trading occurs within two months and insiders take three months to report their transactions to the public, then insider-trading information will be useless regardless of how much profits insiders earn for themselves.

Outside investors know that insider trading is motivated not only by information reasons. Is it possible to separate information-based transactions from those based on manipulation, liquidity, risk bearing, or portfolio adjustment motivated trading by insiders? For instance, potential stock pickers would like to know whether a given stock sale by an insider signals positive or negative future prospects for the stock or whether it simply represents a closing of a previous stock purchase.[15]

Potential stock pickers would also benefit from learning about the risk associated with imitating insiders. Is the probability of success from imitating insiders 90%, 55%, or even 40%? Once again, clearly not all insider trading is motivated by information. If the probability of success from imitating insiders is 90%, outside investors can feel a lot more comfortable in deciding to imitate insiders with a large dollar trade. On the other hand, if the probability of success is worse than a coin toss, most outsiders would not want to bet a lot of money imitating insiders. Hence risk is an important factor in determining the size of the bets outsiders would make on imitating insiders' transactions.

Finally knowledge about insider trading can help with sector investing. For instance, suppose that a sector investor expects interest rates to decline and believes that this should benefit the financial services sector. However, insiders in the financial services industry all seem to be selling stocks of financial intermediaries. Does this mean that this is a bad time to go into the financial services sectors? Alternatively, can there be individual banks that can benefit more from an interest rate decline even if the whole industry does not benefit? We could offer many other examples.

Another group interested in insider-trading activity is the public policy-makers and regulators. Policy-makers are interested in determining the effect of insider trading on the workings of financial markets. One of the most important questions facing policy-makers is whether insider trading is beneficial or detrimental to the economy. The answer to this question determines the degree to which insider trading is restricted and penalized. On the one hand, restricting insider trading can improve the returns to small investors and thereby attract more capital and thus reduce the cost of capital. On the other hand, severe restrictions on insider trading can have motivational problems and could interfere with efficient contracting between managers and owners of the firms. While these issues are very important, this book will not deal extensively with the regulatory issues. Instead, we will highlight some of this debate as it relates to the question of whether insiders are allowed to trade on the basis of special information.

Similarly regulators at the Securities and Exchange Commission are not only charged with some aspects of enforcement of insider trading regulations but also with creating rules that operationalize the statutes. The economic effects of insider trading are important inputs into the design of laws that restrict insider trading. Once again, these issues are beyond the scope of this book. Finally courts and the legal community are also interested in the effects and the enforcement of various insider-trading statutes. We will deal with these issues only to the extent that they have investment implications.

The investment implications of insider trading such as are covered in this book will be extremely useful to potential stock market investors. This book will

- document the magnitude and the duration of the stock price movements following insider trading, determinants of insiders' profits, and the risks associated with imitating insider trading;

- provide an active look at the likely performance of individual firms as well as the overall stock market based on most recent insider-trading patterns; and
- compare and contrast the information content of insider trading with commonly used measures of value such as the P/E and B/M ratios.

This book will help separate fact from fiction regarding insider trading. For instance, a common fiction is that there wasn't a lot of insider-trading activity in the 1980s and 1990s due to the increased regulatory penalties. Another common fiction is that while insider-trading information was very useful in the 1970s, it has much less predictive power in the 1980s and 1990s. As evidence to support their claim, critics point to the less than spectacular performance of the funds managed on the basis of actual insider trading. We will examine the time series patterns in the level and profitability of insider trading from the 1970s to the 1990s.

Most of the results in this book are based on a universal insider-trading data set that covers the period from 1975 to 1996. Care has been taken to clean the data set from reporting errors.[16] While the insider-trading data are compiled from public sources and therefore they are not proprietary, many of the results presented in this book are new and have not been published elsewhere in the literature. This book on the information content of insider trading should be an indispensable guide for your investment decisions.

Investment Intelligence from Insider Trading

1   *Insider-trading patterns*

{

Some preliminaries

This chapter provides the reader with some preliminary building blocks of analysis such as an operational definition of insider trading, how to treat conflicting insider-trading signals, and various statistical properties of insider trading. It will digress briefly on the legal and regulatory issues surrounding insider trading. These preliminaries will help the potential stock market investor better appreciate the investment signals provided by insider trading.

In order to interpret the meaning of a given set of insider transactions, we need first to understand the everyday insider-trading characteristics. For instance, suppose that I would like to use insider trading to help guide my portfolio decisions. The first question I would ask is: How often does an insider trade occur for a typical stock? If an insider trade occurs once every five years, then waiting for insiders to provide investment signals is not going to be very helpful. On the other hand, if an insider trade is expected to occur once every other month, then I would have a sufficient number of buy and sell signals to monitor my portfolio decisions.

Examination of the industrywide or the economywide insider-trading patterns can help us interpret such insider-trading signals. Suppose that most insiders in banks and savings and loans have been sellers for the last ten years, with an average sale of 1,000 shares per month. In this case a sale of 1,000 shares in a bank would not be unusual. It would simply confirm what I already know. However, in this same situation a lack of sales would be a signal of a departure from the recent trends. Alternatively, a larger purchase would be more unusual and would require more attention. We need to examine usual insider-trading patterns in the economy as a whole as well as in each sector before we can interpret any insider-trading signal.

Before we can begin to analyze the historical patterns of insider-trading activity, we need to be more specific about what we mean by insider trading. As was mentioned in the introduction, insiders can acquire and dispose of shares in their own firms through many different vehicles, including open market transactions, private transactions, and option exercises. This book focuses on mostly open market purchases and sales, which refer to trades executed anonymously through a broker.[1] To execute an open market transaction, the insider simply calls a broker and places a buy or a sell order. The broker may know that the order is from an insider of the firm, but the market maker or the trader on the other side of the transaction is not likely to find out who has initiated the transaction. It is this anonymity that allows the insider to exploit special information.

Suppose that the anonymity did not exist. Suppose that insiders were required to register every transaction with the Security and Exchange Commission, say one month *prior* to the trading date. Then it would be very difficult for insiders to trade profitably. When insiders register their intention to trade and announce their upcoming plans, stock prices may rise prior to insiders' purchases or fall prior to insiders' sales, making it difficult if not impossible, for insiders to exploit their special information. Anonymity is therefore essential for profitable insider trading. Hence we focus specifically on open market sales and purchases that allow insiders to trade with anonymity.[2]

Conflicting transactions

A lot of trades by insiders in a given firm and month contain both sales and purchases. One insider may buy stock while another insider may sell stock. Alternatively, an insider-buying month may be followed by an insider-selling month, and vice versa. Not all insider trading is motivated by propriety information, and there is no reason to expect all insider trading to occur in the same direction at a given time.

How do we deal with conflicting insider trades? There is no right way to define insider trading, although there are a number of logical possibilities. In this book we will net out all offsetting transactions in a given firm and calendar month and consider only the *net* number of shares traded. The advantage of this approach is that it gives equal weight to a given share traded regardless of the source of trade. We choose this approach because we believe that the number of shares traded by insiders is an important signal of the quality of the information. We will have more to say about the relation between number of shares traded and future stock returns in chapter 3 of this book.

An example should clarify our procedure: Consider the insider-trading activity in the following hypothetical yet quite likely situation. In January, two different insiders of the ABC firm execute a total of three buy orders of 500 shares, while a third insider has a single sell order for 3,000 shares. How should we classify January for ABC firm? One could say that it represents buying, since two insiders bought shares and only one insider sold shares. One might also consider it a buying month, since two net purchases took place given that three buy orders were executed against only one sell order. Alternatively, one could treat it as a sale month, since insiders sold 1,500 shares on net. What is the best way to define insider trading in this situation? In this book we will define such a month as a net sale month based on the total number of shares sold.

The degree to which our measure of insider trading predicts future stock returns depends on how we define insider trading. As was mentioned above, we will use a definition that places greater weight on larger trade volumes for the most part. As an alternative procedure, we could have used the net number of transactions as a way of defining insider trading. In our hypothetical example above, we would have characterized insider-trading month as a purchase month. This approach would have ignored the information in the number of shares and treated each transaction the same regardless of the number of shares traded. This approach would be superior if the number of shares traded by insiders is not sufficiently informative.

Alternatively, we could have used the number of insiders trading to classify a given insider-trading month. This approach would have ignored multiple transactions by the same insider and treated such transactions as if they were a single transaction. Again this approach would be superior if neither the number of shares traded by insiders nor the number of transactions by a given insider provides any additional information regarding future stock returns.

Finally we could have required unanimity among insiders.[3] For our hypothetical example above, we would have simply ignored this particular calendar month as if no transaction took place. Unanimity would be important when a conflicting transaction signals a liquidity motivation rather than information motivation. We might be interested in restricting our attention to unanimous insider-trading months if we wanted to maximize the information content of a subset of insider transactions. The weakness of this approach would be that it would ignore months when insiders buy say 10,000 shares and sell only 100 shares. In addition a requirement of unanimity might eliminate most of our sample.

What is the best measure of insider trading? To settle this question, we will measure insider trading using *all* of the approaches discussed above and compare the predictive ability of each approach. After examining all of these possibilities, we will settle on the most informative measure. As we mentioned before, for the most part, we will use the net number of shares traded as our measure of insider-trading activity.

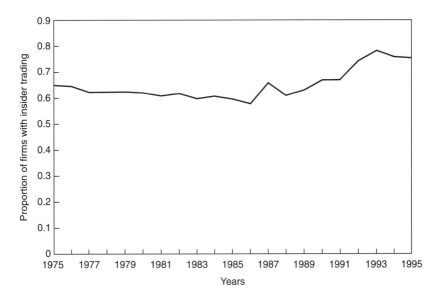

Figure 1.1
Proportion of all firms listed on NYSE, AMEX, and NASDAQ with at least one open
market transaction in a given year

Frequency of insider trading

To be a useful guide in investment decisions, there needs to be a lot
of insider trading in most firms. If only 1% of all firms reported insider
trading in a given year, then insider trading may still be interesting,
but it would not provide much guidance to the potential stock price
performance of the great majority of firms. Hence we must first examine whether there is sufficient insider trading in most firms.

Fortunately (or unfortunately depending on your beliefs about it)
insider trading is a common occurrence. Figure 1.1 shows a graph of
the proportion of all firms trading on the New York Stock Exchange,
American Stock Exchange, and NASDAQ in which insiders trade at
least once in a given year. The proportion of firms with insider trading
varies between two-thirds to four-fifths of all listed firms from 1975 to

1995. There is no decline in the proportion of firms with insider trading in the 1990s. In fact the proportion of firms with insider trading shows a small increase toward the end of the time period. Figure 1.1 demonstrates that insiders trade freely in most firms. This is good news from an investment perspective. Insider trading can guide portfolio management decisions for most firms.[4]

Insider-trading cycles

Is insider trading random across firms? If this were true, then aggregate insider trading would be pretty constant over time and insider trading would only be used for stock picking. Alternatively, there could be correlation between insider trading at industry level or economy level. For instance, at the industry level, if Ford executives are buying their own firm's stock, this can represent either good news (or bad news) for GM and Chrysler stocks.[5] At the economy level, are there periods of general buying and selling activity by insiders? Is it meaningful to talk about insider-trading sentiment across the economy? Finally, if they exist, are the insider-trading cycles related to aggregate stock price cycles? These are all interesting questions for most investors. We begin by examining historical insider-trading patterns.

Aggregate insider-trading activity follows rather slow cycles that are similar to business cycles (figure 1.2). There are periods of four to five years when insiders tend to buy more shares than they sell, and four to five years when insiders tend to sell more shares than they buy. Figure 1.2 indicates that for the five years during 1975 to 1979, the number of firms with net insider buying exceeded the number of firms with net insider selling. The five-year insider buy cycle ended in 1979 following a sharp decline in the number of buying firms and a moderate rise in the number of selling firms. In 1979 insider trading appeared to have been neutral with buying firms about the same in number as the selling firms. In 1980 sellers gained an upper hand over buyers, which they retained until 1987. Except for a slight reversal in 1984,

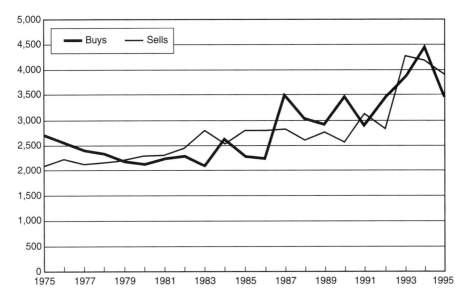

Figure 1.2
Number of firms with insider buying and selling activity

the seven-year period from 1979 to 1986 shows more selling firms than buying firms.

The stock market crash of 1987 ushered in another period of increased insider buying, while the number of sellers remained about the same. Immediately following the stock market crash in October 1987, the number of firms with insider buying almost doubled. During the four years between 1987 and 1990, buyers continued to outnumber sellers by about 500 firms per year. Apparently insiders viewed the stock market crash of October 1987 as a good buying opportunity. We will also explore this issue in a lot more detail later in the book.

Finally the years 1990 and 1991 show the beginning of a significant climb in overall insider-trading activity. Both the number of firms with net buying and selling made a dramatic climb and reached over 4,000 firms each by 1994. The sellers maintained about a 500-firm edge over most of this period. The first few months of 1996 indicate that insider selling was still outpacing insider buying.

This evidence suggests that it makes sense to talk about insider-trading sentiment. There are distinguishable cycles to insider trading. Over the past twenty-one years, aggregate insider sentiment has changed about four times. Our finding suggests that the average life of insider-trading sentiment lasts about four to five years which is similar in length to business cycles. This finding raises the possibility that aggregate insider-trading patterns may reflect the macroeconomic developments and shows relative persistence over time similar to business cycles. This finding also suggests the possibility that aggregate insider trading may be useful in helping the typical mutual fund investor time the market; namely it can help the investor get in or out of the stock market. We will explore the relations between insider-trading cycles, business cycles, and macroeconomic developments a bit more later.

Probability of trading against insiders

There is of course a counter side to the argument that insider trading can be a useful guide to investors. To the extent that insider trading is profitable, insiders impose losses on everyone else. How big are these losses? If insider trading accounts for half of the overall trading volume, what chance does a small investor have in "insider-infested" waters? Is it possible to imitate insiders successfully, even though insiders may be taxing all other traders?

We can gain additional insights into insider trading by examining the intensity of insider sentiment. Our first measure of intensity is the probability of trading against insiders. To compute probability, we divide the number of shares traded by insiders by the total trading volume for that calendar month. If insiders do not report any trading in a given month, the probability of trading against insiders is taken as zero. These proportions are then averaged across all firms trading on the NYSE, AMEX, and NASDAQ for each of the 252 calendar months from January 1975 to December 1995.

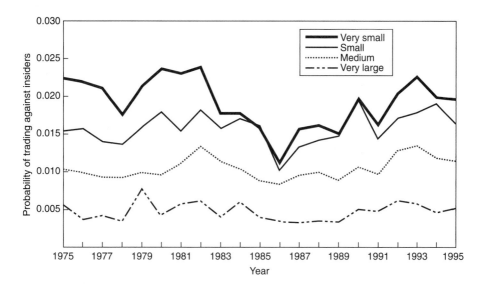

Figure 1.3
Probability of trading against insiders from 1975 to 1995 by firm size

The probability of trading against insiders clearly varies by firm size (figure 1.3). In small firms (market value of equity is less than $25 million), the probability of trading against insiders has averaged around 2% per month, and this probability has varied quite a bit over the past 21 years. In 1986 the probability of trading against insiders fell to its lowest value of 1.1%, while the highest value occurred at 2.4% in 1982.

As firm size increases, the probability of trading against insiders falls. In the largest firm size group (market value of equity more than $1 billion), the probability of trading against insiders has averaged about 0.5%. Hence the probability of trading against insiders has increased fourfold, going from the largest to the smallest firm size groups. Having said that, however, we must put all of the numbers in figure 1.3 in perspective. Overall, the probability of trading against insiders is quite small. A probability of trading against insiders and therefore the likelihood of losing against insiders of only 2% or less is hardly something a typical investor should worry about.[6]

We can also use our evidence to estimate the costs insiders impose on all other traders. If insiders earn 10% abnormal returns when they trade in small firms, the expected losses against insiders will be about 0.2% (10% times 2%). This is not a large cost given all the other trading costs. In large firms the expected losses against insiders will be even smaller. Assuming that insiders earn 5% when they trade in large firms, expected losses against insiders will only be 0.05% (5% times 1.0%). This is hardly noticeable.[7]

The overall probability of trading against insiders is small because the restrictions and sanctions imposed by insider-trading regulations are quite severe. We will discuss these regulations later in this chapter. Absent the regulations, the probability of trading against insiders can easily increase by an order of magnitude. Higher levels of insider trading in small firms are believed to be responsible for decreased liquidity and higher transactions costs, resulting in higher bid-ask spreads for the small investor. Hence the individual investors are right to worry about insider trading.

On average, the probability of trading against insiders is rather small. However, what if insider trading is concentrated in a few months out of a year? After all, we expect insiders to trade only when the stock price diverges from fundamental value. This is also the time when we may want to trade as well. Are there times when the probability of trading against insiders is much higher?[8] Alternatively, we can ask, What is the probability of trading against insiders during those times when insiders are active?

The probability of trading against insiders when insiders are active jumps significantly (figure 1.4). In the smallest firms the probability of trading against insiders is now 12%. This is a sixfold increase from the average probability of trading against insiders. Once again, this probability falls with firm size. In largest firms the probability of trading against insiders (given that insiders are trading) rises to 1%. This represents only a twofold increase from the average probability (figure 1.3).

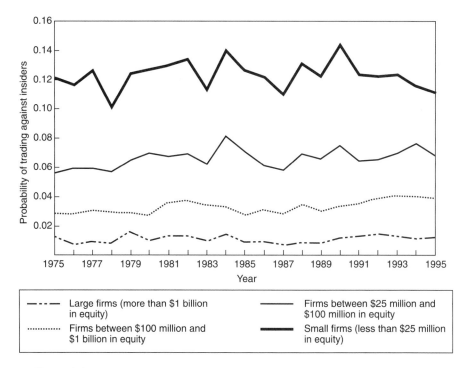

Figure 1.4
Probability of trading against insiders from 1975 to 1995 by firm size given that insiders trade.

Comparing our results with and without active insiders, we see that insiders "cluster" their transactions. Moreover insiders tend to cluster their trading in small firms to fewer months. This finding is consistent with a scenario where more of the insider trading in most firms is information related as opposed liquidity related. We will come back to this issue later in chapter 3.

As a third measure of the intensity of insider trading, we examine the net number of shares traded by insiders. In the 1970s the average shares bought and sold were approximately equal to each other (figure 1.5). For instance, in 1975, the average shares bought by insiders in a typical firm were about 14,000 per month. In comparison, the average shares sold in a typical firm were about 16,000 per month. During the

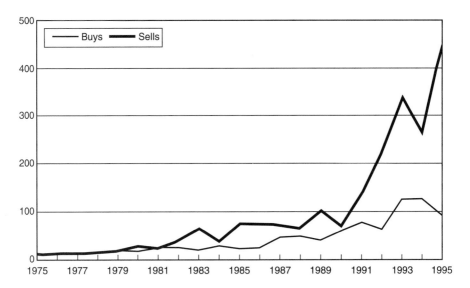

Figure 1.5
Average number of shares bought and sold per firm by insiders (in thousands)

1970s insiders were neither increasing nor decreasing their ownership of corporate assets through open market transactions.

During the 1980s and 1990s insider-selling intensity steadily increased. This trend has been especially strong in the 1990s, as the average shares sold in a typical firm have exceeded the average shares bought in a typical firm, usually by more than 4 to 1. By 1995 the average shares purchased by insiders was just under 100,000, while the average number of shares sold by insiders had grown to about 450,000 shares. This finding suggests that during the rest of the 1990s insider sales will dominate insider purchases in a typical firm. Part of the rationale for this finding is that insiders often receive shares as part of their compensation plans, and they sell these shares on the open market. Hence we should expect less information content to insider sales in large firms.

A fourth measure of insider-trading activity is the frequency of trading measured in firm months. If insiders in a given firm sell during five months and have no transactions during the remaining seven months, then the number of selling firm months contributed by this firm is five. In 1975 the data set contains 8,008 buying months. Given the 2,704 firms reporting buying in figure 1.2, this works out to about three months out of the year. The number of selling months in 1975 equaled 6,131, yielding also about three months out of the year. Hence, on average, half of all months show some trading activity. The frequency of buying and selling shows a gradual increase over time in line with the increase in number of firms trading. By 1995 there were 10,000 buy months and 14,000 sell months. This works out to about 2.4 buying months per firm per year and 3.2 selling months per firm per year, totaling again about six months out of the year. Consistent with figure 1.1, the frequency of insider trading has remained remarkably stable from 1975 to 1995.

Our final measure of insider trading is the total number of shares bought or sold in a year (figure 1.6). This measure summarizes the

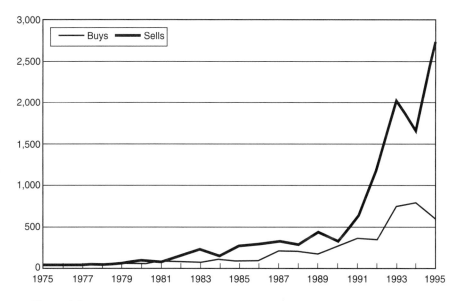

Figure 1.6
Total shares bought and sold by insiders (in millions)

global insider-trading activity. During most of the 1970s, shares bought exceeded shares sold by a small margin. By 1980 total shares sold by insiders substantially exceeded the total shares bought by insiders, and this trend accelerated with each year. By 1995 the total shares sold almost reached 2.7 billion per year. In contrast, shares bought reached only about half a billion by 1995. For the period 1980 to 1995, total shares sold by insiders exceeded the total shares sold by insiders by more than six billion shares. This net disinvestment by insiders in their own firms is too large to be explained by sales of stock that is acquired through option exercises.[9] Whether this disinvestment is a temporary occurrence or a permanent trend remains to be seen.

Normal insider-trading patterns

In order to identify a particular unusual insider-trading activity, we first need to understand the usual or the normal insider-trading patterns in different types of firms. If insiders typically sell 10,000 shares per month in a given firm, a new purchase activity could signal a significant turning point. To identify these turning points, we first document typical insider-trading patterns.

We first group firms by the size of the market value of equity, since different size firms are likely to exhibit different normal insider-trading patterns (table 1.1). The particular division of firm size groups is somewhat arbitrary. We use less than $25 million, between $25 and $100 million, between $100 million and $1 billion, and more than $1 billion. This grouping is intended to produce a differentiation between very small and very large firms. Other categorizations would have worked just as well.

In small firms insiders report a greater frequency of purchases than sales. In large firms the reverse is true. Insiders in large firms are more likely to be given stock options as part of their compensation as compared with insiders in small firms. After exercising their options to ac-

Table 1.1
Distribution of insider trading by firm size groups

Firm size group	Number of buying months	Number of selling months	Shares bought (millions)	Shares sold (millions)
Less than $25 million	51,399	38,563	1,2234.0	1,818.9
Between $25 and $100 million	39,062	41,878	776.2	1,786.1
Between $100 million and $1 billion	41,414	58,869	829.5	2,774.6
More than $1 billion	13,008	24,999	737.0	1,469.3

Table 1.2
Proportion of trading months accounted by net purchases grouped by firm size: All insiders' transactions

Firm size	Number of trading months	Buy proportion
Less than $25 million	89,962	57.1%
$25–$100 million	80,940	48.2
$100 million–$1 billion	100,283	41.3
More than $1 billion	38,007	34.2

quire stock, insiders in large firms often sell these shares. This phenomenon increases the relative frequency of insider sales in large firms. However, across all firms the number of shares sold exceeds the number of shares purchased.

In small firms there are more insider purchases than insider sales (table 1.2). Given at least one transaction, 57% of all months are net purchases, while 43% are sales. Thus the frequency of purchase months outnumbers the frequency of sales months by a 4:3 ratio. As the firm size increases, the buy ratio falls. For the next three size groups, the buy ratio equals 48.3%, 41.3%, and 34.2%, respectively. In the largest firm size category the frequency of sell months outnumbers the frequency of buy months by 2:1.

An important lesson suggested by our evidence is that insiders in large firms normally sell *twice* as frequently as they buy. Consequently, in large firms, an average sell-to-buy ratio of 2:1 should be considered neutral. When selling exceeds buying by significantly more than 2:1, then insiders should be considered bearish. To be considered bullish in large firms, buy-to-sell ratio should be above 0.5.

Another important caveat to keep in mind is that the above rule of thumb does not apply to the smaller firms. For the smallest firms, on average, there is a greater frequency of buying than selling by a ratio of 4:3. Consequently, to be considered bullish in small firms, insider buying must actually exceed insider selling by more than a 4:3 margin. Hence it is important to keep these normal insider-trading patterns in mind before one can assess whether a particular pattern indicates unusual changes in insider-trading activity.

Do insiders worry about the regulatory implications of their transactions? Do they worry more about large transactions? Do they worry more about purchases than sales? If insiders do not worry about regulatory scrutiny, they would not hesitate to trade large number of shares. If they do worry, then they might want to break up their large transactions into smaller lots. One of the indicators the Securities and Exchange Commission uses in order to detect potentially illegal insider trading is unusual trading volume. By breaking up their large transactions into smaller lots and spreading these over a period of time, insiders can reduce some of the regulatory costs.

To address these issues, we analyze the relation between trade size and buy-sell activity. If regulatory concerns are not important at all, there should be no relation between buy and sell transactions and volume of trade. Our data show that small transactions tend to be purchases while large transactions tend to be sales (table 1.3). For those months where the net volume is less than 100 shares, about 80% are purchases. In contrast, when the net trading volume increases, selling becomes more predominant. For those months where the net volume

Table 1.3
Proportion of trading months accounted by net purchases grouped by trade volume: All insiders' transactions

Shares traded	Number of trading months	Buy proportion
1–100	24,278	80%
101–1,000	86,495	58
1,001–10,000	120,160	39
10,001–more	78,260	29

exceeds 10,000 shares, only 29% are net purchase months and 71% are sale months.

One possible explanation for this pattern is that insiders may be worried about regulatory scrutiny of their stock purchases, and therefore they are more likely to submit their purchase orders in smaller, multiple batches. By breaking up their purchase orders into smaller lots over longer time horizons, insiders make it harder for regulators to detect unusual purchase activity. In contrast, insiders are less concerned about the size of their sales transactions. Again, a possible explanation for this finding may be that insiders can easily come up with reasons as to why they need the cash due to liquidity reasons. Making a similar argument for purchases may be more difficult. Insiders have to justify excess liquidity and the fact that they are buying their own firm's stocks as opposed to a mutual fund or a market index fund.

Seasonal patterns in insider trading

What can we learn about seasonal patterns to insider trading? We know that stock returns exhibit seasonal patterns. Historically stocks have done well in January and not so well in September or in October. Does insider trading also exhibit any seasonal patterns? Does it follow the same patterns as stock returns? What do insiders think about these seasonal stock returns?

Our findings show that insider buying peaks in the last quarter of the year. October has the highest buying proportion of any calendar month, followed by the month of December. Buying activity is lowest during the summer months. We also examined the seasonal trading patterns for top executives and found that top executives exhibit similar seasonal trading behavior. Once again, the top purchase month for top executives is December.

The seasonal distribution of insider trading is consistent with the seasonal pattern in stock prices. Between 1926 and 1993, stock prices rose more than 1% in December and between 2% and 5% in January, while stock prices declined by more than 1% in September and October.[10] There is some evidence that these seasonal patterns have become smaller in magnitude in the 1990s. There is less agreement on the underlying cause of these returns patterns. Some authors believe that these seasonal variations represent a profit opportunity due to selling pressure, while others think that it is an artifact of the way prices are recorded or compensation for some unspecified risk factors.

Our evidence suggests that insiders take advantage of these seasonal variations in stock prices: They buy following price declines in September and October. Moreover buying is heaviest just before the large stock price increases in January. The seasonal insider-trading patterns suggest that insiders exploit the seasonal variations in stock returns.

Do insiders manipulate stock prices?

Let us now examine the relation between current insider trading and future insider trading in a given firm to see if insiders manipulate stock prices. If insiders trade their own firm's stock to exploit some nonpublic information, then we would expect insider trading to be concentrated during times of information asymmetries. We would also expect insider trading at a given time to be in the same direction. If insiders buy stock because they expect the fundamental value to be above the current stock price, we would expect insider buying to continue until the stock price rises to the fundamental value. Hence insider purchases would be followed by purchases. Similarly, if the stock is overpriced, insiders would sell, and their sales would be followed by further sales.

Another possibility is that most of the reported insider trading is for liquidity reasons. If this is the case, then, by definition, a given purchase by an insider would be just as likely to be followed by either a purchase or a sale by another executive. In this case there should be no serial correlation between current insider trading and future insider trading.

There is a third possibility. What if insiders manipulate stock prices? If insiders trade strategically, they might also attempt to deceive the uninformed investors. If they receive good news and everyone else expects good news as well, then there isn't much profit to be made by buying the stock. In this case the stock price will already be high reflecting the public expectation of good news. Instead, insiders will have strong incentives to strategically sell a small number of shares to fool uninformed investors. If the revelation of the surprise insider sale causes a large stock price drop, insiders can then go in and buy an even larger number of shares.[11]

In contrast, if everyone else expects bad news and insiders receive good news, the price will already be low, reflecting the public pessimism. In this case insiders will have less of an incentive to manipulate stock prices. Instead, they can make more profit by buying stock based on their positive information.

By examining the time series properties of insider trading, we can also get some idea about whether insiders attempt to manipulate stock prices. If insiders do manipulate stock prices, we should expect a large number of reversals in insider trading. Insiders' purchases should be more likely to be followed by sales than by additional purchases. Similarly insiders' sales should be more likely to be followed by purchases than by additional sales. This is a necessary condition for manipulation, since the first transaction is meant to fool the public and the second transaction in the opposite direction is meant for profits.

Moreover reversals should be accompanied by even larger stock returns than continued insider trading in the same direction. This is expected, since the first transaction is small while the second transaction is larger. Also manipulation involves surprises, while trades in the same direction would have already resulted in partial stock price adjustment.

Third, reversals should be more likely over the short term like a month horizon as compared with a longer term such as one year. This is because over the longer term, additional information will be released, which can undo the effects of insider trading in the wrong direction leaving insiders with losses.

Finally, reversals should be more likely if only the top executive knows about the information. This is because manipulation works best when few insiders have access to the information or if they collude. A given insider trying to manipulate the stock prices is likely to make losses by buying on bad news if all the other insiders sell on bad news.

Stock price manipulation is an important issue from both an investment and a regulatory perspective, and we will come back to it later in chapter 3. We will discuss some insider-trading regulations that reduce insiders' ability to manipulate stock prices. We will consider insider-trading regulations shortly.

There is another reason to examine the time series properties of insider trading. From the typical investor's perspective, it would also be very helpful if we could predict future insider trading. Current insider trading presumably predicts future stock returns. If we can predict future insider trading, then effectively we can predict future stock returns with a substantial lead time which would enable us to accumulate large positions with minimal price impact.

To address the possibility of manipulation, we tabulate next months' insider-trading activity against the current month's insider-trading activity (table 1.4). In a given month we add all shares traded to net out offsetting transactions. If the total net shares traded is positive, we group this month into the buy category. If the total net number of shares traded is negative, we group this month into the sell category.

Table 1.4
Predicting future insider trading from past insider trading

During the past month, insiders	Probability of buying next month	Probability of no trade next month	Probability of selling next month
Buy	38%	51%	11%
Do not trade	7	85	8
Sell	10	49	41

If the total net number of shares traded is zero, then we group this month into the no trade category.

Insider-trading activity is characterized by strong momentum.[12] If insiders buy shares in the current month, the probability they will continue to buy next month is 38%. The probability of a reversal into a sale next month is only 11%. Thus the odds ratio that purchases will be followed by purchases is 4:1. If insiders sell shares during the current month, the probability that they will continue to sell during the next month is 41%. The probability of a reversal into a purchase next month is only 10%. Thus the odds ratio that sales will be followed by sales is also 4:1. There is strong evidence that insider-trading activity is followed by insider-trading activity with the same sign. In addition months with zero insider trading have an 85% probability of being followed by another no-trade month.

Our earlier discussion suggested that if insiders manipulate, it should be more profitable in the short term. Over time additional information arrives, making manipulation potentially less profitable. Hence, if manipulation is present, reversals in insider-trading activity should be more likely in the short run rather than the long run.

To investigate this issue, we examine insider trading over 12-month horizons (table 1.5). Our evidence suggests that insider-trading momentum weakens over the 12 months. If the past 12 months is characterized by net insider purchase, the next 12 months has a 47% chance

Table 1.5
Predicting the 12-month-ahead future insider trading from past 12 months of insider trading

During the past 12 months, insiders	Probability of buying next 12 months	Probability of no trade next 12 months	Probability of selling next 12 months
Buy	47%	27%	26%
Do not trade	14	73	13
Sell	18	24	58

of being a purchase year as well. The probability of following a purchase year by a sale year is only 26%. The odds that purchases during the past year will be followed by purchases during the next year is 2:1. Similarly, if the past year is an insider sale year, the probability that the next year will also be a sale year is 58%. The probability of following a sale year by a purchase year is only 18%. The odds ratio that sales during the past year will be followed by sales during the next year is 3:1.

Our evidence indicates that there is a strong positive correlation between past insider trading and future insider trading. Reversals are more likely in the long run than the short run. This evidence is *inconsistent* with manipulation. For the one-month horizon there is a 4 to 1 chance that purchases will be followed by future purchases. Similarly, there is a 4 to 1 chance that sales will be followed by future sales. For the 12-month horizon, the probability of reversals doubles. There is only a 2 to 1 chance that insider trading will be followed by same sign insider trading. This evidence is consistent with the interpretation that insiders respond to special information signals indicating good buying and selling opportunities over a long period of time.

To get further insights into possible manipulation, we replicated our analysis for top executives' transactions as well. These transactions showed even a stronger pattern of momentum or positive correlation.

The probability of a buy month being followed by another buy month is about 30%. Similarly the probability of a sell month being followed by another sell month is again about 30%. In contrast, the probability of reversals is only about 2%. Hence the odds of reversing a purchase month by a sale, or reversing a sale month by a purchase, are about 15 to 1 against. This evidence suggests that the signals observed by top executives tend to be even stronger, thereby resulting in stronger momentum trading.

Again, our evidence is inconsistent with manipulation. Manipulation should be more likely when fewer insiders know about the information or if they collude. When top executives know about sensitive information not available to other insiders and their information advantage over the general public is small, we would expect them to manipulate the stock prices and trade in the opposite direction only to reverse the direction of their trade later. Our evidence is the opposite of this. Our evidence suggests that such manipulation by insiders is not pervasive. As mentioned earlier, this is likely due to insider-trading regulations.[13]

Overall, the evidence suggests that insiders respond to common signals in their own firms. Positive signals remain positive for a fairly long time period. Similarly negative signals remain negative for a fairly long time. The positive correlation in insiders' transactions over time increases the likelihood that insiders do observe signals allowing them to trade profitably their own firms' stock.

Insider-trading regulations

If you have read this far, you will already know that it is almost impossible to understand and interpret insider-trading patterns without a good understanding of insider-trading regulations. The effects of regulations on insider trading are likely to be complex. Some regulations discourage information-motivated insider trading and therefore reduce the information content of reported insider trading. Other regulations discourage manipulation and therefore increase the information content of reported insider trading.[14]

Having discussed the historical insider-trading patterns, we will now examine the regulatory environment to help put these historical trends in context. In this section we will briefly examine the development of insider-trading regulations from the 1930s to the present. We will also identify the winners and losers and briefly discuss the costs and benefits of insider-trading regulations.

As we have mentioned before, insider-trading laws basically prohibit purchases and sales of stock by any person deemed to be an insider while in possession of material, nonpublic information. Any violations of these provisions are considered criminal infractions. The legal term "material, nonpublic" is not defined in law, and it does not necessarily mean profitable insider trading. Insider-trading restrictions are covered by the antifraud provisions of Section 10 of the Securities and Exchange Act of 1934. Strict enforcement of Section 10 would reduce the information content of reported insider transactions.

In addition Section 16 of the Securities and Exchange Act (1) requires timely disclosure of insiders' transactions within 10 days of the following month in which insiders trade (Section 16a), (2) prohibits insiders from profiting from short-term price movements defined as a profitable, offsetting pair of transactions within 6 months of each other (Section 16b), and (3) prohibits short sales of stock (Section 16c).

The reporting requirement in Section 16(a) forces public dissemination and provides opportunities to detect and punish violations. The enforcement of this provision did not start until the mid-1980s at which time the SEC started handing out fines for late reporting. We will examine the extent of late reporting later in this book.

Section 16(b) is an effective weapon against stock price manipulation. To manipulate effectively, insiders would have to reverse the direction of their trade before other information is released to correct the stock price. If insiders have to wait six months before reversing the direction of their trade, two quarterly earnings announcements would have to be filed. This makes manipulation much less likely, since prices would move against insiders during the interim. This presents a paradox of insider-trading regulations. Holding all else constant, having a stricter enforcement of Section 16(b) should result in an *increase* in the information content of insider trading rather than a decrease by reducing the likelihood of manipulations.[15]

Finally, Section 16(c) prevents insiders from profiting either by manipulation or by deliberate mismanagement. Insiders could replicate a short position by selling call options or purchasing put options. Changes in regulations in the 1980s have ensured that Section 16(c) could not be evaded by creating equivalent option positions. Strict enforcement of Section 16(c) reduces insiders' ability to exploit negative information.

The federal insider-trading laws in the United States were passed in 1934 in response to the crash of 1929 with the aim of protecting small investors. These laws were designed to level the playing field, so to speak, between small, uninformed investors and informed corporate insiders. The aim was to encourage a liquid stock market where the small saver could invest safely.

The federal insider-trading regulations were in fact not actively enforced until the early 1960s. One of the first cases involved the Cady Roberts & Co. (1961) where a director leaked impending news about a dividend cut to his broker who then sold shares. The broker was eventually disciplined. This case was followed by the Texas Gulf Sulfur case where insiders bought 9,100 shares after the company discovered minerals but before the discovery was announced. In 1965 the executives of Texas Gulf Sulfur were indicted and later found guilty of insider trading.

The decade of the 1970s saw increasing involvement in capital markets by small investors following the liberalization of commission fees and increasing the demand for disclosure and control of insider trading. Coincident with the elimination of fixed commission fees in 1975, Section 32 of the Securities and Exchange Act of 1934 was amended to increase the maximum criminal fines to $10,000 and maximum prison sentences to five years. Between 1966 and 1980, the SEC brought 37 insider-trading cases to court, averaging less than three cases per year.

During the 1980s the SEC deemed the level of enforcement insufficient and lobbied the U.S. Congress for increased penalties. These efforts resulted in the Insider Trading Sanctions Act of 1984 (ITSA) and the Insider Trading and Securities Fraud Enforcement Act of 1988 (ITSFEA). These two pieces of legislation increased the criminal fines to $1 million, prison sentences to 10 years, and treble damages for illegal profits. Hence insiders can be made to pay back say $3 million if they illegally make $1 million in illegal insider-trading profit. Moreover the SEC initiated 79 insider-trading cases between 1982 and 1986, averaging about 20 cases per year and signaling a sixfold increase in the enforcement effort. During the 1990s SEC's enforcement efforts have further increased. The SEC now initiates about 40 to 45 insider-trading cases per year, representing more than a fifteenfold increase compared with the 1970s.[16]

Current insider-trading laws treat violations of insider trading almost as seriously as most violent crimes resulting in death or physical injury. Moreover the monetary penalties are substantial and a deterrent. Other aspects of the insider-trading regulations seem just as heavy-handed. For instance, the new legislation has created a bounty program for informants of insider trading. The SEC can recommend a bounty of up to 10% of the illegal insider-trading profits. This provision has increased the number of lawyers chasing after illegal insider-trading profits. The monitoring performed by these specialist lawyers is another important deterrent. The new legislation also holds top management responsible for any insider trading within their firm by any employee. Consequently since 1988 most corporations have formally educated their top employees to stay clear of even an appearance of insider-trading violations. Finally new legislation has created a right of action of traders who lose to insiders. Potential liabilities arising out of such lawsuits can deter most people from even contemplating insider trading.

Has profitable insider trading stopped as a result of the increased sanctions? Some of the critics of insider trading argue that ITSA and ITSFEA, both enacted during the 1980s, eliminated most insider trading in the late 1980s and in the early 1990s. However, as surprising as it seems, figure 1.1 does not show any evidence of a decline in insider-trading activity. Moreover there is no evidence of even a temporary decline in insider trading in 1985 or in 1989 immediately following the passage of ITSA and ITSFEA. Rather, as figure 1.2 shows, the number of firms with insider-trading activity sharply increased over this time. By 1994 our insider-trading data set contains 7,420 firms, about half involved in buying and half in selling.

The lack of a response to the legislation passed in the mid-1980s may seem surprising. One explanation is that insider-trading regulations are weak because there are insufficient penalties to deter insider-trading. However, as we have argued above, this is not the case. What is paradoxical is that severe insider-trading sanctions seem to have produced no visible signs of a decline in reported insider-trading activity.

The simple answer to this question is that a vast majority of the transactions reported by insiders do not even come close to meeting the definition of illegal insider trading. First, as we mentioned earlier, "material, nonpublic information" has never been well defined.[17] Consequently most insiders can provide a number of reasonable explanations as to why they traded. Second, as the criminal penalties for insider trading have been stiffened, the burden of proof has also increased. This is a well-known paradox among legal scholars. To be convicted of an insider-trading violation, guilt has to be proved beyond a reasonable doubt in a court of law.[18] This is a high standard reserved for criminal cases. An administrative judge or a SEC bureaucrat cannot simply hand out criminal sanctions against suspected insiders. Finally, as the penalties have increased, it makes more sense for the accused to defend more vigorously against the insider-trading accusations.

Consequently it would be more difficult to obtain consent decrees or convictions even if the case goes to trial.

Given the lack of an economywide decline in insider trading, do the new sanctions have any effect on insiders' transactions at all? The answer is that they do, but only for selected insider trading. During the 1980s case law in effect defined illegal insider trading as buying and selling activity that takes place immediately prior to important corporate announcements such as takeovers, earnings, and dividend announcements. Evidence shows that following the increases in sanctions, insiders have reduced and in some cases completely stopped trading prior to these important corporate announcements. For instance, in a sample of 2,520 takeover announcements from 1975 to 1989, insiders have significantly reduced their stock purchases during the 30 days prior to takeover announcement. Prior to the mid-1980s insiders exhibited purchases in 14.5% of the takeover announcements. Following the increases in sanctions, insiders purchased stock in only 7.1% of the takeover announcements. Since the late 1980s top executives have almost completely stopped purchases prior to takeover announcements.[19] Hence, following enforcement of the legislation, insider trading was reduced and in some cases completely eliminated.

A side effect of the case law has been to define what is and what is not illegal insider trading. As a result corporate insiders have a better understanding of what trading is allowed. This sharper distinction between legal and illegal insider trading has enabled insiders to increase both the volume and profitability of their transactions. This is why figure 1.1 does not show any decline in insider-trading activity during the 1980s.

Should insider trading be regulated?

Is insider-trading good or bad? Should it be regulated? If so, what are the optimal restrictions on insider trading?[20] Who are the losers and winners from insider-trading regulations? These are difficult questions to answer. There are certainly a lot of arguments on both sides of this debate. These issues are especially important for the institutional investors who may be involved in corporate governance. In addition the desirability of regulations is important for the policy-makers and the regulators. We will first briefly discuss the arguments both for and against restrictions and then offer an evaluation of these arguments.

One group of authors argues that insider trading amounts to the theft of corporate property.[21] This is also referred to as the misappropriation theory. These authors argue that the information insiders use ultimately belongs to the firm and its shareholders. By profiting from this information without shareholder approval or knowledge, the insider violates his/her fiduciary responsibility to the shareholders. Consequently insider trading is tantamount to thievery and should be treated as such.

Another detrimental effect of insider trading is that it can potentially lead to incentives to manipulate the management of the corporation to maximize insider-trading profits. For instance, insiders could time the new stock issuance to maximally benefit themselves. Incentives to accept new investment projects, incentives to engage in corporate acquisitions, stock repurchases, dividend payments, and so on, could potentially be affected by the availability of insider-trading profits.[22]

There are other authors who focus on the informational aspects of insider trading.[23] These authors have argued that insider trading affects information efficiency two ways: First, it brings new information to the markets. Second, it discourages information search by outsiders. The net effect depends on the relative strengths of these two factors. Greater information efficiency increases stock prices and encourages real investments. Greater information inefficiency reduces stock prices and discourages real investments.[24]

Other authors argue that insider trading is unfair. It erodes public confidence in the capital markets while increasing the cost of capital for the firm, thereby making it more difficult for the firm to take on good projects. The argument here goes as follows: If uninformed small investors feel that the stock market is stacked against them, they will choose to invest their funds elsewhere such as savings accounts, government bonds, corporate bonds, and real estate instead of the stock market. This will decrease liquidity of the stock market and thereby increase the cost of raising new funds for the firms. As a result firms would have to forgo many investment projects that would otherwise have been profitable. The reduction in investments will also reduce the level of employment and the competitive position of the U.S. economy as a whole. According to this argument, insider trading has a deleterious effect on the efficiency of the corporate sector. These authors also support regulations and sanctions on insiders.

Not everyone believes that insider trading is bad. An opposing view is expressed by a group of authors who argue that insider trading should basically be governed by a private contract between the shareholders and their managers.[25] After all, insiders work for the shareholders and not for the public at large. By not prohibiting insider trading, shareholders can provide insiders with an efficient compensation contract, whereby insiders can benefit maximally from increasing stock prices, which also helps benefit the long-term shareholders. In addition managers would take into account potential profits from insider trading and be willing to work for lower wages. Since shareholders receive both direct and indirect benefits, insider trading is good. In this view insider-trading laws interfere with the efficient contracting between shareholders and managers and lead to a reduced effort by managers, and consequently reduced output and efficiency of the U.S. economy.

Who are the net beneficiaries of insider-trading laws? The previous discussion suggests that the insider-trading laws have shifted the rules of the game in favor of small, short-term traders against large, long-term investors. Hence a clear winner from insider-trading regulations is the small transient investor. Looking at the history of how insider-trading laws have been enacted also supports this view. Small investors and the securities industry that caters to them want liquidity, which is valuable because it allows diversification and easy exit for small investors. From the securities industry's perspective, liquidity generates larger trading volumes and higher commission fees. Given that insider-trading penalizes liquidity traders, it is not surprising that insider-trading restrictions have increased simultaneously with the importance of small traders.

Who are the losers? One of the losers from insider-trading regulations is the large, long-term investor.[26] As we have pointed out before, owners of more than 10% of the equity are considered insiders, regardless of whether these people have access to private corporate information. The insider status automatically burdens the large shareholders with additional costs such as having to report one's transactions, having to justify one's actions, and potential legal costs. In addition institutional investors who are considered insiders cannot engage in short-term trading which would subject them to the short-swing profit rule under Section 16(b). As a result many large investors prefer to keep their ownership below the 10% level that would trigger the insider status. Given the monitoring role performed by the large, long-term investors, insider-trading laws in fact discourage monitoring. Consequently a serious problem with insider-trading laws is that they reduce the effective controls on the self-serving behavior of the managers. In this view insider-trading laws damage the efficiency of U.S. corporations by interfering with the corporate governance process in order to help out small investors.

What is the answer? Unfortunately, there is no easy answer. All of these views are valid to some extent. Insider trading can have beneficial incentive effects as well as deleterious effects on the information efficiency or the liquidity of the stock market. By making markets more liquid, they also encourage short-term trading mentality rather than favoring long-term investors. Unfortunately, it is difficult to quantify and offset these costs and benefits, and therefore it is hard to conclude whether insider trading is, on balance, beneficial or detrimental. All we can say is that restrictions against short-term profits and short selling are probably beneficial. The restrictions against large shareholders are probably detrimental. In between these extremes, optimal insider-trading restrictions will probably be controversial. Existing laws must be reviewed with an appreciation of the costs they generate as well as any benefits they generate for the small investor. Moreover any expansion of insider-trading restrictions must take into account its deleterious effects on corporate governance. Since these issues are beyond the scope of this book, we do not explore them in detail.

Conclusions and investment implications

We have so far examined the levels and year-to-year changes in insider-trading activity. This book focuses on open market sales and purchases, since these transactions are most likely to contain insider-trading information. Other transactions, such as private trades, option exercises, stock splits, and various other acquisitions and dispositions are excluded. We define insider trading in terms of net number of shares traded. We net out any offsetting transactions in a given firm and month and examine net insider-trading activity. We have uncovered the following characteristics of insiders' transactions:

1. There is a lot of insider trading. During the past 21 years between 65% and 80% of all publicly listed firms report at least one open market transaction by an insider every year. Consequently tracking insider trading is likely to provide useful signals in most firms.

2. There are four- to five-year cycles in overall insider buying and selling activity. In the last 21 years, there were two aggregate buying cycles and two aggregate selling cycles. This finding suggests that insiders are likely to respond to macroeconomic conditions when they trade securities of their firms. The aggregate levels of insider trading should also be kept in mind when evaluating insider-trading patterns in a given firm.

3. The unconditional probability of trading against insiders is small. In small firms insiders account for 2% of the trading volume. With increasing firm size, the proportion of the trading volume initiated by

the insiders falls further. In large firms insiders account for about 0.5% of the trading volume. However, insider trading is concentrated into certain months. When insiders do trade, they account for 12% of the trading volume in small firms. Similarly, when they do trade, they account for 1% of the trading volume in large firms.

4. Despite the significant increases in insider-trading sanctions during the 1980s, there was no decline in the levels of insider trading. If anything, a greater proportion of firms report insider trading in the 1990s than in the 1980s or 1970s. Overall, evidence suggests that most insiders do not worry too much about regulatory restrictions when they buy and sell shares in their own firms. In addition there appears to be a trend toward increasing amounts of insider selling over time. For the period 1980 to 1995, insiders have sold 4.3 billion more shares than they bought.

5. In large firms insiders tend to sell twice as frequently as they buy. In smaller firms insiders tend to execute four purchases for each three sale transactions. These normal levels of insider-trading activity must be kept in mind when evaluating potentially unusual insider trading in a particular firm.

6. Purchases tend to come in small denominations. Sales tend to be more likely when the trading volume increases. This finding suggests that insiders may be breaking up their purchases into smaller lots in fear of regulatory sanctions. Insiders do not seem to worry as much about the regulatory implications of their sales.

7. Insider buying is more likely to occur at the turn of the year. Insider buying is lowest during the summer months. This finding is consistent with the so-called January effect when stock prices of especially small firms rise significantly in January. This evidence suggests that at least some insiders view the expected rise in stock prices in January as a profit opportunity.

8. Insider-trading activity is positively correlated over time. Past insider buying in a given firm increases the likelihood that insiders in

the same firm will continue to buy stock in the future. Past insider selling increases the likelihood that insiders will continue to sell stock in the future. The positive correlation in insider trading suggests that insiders respond to common information signals that change slowly over time.

9. Insiders do not appear to be manipulating stock prices. Manipulation implies reversals in the direction of insider trading. Evidence shows that the probability of reversals is higher at 12 months than at one month. Also, contrary to expectations, the probability of reversals is smaller for top executives.

10. Regulation of insider trading has increased along with the increased involvement of stock investors in the stock market. Insider-trading sanctions now treat illegal insider trading the same as violent crimes. Increased insider-trading regulations have reduced specific instances of insider trading that are most likely to be prosecuted. Neither the volume nor the profitability of everyday insider trading is affected by increased insider-trading sanctions.

11. Insider-trading regulations tend to benefit small, liquidity-concerned investors at the expense of large, governance-motivated investors. Increased restrictions on insider trading is likely to lower the incentives of large shareholders to participate in corporate governance.

2   *Does insider trading predict future stock returns?*

Background

The key question for the readers of this book is: Does current insider trading predict future stock returns? To be a useful investment guide, current insider trading *must* predict future stock returns. Otherwise, most of the interest in insider trading would probably disappear. Presumably, following insiders' purchases, stock prices increase more than one would expect under normal circumstances. Similarly, following insiders' sales, stock prices would increase less than normally expected or even decline.

First, we would like to establish if insider trading predicts future stock returns using our data base.[1] Second, we will also examine sales and purchases separately to see if insider trading predicts both stock price increases and stock price decreases. Third, we would like to document the strength of the predictive ability of insider trading. How large are the stock price changes following insiders' transactions? Fourth, we will examine year-to-year changes in profitability of insider trading to uncover any patterns over time in insider-trading profits. Is the profitability of insider-trading stable over time?

To be a useful guide for potential outside stock market investors, insider-trading information must be a strong and accurate predictor of future stock returns, it must be available in a timely fashion, and any profit obtained from insider trading must cover all costs of active investing. Moreover the risks from imitating insiders must be acceptable. We will examine the first set of issues in detail over the next two chapters. Risk will be examined in chapter 14.

Actively buying and selling of stocks is costly. Active investors incur additional costs by frequently trading stocks that they would not incur with a buy-and-hold strategy. First, there are out-of-pocket costs. Outsiders must consider the commission fee paid to the broker, which can vary up to 0.5% (round-trip) depending on the size of the transaction. The commission fee declines with increasing trade size. In addition to the commission fee, traders must also pay a bid-ask spread, which is the difference between the buying (bid) and selling (ask) prices that the market-maker quotes.[2] Market-makers are willing to sell stocks at a higher price than they are willing to buy the same stock at all times. The difference compensates the market-maker for the cost of carrying an inventory, as well as potentially losing to informed traders.[3]

In addition to the direct and indirect trading costs, outsiders must wait anywhere from a few weeks to a few months for insiders to report their transactions. If insiders report a given transaction late for whatever reason, it is not going to be especially useful for outsiders as an investment tool. After insiders report their transactions to the SEC or the stock exchange, some additional time passes until these transactions are made public. Prior to the advent of electronic on-line data bases, the publication lag could take weeks or months as well. Stock prices can and do change between the time insiders trade and the time insider-trading information becomes public. These delays further reduce the potential profits to outsiders below the level of insiders' own profits.

If outside investors are to have any chance of beating a buy-and-hold strategy net of transactions costs by imitating insiders, then current insider trading must predict the future stock returns. If this relation is particularly strong, then the chances are good that outsiders will be able to obtain real profits after all the costs. If this relation is not strong, then chances are good that after all the costs are subtracted, outsiders will not come out ahead. We will return to these real world complications later in the book (chapter 14).

Stock price movements following insiders' transactions

We begin our analysis by looking at the relation between current insider trading and future stock returns. Our first question is, Does current insider trading predict future stock returns? If so, what is the magnitude of the predicted stock returns?

We first examine the one-year unadjusted stock returns following insiders' transactions for the entire sample, sorted by buy and sell months (table 2.1). The data set contains a total of 144,884 buy months and 164,309 sell months, for a grand total of 309,193 insider-trading months between 1975 and 1994. There are more months with net sales, since the overall sample contains more insider sales than purchases.

To determine whether a given month is to be treated as a sale or purchase month in each calendar month we sum all *shares* traded by all insiders. If positive, this is a buy month. If negative, this is a sell month. If zero, we ignore this month. Profitability is examined over the subsequent 12 calendar months. Suppose that in ABC company, an insider purchase took place sometime in February 1976. We examine the stock returns from March 1, 1976, through February 28, 1977.

Table 2.1
One-year raw returns to the insider trading firms

	Number of trading months	Subsequent 12-month raw return
Buy	144,884	24.0%
Sell	164,309	15.1
All	309,193	19.2

We delay our trading strategy to the beginning of the next month to give ourselves time to observe the total insider-trading activity for the month of February 1976 and to decide whether it is dominated by purchases or sales.

Data show that for those firms reporting insider buying activity, stock prices move up 24.0% during the subsequent 12 months following insiders' purchases (table 2.1). In contrast, for those firms reporting insider sale activity, stock prices move up only 15.1% during the subsequent 12 months following insiders' sales. In contrast, the average stock price movement during the 12 months following the overall sample is 19.2%. Hence insider buying activity signals greater than average stock price increase. Insider selling signals less than average stock price increase.[4]

An interesting conclusion is that an estimate of insiders' profits following a round-trip transaction is 8.9%, which is significant but not huge. We estimate this profit by subtracting the price movements following insiders' sales from the price movements following insiders' purchases. Hence table 2.1 answers our first question. Insider trading is profitable and insiders' current transactions do predict the future stock price movements up to a year ahead.[5] In addition our findings are consistent with those in the finance literature. Numerous studies have confirmed the profitability of insider trading using different sample periods, statistical methodology, and sample selection criteria.[6]

A second conclusion is that both purchases and sales seem to be informative. The future stock price movements following insider purchases exceed the average stock price movements. Also the future stock price movements following insider sales fall short of the average stock price movements. Hence we confirm the popular belief that, on average, insider purchases are good news while insider sales are bad news.

Another interesting observation is that stock prices do not actually decline following insider sales. They only increase less than the average stock price increase. Consequently it would not be appropriate to short-sell firms reporting insider selling if the investors cannot earn interest on the proceeds of the short sale.[7] That is to say, if one does not already own shares in a firm with insider sales and does not have access to the proceeds of the short sale, there is nothing to do. Hence it is more difficult to exploit information contained in insider-selling activity. We will return to this issue later in the book.

Overall, our evidence indicates that the magnitude of insiders' profits from a round-trip transaction is not particularly huge. There are several reasons for the relatively small difference. First, our sample contains *all* insider trading. If some insiders attempt to manipulate stock prices, then eventual stock price reaction will be in the opposite direction of the initial manipulative trade. Also, if some insiders trade for liquidity and portfolio readjustment reasons, as well as information-related reasons, then our sample contains many transactions that are not motivated by information. When they are all mixed together, the information content of the overall sample is expected to be diluted. Nevertheless, the sample contains sufficiently numerous insider transactions motivated by information reasons, that we can still detect profitability.

Second, it is important to keep in mind that our sample contains only those trades that are voluntarily reported to the SEC by legally defined insiders. If a particular insider willfully engaged in an illegal trade by buying or selling stock based on important, material, nonpublic corporate information, then that individual might execute this transaction using friends and relatives and not report this transaction to the SEC. We construct our sample only from reported transactions. Consequently any trades reported are not likely to contain egregious exploitation of confidential, corporate information. Despite this caveat our sample reveals significant profitability following all reported insider trading.

Third, not all insider trading reported in our sample is based on anticipation of favorable future stock price movements. Surely some of these transactions also represent a realization of profits based on past insider trading. For instance, suppose that an insider expects stock price to increase more than the market index and purchases some shares in his firm. A year later events prove the insider right and stock prices do increase. Further suppose that at this point insiders' expectations regarding future stock price movements are in line with the performance of the overall stock market. Many insiders would now be interested in selling their extra shares and realizing their profits. By selling their shares, insiders can then invest the proceeds in the stock market and reduce their extra risk exposure. After all, given that their salaries and bonuses are already influenced by the performance of their firm, insiders would not want keep the additional shares also tied up in their own firms.

The preceding discussion suggests that there are two types of insider transactions that are designed to exploit information. The first type is active in the sense that insiders anticipate future stock price movements and take advantage of them. The second type is passive in the sense that they close a previously opened position to bring the insider to the desired level of stock holdings. Active transactions are undertaken to open new positions. Passive transactions are undertaken to close existing positions to either realize profits or bring the insider to a desired level of stockholdings. Mixing active and passive transactions will also reduce the information content of the average insider transaction.

To get some idea regarding potential biases in our sample, we experimented with alternative horizons and weighting arrangements. Looking at three-, six-, and nine-month horizons corroborates our conclusions. The difference in returns between purchases and sales average 3.5 percentage points, 5.2 percentage points, and 6.2 percentage points after three, six, and nine months, respectively. Insider purchases indicate good news relative to insiders' sales for all intermediate-term holding periods. Instead of putting equal weight on each firm-month, we also averaged the raw returns following insiders' purchases and sales in each firm and then put equal weight on each firm. These tests resulted in stronger insider performance. The raw returns for sales now average 10.7%, while the raw returns for purchases average 22.6%, yielding a difference of 11.9 percentage points.[8]

Relative performance

While our evidence suggests that insider trading is a useful indicator of future stock price movements, it does not take into account the relative market performance. If, for instance, the market portfolio rises by 30% while stocks purchased by insiders go up only 25%, then insider purchases will not appear to forecast relatively good performance. Similarly, if stocks sold by insiders rise 15% while the simultaneous market portfolio has in fact declined, then insiders' sales will also not be a very useful indicator of relative performance.

We measure this relative performance by subtracting from the return to the stock traded by insiders the simultaneous market return.[9] As a measure of the market portfolio, we use the return to the equally weighted index of New York Stock Exchange, AMEX, and NASDAQ stocks. The choice of equally weighted index reflects the fact that insider-trading stocks are also weighted equally to form portfolios.[10]

Insiders outperform a passive buy and hold strategy when they both buy and sell shares (table 2.2). Stocks purchased by insiders perform 4.5% better than the simultaneous market portfolio over the next 12 months. Stocks sold by insiders underperform the simultaneous market portfolio by 2.7% over the next 12 months. Hence insider trading does provide important signals about the relative performance of the stocks.[11]

Table 2.2
One-year returns net of the market returns (defined as the equally weighted index) following insider-trading months

	Number of trading months	Subsequent 12-month net return
Buy	144,884	4.5%
Sell	164,309	−2.7

Another interesting observation can be made by comparing the difference between buying and selling portfolios reported. With raw returns the difference in the 12-month performance between buying and selling portfolios was 8.9 points (table 2.1). When we take into account the market returns, this difference narrows to 7.2 points (table 2.2). What is the significance of this narrowing, if any?

A potential explanation for this narrowing of the profit estimate is the following: When most insiders buy shares in their own firms, the overall stock market itself tends to do well, thereby cutting into the relative performance of the stocks bought by insiders. Similarly, when most insiders sell stock in their own firms, the subsequent market index also does somewhat worse than average. Consequently the relative performance of the stock bought and sold by insiders looks weaker compared with total performance.

To further illustrate the relation between total and relative performance, let's return to tables 2.1 and 2.2. The 12-month raw returns following insiders' purchases is 24.0% (table 2.1), while the return net of the market is 4.5% (table 2.2). Consequently the market return following insiders' purchases must be 19.5%, since we subtract the market return to compute net returns. Similarly the 12-month raw returns following insiders' sales is 15.1% (table 2.1), while the return net of the market is −2.7% (table 2.2). Consequently the market return following insiders' sales must be 17.8%. Hence the market portfolio rises more following insiders' purchases, 19.5% than it does following insiders' sales, 17.8%. This is what we mean when we say aggregate insider purchases predicts a rise in the market index itself.

An interesting conclusion is that *aggregate* insider-trading patterns may predict the overall performance of the stock market. Aggregate insider trading refers to the sum of all shares bought and sold by all insiders in all public firms at a given point in time. The overall market index may go up more when aggregate insider trading is positive, and overall market index may go up less (or it may even go down sometimes) when aggregate insider trading is negative. This is a very important issue, and we will explore it in greater detail later in chapter 4.

Year-to-year profitability of insider trading

A potential investor in the stock market would be more interested in a relatively recent performance. After all, profitability of insider trading in the 1970s may not be indicative of the profitability of insider trading in the 1990s. In chapter 1 we discussed some important insider-trading regulations that were put in effect during the 1980s. What were the effects of these regulations on the profitability of insider trading? Do insider transactions still reflect anticipated future stock price movements?

For each year from 1975 to 1994, the following information is shown: (1) the number of trading months in that year, (2) one-year net stock returns following insiders' purchases in that year, (3) one-year net stock returns following insiders' sales in that year, and (4) the one-year return to the equally weighted market index (table 2.3). Market index matches each insider transaction in calendar time.[12] Net stock returns are computed by subtracting the market returns during the 12 months following the month in which insider trading takes place from the return to the insiders' firm. Hence a positive net return following insiders' purchases means that the stocks purchased by insiders rose more than the market, thereby confirming the information content of insiders' purchases.

Year-by-year returns indicate that both purchases and sales are informative about future stock prices in both up and down years. An example will best illustrate the reported results. In 1975 the net return following insiders' purchases was 1.8%, while the net return following insiders' sales was −10.8%. The average market return following insiders' transactions was 40.8%. To reinterpret the results, stock prices rose approximately by 42.6% following insiders' purchases (40.8% plus 1.8%), and they rose approximately by 30% following insiders' sales

Table 2.3
Distribution of returns following insider trading from 1975 to 1994

Year	Number of trading months	One-year net returns following buys	One-year net returns following sells	One-year market return following all insider trading
1975	14,139	1.8%	−10.8%	40.8%
1976	14,432	8.0	−5.5	18.8
1977	13,130	6.9	−2.0	27.6
1978	13.060	2.5	−4.2	26.7
1979	13,311	−0.6	4.4	29.1
1980	13,795	3.5	−0.9	26.7
1981	13,403	4.4	−3.6	1.4
1982	14,777	−2.1	0.5	63.5
1983	15,261	4.1	−11.4	1.8
1984	15,010	6.8	−2.3	17.8
1985	14,881	7.0	−0.7	23.7
1986	12,628	−2.1	−3.8	13.7
1987	17,930	3.1	−6.7	−0.2
1988	15,455	2.7	−2.4	17.4
1989	15,939	−0.5	3.2	−9.0
1990	17,626	5.6	5.3	18.8
1991	14,993	0.8	−0.2	21.2
1992	20,352	13.5	−4.2	21.5
1993	21,759	5.0	−3.6	7.8
1994	17,312	3.0	−1.6	−1.3

(40.8% minus 10.8%). Hence both insider purchases and sales were informative about future stock price changes.

A visual examination of 20 years of data shows that insiders' purchases are profitable in most years (table 2.3, column 3). Moreover there is no obvious decline in the information content of insiders' purchases over time. The years in the 1990s appear to be just as profitable, if not more profitable than, the 1980s or even the 1970s. The average return for the first five years in the 1990s equals 5.6%, which is greater

than the 4.7% grand average reported in table 2.2. They are characterized by positive net returns, which means that every year the stocks
purchased by insiders rose more than the market index.

There is some evidence that the profitability of sales has declined
recently. The fourth column in table 2.3 shows the net returns following insiders' sales. A positive number means that the stocks sold
by insiders rose relative to the market index, thereby contradicting the
insiders' sales. A negative number means that the stocks sold by insiders fell relative to the market index, indicating underperformance and
confirming the validity of insiders' sales. Examining the fourth column
shows that the 1990s have been a bit weaker than the average information content of insiders' sales over the 20 years. Four of the five years
in the 1990s have negative net returns, for an average underperformance of 0.9%. Recall from table 2.2 that stocks sold by insiders underperform the market by 2.7% over the 20 years.

Our first conclusion is that the profitability of insider trading is alive
and well in the 1990s. There is no compelling evidence of an elimination of the profitability of insider trading in the 1990s despite significantly higher sanctions against insider trading that were enacted
during the 1980s. In addition, increased SEC enforcement efforts
against the insiders in the 1980s and 1990s have not reduced the
profitability of insider trading.[13] This is good news for investors who
are interested in imitating insiders.

The risks associated with insider trading are evident during the period 1975 to 1994. There are 16 years out of the 20 years when the net
returns following insiders' purchases are positive (table 2.3, column 3).
There are only 4 years out of 20 when insiders actually were beaten by
the market index following their purchases. These are 1979, 1982,
1986, and 1989. The magnitude of the largest underperformance is
2.1%, occurring in 1982 and 1986. In both 1979 and in 1989, the underperformance is less than 1%. In contrast, insiders were able to beat
the market index by as much as 13.5% in 1992. Hence, buying stocks
following insiders' purchases is a not risk-free strategy. There is about

a one in five chance of underperforming the market even if the outside investor buys all stocks purchased by insiders in that calendar year. However, the magnitude of the largest underperformance is rather small.

There are also risks of imitating insiders' sales. Once again there are 16 years out of 20 when the net returns are negative indicating that insiders' sales were a good indicator of worse-than-average performance (table 2.3, column 4). There are only 4 years when stocks sold by insiders outperformed the market, which were 1979, 1982, 1989, and 1990. Incidentally, in three of these four years, insiders' purchases also failed to give an accurate signal which suggests that most of the insider transactions in these years probably were not motivated by firm-specific information in insiders' own firms. Other possibilities include liquidity motivated transactions, risk-based portfolio adjustment reasons, or closing out positions established in previous years. Alternatively, insiders may have mistaken signals that relate to their industry or the economy as a whole with the firm-specific performance of their own firms. We will have more to say about these other motivations regarding insider trading. The magnitude of the mistakes following insiders' sales is also larger, with the largest overperformance equal to 5.3%. Nevertheless, there is only about a one in five chance that selling all stocks sold by insiders in that calendar year would provide a wrong signal.[14]

Duration of the stock price reaction to insider trading

Another important question for the potential stock market investor is how long do stock price movements last following insider transactions? Do prices continue to go up following insiders' purchases for a year? Do they continue to increase for two years? If stock price movements are completed quickly, then it would be necessary to imitate insiders as soon as possible. If price movements continue for a year or two years, then urgent imitation of insider trading is not an important consideration.[15]

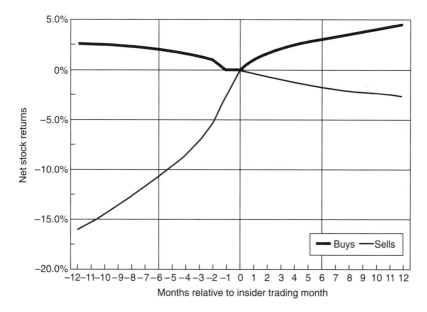

Figure 2.1
Net stock returns around insider trading

A more detailed picture of insiders' motivations can be gauged by examining the net returns for a period 12 months before the insider-trading month to 12 months afterward. Figure 2.1 shows this net return pattern. On the vertical axis are the net stock returns. On the horizontal axis are the months relative to the insider-trading month, which is denoted as month 0. Hence month 6 refers to the sixth month following the insider-trading month. Similarly month −3 refers to third month before the insider-trading month.[16]

We examine net returns separately for purchases and sales (figure 2.1). The net stock return for purchases is indicated by a darker line. Stock prices fall before insider purchases and rise after insider purchases. For sales the pattern is reversed. Stock prices rise before insider sales and fall following sales. Both sales and purchases meet at zero returns for the insider-trading month (month 0). This is by construction to make it easier to measure net stock returns relative to the insider-trading month.

Examining the stock returns following insiders' transactions, we see that following purchases, stock prices rise relatively more sharply for about three to four months and then level off. Similarly for sales, stock prices fall relatively more sharply for about six months and then level off. Nevertheless, the gap between the net returns to purchases and sales continues to widen until 12 months following the insider-trading month. The rather slow and sustained price changes following the insider-trading month in figure 2.1 suggests that insiders tend to exploit relatively long-lived information rather than trying to take advantage some immediate upcoming corporate announcement.

Stock prices continue to drift for at least a year following insiders' transactions (figure 2.1). After 3 months following insiders' transactions, the difference between net returns to buy and sell portfolios grows to 3.1 percentage points. By 6 months this difference reaches 4.8 points; by 9 months, 6.0 points; and by 12 months, 7.2 points. Hence we can make the following inferences: First, stock price reaction continues for at least 12 months following insider trading, since even from month 9 to month 12 there is some drift (albeit small) in stock prices. Second, the rate of stock price drift definitely slows over time. Prices show sharpest reactions during the first 3 months following the insider-trading month. The stock price reaction during the second 6 months is only 2.4%, compared with 4.8% during the first 6 months.

We have also examined longer-term drifts up to five years. Surprisingly, stock price reactions continue to occur after 12 months following the insider-trading month, but at a much slower rate. Prices continue to drift up following insider purchases and drift down following insider sales for about two years. The magnitude of the drift between years one and two is somewhere between one and two percentage points. Beyond year two, stock price drift is minimal. Between two and five years, estimates of abnormal returns is less than one percentage point.[17] Once again, this evidence suggests that insiders are trading on the basis of a general assessment over a two-year outlook for their firms and not specific corporate announcements.

We can draw a couple of important lessons based on our findings. First, it is useful to act on insider-trading information soon, though this is not a critical issue. Within six months of insider-trading month, about two-thirds of the stock price reaction is completed. Subsequent price reaction during the next six months is smaller, and it is not likely to exceed transactions costs (more about this in chapter 14). Second, there is no immediate, large price reaction following insiders' transactions. Instead, there is a gradual (albeit declining) reaction over time. This finding suggests that insiders base their trading not on immediate upcoming corporate announcements (which in fact could be illegal) but rather on a general assessment of the overall direction of their firms over the next two years or so. This second finding also suggests that any outside investors who attempt to imitate insiders can afford to execute their transactions over a period of a few weeks. Instantaneous execution which requires that the investor pay the bid-ask spread does not appear to be critical (also more about this in chapter 14).

Our evidence also shows that that the relative stock price movements *prior* to insiders' transactions are not random (figure 2.1). Instead, relative stock prices decline before insiders' purchases, and they rise before insiders' sales. What is the significance of these patterns? Is there any information here that is useful for the potential stock market investor? We will show that understanding the price movements prior to insiders' transactions can help us separate information-based transactions from liquidity-based transactions. We now turn to this question.

Prior stock price movements

Examining the stock return behavior during the 12 months prior to insiders' transactions, we see that insiders' purchases are preceded by an average *negative* net return of about 2.5%. In contrast, insiders' sales are preceded by an average positive return of about 16%. Moreover biggest price changes occur immediately before the insider-trading month. Why are there such systematic and significant stock return patterns prior to insiders' transactions?

One potential explanation for these intriguing stock return patterns is the following: Insiders may exploit a given piece of information by actively trading on it, or specifically by buying stock before the good news is announced and by selling stock before bad news is announced. This is the usual way that insiders exploit their special information. However, there is another, more subtle way that insiders can exploit their special information without ever running afoul of insider-trading restrictions. We call this *passive trading*. Suppose that a given insider has planned to buy stock but also expects some type of negative news to be released. If the insider buys immediately, the subsequent stock price fall will subject the insider to an immediate capital loss. To avoid this problem, she can simply refrain from buying until after the negative news is announced. In this way the insider avoids having to buy the stock at a high price and thereby avoids the subsequent stock price fall. Since negative news comes before the insider's purchase, the purchases should be preceded by stock price falls as they are in figure 2.1. Notice that since the insider does not trade, she cannot get into legal trouble for postponing a previously planned purchase.

A similar argument can be made for insiders' sales. As figure 2.1 shows, insiders' sales are preceded by a positive net returns of about 16%; hence stock prices rise before insiders' sales. If the insider wants to actively exploit a piece of negative news, she would sell stock before the negative news is released. Alternatively, suppose that the insider has already planned a sale, and she suddenly expects the release of some good news. If she sells immediately, the price would be too low and she would miss the opportunity to sell at a higher price later. Once again, she can simply postpone the sale and wait until after the good news is announced. Since the good news would come before insider sales, they should be preceded by a rise in stock prices as they are in figure 2.1. The passive trading activity for sales here is especially important since the stock price rise before insiders' sales exceeds 15% over a 12-month period. In the last six months before a sale, stock prices rise by about 10%, with half of this occurring in the last two months alone.

One difficulty with the explanation above is that the rise in stock prices before insider sales or the fall in stock prices before insider purchases takes place over a 12-month period. Why do insiders wait so long to execute their passive transactions? Another way of looking at this issue is in terms of active and passive trading framework we discussed earlier. An active trading strategy anticipates future stock price movements and buys and sells stock based on these stock price movements. Suppose that insiders expect better than average performance and buy shares in their own company. A year later, the good news is gradually realized, and insiders close their positions by selling the extra shares purchased and thereby return to the desired level of stockholdings. The first purchase is an *active* transaction. It is forward-looking. It is executed in anticipation of better than average stock price appreciation. The second sale transaction is *passive*. Following their sales, insiders do not necessarily expect negative future performance. They only know that past expectation of good performance is completed and the stock price fully reflects insiders' expectations. However, the level of their stockholdings is above what they would normally hold; therefore they sell the extra shares purchased. In this example the second, closing transaction has no implications for future stock price performance.

We next test our conjecture regarding active and passive trading. If our conjecture is correct, then only active transactions should predict future stock returns. In contrast, passive transactions should not predict future stock returns at all. A second implication of our conjecture is that the probability of an insider sale should be influenced by the current stock price movements. The probability of an insider sale should increase following increases in stock prices. Similarly the proba-

Table 2.4
Prior 6-month net stock return and subsequent trading activity by all insiders

	Stock is up 10% during the past 6 months	Stock is down 10% during the past 6 months
Probability of insider buying	39.9%	49.0%
Probability of insider selling	60.7%	51.0%
Number of shares traded	−17,214	−7,758
Number of events	117,308	136,608

bility of an insider purchase should increase following decreases in stock prices.

To test our conjecture regarding active and passive trading, table 2.4 groups all insiders' transactions by the previous stock price movements. Using previous stock price movements as a classifying variable should bring the difference between active and passive insider trading into much sharper focus. If the stock price outperforms the market index by 10% or more during the six months prior to an insider trade, then we include this observation in the first column. If the stock price underperforms the market index by 10% or more during the six months prior to an insider trade, then we include this observation in the second column. If the net stock price movement during the six months prior to an insider trade is between −10% and +10%, then we exclude these observations.

Our evidence suggests that increases in stock prices makes sales more likely. Similarly declines in stock prices make purchases more likely (table 2.4). The probability of an insider sale increases to 60% following stock price run-ups of 10% or more. The probability of an insider purchase following stock price run-ups is only 40%. Following stock price declines, the probability of buying stocks is about as likely as the probability of selling stocks.

The intensity of trading activity also follows the probability of sales and purchases. The net number of shares traded is significantly related to prior stock price movements. Following price run-ups, insiders sell an average of 17,124 shares. Following price declines, insiders sell an average of only 7,758 shares.

Our evidence is consistent with the conjecture that we can separate active and passive transactions by examining the prior stock price movements. Our findings suggest that many of the sell transactions are likely to be passive. Insiders tend to buy on good news, wait until after the good news is realized, and then sell the stock. Hence, on average, transactions are preceded by stock price increases.

Are there differences in the likelihood of passive transactions for different classes of insiders? If the answer is yes, then we can separate insiders' transactions into active or passive transactions and focus only on the information-related, forward-looking transactions. To the extent there are differences among different classes of insiders, our ability to pinpoint information related transactions would be further enhanced.

The insiders group examined in table 2.4 includes large shareholders many of whom are other corporations whose transactions may be strategically motivated to a lesser extent. Moreover passive transactions are also motivated by risk-aversion, which is more important for individuals rather than institutions. As we stated before, an executive would want to sell the extra shares bought to exploit a given piece of information after prices rise. Corporations may not care as much about the average level of their shareholdings. To examine these differences, we replicate the tests in table 2.4 using only the transactions of the top executives.

When we examine the active and passive transactions by top executives, the relation between prior price movements and insider trading gets even stronger (table 2.5). A price run-up of 10% or more during the past six months increases the probability of selling by top executives to over 68%. Following stock price declines, the probability of purchases and sales are again similar. Also the net number of shares traded by top executives shows a strong negative relation with the prior stock

Table 2.5
Prior 6-month net stock return and subsequent trading activity by top executives

	Stock is up 10% during the past 6 months	Stock is down 10% during the past 6 months
Probability of buying by top executives	31.4%	47.5%
Probability of selling by top executives	68.6%	52.5%
Number of shares traded	−22,675	−12,177
Number of events	29,859	32,041

price movements. Top executives sell an average of 22,675 shares following price run-ups. They sell only an average of 12,177 shares following price declines. Overall, the evidence suggests that selling by top executives is strongly related to previous stock price increases.

This finding is good news for the potential stock picker. Since many of the transactions by top executives represent closing of previous positions, eliminating passive transactions should eliminate a greater proportion of top executives' transactions. The remaining sample of active transactions should be most likely due to information reasons. We now examine the profitability of active and passive transactions.

Profitability of active and passive transactions

The discussion in the previous section suggests that there are two fundamentally different reasons for insider transactions. An active transaction opens a new position for insiders. It is forward looking and it is undertaken with the anticipation of future stock price movements. A passive transaction closes a previous position. It is backward looking and it is undertaken following stock price movements.[18]

As stated earlier the active strategies are expected to be much more profitable than the passive strategies. In fact, if we could separate active and passive motives perfectly, then passive transactions should have no information content for future price movements and therefore have no predictive ability whatsoever. Clearly perfect separation requires that we know why the insiders engaged in each and every transaction, which is not feasible. However, we might be able to obtain an approximate separation by looking at stock price movements prior to the insider-trading month. If insiders' purchases are preceded by greater than average stock price falls, we can classify these transactions as passive transactions. Similarly, if insiders' purchases are preceded by less than average stock price falls, we can classify these transactions as active transactions. For sales we use a similar logic. Sales that are preceded by greater than average price rises are classified as passive, and sales that are preceded by less than average price rises are classified as active.

To operationalize the logic above, we examine the net stock returns to the security traded by insiders during the past six months. In addition we use historical average prior net stock returns to separate active and passive transactions. The choice of six months and historical average net returns are arbitrary. However, our aim here is not to find the optimal cutoff point. Instead, we want to illustrate whether or not such a simple classification scheme works at all.

Average net stock return for the six months preceding insider sales is about 10% (from figure 2.1). If for any particular insider sale, the net stock price rise during the six months prior to insider-trading month is less than 10%, then such a transaction is classified as an active transaction. If the net stock return during the six months prior to the insider-trading month is more than 10%, then such a transaction is classified as a passive transaction. As explained before, large price changes prior to the insider-trading months suggest passive transactions. Small price changes suggest active transactions.

A similar logic is used for insiders' purchases, for which the average net stock return during the past six months is -2% (figure 2.1). All transactions with more than 2% decline are classified as passive, and all transactions with less than 2% decline are classified as active. It should also be noted that this classification scheme uses only publicly available information, and it is therefore feasible for outside investors

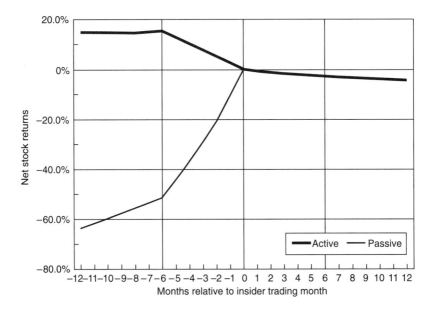

Figure 2.2
Net stock returns around insider sales

to imitate. By the time insiders' transactions are publicly announced, both the stock returns and the index returns are also publicly available; therefore it is possible to classify insiders' transactions into active and passive groups.

The results of such a classification scheme are shown in figures 2.2 and 2.3. Figure 2.2 shows the net stock returns for insiders' sales separated for active and passive transactions. Active sales are shown with a darker line, while passive sales are shown with a lighter line. Since we have classified active and passive sales based on past net returns, prior stock returns are now exaggerated. For active sales, prices decline by about 18% during the six months preceding the insider-trading month. For passive sales, prices rise by over 50% during the past six months.

Looking at the *subsequent* 12-month stock price changes, figure 2.2 shows that for passive sales, there is literally no stock price decline.

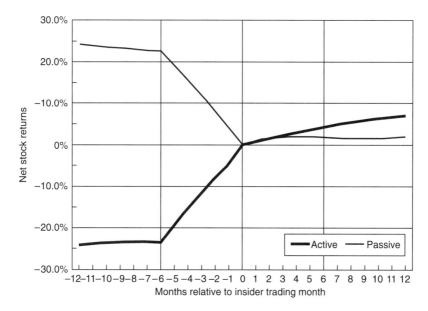

Figure 2.3
Net stock returns around insider purchases

The line for passive sales overlaps with the horizontal axis. As suspected, these are backward-looking transactions, and therefore they are not informative regarding the *future* stock price changes. In contrast, active sales are characterized by about 5% net stock price decline during the next 12 months. Hence grouping sales into active and passive categories using a very crude measure has been able to double the information content of insiders' sales.

Figure 2.3 shows the stock returns around active and passive purchases. Once again, active purchases are indicated by a darker line, while passive purchases are indicated by a lighter line. Stock prices rise about 24% prior to active purchases, and they fall about 22% prior to passive purchases.

Examining the *subsequent* 12-month changes for active and passive purchases, both groups show positive net returns. Passive insider purchases are characterized by a small stock price increase of about 2% for the next 12 months following the insider-trading month. In contrast, active insider purchases shows about 7% net stock price increase. Clearly our separation scheme is not perfect, since even the passive transactions show a small stock price increase. However, our simple classification scheme works reasonably well to separate the passive transactions from active transactions.

Our findings so far suggest that outsiders can almost *double* the information content of insiders' transactions by focusing on active insider trades instead of all trades. From table 2.2 the difference between the 12-month net stock returns to buy and sell transactions for the entire sample was 7.2% (4.5% for purchases 2.7% for sales). By focusing on active buys and sells alone, the difference between buys and sells rises to about 12% (recall from figure 2.2 that prices fall by 7% following active sales and from figure 2.3 that they rise by 5% following active purchases).

The evidence we have presented so far is great news for an outsider interested in imitating insider trading. By engaging in a round-trip transaction following active insider buying and selling, the outside investor can add an extra 12% to his/her portfolio returns (before transactions costs). Given that the market portfolio has averaged about 12% annual return over the past 70 years, this is a substantial advantage over a naive buy and hold trading strategy.[19]

Stronger insider-trading signals

Our evidence so far has shown that insider trading does a very good job of predicting future stock returns. At this point we would like to explore whether it is possible to focus on a subset of the overall sample in an attempt to improve the predictive power of insider-trading activity. We will concentrate on developing a few rules because there are a large number of possibilities to evaluate.

The tests discussed so far still consider a given calendar month in isolation. If the number of shares bought exceeds the number of shares sold in that calendar month, then that month is considered a *purchase month*. If the number of shares sold exceeds the number of shares bought in that calendar month, then that month is considered a *sale month*.

We have so far completely ignored whatever else may be going on during the previous calendar months to formulate our trading strategy. For instance, insiders may be buying shares this month but have sold shares the previous month. Our tests have treated these as independent observations. Can we do better by enlarging our horizon and taking into account insiders' actual trading behavior during the previous months? If yes, how much?

Let's first consider a three-month horizon. The simplest way of strengthening a given insider trading signal is to require that there be no conflicting signals during the previous two months. Specifically, we can require that a buying month not be preceded by a selling month during the previous two months. If it is, then we simply ignore such observations as conflicting signals. This rule will ensure that insider trading over a *three-month* period provides a clear buy or sell signal.[20]

To identify stronger insider-trading signals, we require that there be no conflicting signals during the past three months. For instance, if for a given purchase month any of the past three months exhibits net selling, then that purchase month is excluded. No trading or other purchases during the past three months are allowed. Similarly for sales months it is required that none of the past three months exhibit any net purchases.

The results of the strengthening restrictions are shown in table 2.6. To provide continuity with the preceding discussion, any passive transactions are also excluded. Table 2.6 shows that there are still 85,344 active trading months that satisfy the no conflicting signal criterion discussed above. Of these, 38,473 are buy months and 46,871 are sell months. When compared with the original sample in table 2.1, these restrictive criteria exclude 223,849 trading months, or 72% of the origi-

Table 2.6
One-year raw returns to insider trading firms

	Number of trading months	Subsequent 12-month raw return
Buy	38,473	29.6%
Sell	46,871	10.9
All	85,344	18.7

Note: All insider purchase months that are preceded by a selling month over the past 3 months are excluded as are all insider sales months that are preceded by a purchase month over the past 3 months and all *passive* transactions.

nal sample of 309,193. Though restrictive, there are nevertheless more than 4,000 firm-months per year still available.

Eliminating conflicting and passive transactions improves the information content of insider trading (table 2.6). Stocks actively purchased by insiders that do not have a conflicting signal over the past three months exhibit a 29.6% price appreciation over the next 12 months. In contrast, stocks actively sold by insiders without a conflicting signal over the past three months show a price appreciation of only 10.9% over the next 12 months. The average price appreciation for all transactions in this subsample is 18.7%.

In table 2.6 the difference in 12-month holding period returns between purchases as sales has now increased to 18.7 percentage points (which is the difference between 29.6% and 10.9%). In contrast, this difference for the entire sample of 309,193 trading months is 8.9 percentage points (from table 2.1). Hence we have been able to more than double the information content of insider trading by requiring (1) no conflicting signal over the past three months and (2) no passive transactions. This finding is especially important for those investors who may be interested in imitating insiders.

We have also examined the *relative* performance of stocks actively traded by insiders in the absence of conflicting transactions. Relative stock returns are measured net of the market index for the three months. Net returns are computed by subtracting from the return to

Table 2.7
One-year returns net of market returns (defined as the equally weighted index)
following insider trading months

	Number of trading months	Subsequent 12-month net return
Buy	38,473	7.5%
Sell	46,871	−6.1

Note: All insider purchase months that are preceded by a selling month over the past
3 months are excluded as are all insider sales months that are preceded by a purchase
month over the past 3 months are excluded and all *passive* transactions are excluded.

each stock the contemporaneous return to the equally weighted market index. We use the equally weighted average of the NYSE, AMEX, and NASDAQ stocks.

Firms with active insider purchases outperform the market index by 7.5%, while firms with active insider selling underperform the market index by 6.1% (table 2.7). The difference in net returns has now increased to 13.6 percentage points, compared with 7.2 percentage points for the overall sample (from table 2.2). Once again, requiring all active transactions and no conflicting signal has approximately doubled the information content of insider trading.[21]

Do insiders manipulate stock prices?

In chapter 1 we provided some evidence on the time series properties of insider trading which suggested that insiders do not engage in extensive manipulation. However, this was indirect evidence. It is now time to examine this issue directly. We would like to know if insiders engage in manipulation at all. If so, what are the profits they obtain from manipulation? What signals should outside investors look out for to detect manipulation?

If insiders manipulate stock prices, we will expect them to send out a wrong signal every once and a while. Insiders will have an incentive to manipulate stock prices when their information advantage is small, and market participants pay attention to what the insiders are doing. If the market participants are optimistic and insiders receive a positive signal, they will have incentives to manipulate. In this case insiders might sell some shares, disclose their sales, drive the price down, and later buy a much larger volume of shares at the lower price. Similarly, if the market participants are pessimistic and insiders receive a negative signal, they will have incentives to buy some shares, disclose their purchases, drive the price up, and later sell a much larger volume of shares at the higher price.

If insiders manipulate, we expect reversals in insider trading to be associated with much larger stock price reactions. We also expect higher volume of trading to follow a smaller volume in the opposite direction. Finally we expect manipulation to be more important in the short run and for top executives who are more likely to have sole possession of the special information.

Our evidence indicates that insiders do not try to manipulate stock prices (table 2.8). First, our sample contains 16,665 instances where a given insider-trading month is preceded by a smaller volume of trading in the opposite direction. Hence reversals are not frequent. Second, for the overall sample, insider profits for the 12-month holding period is −0.1%. For the 10,919 sales, stock prices rise more than the market index by 1.1%. This price reaction is in the wrong direction. For the 5,746 purchase months, net stock returns are only 1.7%. Overall, there

Table 2.8
One-year profits to insider trading firms following reversals in insider trading

Insider trading in the current month	Number of trading months	Subsequent 12-month profit
Buy	5,746	1.75%
Sell	10,919	−1.10
All	16,665	−0.13

Note: To be included, insider trading in the current month must be preceded by a smaller volume of trading in the opposite direction the previous month.

is no evidence at all that insiders engage in manipulation. We have reproduced the tests in table 2.8 for top executives as well. Once again, the evidence was similar to that for all insiders and inconsistent with manipulation.

We have also examined the issue of manipulation by looking at volume of trading. While the overall sample may not show any manipulation, larger volume of trading may still be associated with manipulation. The answer to this question is also negative. Even for large volume insider trading that shows reversals from an earlier month, insiders' profits are always less than the overall average profits and much less than the profits when previous month of insider trading is in the same direction.

Conclusions and investment implications

In this chapter we have examined the profitability of insider trading. Profitability is measured both by raw returns as well as market-adjusted returns. We can summarize our findings and recommendations as follows:

1. Stock prices rise following both purchases and sales by insiders. However, stock prices rise more following insiders' purchases than they do following insiders' sales. Hence insiders earn significant profits from trading in their own firms. The stocks purchased by insiders outperform the market by 4.5%, and the stocks sold by insiders underperform the market by 2.7%. Overall, insider purchases are good news, while insider sales are bad news for future stock price performance.

2. The profitability of a typical insider trade is small. For a potential stock market investor, the finding of small profits implies that he/she should not take large positions based on a few transactions by insiders. In addition investors are advised not to short sell stocks following insiders' sales unless they can invest the proceeds of the short sale.

3. Insider trading is profitable in most years. Moreover profitability of insider trading has not diminished over time. Insider trading in the 1990s is just about as profitable as it was in the 1980s and 1970s.

4. There are risks to imitating insiders. Even if an outsider were to buy all stocks purchased by insiders in that year and sell all stocks sold by insiders in that year, there is still about a one in five chance of making mistakes. The magnitude of these mistakes does not appear to be large. Nevertheless, a typical outsider should diversify his/her transactions over a period of years and obtain additional information about the stock before taking on significant exposure based on insider-trading information.

5. Stock price reactions to insiders' transactions appear to occur rather slowly over a 12-month period. In fact stock prices continue to drift in the direction of insiders' transactions even after 12 months but at a slower rate. Also there is no immediate reaction to insiders' transactions. These findings suggest that insiders do not exploit the upcoming corporate announcements as a basis for their transactions. Instead, insiders appear to use their long-term expectations of the prospects for their firms. This finding suggests that immediate imitation of insider trading patterns should not be an overriding concern to outsiders.

6. We have identified active and passive trading strategies. Active transactions tend to be forward-looking, and they open new positions. Passive transactions are backward-looking, and they close previously opened positions. Following large stock price increases, insiders tend to sell stock to close previously opened positions. Following large stock price declines, insiders buy stock to restore previously sold stock.

7. We have discovered that passive trading does not have much future predictive power because they are backward-looking. Eliminating passive transactions increases the predictive power of the remaining transactions. Hence stocks actively purchased by insiders outperform the market by about 7% over the next 12 months, and stocks actively sold by insiders underperform the market by about 5% over the next 12

months. Considering that the market portfolio has averaged about 12% return over the past 70 years, an investor following active insider trading can just about double the returns to a buy and hold strategy before transactions costs.

8. It is possible to further improve the predictive ability of insider trading by focusing attention on a subsample of transactions that are not preceded by conflicting signals. For instance, firms exhibiting insider purchases that are not preceded by any sales over the past 12 months tend to appreciate 30.5% during the subsequent 12 months. Similarly firms exhibiting insider sales that are not preceded by any purchases over the past 12 months tend to appreciate only 9.5% during the subsequent 12 months. The difference between purchases and sales reaches an incredible 21.0%. Hence outside investors who are interested in imitating insiders are advised to look for insider trading that is not preceded by past conflicting signals.

9. Our evidence is also inconsistent with the conjecture that insiders manipulate stock prices. Stock price reaction is much smaller and in some cases in the wrong direction following reversals of insider trading.

3   *A stock-picking strategy*

Additional indicators of profitability

In the previous chapter, we showed that active and passive nature of insider trading and lack of conflicting signals are important indicators of the quality of insiders' information. In this chapter we analyze five additional indicators of the quality of insiders' information: (1) the identity of the traders, (2) number of shares traded, (3) firm size, (4) sales and purchases, and (5) the existence of consensus among insiders. Our goal in this chapter is to flesh out a stock-picking strategy that identifies the most profitable insider trading.

We first begin by examining the profitability of each of these indicators one at a time. It is important to understand just how important each of these factors is in predicting future stock price movements. However, a coherent stock-picking strategy must also examine the interactions between these indicators of profitability. For instance, volume of trade may be an important determinant of the future profitability of insider trading. We must also examine whether this is true for all types of insiders, sales and purchases, and small and large firms. It is quite possible that for top executives, volume of trading may provide an important additional signal of profitability; however, for large shareholders volume may not add much or it may be in the opposite direction. To form a stock-picking strategy, we need to understand these interaction effects between each of our indicators of quality.

Another word of caution is appropriate at this stage. We are working with seven predictors of profitability of insider trading. Astute readers will recognize that there will be over 2,000 combinations of these predictive variables.[1] A fuller treatment of these effects requires statistical tools beyond the scope of this book. In this chapter we will provide general descriptions of the two-way and three-way interactions between various predictive variables. In chapter 14 we will attempt a fuller treatment of the interactive effects. We now turn to the additional determinants of the profitability of insider trading and start with the identity of insiders.

Identity of insiders

As described earlier in the book, there are four general classes of insiders: executives, top executives, members of the board of directors, and large shareholders who own more than 10% of any equity class of securities. We first examine whether the quality of information possessed by these four classes of insiders is different.[2] If the answer is yes, how big are the differences? Is a trade by a large shareholder more important than a trade by an officer? To answer this question and interpret our findings, we must first examine where these insiders might receive their special information.

Insiders who are executives of the firm receive information regarding the future potential of their firms as part of their daily involvement with all operational, financial, accounting, marketing, human resource and strategic planning activities of the firm.[3] Top-level executives plan and execute all major decisions involving the firm. They are also first to find out about all developments regarding their firm. Their in-depth knowledge of their firm and the industry allow them to interpret and understand publicly available information that may be meaningless to outsiders. Consequently there is ample reason to expect that executives, and especially top executives, have a better idea as to where their firm is headed than the average stock market investor.

Insiders who are on the board of directors are one step removed from the day-to-day activities of the firm. Nevertheless, members of the board of directors approve or reject all major initiatives of the firm before they are undertaken, declare or skip a dividend, set the compensation package of top executives, and hire and fire chief executive officers. While they will not be as knowledgeable about the details of the day-to-day business, they certainly receive information about major issues regarding the firm before the average investor in the stock market.

The last group of insiders is the large shareholders. On average, these insiders do not have contact with the daily operations of the firm. Instead, they may have an occasional meeting with the high-level executives of the firm. Depending on the size of their holdings, they may have nominated a member of the board of directors with whom they may communicate periodically. Alternatively, these investors may also trade the securities of the firm and be familiar with changes in order flows. Overall, large shareholders are expected to be farthest away from the day-to-day business of the firm.

Our first task is to discover just how profitable trading by each of these groups of insiders is. This information is important from the perspective of the outside investor in interpreting the various signals given by these groups. If, for instance, a member of the board of directors buys 1,000 shares, is that any different than the information that a large shareholder bought 1,000 shares? Is the information that a member of the board bought 1,000 shares a more important signal than for instance 10,000 shares bought an officer? These are typical questions that potential stock market investors must answer before they can decide whether to imitate insiders.

A second interesting question is the source of insiders' advantage. If the top executives of the firm are most successful in predicting the future direction of their stock, then it is most likely that insider information arises from day-to-day operations of the firm. After all, these insiders are closest to the detailed day-to-day decision making in their firms. If, however, the members of the board of directors happen to be the best predictors of the future stock returns, then insider information most probably arises from familiarity with the major initiative of the firms, changes in dividends and earnings information, and changes in management incentives. On the other hand, if the large shareholders are the most successful group, then it is unlikely that insider information could be attributed to either of these sources. The most likely explanation has to be an information about order flows. After all, large shareholders get their operational and strategic information regarding the firm through secondhand information from the top executives or the members of the board of directors. However, large shareholders will be the only ones to know if they will increase or decrease their stockholdings. Hence information about the order flows is where large shareholders have an advantage over the other insiders.

To address these issues, we have computed the profitability of insider trading separately for each class of insiders. Large shareholders are defined as those insiders who are only large shareholders. If a large shareholder holds executive office in addition, then he or she would be included with the officers group. Similarly directors are those who only hold a position on the board of directors. If a director is also an executive of the firm, then he or she is also included with the officers group. The officer group is a catchall category. Regardless of their other affiliations, if insiders hold an executive title, they would be included in the officer category. Table 3.1 includes a separate group for top executives. To be included in this group, the insider must possess one of the following titles: chief executive officer, chairman of the board of directors, chief financial officer, president, officer and a member of the board of directors, general partner or controlling person. Since these classifications allow overlap (e.g., officer group also includes all top executives), the number of trading months do not add up exactly to the total of 309,193 trading months. Moreover, in a given firm and calendar month, there may be separate transactions by a large shareholder as well as a top executive, thereby leading to double counting. Hence no attempt has been made to obtain a nonoverlapping partition of the total insider-trading months.

We first examine the profitability for different classes of insiders. Once again, insiders' profit is defined relative to the market returns. For purchases, insiders' profit equals the 12-month holding period return to the stock minus the 12-month holding period return to the market index. If the stock purchased by insiders outperforms the market, the difference constitutes insiders' profit. For insiders' sales, profit is defined as the loss avoided again relative to the market. Hence profit equals the negative of the 12-month holding period return to the stock minus the 12-month holding period return to the market index. Following sales, if insiders' stock underperforms the market, this difference is the loss avoided and constitutes insiders' profit.

For all insiders the 12-month profitability equals 3.5% (table 3.1). Interestingly the large shareholders possess hardly any information at all. On average, they earn 0.7% from their transactions. Given the large sample size (32,976 trading months), we can say with a high degree of statistical confidence that large shareholders are, on average, uninformed. This finding suggests that not all insiders have equal access to information. Being classified as an insider by the insider-trading regula-

Table 3.1
Insider trading profits grouped by the identity of traders

	Number of trading months	Subsequent 12-month net profit
All insiders	309,193	3.5%
Large shareholders	32,976	0.7
Directors	140,824	3.6
Officers	277,951	3.9
Top executives	78,403	5.0

tions does not entitle an individual to important, corporate information.

Before we get too excited about the lack of information possessed by large shareholders, a word of caution is in order. We should nevertheless point out that the finding in table 3.1 does not mean that *all* transactions by large shareholders are noninformative. It simply says that the typical transaction by a large shareholder is noninformative. It is still quite possible that large transactions (e.g., 10,000 shares or more) by large shareholders may still be informative. We will examine this issue in more detail later.

Our evidence shows that directors are better informed than large shareholders (table 3.1, row 2). Our sample contains 140,824 firm-months with at least one transaction by a director. On average, the directors earn 3.6% profits over the subsequent 12 months.

The next group of insiders is the officers, who have 277,951 trading months in our sample. Officers earn 3.9% from their transactions in their own firms. Hence officers are even better informed than the directors.

As expected, top executives have the most accurate, most valuable information, and they are not hesitant about using this information in their everyday transactions. The top executives have traded at least once in 78,403 occasions, which accounts for 25% of the overall insider trading sample. Moreover top executives earn 5.0% from their typical transaction. In comparison with the large shareholders, the profitability of trading by top executives is more than seven times the profitability of the typical transaction by a large shareholder.[4]

Our evidence so far indicates an important hierarchy of knowledge, with large shareholders at the bottom and top executives at the top. We need to make sure that looking only at the 12-month horizon gives us an accurate picture of the overall informational differences. Is it possible that the ordering is reversed if we look at the 3-month or the 6-month horizon? To examine this issue in more detail, let us look at figure 3.1 which presents net stock returns during the 12 months be-

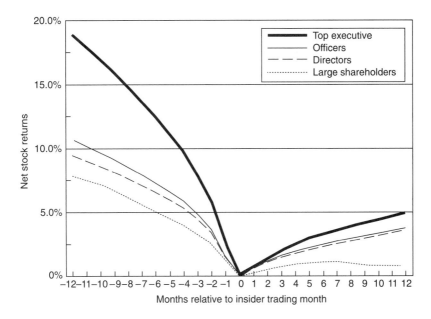

Figure 3.1
Insiders' profits grouped by the identity of insiders

fore to the 12 months after the insider-trading month. Net stock returns for insider sales are normalized to match insider purchases by
multiplying by minus one.

There is nothing unusual about the 12-month holding period. Indeed the profitability of top executives' transactions dominate the
other groups as early as 3 to 4 months following the insider-trading
month (figure 3.1). Over time the difference between the profitabilty
of top executives' transactions and other groups increases. Similarly
the profitability of officers' and directors' transactions exceeds the
profitability of the large shareholders' transactions immediately following the insider-trading month.

Stock price reactions *prior* to the insider-trading month follow a similar pattern. Moreover price patterns before the insider-trading months
are much more pronounced than those following the insider-trading

month. Price declines before purchases (or price increases before sales) are largest for top executives, followed by officers, directors, and large shareholders. These patterns indicate that top executives trade on most valuable information and they are also most likely to return to their preferred level of stockholdings following an information-motivated transaction. As we discussed in the last chapter, risk-aversion probably plays an important role here.

Our evidence clearly points out a hierarchy of knowledge.[5] Large shareholders are at the bottom of the hierarchy with hardly any information at all. From the perspective of a potential stock market investor, a typical transaction by a large shareholder is best ignored. Directors and officers have similar types of information. The information content of their transactions reflects the typical insider transaction. Finally at the top of the hierarchy are the top executives. From the perspective of the outside market investor, this is the most informed group and the type of insider they should most closely imitate.[6]

Volume and profitability of insider trading

Another important observable characteristic of insider trading is the number of shares or the dollar volume of trade. A greater dollar volume of trade indicates greater potential dollar consequences for the insiders. If insiders trade $1,000 worth of shares and prices move 10% in their favor, insiders gain $100. However, if insiders trade $1,000,000 worth of shares and prices move the same 10%, then the dollar gain to the insiders would be $100,000. Hence insiders are a lot more careful when they trade one million dollars worth of stock than when they trade only a thousand dollars worth of stock. Greater dollar trading volumes increase both the positive and negative consequences for insiders.[7]

Does the quality of insiders' information increase with the dollar volume of trade? This is an important question for outsiders who are interested in mimicking insiders. If higher dollar volume signals more valuable information, then outsiders can use the dollar volume of trades to determine whether or not they might imitate insider trading. If not, then outsiders can avoid making mistakes by not focusing exclusively on the large transactions by insiders.

We can think of numerous reasons why one could expect either a positive or a negative relation between volume and profitability. If insiders do not at all worry about potential regulatory sanctions, then they would clearly trade a larger volume of shares when they have more valuable or more precise information. For instance, if insider information implies that their firm's stock price will outperform the market by 20%, we expect that they would trade a greater number of shares than if their information implied only a 2% relative good performance. Similarly, as insiders feel more confident about the precision of their information, they would trade a greater number of shares.

We can also think of situations where larger trade volume could signal less information. Suppose that trading greater number of shares will subject insiders to greater scrutiny by regulatory agencies. In this case greater trading volume would impose greater regulatory costs on insiders. In fact market surveillance programs conducted by the Securities and Exchange Commission watch out for unusually high volumes around important corporate events to look for potential insider-trading violations. Therefore insiders will be less enthusiastic about trading larger volumes of shares to take advantage of a given situation. Instead, they would break up their total trade into smaller trades over a longer time horizon to escape potential regulatory costs.

Another situation where increased volume can signal less valuable information can arise when different insiders trade different volumes of shares. In the previous section we found that large shareholders possess almost no information. If large shareholders also tend to trade much larger volumes than top executives (which they do), then we might find no relation or even a negative relation between dollar volume of trade and the value of insiders' information. However, this does not mean that a given insider would trade fewer shares when they have more valuable information. Instead, this result would suggest that we have not controlled for other important determinants of the value of insiders' information.

There are other situations where increased trading volume can signal less valuable information. Suppose that insiders in large firms tend to trade much larger volumes than insiders in small firms (which they do). Let's also assume that insider trading in smaller firms is most valuable. If we only segment by volume of trade, once again we might find no relation or even a negative relation between volume and profitability since large trades will tend to be dominated by insider trading in large firms. This reasoning suggests that when we segment the data by volume of trade, it is also important to segment by firm size and by class of insiders.

The preceding discussion suggests that we cannot answer the question regarding the relation between volume and profitability by reasoning alone. In this book we define volume of trading by the number of shares traded. Clearly there are a number of ways we can define trading volume. We could also define it as the dollar volume of trade, proportion of the outstanding shares traded, proportion of the daily trading volume, or the proportion of the overall market volume. Each of these measures puts different weights on the shares traded. Since we will separately examine the effect of firm size and market factors, we prefer to define trading volume as simply number of shares traded.

To examine trade volume effects, we use four groups based on net number of shares traded by insiders in a given calendar month: 100 shares or less, between 100 and 1,000 shares, between 1,000 and 10,000 shares, and more than 10,000 shares traded (table 3.2). In each month, offsetting transactions by insiders in each firm are first netted out. Hence volume denotes net trading volume by insiders.[8]

The results show a uniformly positive relation between volume and profitability for the four volume groups. When insiders trade a round lot or less (100 shares and less), there is hardly a price movement over

Table 3.2
Distribution of insider trading profits grouped by net shares traded

Shares traded	Number of trading months	12-month net profit
1–100	24,278	0.8%
101–1,000	86,495	2.9
1,001–10,000	120,160	4.0
10,001–more	78,260	4.4

the subsequent 12 months. These transactions result in a profit of only 0.8%. As the net number of shares traded by insiders increase, so does profitability. When insiders trade between 100 and 1,000 shares, profitability increases to 2.9%. When insiders trade between 1,000 and 10,000 shares, profitability rises to 4.0%. Finally, when insiders trade more than 10,000 shares, profitability reaches 4.4%. The difference between the profitability of the largest and the smallest trade groups equals 3.6 percentage points (4.4% minus 0.8%).[9]

To get a complete picture, we also examine the net stock returns (normalized for sales by multiplying by minus one) from 12 months before to 12 months after the insider-trading month grouped by the volume of trading (figure 3.2). Even if we focus on relative profitability ordering for 3-, 6-, or 9-month holding periods, insiders' profitability still increases with the trading volume. Moreover *prior* stock price movements are also ordered by the volume of trading. This finding once again corroborates our earlier interpretation: As the volume of trading increases, insiders are more likely to engage in an offsetting transaction after the stock price reactions have been completed. Following a large purchase by insiders, stock prices go up, and insiders realize their profits by selling the shares. Hence large sales are more likely to be preceded by large price increases.

What are the implications for the potential stock market investor? First, volume contains useful investment information. Insiders trade

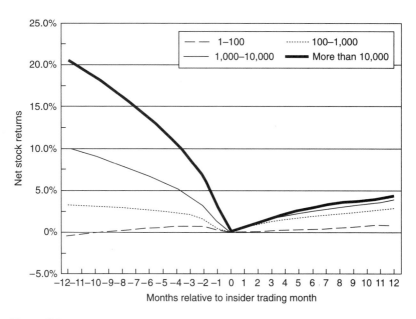

Figure 3.2
Insiders' profits grouped by the number of shares traded

larger volumes to exploit more valuable information. For an outside investor who is interested in imitating insiders, greater number of shares traded by insiders is an important signal of the quality of insiders' information. Second, there is a monotonically positive relation between volume and profitability. Hence there is no critical threshold level where volume begins to signal more valuable information. Instead, there is a gradual positive relation. Third, the relation between volume and profitability is quite strong. Consequently the positive relation between the volume of trade and profitability comes through even before we control for other determinants of the value of insiders' information.

Our evidence also suggests that insiders do not seem to be overconcerned about the regulatory implications of their transactions. If the regulatory considerations had been paramount, we might have found a zero or even a negative relation between profitability and number of shares traded. The positive relation between volume and profitability holds even after regulatory sanctions have been increased significantly in the mid-1980s.

There are also a couple of caveats suggested by the relation between volume and profitability. First, this positive relation is *not* linear but simply monotonically increasing. A trade of 20,000 shares signals more valuable information than a trade of 1,000, but the difference is small and certainly not a 20-fold increase. Hence a simple rule of thumb suggested by the data is that a doubling of trading volume implies much less than a doubling of the information content.

Second, we have only examined trade volume up to 10,000 shares. An interesting question not addressed so far is whether the value of insiders' information keeps increasing at very high levels of trade. This issue is also important because some publications such as the Wall Street Journal publish only extremely large volumes of trade, usually exceeding one million shares. To address this question, we broke down the large transactions into finer subgroups.

The profitability of extremely large transactions follows an inverse-U shape (table 3.3). Profitability first increases and then decreases with trade volume. Profitability of insiders' transactions continues to increase up to 100,000 shares. For months involving between 20,000 and 100,000 net shares traded, the 12-month profitability reaches 4.8%.

Table 3.3
Distribution of insider trading profits grouped by net shares traded for very large transactions

Shares traded	Number of trading months	12-month net profit
10,000–20,000	26,243	4.1%
20,001–100,000	37,049	4.8
100,001–1,000,000	13,185	3.8
1,000,001–more	1,783	0.5

After 100,000 shares profitability begins to decline. For months involving between 100,000 shares and 1 million shares, the 12-month profitability declines to 3.8%. Most surprising are the extremely large transactions involving more than 1 million shares. The 12-month profitability equals a paltry 0.5%. As argued before, such large transactions are most visible and will invite increased regulatory scrutiny. As a result these transactions are not motivated by nonpublic information. An additional rule of thumb suggested by these data is that at very high levels of volume (e.g., more than 100,000 shares), the information content of insider trading begins to fall and profitability almost completely disappears at about 1 million shares.

Earlier we argued that both the class of insiders and firm size can affect the relation between volume of trade and profitability. Consequently, to identify just how much an insider in a given firm might respond to various types of information, we need to also control for the identity of insiders and firm size. Hence the next group of tests examines the relation between trading volume and profitability separately for each class of insiders. This analysis will tell us whether or not each class of insiders trade larger volumes of shares when they have more valuable information. This analysis will also help us compare the value of information when, say, 100 shares are traded by top executives as compared with 100 or 1,000 shares traded by officers.

Interaction between volume and identity of insiders

So far we have determined that both the identity of insiders and the volume of trade matter. We now ask a related question. Does increasing volume signal higher quality of information for all classes of insiders? If so, up to what level of volume? Alternatively, is there a critical trading volume for a give type of investor which signals special information? We now examine the interaction between the identity of insiders and trading volume.

Table 3.4
Large shareholders' trading profits grouped by shares traded

Shares traded	Number of trading months	12-month net profit
1–100	883	3.5%
101–1,000	3,905	0.7
1,001–10,000	10,856	0.6
10,001–more	17,332	0.7

We first focus on the large shareholders. We would like to find out whether higher trade volume increases the quality of large shareholders' information. To address this issue, table 3.4 shows the profitability of large shareholders' transactions grouped by number of shares traded. The grouping for number of shares is the same as the previous tests.

Our sample contains 32,976 trading months by large shareholders. Of this total, 4,788 trading months (14%) involve 1,000 shares or less, while 28,188 trading months (86%) involve more than 1,000 shares. Moreover more than half of the entire sample involves more than 10,000 shares. Large shareholders are also responsible for most trading months that contain more than one million shares. The most likely trade by a large shareholder involves more than 10,000 shares.

Given the dominance of large trading volume for large shareholders, our previous caution about controlling for the identity of insiders appears to be well placed. Without this control large volume of trade will tend to come from large shareholders, who tend to be mostly uninformed. Hence including all the data together would reduce the importance of the number of shares traded for most classes of insiders.

The profitability results for large shareholders are consistent with previous findings. When large shareholders trade 100 shares or less, the 12-month profitability equals 3.5%. However, there are only 883 trading months in this category, so these results should be viewed with caution.[10] For all larger size transactions, profitability remains between 0.6% and 0.7%. Hence, when large shareholders trade 10,000 shares or more, the profitability is still 0.7%.

Given the small number of observations in the 100 shares or less category, it may be ignored. The remaining results in table 3.4 suggest that regardless of the volume of trade, large shareholders do not seem to possess special information. From the perspective of an outside stock market investor in the United States, *all* transactions by large shareholders may be safely ignored.

Why do large shareholders fare so miserably even for large transactions? The most likely answer is that given our definition of no executive officer relationship, these large shareholders are not close to corporate decision-making. Remember that if a large shareholder also holds an officer position, we treat him/her as an officer. Consequently the fact that the law defines them as insiders does not make them insiders in reality. Many of the large shareholders are other corporations, employee stock option plans, or pension funds, who are too far removed from day-to-day operations of these firms. In short, large shareholders do not have regular access to privileged corporate information. The important lesson for the outside stock market investor is to ignore all transactions by large shareholders.

The evidence presented so far points out a potential trap many publications (including *Wall Street Journal*) fall into when they screen insider-trading information. These publications report only the largest trading volumes that extend into millions of dollars by a single insider. As the dollar volume of reported trade increases, individual insiders are less likely to be represented, and corporations that are shareholders in other corporations are more likely to be represented. Hence using extremely high screens for trading volume will have the effect of eliminating officers', directors', and top executives' transactions and focus mostly on the transactions of large shareholders. However, the identity of traders is very important (table 3.4). In particular, large shareholders do not trade on the basis of important information. Even a 100,000 share by a large shareholder does not contain any important information about the future direction of stock prices.

Volume and officers and directors

We next turn to the relation between trade volume and profitability for the officers' group and analyze the profitability of officers' transactions grouped by trade size. We use the same trade size groups as before. Recall that officer class is a catchall group that includes every insider who holds an officer position regardless of their other associations with the firm. If a given calendar month includes at least one transaction by any officer, it is included in our sample. Our total sample contains over 270,000 trading months by officers.

The profitability of officers' transactions increases monotonically with volume of trade (table 3.5). For small transactions, profitability is small. As the trading volume increases, so does profitability. When officers trade 100 shares or less, the subsequent 12-month profitability equals 0.7%. For transactions involving more than 10,000 shares, profitability reaches 5.4%. The difference between the smallest and largest trade size now reaches 4.7 points, as compared with 3.6 points for the overall group.

Once again, officers trade more shares when they have more valuable information. Again, this is good news for outsiders who are

Table 3.5
Officers' trading profits grouped by shares traded

Shares traded	Number of trading months	12-month net profit
1–100	24,160	0.7%
101–1,000	84,233	3.0
1,001–10,000	109,799	4.4
10,001–more	59,759	5.4

interested in imitating officers' transactions. Hence, on average, the greater the number of shares, it is more likely that the officers act with more valuable information. Outside stock market investors should pay special attention to officers' transactions that are more than 10,000 shares.

We replicated our analysis for directors. Our findings are similar to those of the officers, and therefore they are not shown in detail. There is again a positive relation between volume and profitability. For large transactions (volume more than 10,000 shares), profitability of directors' transactions reaches 4.9%, which is similar to the profitability of officers' transactions. Our analysis indicates that directors also trade a larger volume of shares when they have more valuable information.

Volume and top executives

Our final group of insiders is the top executives. Remember that top executives group include only those individuals with the decision making authority over the entire firm. This class of insiders has engaged in at least one transaction in more than 78,000 firm-months. The most frequent transaction by this group is more than 1,000 and less than 10,000 shares traded, which contains 30,373 firm-months (39%).

The profitability of top executives also rises with the level of trade (table 3.6). What is surprising about the top executives is that even the

Table 3.6
Top executives' trading profits grouped by shares traded

Shares traded	Number of trading months	12-month net profit
1–100	7,137	1.1%
101–1,000	18,314	4.4
1,001–10,000	30,373	5.5
10,001–more	22,579	6.1

smallest transactions by top executives exhibit profitability. For instance, for transactions involving 100 shares or less, the average profitability is 1.1%. Hence a 100-share transaction by top executives provides more valuable information than a 10,000-share transaction by a large shareholder (0.7% from table 3.4). This finding points out the importance of the information held by different classes of insiders.

The profitability of top executives' transactions rises most sharply with the volume of trade. For large transactions involving more than 10,000 shares, profitability reaches 6.1%. Table 3.6 indicates that the difference between the profitability of the largest and the smallest trade size groups now equals 5.0 percentage points (6.1% minus 1.1%). This value is greater than the 3.6 points for the overall groups as well as each of the three other classes of insiders. This evidence suggests that top executives' transactions are most sensitive to the value of their information. Top executives are willing to trade significantly larger volumes when they have more valuable information than the each of the other classes of insiders.

From the perspective of a potential stock market investor, top executives' transactions provide the best news yet. Any transaction by top executives involving more than 100 shares is highly profitable (table 3.6). The profitability increases monotonically by volume of trade. Outside stock market investors should pay special attention to transactions by top executives that involve more than 1,000 shares.

The analysis presented so far raises a new question. Earlier we showed that profitability of large transactions increases up to 100,000 shares traded and then begins to decline. For extremely large volumes such as transactions over 1 million shares, there is no profitability whatsoever. We argued that most of these extremely large transactions come from large shareholders who are not informed to begin with. If our interpretation is correct, extremely large transactions from top executives should continue to be profitable. If so, what is the magnitude of their profitability? Second, do top executives worry about the regulatory impact of extremely large transactions?

Extremely large transactions by top executives show a continuing, monotone increase in profitability. Profitability rises from 5.0% for transactions between 10,000 and 20,000 shares to over 7.5% for transactions involving more than 1 million shares. Hence top executives continue to trade extremely large number of shares to exploit their most valuable information. So far this finding is consistent with our previous interpretation.[11]

Once again, what are the implications for the typical stock market investors? Except for large shareholders, who do not appear to possess any special information anyway, identity of insiders and the volume of trade appear to exert independent and additive influence on the quality of insiders' information. For each of the three informed classes of insiders, higher trading volume indicates monotonically more valuable information. Top executives combined with large trading volumes give the most reliable signals about profitable insider trading.

Sales versus purchases

Another observable characteristic of insiders' transactions is whether insiders are buying or selling shares. In chapter 2 we already demonstrated that both insiders' purchases and sales signal information about the direction of future stock price changes. Prices go up more than expected following insiders' purchases and prices go down more than expected following insiders' sales. Our evidence also indicated that the profitability of insiders' purchases exceeds the profitability of insiders' sales. Our objective in this section is to examine the interactions by volume of trade, identity of insiders and purchases and sales.

We begin by examining the profitability of insiders' transactions grouped by volume of trade and by sales and purchases. The results suggest that for both sales and purchases, higher volume is more infor-

Table 3.7

Net 12-month stock returns grouped by net number of shares traded and by sales, purchases

Shares traded	Sales	Purchases
1–100	−1.1%	0.8%
101–1,000	−0.8	4.3
1,001–10,000	−2.4	6.4
10,001–more	−4.5	3.9

Table 3.8

Top executives' profits (losses avoided) following large transactions

Trade type	Number of months	12-months
Buy	4,543	8.9%
Sell	18,036	−5.4

Note: Top executives trade more than 10,000 shares in a month.

mative (table 3.7). Net stock price reaction ranges from −1.1% for small sales to −4.5% for large sales. Similarly net stock price reaction ranges from 0.8% for small purchases to 3.9% for large purchases. Our evidence also indicates that insiders make profits following both small purchases and small sales. This evidence once again suggests that insiders do not attempt to manipulate stock prices by trading a small number of shares in the opposite direction of the information they receive to fool the uninformed traders.

Next we combine identity of insiders, volume of trade, and sales and purchases. Given that the highest level of profitability is shown by large transactions of top executives, it is instructive to separate these trades into sales and purchases to see whether there is profitability for both classes of trades. Table 3.8 shows the breakdown of the profitability of large trades (more than 10,000 shares) by top executives into sales and purchases. Approximately 20% of these trades are purchases, while 80% are sales. As for profitability, stocks purchased by top executives outperform the market index by 8.9%, while stocks sold by top executives underperform the market index by 5.4%. Hence, while both types of trades are highly informative, large purchases by top executives appear to be somewhat more informative. This evidence also agrees with the overall greater profitability of insider purchases discussed in chapter 2.

The implications of these findings for the potential stock market investor is clear. First, volume is informative whether insiders are buying or selling. Second, for all classes of trading volume, stock price changes agree with the direction of insider trade. Third, both large sales and large purchases by top executives are informative.

Earlier we reported that extremely large transactions by all insiders (over 100,000 shares traded) show declining profitability. To get a clearer picture as to why the information content of extra large transactions falls, we have also re-examined these extra large transactions for top executives separated by buying and selling months as well as firm size.

Our evidence suggests that top executives in small firms definitely base extra large transactions (over 100,000 shares) on nonpublic information. Following such trading months, top executives earn more than 10% profits in small firms. The main problem appears to be in large firms. Top executives in large firms make almost no profit at all (0.8%) from extra large transactions in large firms.

Hence this evidence suggests that firm size plays an important role in determining just how aggressively insiders will exploit a given piece of information. It is likely that the top executives of large firms particularly feel that they are subject to greater public scrutiny. In these firms an appearance of impropriety may be just as important as impropriety itself. As a consequence top executives take additional precautions prior to highly visible, very large transactions in large firms. The fact that financial publications such as the *Wall Street Journal* focus mostly on very large transactions in their weekly insider-trading column may further contribute to this restraint. In contrast, such a restraint does not appear in the top executives of small firms.[12]

Firm size and profitability of insider trading

Our fourth observable characteristic of insider trading is the firm size. Earlier we mentioned that firm size may also affect the profitability of insiders' transactions. We now formally analyze both the conceptual and the empirical relations between the profitability of insider trades and the size of insider firm.

Why should firm size matter? We expect that in large firms, a given piece of information is less likely to have a major impact on the stock price. For instance, suppose that top executives in a large firm such as Merck & Co., which is a major health care firm, receive good news that a particular test drug had a successful clinical trial. This new drug is expected to have sales of $500 million per year and generate a net profit of $100 million per year, which is a substantial amount for a single drug. However, Merck's 1996 sales level was around $16 billion with a net income of more than $3 billion. Hence this major new product would represent only about 3% of Merck's sales and income and would have a small impact on the stock price on announcement. As a result insiders in large firms such as Merck & Co. cannot expect to profit very much from insider trading.[13]

Now assume that the same drug mentioned above is launched by a small firm with $3 billion in sales and $100 million in annual income. For this firm the same drug implies a doubling of income. Hence, for a small firm with few existing products, new developments can have a major impact on the stock price, thereby generating more profitable insider trading opportunities.

Just how large are these profit opportunities in small firms? A potential stock market investor interested in imitating insiders would like to find out just how profitable is insider trading in small firms. This information will help outsiders determine how aggressively he or she

Table 3.9
Insiders' profits grouped by firm size

Firm size	Number of trading months	12-months
Less than $25 million	89,239	6.2%
$25–$100 million	80,940	3.1
$100 million–$1 billion	100,283	2.3
More than $1 billion	38,007	1.7

would imitate insider trading. Breaking insider trading in small firms to subgroups such as identity of insiders and number of shares traded can provide further guidance in this regard.

The above discussion suggests that the profitability of insider trading should be inversely related to firm size. Insider trading should be most profitable in small firms and least profitable in large firms. However, while this reasoning seems plausible, we need to examine the data to be sure.[14]

For the purpose of this analysis, small firms are defined as those firms with less than $25 million in equity. The next group includes firms between $25 and $100 million, firms between $100 million and $1 billion, and finally firms with more than $1 billion in equity. While arbitrary, these choices try to balance the distribution of insider trading observations across different size firms, and they simply illustrate the basic relation between firm size and profitability.

Our evidence shows a strong negative relation between firm size and profitability of insider trading (table 3.9). Insiders in the smallest firm size group have 89,239 months with at least one transaction. For the 12-months following these trading months, insiders in small firms earn an average profit of 6.2%. As firm size increases, profitability of insider trading decreases monotonically. For firms between $25 and $100 million, there are 80,940 trading months. The average insider trading profits in this group equal 3.1%. For firms between $100 and $1 billion,

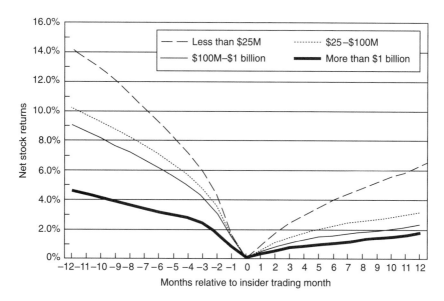

Figure 3.3
Insiders' profits grouped by firm size

there are 100,283 trading months. The insider profits in this group average 2.3%. Finally, for firms with more than $1 billion in equity, there are 38,007 trading months. In these large firms insiders earn a mere 1.7%.[15]

To ensure that the negative relation between firm size and profitability hold for all holding periods, we have examined profitability from 12 months before to 12 month after the insider-trading month grouped by firm size (figure 3.3). Net stock returns for sales are normalized to match purchases by multiplying by minus one. Our evidence indicates that insider trading in small firms is more profitable for all holding periods. Consequently, by focusing on the 12-month horizon, we have not picked an unusual pattern. In addition stock price reactions before the insider-trading month are also ordered by firm size. This finding indicates that passive trading is also inversely related to firm size.

Overall, our evidence shows that insiders in all firms trade profitably. Second, the average profitability of insider trading in small firms is very high. Remember that insider-trading activity includes *all* transactions regardless of the true motive. Despite including all transactions, insiders in small firms are able to earn almost twice the average insider profits and four times the profits of insiders in large firms. Third, insiders in large firms are also able to earn positive profits, although this magnitude is a lot smaller.[16]

What are the implications for stock market investors? First, outside investors are best advised to follow insider trading in small firms, preferably those firms with equity less than $100 million. While profitable such a strategy is not without any drawbacks, since trading in shares of smaller firms will have significantly higher costs. The bid-ask spreads which represent the differences between buying and selling prices tend to be significantly higher in shares of smaller firms. Moreover the shares of smaller firms tend to have thinner trading volumes. As a result the price impact of a given transaction tends to be higher. Outside stock market investors need to take into account all of the trading costs before they can implement profitable trading strategies. We will return to these issues in greater detail later in chapter 14.

Interaction among identity of insiders, firm size, and volume of trade

While our analysis so far answers a fundamental question regarding firms size and profitability, it also raises new questions. The average insider transaction in large firms appears to signal smaller profitability (table 3.9). However, this does not necessarily mean that *all* insider transactions in large firms can be ignored. For instance, it is possible that large transactions in large firms or the large transactions by officers or top executives in large firms can be quite profitable. This brings us to our next question. What is the interaction between identity of insiders, firm size, and volume of trade? For instance, what is the profitabil-

Table 3.10
Officers' profits grouped by firm size

Firm size	Number of trading months	12-months
Less than $25 million	78,479	7.0%
$25–$100 million	73,166	3.4
$100 million–$1 billion	91,500	2.5
More than $1 billion	34,805	2.0

ity of a large trade by officers in small firms? Given that we have 4 types of insiders, 4 firm size groups, and 4 trading volume groups, the total number of subgroups already reaches 64. To keep our analysis tractable, we will focus only on the most profitable subgroups including officers and top executives.

We start our analysis by examining the interaction between identity of insiders and firm size. Specifically we would like to know what is the profitability of each class of insiders in different size firms. Since officers and top executives are the most successful insiders, we start with officers.

Our evidence shows that the profitability of officers' transactions declines with firm size, starting at 7.0% in the smallest size firms (table 3.10). In the largest firm size group, officers' trades show a profitability of 2.0%. Each firm size group contains a large number of trading months. Also officers' transactions in all firm size groups are profitable. In addition officers' transactions are more profitable in every firm size category than the overall sample.

The profitability of top executives' transactions also declines with firm size, ranging from 7.8% in the smallest firm size group down to 3.9% in the largest firm size group (table 3.11). Once again insider trading in the smallest firms is the most profitable. Nevertheless, the evidence suggests that top executives even in large firms are able to trade profitably. In addition the profitability of top executives' transactions

Table 3.11
Top executives' profits grouped by firm size

Firm size	Number of trading months	12-months
Less than $25 million	28,239	7.8%
$25–$100 million	21,307	4.0
$100 million–$1 billion	22,444	2.9
More than $1 billion	6,413	3.9

in large firms is almost double the level of profitability of all insider transactions in large firms.

Our data corroborate an important finding we discussed earlier. Similar to the interaction between identity of insiders and trading volume, identity of insiders and firm size appear to exert independent and additive influences on the quality of insiders' information. There is a negative relation between firm size and profitability of insider trading. This negative relation holds true separately for both officers and top executives.

We next bring in all three factors; identity of insiders, firm size, and volume of trade. Since space limitations do not allow us to discuss all possible combinations of these three factors, we focus on selected combinations. We begin with top executives' transactions in large firms, separated for all four, volume groups.

First, we examine the profitability of top executives' transactions in large firms, grouped by trade size (table 3.12). Small transactions by top executives have minimal profitability as usual. As the trade size increases, profitability also increases. For trades between 101 and 1,000 shares, profitability rises to 3.7%. For trade size between 1,001 and 10,000, profitability further rises to 4.9%. Finally, for very large volumes exceeding 10,000 shares, profitability equals 3.7%.

Our evidence shows that top executives in large firms *do* trade with information. A large transaction by a top executive in large firms (more than 1,000 shares traded) is in fact more informative than an average

Table 3.12

Top executives' profits (losses avoided) in the largest firm size group (firms with market value of equity more than $1 billion)

Shares traded	Number of trading months	12-month net profit
1–100	527	0.3%
101–1,000	1,248	3.7
1,001–10,000	2,224	4.9
10,001–more	2,414	3.7

transaction by an officer in all firms (3.9% from table 3.1). Second, the potential stock market investor must be highly selective when imitating insiders in large firms. The large transactions by top executives represent only about 10% of all transactions in large firms by all insiders. Finally one should not always view higher volumes as profitable. The profitability of trades exceeding 10,000 shares is *less* than the profitability of trades between 1,000 and 10,000 shares. We have also examined profitability beyond 10,000 shares. Our evidence shows that profitability falls further as the trading volume increases beyond 10,000 shares.

In short, our evidence suggests that it is feasible for outsiders to imitate insider trading in *large* firms. However, outsiders must confine their attention only to the transaction of top executives in large firms. Moreover the trading volume that signals the most valuable information appears to be those more than 1,000 shares and less than 1 million shares. At very high levels of trading volume (more than one million shares), caution is advised.

We next turn our attention to exploring the interaction between identity of insiders, and buy-sell decisions in the smallest firm size group. The first striking finding is that insiders' buy orders in smallest firms tend to be a lot more profitable than insiders' sell orders (table 3.13). Profitability of buy orders exceeds 10% for all three classes of insiders while the profitability of sell orders is less than 3.0%. Sec-

Table 3.13
Net stock returns around insiders' trades in the smallest firm size group (size less than $25 million)

Traders	Type of trade	Number of trading months	Net returns for 12-months ahead
All	Buy	51,399	10.4%
insiders	Sell	38,563	−0.8
Officers	Buy	44,264	11.9
only	Sell	34,215	−0.9
Top executives	Buy	15,465	12.3
only	Sell	12,774	−2.8

ond, all three classes of insiders appear to predict the future direction of stock prices very well. For instance, 51,399 buy months for all insiders category shows an average profitability of 10.4%. If we remove the 15,465 buy months for top executives, the profitability of the remaining 35,934 buy orders is still 9.6%. Hence selectivity with respect to the class of insiders is not an important consideration in small firms. However, the lack of information content of the sell orders in small firms is especially noteworthy. This difference between the profitability of insiders' purchases and sales appears to be general phenomenon that stands out clearly in our analysis so far.

Our final interaction tests focus on the top executives' transactions in small firms. Our objective here is to determine the greatest profitability levels by combining the three most important determinants of the quality of insiders' information: (1) top executive class, (2) small firms, and (3) large trading volumes.

Our earlier evidence indicated that top executives in small firms earn an average of 7.8% trade from a typical trade in small firms (table 3.11). When we group top executives' transaction in small firms by number of shares traded, we find that trades of 100 shares or less earn 4.3% (table 3.14). With increasing trade volume, profitability rises monotonically. When top executives trade more than 10,000 shares, profitability rises to 9.8%.

Table 3.14

Top executives' profits (losses avoided) in the smallest firm size group (firms with market value of equity less than $25 million)

Shares traded	Number of trading months	12-month net profit
1–100	2,310	4.3%
101–1,000	7,424	6.8
1,001–10,000	11,683	8.2
10,001–more	6,822	9.8

Top executives in small firms can predict the direction of future stock price movements rather well. All transactions are profitable. Second, even the smallest transactions are highly profitable. In fact a 100-share trade by a top executive in small firms is just as profitable as a typical 10,000-share trade by an officer in a average size firm (table 3.5). Large transactions by top executives in small firms are the most profitable.

Before we leave this section, it is instructive to reflect on our evidence so far. Our indicators of quality exert pretty much independent and additive influence on the quality of insiders' information. For instance, insiders' purchases are more profitable than insiders' sales. This conclusion is also true for all three classes of insiders as well as for different size firms. Similarly higher volume of trade indicates higher quality of insider information for all three classes of officers and directors. Third, insider trading in small firms is most profitable, holding trading volume and class of insiders constant. When we combine these four indicators of profitability, each of them retains and reinforces the information content of the other predictors.

These findings are good news for the outside investor. The fact that predictors of the profitability of insider trading do not show complex interactions makes it easier to replicate most profitable trading. In general, regardless of what else is going on, top executives have the best information. Also, holding all else constant, insiders in small firms do the best. Finally, holding all else constant, higher volume signals the more valuable insider information. To increase the profitability of their transactions, outsiders would do well to focus on decision-making authority of the insiders, volume of trade, and firm size.

Consensus among insiders

Our fifth observable characteristic of insider trading is the consensus among insiders. Consensus refers to the degree of agreement or disagreement among different insiders. We have already made use of a related idea when we discussed possible conflicting signals over a period of back to back months.

We define consensus as the degree of agreement among insiders at a given time. The idea is that as more insiders buy shares (or sell shares) at the same time, the greater the likelihood that they are motivated by information rather than liquidity or personal reasons. Hence we expect that 5,000 shares bought by five separate insiders in a given firm could signal more valuable information than a 15,000-share purchase by a single insider. After all, as the number of insiders trading in the same direction increases, it makes it less likely that that the observed trade could be due to a unique, noninformation related reason.

Consensus may be defined a variety of ways. In the book we define consensus as the net number of transactions in a given direction in the same calendar month. Hence, if four insiders sell stock and one purchases stock in the same calendar month, we define a consensus value of -3. Similarly, if three insiders sell stock and no one purchases stock in the same calendar month, once again the consensus figure is defined as -3. When, say, three insiders buy stock and three insiders sell stock (regardless of the number of shares traded), consensus is defined as zero.

Insiders' profitability increases with selling consensus. When three or more insiders are net sellers in a given month, insiders' profits average 4.6% for 48,560 trading months (table 3.15). As the selling consensus declines to zero, so do average profits. With a zero consensus,

Table 3.15
Insiders' profits grouped by the net number of insiders trading: Consensus among all insiders

Net number of insiders trading	Number of trading months	12-month net profit
−3 or more	48,560	4.6%
−2	30,556	3.2
−1	74,006	1.8
0	15,533	0.2
1	79,023	4.2
2	26,562	5.6
3 or more	34,953	4.7

insiders' profits average only 0.2% following 15,533 trading months. Hence selling consensus seems to be strong predictor of the quality of insiders' information. With an increase in consensus from −1 to −3, the profitability of insider trading increases by 2.8 percentage points (4.6% minus 1.8%).

Buying consensus is a bit less strong. When the buying consensus is +1, insiders' profit equals 4.2%. When the buying consensus equals 2, insiders' profit further increases to 5.6%. However, insiders' profit declines slightly to 4.7% when the buying consensus equals +3 or higher. Hence an increase in consensus from +1 to +3 increases the profitability of insider trading only by 0.5 percentage point.[17]

Consensus among different insiders is an important factor that determines the quality of insiders' information. Higher consensus generally leads to more valuable information. Overall evidence suggests that selling consensus is somewhat more important than buying consensus. While not shown here, additional consensus levels are also analyzed. The results suggest that consensus levels up to five provide consistent information regarding the quality of insiders' information. Consensus levels beyond 5 are quite erratic to be consistently useful.[18]

In this chapter so far we have identified five important determinants of the quality of insiders' information. These are (1) identity of insiders, (2) trading volume, (3) buy versus sell transactions, (4) firm size, and (5) consensus. In chapter 2, we earlier identified two other variables that affect the quality of insiders' information: (6) active and passive transactions and (7) conflicting transactions. To the extent possible we have also explored the interaction between some of these variables. However, we have not explored all of the possible interactions between all the variables. With 7 quality variables the total possible combinations between these variables exceed 1,700. Clearly we cannot examine all possible combinations of the quality variables. Such an undertaking would require the use of some statistical tools, which are beyond the scope of this book.

Insiders' option exercises and other transactions

So far we have dealt only with insiders' open market sales and purchases. However, as we discussed before, insiders report many other categories of transactions. For instance, insiders can acquire or dispose of shares by exercising stock options, warrants and convertible securities. Gifts, private transactions, redemptions, stock splits, employee benefit plans, tender offers, dividend reinvestment plans, and inheritance represent just some of the other ways insiders can acquire and dispose of shares.

Should outsiders pay attention to insiders' option exercises? If so, what is the information content revealed by insiders option exercises? Is it good news or bad news? What is the magnitude of the stock price movements following insiders' option exercises? We now turn our attention to these and related questions.[19]

In this section we will briefly examine the profitability of insiders' option exercises and other transactions. Unlike most of the other transactions listed above, option exercises are important, since they represent a voluntary transaction by the insider. In this sense option exercises are similar to open market sales and purchases and they deserve special attention.

First some preliminaries are in order. There are two kinds of options. An option to buy shares (call option) allows an insider to purchase shares at a fixed price (called the exercise price) during the life of the option. If the stock price rises above this exercise price, then the insider can exercise the option and acquire shares at a below market price. If the stock price falls, then the call option is less valuable.

An option to sell shares (put option) allows an insider to *sell* shares at a fixed price (called the exercise price) during the life of the option. If the stock price falls below the exercise price, then the insider can exercise the option and sell shares at a price above the current market price. Hence increases in the stock price will reduce the value of the put option.

Most of the call options (to purchase shares at a fixed price) are given to the insiders as a result of their employment with the firm. These options cannot be resold in the market. Nevertheless, insiders must report any shares acquired by exercising these options.

Insiders may also purchase call or put options in the marketplace. One way to realize their profit from these options is to exercise these options and acquire and dispose shares of their firm. Alternatively, insiders may simply sell these options in the open market.

The regulatory treatment of option exercises is also important in determining their signaling value. Insider-trading regulations before May 1991 required that insiders must hold on to the stock acquired by option exercises for at least six months. If an insider sold the stock acquired from an option exercise before this mandatory six-month holding period, then he/she would be subject to short-term swing profits rule (Section 16(b) of the Securities and Exchange Act).[20] Consequently, if an insider expected price declines starting somewhere after the next six months, he/she might exercise the options, especially nonmarketable options since they cannot be sold otherwise, acquire the stock, and start the six month clock so that the stock could then be sold safely. However, if the stock price decline were to occur immediately, then exercising the option would not protect the insider since the stock must be held for another six months. Hence prior to May 1991, option exercises could be viewed as a weak signal.

Since 1991 the Securities and Exchange Commission relaxed the option exercise rules. After May 1991 the six-month clock starts from the time the option becomes exercisable. Insiders do not also have to hold the stock acquired for six months. In this case, if insiders expect stock price declines short term or long-term, they can exercise the option and immediately sell the stock at the current high stock price. Consequently, after 1991, option exercises ought to be viewed as a stronger negative signal.

For put options (options to dispose of shares), the signal value is more clear. These put options allow insiders to sell the stock for a fixed price. Hence, as the stock price falls, the put option becomes more valuable. When stock prices rise, put options become less valuable. Consequently, if insiders expect a rise in stock prices, we would expect them to exercise their put options and dispose of shares. They can of course also replace these shares at the current low market value before they rise in price.

Do insiders time their option exercises? If so, what is the level of profits? Have changes in regulatory requirements changed the way insiders view option exercises? Most academic finance studies exclude option exercises. As a result there are no good guides to help answer these questions. It is time to look at the profitability of insiders' option exercises.

Most options involve call options, which give the insiders the right to buy shares at a fixed price (56,030 trading months). Stock prices rise 1.0% during the following 12 months following the option exercises (table 3.16). Our earlier discussion suggested that call option exercises would be more likely if insiders expect a fall in stock price. Hence, for the entire sample that includes pre-1991 data, acquiring shares

Table 3.16
Net stock returns following insiders' option exercises

Type of trade	Number of trading months	12-month net stock returns
Exercise call options to acquire shares	56,030	1.0%
Exercise put options to dispose of shares	1,832	9.3

through option exercises is inconsistent with our reasoning given earlier. Nevertheless, the magnitude of the price change is rather small.

Our sample contains 1,832 exercises of put options. Stock prices rise 9.3% following insiders' exercises of put options. This finding confirms our reasoning given earlier. Had insiders waited and not exercised their options, the rise in stock prices would have reduced the value of their put options. Hence, the evidence is consistent with insiders' timing the exercise of their put options.[21]

Our reasoning given earlier regarding the changes in regulation of option exercises suggests that exercises of call options should be viewed as more of a negative signal after 1991. If insiders possess negative information, they would immediately exercise their call options, acquire the stock, and sell the stock at the current high price. Consequently we might be able to clarify the information content of call option exercises by limiting the sample period to post-1991 data only.

We also examined the net stock price movements following option exercises for top executives after May 1991. As argued above, the stock prices in fact do decline by 0.8% (underperform the market) following insiders' call option exercises. However, limiting the data to post-1991 period also eliminated most of the sample. For the put option exercises, stock prices again rise. Once again, restricting the data to post-1991 period has eliminated most of the sample. Overall, the evidence suggests that insiders do time their option exercises. The evidence appears to be stronger for put option exercises than it is for call option exercises.[22]

Conclusions and investment implications

We have examined the determinants of the profitability of insiders' open market transactions in detail. We have defined profitability with respect to the market index. If the stock price of a firm purchased by insiders outperforms the market index, we declare the purchase to be profitable. Similarly, if a stock price of a firm sold by insiders underperforms the market index, we declare the sale to be again profitable. We have examined profitability of insider trading with respect to the class of insiders, buy-sell transactions, number of shares traded, firm size, and consensus among insiders. Our findings are as follows:

1. Of the four different classes of insiders, top executives are most informed, followed by officers and directors. Large shareholders appear to be the least informed. These findings suggest that insiders' private information comes from the day-to-day contact with all operations of the firm, rather than changes in corporate strategies, potential acquisitions or dispositions, or changes in market volume.

2. On average, all insiders trade a greater number of shares when they have more valuable information. However, at extremely high levels of trades, profitability falls. In fact profitability of trades exceeding 100,000 shares is less than the profitability of trades between 10,000 shares and 100,000 shares. At extremely high trade levels, greater regulatory scrutiny becomes an important concern. The concern about highly visible 100,000 plus-share trades are especially important in large firms. It is likely that all insiders and especially top executives in large firms feel that they are subject to greater public scrutiny.

3. When examining only large trades by insiders, it is extremely important to focus only on transactions by officers, directors, and top executives. Large trades by large shareholders do not contain any information.

4. Insiders' purchases are more profitable than insiders' sales. This conclusion holds regardless of the type of insiders or firm size.

5. Insider trading is a lot more profitable in small firms than it is in large firms. Insiders earn an average of 6.2% in small firms as compared with 1.7% in large firms. For outside stock market investors who are interested in imitating insiders in large firms, selectivity is required. Outside investors are cautioned to restrict their attention only to top executives who trade more than 1,000 trades.

6. In small firms all classes of insiders appear to trade profitably. Hence distinguishing between different classes of insiders does not improve performance much. However, purchases in small firms appear to contain more information than sales. In particular, small sales volumes do not seem to have any predictive ability. Both large purchases and large sales are informative. A large purchase by a top executive in small firms outperforms the market index by 14.7% over 12 months. A large sale by a top executive is associated with 7.8% average profit.

7. Consensus among insiders also plays an important role in determining the quality of insider-trading signals. As more insiders trade in a given direction, the value of insider-trading information increases.

8. Insiders do appear to time the exercises of their stock options. Stock prices rise following insiders' exercises of put options while stock prices decline following the exercises of call options (after 1991). Hence insiders' option exercises also contain important information regarding the future direction of stock price changes. Moreover exercises of put options seem to provide stronger signals. However, other types of transactions by insiders do not appear to provide strong signals regarding the direction of future stock price changes.

9. Interaction effects between sales-purchases, identity of insiders, volume of trade, and firm size are mostly unimportant. Each of these variables exerts an independent and additive influence on the profitability of insider trading. This is good news for the stock pickers, since it simplifies the stock selection criteria.

4   *Predicting future market returns*

Market timing

We have so far discussed whether insider trading in a given firm predicts the future stock returns in that firm. This information is useful to outside investors who like to pick stocks since they can use insider-trading information to decide which stocks to buy and sell. However, most investors do not trade individual stocks. Instead, they invest in mutual funds that are either managed or indexed portfolios that contain thousands of stocks. Hence insider-trading activity in an individual stock is not terribly relevant for an investor who owns stocks through mutual funds.

What sort of information would mutual fund investors find useful? Mutual fund investors ultimately care about whether the overall stock market is going to go up or down. Since the stock market anticipates the developments in the underlying real economy, mutual fund investors also care about macroeconomic developments such as changes in gross national product, index of industrial production, index of consumer confidence, applications for first time unemployment benefits, interest rates, exchange rates, market dividend yields, and market book-to-price ratios, to name a few. The key question for the reader of this book is whether there is any information in insider-trading signals that is useful for the likely performance of mutual funds? The answer to this question is an emphatic yes. This chapter will show the reader how to extract marketwide signals from insiders' transactions.

We can also group mutual fund investors into active and passive investors. Some mutual fund investors can passively invest in a well-diversified portfolio of stocks and bonds and hold it until retirement. These long-term, passive investors would not care about short-term developments such as whether the market is likely to increase or decline next year, recent changes in the relative strength of the dollar, or the latest change in unemployment figures. Instead, they would buy and hold a diversified portfolio and guarantee themselves the average market returns in good times and bad times. I would advise and encourage this kind of discipline on all investors. However, this book does not offer any advice to passive mutual fund investors.

Many mutual fund investors are not interested in passive investing. These investors enjoy actively managing their portfolios. This active management may be simply reading about star portfolio managers and shopping for the best portfolio manager, delaying or accelerating investments into a retirement portfolio, or actively shifting between different types of mutual funds depending on their outlook for the economy. This process of always looking for the highest returns and getting in and out of the stock market is called *market timing*. For market timers, once again, macroeconomic information is paramount.

Investors have many choices of mutual funds such as a government or a corporate bond fund or a stock fund. Among stock funds, investors can choose between aggressive, growth-oriented risky mutual funds or less risky, income-producing, value-oriented mutual funds. In addition, depending on their outlook, investors can choose sector portfolios that specialize in a particular industry, such as health care, precious metals, or oil-related funds, or stocks that have a common characteristic such as high-technology or consumer nondurables. What types of mutual funds are best depends on how risk-averse investors are as well as their outlook for the economy and its various sectors.

Market timers evaluate all macroeconomic developments, assess whether the stock prices are going to go up or down and then position their assets in such a way as to maximally benefit from expected future economic changes. In good times, stocks are more likely to outperform bonds due to increasing corporate cash flows. If the macro information suggests an economic upturn, then the market timer can switch from cash or a low-risk bond portfolio to a higher-risk stock portfolio. If the market timer already holds a stock portfolio, then she can switch to a more risky, aggressive growth mutual fund, which would benefit more from a rising stock market. Depending on her taste for risk, a market timer can also buy index futures that will also pay off positively when stock prices rise. Alternatively, if the macro information signals an economic downturn, then safer assets are likely to outperform riskier assets. In this case the market timer can either shift away from the stock market into bonds and cash, or she can establish a short position in the market portfolio by using options or index futures, thereby avoiding the negative future market returns.

Aggregate insider trading

How does insider trading fit in this picture? Do corporate insiders possess macroeconomic information, which they reveal through their transactions in their own firms? If so, where do insiders get their macroeconomic information?[1]

On the face of it, a proposition that insider trading can predict market returns seems rather implausible. After all, the information that insiders possess is related specifically to their own firms. Insiders possess no more special information regarding interest rate movements, monetary targets, aggregate employment, or the growth rate of the Gross National Product any more than you and I do. What insiders do know are things like whether their firm is doing a good job of controlling expenses, whether they are facing increasing or decreasing product market competition, and whether sales are likely to improve or worsen over time. None of this information directly relates to macroeconomic conditions. Hence where could insiders get nonpublic macroeconomic information to help them predict future market returns?

There is a way out of this paradox. While insider information does not pertain directly to the macroeconomy, the signals insiders observe *are* affected by macroeconomic developments. Consequently there should be some relation between insider trading and macroeconomic developments. For instance, changes in interest rates affect the firm's sales levels, profit margins, and the ability of the firm to borrow additional capital. While insiders do not know what will happen to future interest rates, they do observe the effects of recent interest rate changes in their own firms before other market participants do. Consequently the signals on which insiders base their trading decisions are affected by macroeconomic developments.

Second and more important, insiders are best positioned to interpret the implications of macroeconomic developments for their own firms. It is difficult for outsiders to infer the implication of events such as interest rate changes or exchange rate changes on the profitability of a given firm without knowing specifically how the firm is financed. For instance, suppose that short-term interest rates have risen by 100 basis points over the past six months, while the long rates have remained constant. Also suppose that an auto manufacturer has recently taken a long-term bank loan and retired its short-term bank loan. In this case the increases in short-term interest rates may have less of an effect on the profitability of the firm. Consider the situation of an executive in our auto manufacturing firm. This officer is best suited to understand the extent to which such an increase in short-term interest rates will cause a squeeze on her firm's profit margins, reduce the sales volume, or favor their competitors. Outsiders who do not have access to this information will have a hard time understanding the implications of changes in short-term interest rates for the profitability of this firm. Hence an outsider and an insider can observe the same publicly available information about changes in interest rates; yet she will understand what this means for her firm while the outsiders will be at a disadvantage.[2]

The preceding discussion suggests that insiders are best positioned to observe the effects and understand the implications of macroeconomic developments for their own firm's stock price. Insider trading at a given point in time represents a forecast of how insider-firm's stock price is going to fare in the future. When we aggregate all individual stocks into a portfolio, we get the market portfolio. Hence aggregate insider trading across all firms should predict the aggregate market returns. The conjecture that aggregate insider trading should forecast the future market returns is not only plausible, but it is also quite compelling. Ultimately whether insider trading in reality predicts future states of the economy and through this channel also predicts the future market returns is an empirical question. Our discussion so far suggests that it has the possibility of predicting both. The next step is to actually examine whether our conjecture is borne out by the facts.

Aggregate insider trading and future real activity

We have argued so far that aggregate insider trading has the potential to predict future market returns and the future state of the economy. We have argued that insiders can observe the effects of future changes in the real activity in their own firms before other market participants and trade on the basis of these signals. To test these conjectures, we need to flesh out what we mean by future state of the economy.

We will measure the state of the economy by three variables: The growth rates of gross national product (GNP), the index of industrial production (IIP), and the corporate profits. We use these three different measures for real activity to make sure that we are genuinely measuring economic growth rather than a particular characteristic of the measured data. These three different variables capture different aspects of

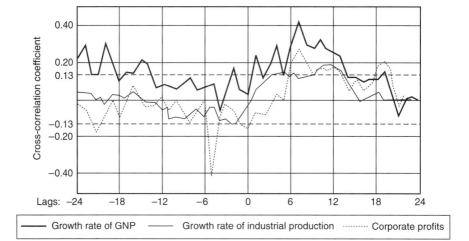

Figure 4.1
Cross-correlations of the aggregate insider trading at time *t-LAG*, with the growth rate of GNP, growth rate of index of industrial production, and the growth rate of after-tax corporate profits at time *t*.

economic growth. The proposition that the aggregate insider trading reflects insiders' view about the future real activity is testable. We now test our conjecture.

We examine the contemporaneous, lagged, and leading correlations between aggregate insider-trading activity and real activity (figure 4.1). As before, aggregate insider-trading activity is measured by the proportion of stocks purchased by insiders in each calendar month. Real activity is measured by the continuously compounded growth rates of GNP, IIP, and after-tax corporate profits after inventory and capital consumption adjustments.

Our evidence shows that current aggregate insider trading is generally positively correlated with the growth rates of GNP from 24 months before the insider-trading month to 24 months following the insider-trading month.[3] The cross-correlations between aggregate insider trading and the growth rate of GNP are *significantly* positive from two years before to about one year before the insider-trading month. Similarly the correlation between aggregate insider trading and the growth rate of GNP are *significantly* positive from one month following the insider-trading activity and up to 19 months ahead. Maximum correlation occurs at about 7 months ahead. Hence current aggregate insider trading is strongly positively correlated with insiders' views regarding future GNP growth rate. Overall, our evidence tells us that insiders buy stock up to 20 months before an increase in real activity, and they sell stock up to 20 months before a decline in real activity.

We also examine the cross-correlations with aggregate insider trading and the past and future growth rates of the IIP, which reflects the performance of the manufacturing sector. These correlations are generally weaker than those for the GNP. Given that service sector has become the most dominant part of the U.S. economy, weaker correlations for the index of industrial production should not be surprising. Nevertheless, the positive correlation between aggregate insider trading and growth rates of IIP become significant at about 3 months, and they remain significantly positive up to about 14 months ahead.

Finally we examine the cross-correlations between aggregate insider trading and the corporate profit variable. These correlations fall in between those for the GNP and IIP in strength. Once again, the relation between current aggregate insider trading and future corporate profits is positive. These correlations attain significance at about 6 months and remain significantly positive past 20 months. Hence insiders buy before an increase in corporate profits and insiders sell before a decrease in corporate profits.

Interestingly our evidence also shows that there is a significant negative correlation between current insider trading and *past* corporate profits. Hence insiders buy following a decline in corporate profits, and insiders sell following an increase in corporate profits. These negative correlations may underlie the reversals of insider-trading patterns we have seen in chapters 2 and 3.

The evidence we have presented so far suggests that indeed insiders receive signals about the effects of macroeconomic changes in their own firms before other market participants and trade on the basis of these signals. Studies from finance literature show that stock prices are also a leading indicator of future real activity. In fact studies have shown that stock prices reflect future changes in real activity up to one year ahead. We have demonstrated that aggregate insider trading reflects changes in future real activity up to two years ahead (figure 4.1). Consequently it should come as no surprise that aggregate insider trading could potentially forecast future stock returns. This is the task we now return to. Our next set of tests examines the relation between current aggregate insider trading and the future market returns.

50%–50% rule

Our first order of business is to operationalize a procedure to extract economywide signals from observed insider trading. We do this by summing insiders' transactions at a given time across all the firms in the economy. This aggregation process eliminates firm-specific reasons for insiders' buy and sell transactions and extracts a common, marketwide component. Hence by aggregate insider trading we mean the sum of all insiders' trades across all firms at a given point in time.

Let's be more specific. What exactly do we mean by aggregate insider trading? There are a number of ways we can define and aggregate insider trading. We can refer to number of firms with insider trading, the number of insiders, number of transactions, or number of shares traded. Each of these will capture a different aspect of aggregate insider-trading activity. In this book we again use the number of shares to decide whether a given firm is a buyer or seller. We then sum up the number of firms to decide if there is an economywide buy or a sell signal.

An example should clarify our procedure. Let's compute the aggregate insider-trading signal for the month of January 1976. Consider General Motors Corporation as an initial example. If the total shares bought by all insiders in GM exceed the total shares sold by all insiders in GM during January 1976, then we consider GM as a buyer and assign GM a weight of +1. If the shares sold by insiders exceed the shares purchased, then GM is considered a seller and it receives a weight of −1. If the shares sold exactly equal the shares purchased, or if there is no transaction by insiders, then GM gets a weight of zero.[4]

Having examined insider trading in one firm, we then repeat this procedure for all publicly held firms in January 1976 and assign weights of +1, −1, or 0 to all firms. Next, we sum these weights for all firms for the month of January 1976 separately for purchases and sales. For instance, in January 1976 there were 685 firms as buyers and 646 firms as sellers, yielding a net number of buyers of 39 (685 minus 646). Hence, using the net number of firms buying, January of 1976 was an aggregate-buying month.

We then look back 3 months, 6 months, 9 months, and 12 months and sum the number of buyers and sellers for each month during these observation periods. If over the past *three* months, for instance, the number of buying firms exceeds the number of selling firms, then we declare that an aggregate insider buy signal has been obtained for the last three months. Similarly, if the number of selling firms exceeds the number of buying firms, we declare an aggregate sell signal for the last three months. Since we declare an observation period as a buy month if 50% or a greater proportion of firms are net buyers or a sell period if 50% or a greater proportion of firms are net sellers, we call this rule the 50%–50% rule. We also repeat this procedure for six, nine, and twelve month observation periods. Finally we repeat this procedure for every possible month from 1975 to 1994.

Our procedure to compute aggregate insider trading outlined above has a number of advantages and disadvantages. First, our procedure focuses on firms that actually report insider trading and ignores firms that have no insider trading. Whether 20% or 70% of the firms are trading at a given point in time does not affect our aggregate insider-trading measure. One can argue that the quality of the insider-trading signals increases in the proportion of the firms trading. Using this logic, we should give a greater weight to those months with a greater proportion of firms reporting insider trading. We will come back to this refinement later.

In addition our conclusions are not affected by the number of firms since we examine the *proportion* of firms with insider trading at a given point in time. Consequently the fact that the number of firms with insider trading has increased from 3,000 in 1975 to over 7,000 in 1996 does not adversely affect our classification procedure. As a result we can compare aggregate insider sentiment in January of 1976 with that of January 1994 without introducing obvious biases. This is a clear advantage of our procedure.[5]

Our procedure described above explicitly assigns each firm an equal weight. Presumably the ability of insiders to observe the effects of macroeconomic signals in their own firms need not be the same in every firm. In fact we would expect that in firms that are more sensitive to business cycles (high-risk firms), insiders would be more likely to observe and act on the basis of economywide signals. This line of reasoning suggests that an improved measure might weight each firm differently. Firms that are more sensitive to business cycles would receive a greater weight. Firms that are insensitive to business cycles might receive a smaller weight. Moreover the weights can be constructed to be proportional to each firm's sensitivity to business cycles. We have not pursued this improvement in this book, since our aim is to show that even a crude measure of aggregate insider trading has significant forecasting ability. Such an improvement would only result in increased forecasting power.[6]

In addition the 50%–50% cutoff proportion that we use is arbitrary. We could have also required insiders to buy in 55% of the firms to declare a buying period, or to buy in 45% of the firms to declare a selling period. In fact, later in this book, we will examine the forecasting characteristics of additional rules such as 55%–45% or 60%–40%. Empirically it turns out that the results are not extremely sensitive to particulars of how we define aggregate insider-trading signals. This in-

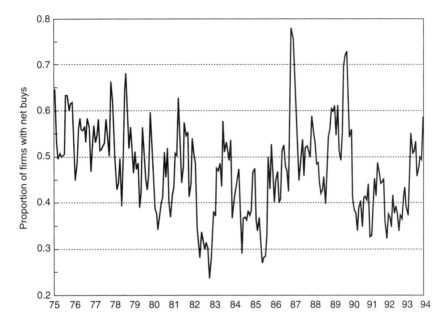

Figure 4.2
Proportion of firms with net insider buying for 1975 to 1994

sensitivity gives us more confidence that our findings are robust, and they do not depend on the particular way we measure aggregate insider-trading signals.

Let's start by examining the aggregate insider trading patterns from 1975 to 1994 (figure 4.2). The average proportion of firms with net buying is slightly under 50%, or at 47.2%. Hence, given our definition of buy and sell signals, sellers have a slight advantage over buyers for the 1975 to 1994 period.

Data also indicate that the aggregate buy proportion moves rather slowly. When the buy proportion is above the sample average of 47%, it spends a long time above the sample average and then returns to the sample average. Similarly, once the proportion moves below 47%, it spends a long time below the sample average and then returns to the sample average. This observation suggests that the proportion of firms with net buying is a mean-reverting process. Namely, when the buying proportion moves away from the sample average, it is more likely to return to the sample average rather than move further away.

There is also significant variation in the net proportion of firms over the sample period. The minimum value of buyers reaches 25% while the maximum value of buyers reaches 78%. This large variation in aggregate insider-trading signals increases our confidence that it has a chance to forecast future economic developments. If in contrast, the proportion of buyers were to vary between 46% and 48%, it would almost be a constant, incapable of predicting any variable.

Examining the year-to-year trends shows that the net proportion of buyers starts out about 65% in 1975, and fluctuates around 50% until late 1981. In 1982 the proportion of net buyers starts a sharp decline and reaches the sample low of 25% by late 1982. The proportion of net buyers remains below 50% until late 1987. The crash of October 1987 is associated with a huge increase in buying activity and the proportion of net buyers jumps to the sample peak of 78%. The middle of 1990 witnesses another sharp decline in insider buying which sends the ratio of net buyers to below 40%. Net buyers remains low until 1994, when it finally rises over 50%.

Our thesis is that buy and sell signals obtained from aggregate insider-trading activity will predict the overall future stock market returns. To measure the overall stock market returns, we use the equally weighted average of all New York Stock Exchange (NYSE), American Stock Exchange (AMEX), and over-the-counter (NASDAQ) firms. This index contains over 8,000 firms and weights the returns to each firm equally. As for holding periods, we look ahead 3, 6, 9, and 12 months following the month in which an aggregate insider-trading signal has been obtained.

Our prediction is that an increase in aggregate insider purchases will signal an increase in the market portfolio over a variety of holding periods. An increase in aggregate insider sales will signal a decrease in the market portfolio over a variety of holding periods. To begin our

Table 4.1
Market returns following aggregate insider trading signals

Aggregate insider trading during the past 3 months	Number of quarters	Subsequent 3-month raw return to equally weighted index	Probability of up market
Buy	31	5.7%	74.2%
Sell	48	3.9	62.5

Note: A buy signal is obtained if 50% or more of the firms report net buying activity during the past 3 months.

analysis, we choose past three months to measure aggregate insider trading and examine the future aggregate market returns over the next three months using the 50%–50% rule. Our 20-year sample period from 1975 to 1994 is broken into 80 nonoverlapping 3-month periods. We lose the first 3-month period to compute past aggregate insider-trading activity. Hence there are 79 prediction periods. Thirty-one of these were aggregate insider buy periods, and 48 were aggregate insider sell periods.

Market returns are predictable using the past aggregate insider-trading activity (table 4.1). Following past insider buying periods, stock prices increase by 5.7%. Following past insider selling periods, stock prices increase only by 3.9%. Hence, a positive aggregate insider-trading signal is associated with a 1.8-point (5.7% minus 3.9%) additional market return than a negative aggregate insider-trading signal.

In addition to the magnitude of market returns, the *probability* of a stock price increase is also higher following positive aggregate insider trading. The probability of a positive three-month return on the equally weighted portfolio is 74.2% (23 out of 31) following positive insider-trading signals (table 4.1). The probability of positive three-month market returns falls to 62.5% (30 out of 48) following negative insider-trading signals. Hence both the average returns and the frequency of positive returns is enhanced with a positive aggregate insider trading signal.

This first set of results confirms our thesis. Aggregate insider-trading activity is a useful signal to predict future market returns. On average, the stock market increases more following insiders' buy signals than it does following insiders' sell signals. Moreover the probability of a stock market increase is also higher following aggregate insider purchase activity.

Does the predictive power of the aggregate insider trading hold over other observation periods? The use of a longer time period to aggregate insider-trading activity is more likely to cancel out insider trading that is not related to macroeconomic movements and thereby provides a more accurate signal. To test this conjecture, we examine a six-month measurement period. Aggregate insider trading over the past six months is computed and the return to the equally weighted market index is observed over the next six months. Our 20-year sample period contains 40 six-month periods. Since we lose the first 6-month period to compute the past insider-trading signal, we only have 39 holding periods.

There are 18 periods where the six-month aggregate insider trading provides a positive signal (table 4.2). Following these periods, the equally weighted market index has risen 10.7% over the next six months. In contrast, there are 21 six-month periods with a negative insider-trading signal. The equally weighted index has risen only 7.4% following these periods. The difference equals 3.3 points (10.7% minus

Table 4.2
Market returns following aggregate insider trading signals

Aggregate insider trading during the past 6 months	Number of 6-month periods	Subsequent 6-month raw return to equally weighted index	Probability of up market
Buy	18	10.7%	66.7%
Sell	21	7.4	71.4

Note: A buy signal is obtained if 50% or more of the firms report net buying activity during the past 6 months.

Table 4.3
Market returns following aggregate insider trading signals

Aggregate insider trading during the past 9 months	Number of 9-month periods	Subsequent 9-month raw return to equally weighted index	Probability of up market
Buy	8	16.7%	87.5%
Sell	17	8.6	70.6

Note: A buy signal is obtained if 50% or more of the firms report net buying activity during the past 9 months.

7.4%). The predictive power of the aggregate insider trading is far from perfect. The probability of an up-market was slightly lower following positive insider-trading signals than following negative insider-trading signals (66.7% versus 71.4%).

We next increase both the aggregation period and the holding period to nine months (table 4.3). Following eight periods with positive insider-trading signals, the equally weighted market index rises by 16.7% (87.5% probability of an up market). Following sell signals, the equally weighted market index rises only by 8.6% (probability of an up market is 70.6%). Using a longer holding period now increases the difference in market returns to 8.1 points (16.7% minus 8.6%).

Based on our results so far, we would expect the information content of the aggregate insider-trading signal to increase with the length of the aggregation period. Next, we examine a 12-month aggregation period to compute the aggregate insider-trading signals. Using a longer aggregation period, we can also compare whether longer-term aggregate insider trading does a better job of forecasting the shorter-term market returns than a shorter-term aggregate insider-trading signal. Hence we aggregate insider trading over the past 12 months and also re-examine the returns for the equally weighted index for the future 3-month, 6-month, and 12-month periods.

Following 29 positive insider-trading signals during the past 12 months, the market index rises 6.2% over the next *three* months

Table 4.4

Market returns following aggregate insider trading signals

Aggregate insider trading during the past 12 months	Number of 3-month periods	Subsequent 3-month raw return to equally weighted index	Probability of up market
Buy	29	6.2%	75.9%
Sell	47	3.6	61.7

Note: A buy signal is obtained if 50% or more of the firms report net buying activity during the past 12 months.

(table 4.4). Following 47 negative signals, the market index rises only by 3.6% over the next three months. Insider trading also forecasts the probability of market returns rising or falling. The probability of up markets is 75.9% versus 61.7%, respectively.

Comparing the results with earlier results shows that the 12-month aggregate insider trading does a better job of forecasting the 3-month-ahead returns to the equally weighted index than the 3-month aggregate insider trading. The difference in market returns is 2.6 points using the 12-month aggregation period, while the difference is only 1.8 points using the 3-month aggregation period (tables 4.1 and 4.4). Hence greater aggregation of insider-trading activity over the past 12 months produces more reliable buy and sell signals even for the short-term market returns.[7]

This finding once again confirms our earlier interpretation. Insider trading is capturing changes in the economy that is likely to take place over the next one or two years. As a result most recent changes in insider trading are not designed to exploit events that will take place over the next three months but rather events that will take place over the next year. Consequently the 12-month moving average of insider trading is much more informative than the 3-month moving average.

We now use the 12-month aggregate insider-trading signal to predict the 6-month-ahead returns to the equally weighted index. Following 15 periods with a positive insider signal, the equally weighted index

Table 4.5
Market returns following aggregate insider trading signals

Aggregate insider trading during the past 12 months	Number of 6-month periods	Subsequent 6-month raw return to equally weighted index	Probability of up market
Buy	15	14.1%	80.0%
Sell	23	6.2	65.2

Note: A buy signal is obtained if 50% or more of the firms report net buying activity during the past 12 months.

Table 4.6
Market returns following aggregate insider trading signals

Aggregate insider trading during the past 12 months	Number of 12-month periods	Subsequent 12-month raw return to equally weighted index	Probability of up market
Buy	7	28.7%	100.0%
Sell	12	12.9	66.7

Note: A buy signal is obtained if 50% or more of the firms report net buying activity during the past 12 months.

rises 14.1% during the next 6 months (table 4.5). Following the 23 periods with a negative insider-trading signal, the equally weighted index rises only 6.2% during the next 6 months. The difference in returns now reaches 7.9 points. Once again, compared with earlier results, the 12-month aggregate insider-trading signal does a much better job of forecasting the 6-month-ahead returns than the past 6-month aggregate insider-trading activity.

Finally, we use the 12-month aggregate insider-trading signals to forecast the returns to the equally weighted index for the next twelve months. With annual forecasting, there are only 19 years to forecast. Following the 7 years with positive insider trading, the equally weighted index rises by 28.7% during the next 12 months (table 4.6). Following the 12 years with a negative insider-trading signal, the equally weighted index rises only 12.9% during the next 12 months. The difference in market returns now reaches 15.8 points. This represents an incredible predictive ability. Moreover the return to the market index is positive for each of the 7 years (100%) with a preceding positive insider-trading signal. In contrast, only 8 of the 12 years (66.7%) with a preceding negative aggregate insider-trading signal has a positive market return.

The results so far show a strong positive relation between aggregate insider activity and the future market returns.[8] These findings support our conjecture that the signals insiders observe are affected by macroeconomic events. Moreover insiders best understand the implications of macroeconomic events for the performance of their own firms. Consequently the aggregate insider trading captures an important component of the future market returns.

Our findings so far indicate that when aggregate insider trading is positive, namely when insiders in different firms happen to buy the shares of their own firms, the future market returns tend to be strongly positive. However, the converse is not true. Namely, when insiders in aggregate sell the stock of their own firms, the future market return is not negative. Instead, it is a smaller positive amount. Hence aggregate insider sales do not predict a decline in the stock market, only a smaller increase than the average. For instance, using the annual returns, an aggregate insider sell signal means a stock market increase of 12.9% over the next year.

Implications for the mutual fund investor

How can an active mutual fund investor exploit the information contained in the aggregate insider-trading signals? One way to exploit the aggregate insider-trading signals is to take an aggressive bullish posture when aggregate insider signal is positive. An aggressive bullish posture can be taken by switching from a money market mutual fund or a short-term bond portfolio to a stock portfolio. Since stocks do better than bonds when the market is increasing, the active investor will benefit from such a switch. Second, the active investor can switch into a more risky stock portfolio (e.g., an aggressive growth mutual fund) that will rise even more when the market returns are positive. Third, the active investor can leverage the investment in the market portfolio by buying on margin, or by buying options on stock market indexes, or buying stock index futures.

On the converse side, a negative insider signal should bring caution and more conservative posture. A more conservative position can be taken by eliminating the margin position and investing in less risky portfolios (e.g., short-term bond funds, money market funds, or a value-based mutual fund). Another implication of our findings so far is that one cannot short-sell the market portfolio based on negative aggregate insider sell signals. Such a strategy would lose money since the market returns are still positive, albeit smaller.

Other cutoff rules

Until now, we have used the cutoff proportions of 50%–50% to decide whether the insider trading signal is positive or negative. With a 50%–50% rule for both buys and sell signals, a small number of firms can shift the insider trading signal from a buy to a sell, and vice versa. Given that there are only 20 years in our sample period, this sensitivity can lead to additional noise in our signals. Moreover, when the number of firms with net insider buying is close to the number of firms with net insider selling, we would not expect a strong signal regarding the future performance of the stock market index. Hence there is no need to limit ourselves to such arbitrary cutoff proportions of 50%–50%. In particular, we may be able to increase the information content of buy and sell signals by requiring more extreme insider-trading activity.

As a second screen we use the 55%–45% rule. In this case we exclude all periods when the buy ratio varies between 45% and 55%. An insider-trading period is considered as a buying period only if 55% or

Table 4.7
Market returns following aggregate insider trading signals

Strong aggregate insider trading signals during the past 12 months	Number of 3-month periods	Subsequent 3-month raw return to equally weighted index	Probability of up market
Buy	11	10.2%	72.7%
Sell	29	4.0	65.5

Note: A buy signal is obtained if 55% or a greater proportion of the firms report net buying activity during the past 12 months. Similarly a sell signal is obtained if 45% or a smaller proportion of the firms report net buying activity during the past 12 months.

a greater proportion of the firms are net buyers. Similarly an insider-trading period is considered as a selling period only if 45% or a smaller proportion of the firms are net buyers. This more-strict grouping should allow us to examine the performance of more extreme movements in insider-trading activity and thereby provide a stronger signal regarding the future stock market performance.[9]

With the 55%–45% rule there are 11 three-month periods that are preceded by a 12-month strong insider buy signal (table 4.7). The equally weighted market index has risen in 8 of 11 years (72.7%), for an average return of 10.2% for these periods. In contrast, there are 29 three-month periods preceded by a 12-month aggregate strong insider-selling signal. The market index has risen in 19 out of 29 years (65.5%), with an average return of only 4.0%. Hence, once again, both the average returns and the probability of positive market returns are greater following aggregate insider-buy signals.

The results of strong insider signals are easily comparable to the 50%–50% signals. Using the 55%–45% rule produces a returns differential of 6.2 points between aggregate insider buy and sell signals (table 4.7). In contrast, the 50%–50% rule produces a return differential of only 2.6 points between aggregate insider buy and sell signals (table 4.4). Hence using stronger insider-trading signals more than doubles

Table 4.8
Market returns following aggregate insider trading signals

Strong aggregate insider trading signals during the past 12 months	Number of 6-month periods	Subsequent 6-month raw return to equally weighted index	Probability of up market
Buy	5	19.5%	80.0%
Sell	15	8.1	66.7

Note: A buy signal is obtained if 55% or a greater proportion of the firms report net buying activity during the past 12 months. Similarly a sell signal is obtained if 45% or a smaller proportion of the firms report net buying activity during the past 12 months.

the predictive power of aggregate insider-trading activity. This finding is reassuring, since it suggests that our findings are less likely to be due to noise or lack of a large number of observations.

We next examine the performance of the six-month-ahead forecasting horizon using the 55%–45% rule (table 4.8). There are 5 six-month periods that are preceded by a twelve-month insider buy signal. The equally weighted index has risen in four out of five of these years (80%), with an average return of 19.5%. There are 15 six-month periods that are preceded by a 12-month insider sell signal. The market has risen in 10 of the 15 years (66.7%) for an average return of only 8.1%. The difference between buy and sell signals has now risen to 11.4 points (19.5% minus 8.1%) for the six-month-ahead forecasting horizon.

Once again, the 55%–45% rule results in a strengthening of the information provided by the aggregate insider-trading signal. With the 50%–50% rule the difference between buy and sell signal is only 7.9 points (table 4.5). With the 55%–45% rule the difference between buy and sell signals has now grown to 11.4 points (table 4.8). By focusing in only the stronger insider-trading signals, it is possible to improve the performance of market timing strategies.

Our next tests examine the performance of the 55%–45% rule for 12-month-ahead forecasting horizons (table 4.9). There are only three

Table 4.9
Market returns following aggregate insider trading signals

Strong aggregate insider trading signals during the past 12 months	Number of 12-month periods	Subsequent 12-month raw return to equally weighted index	Probability of up market
Buy	3	36.6%	100.0%
Sell	8	10.7	62.5

Note: A buy signal is obtained if 55% or more of the firms report net buying activity during the past 12 months. Similarly a sell signal is obtained if 45% or a smaller proportion of the firms report net buying activity during the past 12 months.

12-month periods that are preceded by a 12-month insider-buying signal. The equally weighted index has risen in all three occasions for an average of 36.6%. In contrast, there are eight 12-month periods that are preceded by a 12-month insider sell signal. The equally weighted index has risen in five out of eight of these years for an average of 10.7%. The difference between buy and sell signals has now risen to a whopping 25.9 points. This is the best evidence to date that aggregate insider trading provides a strong signal that can help predict the future market returns.[10]

Other market-timing strategies based on aggregate insider trading

Our results so far show that aggregate insider trading does a very good job of forecasting future stock market returns. What we do with this information clearly depends on the nature of the signal. When the insider-trading signal remains between 45% and 55%, the signal quality is weak, so it requires a cautious approach. When the insider-trading signal is strong, less than 45% or greater than 55%, it is possible to take a more aggressive posture.

Moreover there is no need to limit our analysis to predicting the overall stock market. Instead, we could examine insider trading in interest rate sensitive stocks and investigate the forecasting characteristics of such an aggregate insider-trading variable for future short-term, intermediate-term, or long-term bond returns. These signals would be most useful for active investors who trade bond portfolios. We can also construct sector portfolios such as the automotive sector, oil-related firms, health care related firms, or the banking sector. For instance, an insider sentiment index covering automotive stocks can be constructed by examining insider-trading patterns in automobile manufacturers and other automotive related firms. Such an index is expected to track developments in the automotive sector, in conjunction with firm specific insider trading and aggregate insider-trading activity. Finally we can construct broad portfolios based on commonly used characteristics such as consumer durables, consumer nondurables, technology sector, or firm size.

As a test of the above conjecture, we constructed an index of small firm stocks (average market capitalization less than $25 million) and forecast its 12-month-ahead future return using the past 12-month aggregate insider-trading index. Our results indicated stronger forecasting ability for the index of small firms than for the equally weighted market index. With a positive insider-trading signal, future 12-month returns to small firms average 30%. With a negative insider-trading signal, future 12-month returns to small firms average only 9%.[11]

Finally we can explore various interactions between firm-specific, industrywide, and marketwide insider sentiment indexes. For instance, before we decide to imitate insider trading in, say GM, we can require a positive firm specific signal, combined with a positive automotive sector signal, as well as a positive marketwide aggregate insider-trading signal. For firm-specific signals, we have identified seven different variables that signal the quality of insiders' information in chapter 3. We can further use these variables to stratify the firm-specific signal as well. The possibilities are indeed plentiful.

Space restrictions prevent us from fully exploring these additional
forecasting characteristics of aggregate insider trading. Having said
this, the possibility of combining firm specific signals with aggregate
trading signals is too tempting to resist totally. Hence we explore this
question next. Can we further increase the strength of the insider-
trading signals by combining firm specific signals with aggregate
insider-trading signals? If so, what is the magnitude of the predicted
future stock returns?

To combine the firm-specific signals with aggregate insider-trading
signals, we follow the following approach. At a given calendar month,
we examine all firms for insider buying and selling signals. In some
firms insiders will be buying, in others they will be selling. We then
also examine the aggregate insider-trading activity over the past 12
months. Let's suppose that insiders are net buyers over the past year.
In this case we buy the shares of firms currently exhibiting insider purchases and ignore those firms with current insider selling. Similarly, if
the aggregate insider-trading signal over the past year is a sell, then we
simply sell stock in firms currently exhibiting insider sales and ignore
the firms with current insider purchases.

The combined strategy produces more sell signals than buy signals
(table 4.10). There are 57,116 instances where insiders buy stock in

Table 4.10
Market and firm-specific signals are combined

	Number of trading months	Net returns during the next			
		3 months	6 months	9 months	12 months
Insiders buy with aggregate buying	57,116	2.1%	3.2%	4.0%	4.9%
Insiders sell with aggregate selling	106,029	−1.2	−2.2	−2.9	−3.5

Note: Holding period returns are computed net of the equally weighted market index
return.

their own firms when aggregate insider-trading signal is also a purchase. Similarly there are 106,029 instances where insiders sell stock in their own firms when the aggregate insider-trading signal is also a sell.

Using the combined strategy results in improved forecasting performance (table 4.10). Following purchases, stock prices now outperform the market index by 4.9% over the next 12 months. Following insider sales, stocks underperform the market index by 3.5%. Comparing with earlier results shows that adding aggregate insider-trading signals indeed improves the forecasting ability of insider-trading signals. The net stock returns following insider purchases rises to 4.9% from 4.5% (see table 2.2). Similarly the underperformance following insider sales is now 3.5%, up from 2.7%. Hence it is indeed not only possible but quite desirable to combine various insider-trading signals.

Predicting industry returns

A relatively recent phenomenon in investing is called sector investing. Many mutual funds offer portfolios that specialize in a given sector or industry. The objective of these mutual funds is not to beat the sector but to mimic it as closely as possible. Individual investors can then use these specialized sector funds as building blocks to overweigh or underweigh various sectors of the economy such as automobile manufacturing, oil and gas production, and computer hardware or software.

The availability of the sector funds raises the natural question of whether it is possible to predict the industry or sector returns. If investors can predict industry returns, then they can increase or decrease their exposure to a particular industry using these specialized portfolios. This is similar to market timing. Instead of timing the entire stock market, investors would be timing a given sector.[12]

One difficulty in predicting industry returns is that stocks in a given industry can be positively or negatively correlated. If the overall industry is mature and stable, then firms within the industry prosper usually at the expense of each other. In this case stock returns for firms within the industry would be negatively correlated. In contrast, when the entire industry is expanding or contracting, all firms can prosper together or decline together. In this case stock returns within the industry are more likely to be positively correlated.

Before we can use insider trading to predict industry returns, we need to establish the within-industry correlations. If insider trading among different firms in the same given industry is positively correlated, then aggregating insiders' transactions will help predict industry returns. If insider trading is negatively correlated, then it cannot just be aggregated across firms. Insider purchases in one firm is good news for that firm and may be bad news for its competitors. In this case we need to first establish the correlation structure of insider trading across different firms in the same industry.

As an example of predicting industry returns, we have examined the automobile industry, using Ford Motor Company, General Motors Corporation, and Chrysler Corporation. The auto industry is a relatively mature industry, suggesting the possibility that any one firm's gain may be at the expense of the other two. Nevertheless, all U.S. auto manufacturers also experienced difficulties in the 1980s due to increased competition from the Japanese manufacturers. This competition produced shocks that affected all U.S. manufacturers in the same way. Moreover in the 1990s all U.S. auto companies bounced back led by the increased popularity of minivans and sports utility vehicles. Overall, it is hard to predict whether common factors or competitive factors dominate the U.S. auto industry.

Our evidence indicates strong positive correlations between insider trading in Ford, GM, and Chrysler (table 4.11). The proportion of months when insider trading in any two auto companies is in the same direction outnumbers the months with opposite transactions 320 to 95, or with an odds ratio of 3.4:1. When we consider only large insider transactions, the odds ratio for agreements to disagreements is 3.9:1.[13] From insiders' perspective, what is good for GM is also good for Ford and Chrysler.

Table 4.11
Insider trading in Ford, GM, and Chrysler corporations

	All trading	Large volume trading
Agree	320	229
Disagree	95	59
Odds ratio	3.4:1	3.9:1

Note: When insiders in any two of the three auto firms trade in the same direction, it is included in the "agree" cell. If insiders in any two firms trade in the opposite direction, it is included in the "disagree" cell.

Given the positive correlations, we have then forecast stock returns in a given auto company three ways: (1) insider trading in that company, (2) insider trading in the other two companies only, and (3) insider trading in all three companies. The first method is called direct forecasting, while the second method is called indirect forecasting. When we have aggregated insider trading in all three auto companies, we forecast the industry returns for all three firms. This is called the *industry-aggregate method*.[14]

The direct forecasting ability of insider transactions in auto companies is rather small. Insiders in auto firms earn about 2% abnormal profit from their sales and purchases in their own firms over a one-year period (table 4.12). When we use only the indirect approach, profitability improves to 6.1%. Hence insider trading in competitors is even more informative than insider trading in a given auto company.[15] Finally, when we follow the industry-aggregate approach, profitability further improves to 7.0%.

Overall, our evidence suggests that it is possible to time industry returns as well. By aggregating insider trading across firms in the same industry, we can eliminate some of the liquidity-related trading across firms and reinforce the information component of insiders' transactions. In some instances, looking at insider trading in competitive firms gives better signals than insider trading in any one firm. However, before we can implement the industry-timing approach, we need to

Table 4.12
Profitability of insider trading in Ford, GM, and Chrysler corporations

	One-year holding period	Two-year holding period
Direct	2.0%	2.0%
Indirect	6.1	7.0
Industry	7.0	7.6

Note: Direct method looks at the usual profitability of insider trading. Indirect method buys stock of Ford if insiders in GM and Chrysler are on net purchasers. Ford stock is sold if insiders in GM and Chrysler are on net sellers. We repeat the same approach for GM and Chrysler. Industry method sums up insider trading in all three firms. If there is net buying, all three stocks are purchased. If there is net selling, all three stocks are sold.

measure the correlation of insider trading across firms in the same industry.[16]

Conclusions and investment implications

In this chapter we have examined the predictive ability of aggregate insider-trading signals. By aggregate insider trading we mean the net proportion of firms exhibiting insider buying. Our findings indicate that aggregate insider trading is a reliable predictor of the future market returns.

1. Aggregate insider trading predicts aggregate stock returns. The overall stock market increases more if the past aggregate insider trading is positive than it does if the past aggregate insider-trading signal is negative. However, stock prices do not decline following insider sell signals. They simply rise less than those following positive aggregate insider-trading signals.

2. The strength of the aggregate insider-trading signals increases with the aggregation period. Hence aggregating insider-trading signals over the past 12-month period gives more reliable signals than aggregating insider-trading signals over the past month or the past 3 months.

3. Using 12-month aggregate insider trading and a 50%–50% rule to identify buy and sell signals, stock prices increase by 28.7% following the past 12-month aggregate insider buy signals. Moreover the market rises following each of the seven years when aggregate insider trading signal is positive. In contrast, the market rises only by 12.9% following the 12 years when the past 12-month aggregate insider-trading signal is negative. Hence using aggregate insider trading predicts an additional 16-point extra return to the market portfolio.

4. Using more extreme insider-trading signals further improves the predictive content of insider trading. Using 55%–45% rule to identify buy and sell signals, the difference in market returns following positive and negative aggregate insider-trading signals grows to almost 26 points.

5. Combining firm-specific insider-trading signals with the aggregate signals leads to better forecasting of future stock returns.

6. Aggregate insider trading predicts changes in future economic growth up to two years ahead. Other studies have also shown that stock returns are also a leading indicator of future real activity up to one year ahead. Consequently it should not be surprising that aggregate insider trading forecasts furture stock returns up to one year ahead.

7. It is also possible to time industry returns using industrywide insider trading. Our results indicate that U.S. auto stocks are better predicted by using the aggregate industrywide insider trading instead of the firm-specific insider trading in each firm.

5   *Crash of October 1987 and insider trading*

Why did the stock market crash in October 1987?

The stock market crash of October 1987 was a rare and frightening event for investors. The Dow Jones Industrial Average dropped by a record 508 points or 22.6% in one day on October 19, 1987. The sharp drops in stock prices in the United States were also accompanied by similarly sharp drops in stock prices world wide. Following the stock market crash, prices fluctuated wildly from day to day with no clear direction, thereby increasing expectations of volatility over the future stock prices as well as the economy as a whole. The crash caused many investors to lose confidence in the stock market and withdraw from equity markets with large losses. Finally the crash produced doomsday scenarios for the United States and, to some extent, for the world economic outlook.

What produced the crash? We can posit various scenarios. Were the stock prices bid up artificially high prior to the crash? If this scenario is true, then some triggering event would have brought prices down to realistic levels. There is some evidence to support this view. After all, the stock market had risen sharply over 1986 and the early part of 1987. For instance, from January 1986 to September 1987, the equally weighted index of NYSE, AMEX, and NASDAQ stocks rose 46% while the value-weighted index rose 55%. An alternative scenario is that the crash was a rational response to *new* information suggesting slower economic growth rates or higher interest rates. If so, what was this new information? Understanding why the crash occurred can help us understand the conditions that lead to future crashes. No one really knows the answers to these important questions. Moreover, despite the passage of time and significant research, financial economists remain in disagreement about the cause of the crash.[1]

There are basically three possible scenarios that can explain what happened during the crash. First, it is possible that stock prices were valued correctly before, during, and after the crash. In this case some negative information arrived during October 1987 and prices fell sharply and rationally as a result. This negative information may have to do with slower economic growth, legislative changes or higher interest rates. Some authors have argued for instance that potential changes in tax law that would eliminate interest deductions for highly leveraged takeover transactions was the trigger for the crash.[2] Others have argued that realization of slower economic growth triggered the crash.

A second scenario is that the high stock prices prior to the crash were *unjustified* based on fundamentals. Investors bid up prices artificially high simply expecting to sell to a greater fool before everyone else realized what was going on. In this case some new event in October 1987 triggered the widespread realization that the market was overvalued and the stock prices fell sharply and justifiably as a consequence. An example of such a realization may be that investors were unaware of the amount of portfolio insurance that was driving prices up before the crash.[3] Once investors realized this, they adjusted the stock prices downward.[4]

A final scenario is the following: Stock prices prior to the crash were justifiably high on the basis of fundamentals. Some event triggered panic among investors and caused massive selling.[5] As a result stock prices fell below fundamental values following the crash. In this scenario, stock prices would be expected to rebound after a while as investors realize the true fundamental values once again. Some authors have argued that the sustained decline in stock prices during the two weeks prior to the crash caused investors to panic and served as such a trigger.[6] Moreover program trading activity such as portfolio insurance schemes in effect at that time also triggered additional stock sales as prices declined, causing further price declines and thereby contributed to the crash.

What we hope to do in this chapter is to examine what corporate insiders thought about the crash, how they responded to falling prices, and how they fared over the next year or so. In the process we hope to present some evidence on the likelihood of each of the three scenarios outlined above. The answer to this question will help illuminate why some crashes occur and also provide the best response in a future crash. While we cannot be certain that insiders have all the answers, at least it would be comforting to know how some of the most informed people reacted to the crash. What did corporate insiders think about the crash? Were they selling stock prior to the crash? Did insiders buy stock or did they also bail out during the crash? What did they do following the crash?

Say the first scenario is true, namely that the stock market was correctly valued before and after the crash and the crash is due to some negative information. Then we would not expect strong insider trading before, during, or after the crash, since the market is always properly valued. However, if insiders could have advance information regarding the negative fundamentals, then we would expect them to be selling stock before and during the crash. If the crash of stock prices was a rational response to negative information regarding slower economic growth or higher interest rates, then we would probably expect that insiders would also sell their investments in their own firms right before the crash. In this case we would also expect that insiders would sell more of the stocks that declined more during the crash.

Say the second scenario is correct and the stock market was overvalued before the crash. We would expect insiders to sell their own investments before the crash, since insiders are best positioned to evaluate this overvaluation. We expect the insider selling to be spread throughout 1986 and 1987. Moreover the stocks sold to a greater extent by insiders prior to the crash should fall more in price during the crash. Since prices following the crash are justified by fundamentals, we would not expect insiders to exhibit strong trading patterns following the crash.

Finally, say the third scenario is correct. Suppose that most individual investors got spooked, so they wanted to get out of the market, albeit irrationally. In this scenario we would expect insiders to be buying their own firms' stock immediately following the crash. After all, if the fundamentals did not change yet prices are 20% to 30% cheaper, insiders are best positioned to evaluate and act on this information. In this case we would expect insiders to buy more of the stocks that declined the most. So in this scenario we would expect insider buying to continue in the postcrash period as long as stock prices remain low.

We hope that investigating insiders' reaction to the crash will improve our understanding of the causes of the crash. In the previous chapter we learned that insiders' transactions can tell us quite a bit of information about the future direction of the overall stock market. Let us see if insiders' transactions during the crash also prove to be a useful guide. Understanding what insiders did during the crash will perhaps help the average investor sort things out better in a future crash.

Anatomy of the crash

Even though the stock market crash culminated on October 19, 1987, it actually started on Tuesday, October 6, 1987. The value-weighted index dropped for four consecutive days starting with October 6, producing a loss of 4.7% for the week. The following week, from October 12, 1987, through October 16, 1987, the stock prices continued to fall. Prices again fell for four out of five days, registering an additional loss of 8.7%. The fall on October 16 alone was almost 5%. Hence, by the time the market had opened on October 19, 1987, the value-weighted index had fallen a total of 13% in two weeks. Also the returns were negative eight out of ten trading days.

The news of continually dropping stock prices produced an avalanche of sell orders on October 19. Most individual investors were concerned about future declines, so they wanted to get out of the stock market. Second, many institutional investors had been engaging in computer-traded portfolio insurance. This strategy automatically buys stocks when stock prices increase and automatically sells stocks when stock prices decline. As prices declined over the past two weeks, computer-driven portfolio insurers churned out more sell orders. This combination of huge sell orders from both individuals and institutions caused a serious burden on the ability of the system to handle the order flow. Inability to execute the sell orders as well as the fear that the sellers might know something that they did not, only intensified a typical investor's desire to get out, culminating in additional rounds of falling prices and increasing sell orders from both individuals and institutions.[7]

On October 19, 1987, stocks opened lower and headed south. For a while, it seemed like the stock prices were in a free fall. By the end of the day on October 19, 1987, the speed and magnitude of the stock price drop simply amazed and mesmerized people whether or not they had invested in the stock market. Moreover the crash brought home the dangers of investing in the stock market. If prices could drop by more than 20% in a single day, how much could it fall in a year? For many investors the crash shook their confidence in the stock market.[8]

What happened to the stock prices *following* the crash? For our overall sample of 6,135 firms, the stock price drop for the entire month of October 1987 is 27.2% (table 5.1). Over the next 14 months, until the end of 1988, the average stock bounced back by 17.1%.[9] Hence some of the crash losses were eliminated over the next 14 months. This evidence suggests that at least part of the crash returns may have been a temporary adjustment rather than a permanent loss.

Table 5.1
Net stock returns (net of the market returns) grouped by the average return during October 1987

Crash returns	Number of firms	October 1987 returns	Subsequent 14-month raw return (11/87–12/88)	Subsequent 14-month net return (11/87–12/88)
Biggest declines	2,024	−42.2%	20.8%	1.4%
Medium declines	2,067	−28.0	19.2	0.0
Small declines	2,044	−11.6	11.0	−8.4
All firms	6,135	−27.2	17.1	−2.4

If the crash represents an irrational exodus (scenario 3), then stock price declines ought to be temporary. Stocks that declined more during the crash ought to bounce back more later on. To test this story, we sort stocks according to how much they fell during October 1987 (table 5.1). Specifically we sorted stocks into three approximately equal sized categories, biggest price drops, medium price drops, and small price drops. The average October 1987 returns for the three categories are −42.2%, −28.0%, and −11.6%, respectively.

The typical stock bounced back by 17.1% from November 1987 through December 1988. Moreover the stocks that declined more during the crash rebounded more during the subsequent 14 months. For the biggest decliners, the rebound equals 20.8%. While these firms did not completely make up the loss of October 1987, they recouped about half the loss. The rebounds for the other groups are smaller. For the medium decliners, the rebound equals 19.2%. For the smallest decliners, the rebound equals only 11.0%.

Once again, when we examine the subsequent performance of these three groups, we find some mean reversion or evidence for overreaction. The stocks that dropped the most during October 1987 rebounded a bit more than the equally weighted index, while the stocks that dropped the least rebounded less than the equally weighted average during the next 14 months. Specifically the stocks that dropped the most during October 1987 outperformed the equally weighted index by 1.4 points. In contrast, the stocks that dropped the least during October 1987 underperform the equally weighted index by 8.4 points.

How do we interpret this evidence? First, the results suggest that there is some overreaction. Stocks that fell the most bounced back the most following the crash. Similarly stocks that did not fall very much underperformed the market index subsequently. This evidence suggests that the third scenario is likely to be involved. However, the evidence also suggests that not all of the decline during the crash can be attributed to overreaction. Some of the losses are permanent. Specifically stocks fell 27.2% during October 1987 but bounced back only 17.1% during the subsequent period. Hence some of the losses were not recovered. This evidence also suggests that scenario one may also be involved. Consequently looking only at the stock returns does not help us separate the three stories. To get a better picture, we need to examine the insider-trading information.

Insider trading around the crash of October 1987

To understand the insider-trading patterns during October 1987, it is instructive to go back and re-examine the insider-trading behavior for every month from 1975 to 1994. Let us first understand the normal insider-trading patterns so that we can evaluate the unusual insider-trading activity during the crash.[10] The monthly proportion of firms with net insider buying is shown in figure 4.2. For convenience, this figure is again reproduced as figure 5.1.

For the 20 years from 1975 to 1994, the highest monthly proportion of buying occurs in October 1987. This proportion of buying firms reaches 78%. While figure 5.1 does not distinguish between insider buying before and after October 19, most of the buying occurs on and after October 19, 1987. Using an alternative definition of insider trading, such as the ratio of buy transactions to total transactions,

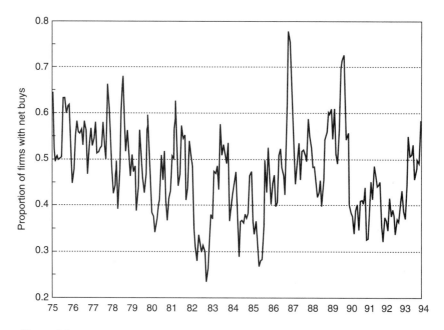

Figure 5.1
Proportion of firms with net insider buying for 1975 to 1994

the buy ratio almost reaches 90% on and immediately following October 19, 1987. If we repeat our analysis using *daily* insider-trading patterns instead of monthly insider-trading patterns, a similar picture emerges. In fact insider buying on October 20, 1987, also constitutes a record buying for any day between January 1, 1975, and December 31, 1994.

To give some indication of the magnitude of insider trading, during the eight months from January 1987 to August 1987, insiders sold a total of 170 million shares for their personal accounts. During the four months starting with October 1987, insiders *purchased* 70 million shares. This represents a turnaround of 240 million shares. During October 1987 alone, insiders purchased approximately 25 million shares.[11]

Data clearly show that in fact insiders were buyers of their own firm's stock in record numbers immediately following the crash. This suggests that insiders must believe that the magnitude of the stock price fall was somewhat unjustified. Based on their knowledge of the fundamentals and the stock price falls, insiders apparently viewed the events of October 19 and October 20 as good buying opportunities.

Overall, this evidence suggests that the third scenario is the most likely explanation for the crash of 1987. While some investors got spooked and drove stock prices down, insiders were not frightened by the crash. They viewed the decline as a temporary decline, and they supported the market in record numbers with their own money while individual and some institutional investors were trying to get out. Further supporting this view is the continued insider buying for about three months until the beginning of 1988 (figure 5.1). Insider buying only slowed down as stock prices climbed and stocks became less attractive purchases.

Did insiders buy indiscriminately or could they distinguish between the good and the bad even during the crash? If insiders bought stocks indiscriminately, then this would suggest that all stocks fell unjustifiably. This evidence would suggest pure overreaction. Instead, if insiders bought stocks only in those firms that would bounce back in the future, then we cannot completely rule out a fundamental bad news scenario as in scenario one.

To investigate the predictive ability of insider trading during the crash, we examine the relation between insider trading, crash returns, and subsequent stock price reactions. To get a better grasp on insiders' reaction to the crash, we only use post crash insider trading for the two-week window from October 19, 1987, to October 31, 1987. Based on postcrash transactions, insiders sold shares in 251 firms and bought shares in 1,559 firms (table 5.2). Hence the ratio of net buying to total trading is 86%. In 4,325 firms there is no insider trading.

Let's take the nontrading firms first. The lack of insider trading in 4,325 firms raises an interesting question. Why didn't insiders buy any shares in these firms when they were buying shares in record numbers? The answer probably has to do with the legal restrictions on insider

Table 5.2
Net stock returns (net of the market returns) grouped by the insider trading activity from October 19, 1987, to October 31, 1987

Insider trader activity	Number of firms	October 1987 returns	Subsequent 14-month net return (11/87–12/88)
Insiders sell	251	−28.4%	−11.6%
No trade	4,325	−26.7	−4.7
Insiders buy	1,559	−28.5	5.1

trading. As we discussed earlier, Section 16(b) of the Securities and Exchange Act prohibits short-swing profits, which is defined as a buy-and-a-sell, or a sell-and-a-buy combination within six months that results in a profit. In this case the profit must be returned to the corporation. Consequently, if insiders have sold stock any time during the six months prior to the crash, then they would be subject to the short-swing profits rule if they were to purchase stock immediately after the crash. This legal restriction probably explains the lack of greater buying by insiders.

Interestingly, there is no meaningful difference between the crash returns among firms purchased, sold, or not traded by insiders during the crash month (table 5.2). Regardless of whether insiders bought, sold, or did not trade, the stock returns average about 28%. Hence this evidence suggests that insiders did not exclusively rely on the stock price declines in their trading decisions. Instead, they probably used the difference between their new estimates of the fundamental value of the firm postcrash and the postcrash stock price. This evidence suggests that the entire crash experience cannot be explained completely by an overreaction story. If this were the case, we would have found insider selling only in a few firms which experienced stock price increases, and massive insider buying in those cases where the stock prices fell much more than average.

The stocks sold by insiders during the two weeks immediately following the crash underperformed the market index by an amazing 11.6% over the next 14 months. Hence insiders could identify firms that fell justifiably, and would even fall more relative to the overall market index. The stocks that insiders did not trade underperformed the market index by 4.7%. Finally the stocks that insiders purchased (1,559 stocks) during the two-week postcrash window outperformed the market index by 5.1% over the next 14 months. Clearly, insiders could identify those stocks that fell unjustifiably during the crash.

To get a more detailed picture of insider trading behavior during the crash, we repeat our analysis using only the top executives' transactions. Since top executives tend to be better informed, we can increase our confidence in the interpretation of the overall insider trading patterns. It appears that top executives traded in only 181 firms during the two weeks following the crash (table 5.3). The ratio of net buys to total transactions is exactly the same as overall insiders, or 86%. There is no trading by top executives in 5,954 firms.

Top executives had a slight preference for purchasing stocks that declined more during the crash. Stocks that top executives sold declined 28.1%, while the stocks that top executives bought declined 31.2%. However, given the small sample size, the differences are not economically meaningful.

The subsequent performance of stocks over the next 14 months

Table 5.3
Net stock returns (net of the market returns) grouped by the top executive trading activity from October 19, 1987, to October 31, 1987

Top executive trading activity	Number of firms	October 1987 returns	Subsequent 14-month net return
Top executives sell	26	−28.1%	−14.3%
No trade	5,954	−27.1	−2.5
Top executives buy	155	−31.2	5.3

shows even greater predictive ability for top executives. Stocks sold by top executives underperform the market index by 14.3 points. Stocks purchased by top executives outperform the market index by 5.3 points. Hence top executives are more successful and more selective than overall insiders with their trading decisions in the immediate postcrash period.

The evidence that we presented so far suggests that insiders, including the top executives, viewed the overall stock market crash as less than fully justified. On average, they bought stocks in record numbers. Finally, the stocks that insiders purchased during a two-week window following the crash significantly outperformed the market index over the next 14 months.

Another question raised by the crash is the following: Which is a better predictor of future stock returns, returns during the crash month or insider-trading activity in the immediate postcrash period? To get an answer to this question, we now examine the interaction between the crash returns and postcrash insider trading.

Our evidence suggests that insider trading is a good indicator of future stock returns regardless of the October 1987 returns (table 5.4). Looking at the first column, stocks sold by insiders underperform the market index whether they declined a lot or a little during the crash. Similarly stocks bought by insiders postcrash do better than the market index regardless of the crash returns. The only exception is the group

Table 5.4
Net stock returns (net of the market returns) from November 1987 to December 1988 grouped by the average return during October 1987 and insider trading activity from October 19, 1987, to October 31, 1987 (number of firms in parentheses)

Crash returns	14-month returns insiders sell	14-month returns insiders buy
Biggest declines	−11.9% (86)	7.9% (538)
Medium declines	−5.5 (94)	8.9 (557)
Small declines	−19.7 (71)	−2.6 (464)

Table 5.5
Net stock returns (net of the market returns) during the 14 months following the crash grouped by the number of shares traded by insiders from October 19, 1987, to October 31, 1987 (number of firms in parentheses)

Shares traded	Insiders sell	Insiders buy
1–100	−16.1%	3.8%
	(6)	(69)
101–1,000	−4.7	5.6
	(48)	(463)
1,001–10,000	−13.5	5.2
	(105)	(659)
10,001 or more	−12.6	4.7
	(92)	(368)

with small crash declines and insider purchases. This group underperformed the market index by 2.6%.

Finally we examine the relation between number of shares traded by insiders during the immediate postcrash period and the subsequent performance (table 5.5). Somewhat surprisingly, the relation between number of shares traded and subsequent performance is weak, especially for insiders' sales. However, the sample sizes in some cells are very small. Consequently it is difficult to get too excited about the role of numbers of shares in this context.

Conclusions and investment implications

In this chapter we attempted to use insider trading to help us better understand the causes of the stock market crash of 1987. We have examined the subsequent performance of the stocks based on the amount of decline during the crash and trading behavior of all insiders as well as top executives. Our findings are as follows:

1. Insiders responded to the crash by buying stocks in record numbers immediately following the crash. Similarly top executives bought

stocks in record numbers. The proportion of firms purchased by insiders reached almost 90%. The insider buying on October 20, 1987, exceeds that of any day between January 1, 1975, and December 31, 1994. Hence insiders regarded the crash returns as temporary, and they supported the market when few others were willing to.

2. Based on insider-trading behavior, we can say that an important contributor to the crash of 1987 was overreaction to the stock price declines over the previous two weeks. Our evidence is consistent with the view that the typical investor got spooked by the price declines during the two weeks that preceded the crash.

3. The record amount of insider buying during and after the crash serves an important public interest by stabilizing stock prices. Not only did insiders provide liquidity to the market, but they also increased the confidence of individual investors in the stock market as insider purchases became publicly known. This finding suggests that extreme restrictions on insider trading can have some deleterious effects on the efficient functioning of the stock markets.

4. Stocks purchased by insiders during the two-week postcrash period significantly outperformed the market over the next 14 months. Stocks sold by the insiders during the same window significantly underperformed the market index over the next 14 months. Hence subsequent developments proved insiders' evaluations of the crash events as accurate.

5. Insiders did not rely too heavily on the amount of the stock price declines in their trading decisions. There is not much difference in the price declines of stocks purchased and sold by insiders. Instead, insiders brought additional information to make their trading decisions. Hence insiders did not act as naive, mean-reversion believers simply buying stocks that declined more during the crash.

6. A lesson suggested by the crash of October 1987 is that when a lot of people panic, it pays to know what the insiders are doing.

6   *Dividend yields and insider trading*

Dividend yields and future stock returns

In this chapter we compare the predictive ability of insider trading with various other measures of valuation that are typically used in practice. Our objective is to see how insider trading stacks up against these other measures of valuation. We start out with the dividend yields.

In the finance literature, dividend yields have been used to forecast future stock market returns. Empirical studies have shown that the periods when the dividend yields are higher are followed by higher future stock returns and that the periods when the dividend yields are lower are followed by lower stock returns.[1] Consequently dividend yields have been used to judge whether the market is fairly valued: If the current dividend yield is low, then the market is said to be overvalued, since the future returns following periods of low dividend yields are expected to be below average or sometimes negative. If the current dividend yield is high, then the market is said to be undervalued, since the future returns following periods of high dividend yields are expected to be above average.

The predictive ability of the dividend yield is quite important, since it provides a simple and convenient yardstick for potential investors to judge whether to invest in the stock market. It also raises numerous

questions regarding the pricing of the stocks: How good a yardstick is
the dividend yield variable for a recent time period? Why do dividend
yields predict future stock returns? Does the predicted variation in future stock returns represent a profit opportunity or simply compensation for risk taking? Is the predictive ability of dividends related to
other predictors of the stock returns? If so, what are these relations?
All of these are interesting and important questions for the typical
stock market investor, and we will attempt to provide some answers
in this chapter.

In chapters 4 and 5 we established that aggregate insider trading is an
important predictor of future market returns. Aggregate insider buying
indicates higher than average future market returns, and aggregate insider selling indicates lower than average future market returns. Another interesting question that is raised by these findings is whether
dividend yields and aggregate insider trading are separate and independent predictors of future stock returns and whether these two variables
can be combined to provide even stronger predictors or the future market returns. If dividend yield and aggregate insider trading are independent predictors of future stock returns, then we can improve our
predictive ability by using both variables. However, if one variable depends on the other, then combining them will not yield greater predictive ability. In this case it would be interesting to know which
variable is the dominant predictor. Hence we will also examine the
relation between dividend yields and aggregate insider trading and
compare their predictive ability for future market returns.

We begin our analysis by examining the ability of past market dividend yields to forecast future market returns for the sample period
1975 to 1994. This analysis will also demonstrate the strength of the
predictive ability of the dividend yield variable. Second, we examine
the interaction between aggregate insider trading and the market dividend yield. Is the aggregate insider-trading variable an independent
predictor of future stock returns? Alternatively, does the insider trading
sentiment already reflect the predictive ability of the dividend yield

variable? For instance, do the higher market dividend yields forecast higher future stock market returns even if insiders in aggregate are selling stock? Do the low market dividend yields forecast lower future stock market returns even when insiders in aggregate are buying stock? These are some of the additional questions we will attempt to answer in this chapter.

After examining the time series predictive ability of market dividend yields, we focus our attention on the cross-sectional predictive ability of dividend yields. By cross-sectional analysis we examine the distribution of returns across stocks at a given time. Hence we would like to know at a given time, whether stocks with higher dividend yields have higher expected future returns than the stocks with lower dividend yields. We then investigate the interaction between firm-specific dividend yields and firm-specific insider trading. Once again, we examine whether firm-specific dividend yields and firm-specific insider trading exert separate and independent influences on future stock returns or whether these variables proxy for one another.

Predictive ability of the market dividend yield

Let's begin by defining what we mean by market dividend yield. Market dividend yield is measured as dollar dividends paid over the past year divided by the current stock price. Some studies use the forecasted dividends that are expected to be paid over the next year instead of the trailing dividends in computing dividend yields. In this book we always use the trailing dividends because this obviates the need for estimating future dividends.

There are a variety of ways of measuring the market dividend yield. In this book we work with the dividend yield on the value-weighted market index. We choose a value-weighted average of dividends because this gives a good picture of the total dividends paid in the U.S. economy as a whole. The daily dividend yield on the value-weighted index is computed as the total dollar dividends paid on all NYSE,

AMEX, and NASDAQ stocks on each calendar day divided by the closing market value of the NYSE, AMEX, and NASDAQ stocks on that day. We then simply sum the daily dividend yields within each calendar month to compute the monthly dividend yield. From now on, we simply refer to this measure as the market dividend yield, or simply as the dividend yield.

Why do dividend yields predict future market returns? There are two potential explanations. The first explanation suggests that higher dividend yields capture periods of higher risk and thereby provide compensation for bearing risk. The second explanation suggests that dividend yields may help identify periods of irrational stock price behavior.[2] Let's examine these two potential explanations in detail.

The first potential explanation for the predictive ability of market dividend yields is that it captures the variations in required stock returns as a result of changes in risk. When the risk in the economy increases, stock prices must fall, since lower stock prices are necessary to induce risk-averse investors to hold stocks in a more risky environment. Lower stock prices in turn cause expected stock returns to rise in the future, since investors now pay less to purchase the same stockholder profits. Hence higher risk in the economy increases the expected stock returns in the future. At the same time, falling stock prices also increase the current market dividend yield.[3] This intuition suggests that higher dividend yields should be associated with higher future stock returns. A similar argument can be made for a reduction in the risk level of the economy. Consequently changes in market dividend yields should predict the changes in future expected market returns. This line of reasoning suggests that the predicted changes in future stock returns simply represent varying compensation for risk.

There is an alternative way of viewing the positive relation between dividend yields and future stock returns. Suppose that stock prices do not always reflect fundamental values but sometimes overreact to news. Specifically assume that stock prices have overreacted to negative news and have fallen below the fundamental values. For a given dollar dividend payout the fall in stock prices will increase the dividend yield. Also assume that after a while market participants will realize the undervaluation and revalue the stock appropriately. Hence positive stock returns will follow high dividend yields. In this case a high dividend yield signals that the current stock price is irrationally low and is expected to rise in the future. A similar argument can be made with good news as well. This second line of reasoning suggests that the predicted change in future stock returns represents irrational pricing or a profit opportunity.

The preceding discussion suggests that there are two alternative ways of interpreting a positive relation between current dividend yields and future stock returns. One is based on changes in risk, and it is consistent with rational pricing. The other interpretation is based on irrational pricing. Ultimately it is not obvious that the typical stock market investor would care as to why there is a relation. Regardless of the true process that produces this positive relation between dividends and future market returns, investors can expect to earn higher returns when the dividend yields are high. From an academic perspective it is also quite difficult to distinguish between these alternative interpretations. Consequently we will focus more on the strength of the relation between dividend yields and future stock returns rather than the process that generates the relationship.

Forecasting characteristics of dividend yields

Figure 6.1 shows the time series behavior of the market dividend yield from 1975 to 1994. The overall picture of dividends shows a very slow-moving, low-frequency series. The changes in market dividends from one month to the next month are a lot smaller than the movements over the entire 20-year period. The market dividend yield starts out at about 4.4% in 1975. It dips slightly below 4% by 1977 and then rises to over 5% by 1980. It stays around 5% until 1982, when it takes a sharp downturn and declines to almost 2.5% by the beginning of 1994.

Figure 6.1
Market dividend yield for 1975 to 1994

By the end of 1994, the market dividend yield increases slightly to about 3%.

A careful examination of figure 6.1 shows that the dividend yield does not seem to fluctuate around an average value at least during the 1975 to 1994 period. Instead, it wanders around aimlessly without any affinity to a particular yield or a range of yield values.[4] Consequently it does not make sense to talk about an average dividend yield during 1975 to 1994 because it keeps changing. Instead, it is more meaningful to talk about *changes* in the level of dividends. Consequently we will examine the predictive ability of both the levels of dividend yields as well as the changes in dividend yields.

As we have discussed earlier, previous researchers have examined the predictive ability of the level of the dividend yield. The basic forecasting characteristics of the levels of the market dividend yields are explored using a time series approach. The sample period is 1975 to 1994, which contains 240 calendar months. We first measure the market dividend yield for a given month. We then look forward to the next three months and measure the market return over this three-month period. We then move forward one month and repeat this exercise. Hence there are 237 observation periods, since we lose a three-month forward window to measure the last three-month stock returns (we also measured the first dividend for the month of December 1974).

We sort the monthly market dividend yields into five equal-sized groups (table 6.1). This simple classification is intended to provide the reader with a general distribution of the market dividend yield for the period 1975 to 1994. The average market dividend yield for the lowest group is 2.9%. The average market dividend yield for the middle group is 4%. Finally the average market dividend yield for the highest group is 5.1%.

Table 6.1
Returns to the 3-month-, 6-month-, and 12-month-ahead equally weighted market index grouped by the past dividend yield for the market portfolio

Dividend level	Average yield	Subsequent 3-month market returns	Subsequent 6-month market returns	Subsequent 12-month market returns
Lowest dividend yield months	2.9%	2.2% (45)	5.1% (42)	12.9% (36)
Second dividend yield months	3.6	2.6 (48)	5.4 (48)	11.4 (48)
Third dividend yield months	4.0	3.6 (48)	7.8 (48)	14.1 (48)
Fourth dividend yield months	4.5	5.6 (48)	9.6 (48)	25.4 (48)
Highest dividend yield months	5.1	9.1 (48)	18.2 (48)	31.5 (48)

We now examine the relation between past market dividend yields and future market returns (table 6.1). As a measure of the market return, we use the returns on the equally weighted average of NYSE, AMEX, and NASDAQ stocks. The data reveal a strong, positive and monotone relation between past market dividend yields and future market returns. When the dividend yield is low (the first group), the three-month ahead future stock returns average only 2.2%. As dividend yields increase, so do the future stock returns. For the middle groups of dividend yields, the three-month-ahead stock returns average 3.6%. Finally, for the highest dividend yield group, the three-month-ahead stock returns average 9.1%.

We have the answer to our first question. The positive relation between the market dividend yields and future stock returns discussed in the finance literature also holds over the recent 1975 to 1994 time period. Moreover this relation appears to be quite strong. Going from the smallest dividend yield group to the highest dividend yield group, stock returns more than quadruple from 2.2% to 9.1% over a three-month holding period, giving a 6.9-point additional return based on the level of the dividend yield.

Since there is nothing special about a 3-month holding period, we also repeated this analysis for 6-month-ahead holding periods and 12-month-ahead holding periods. These results are also similar to those for the 3-month holding period. The predictive ability of the dividend yield variable appears to grow stronger with the longer holding periods.

For the 6-month-ahead holding periods, the future stock returns for the lowest dividend group starts out at 5.1%. This increases to 7.8% for the middle group. For the highest dividend group, the future stock returns average 18.2%. The difference in future stock returns for the highest and lowest dividend yield months equals 13.1 points. Once again, there is a strong positive relation between past dividend yields on the market portfolio and expected future stock returns.

For the 12-month-ahead holding periods, a similar yet even stronger picture emerges. For the lowest market dividend group, the future stock returns average 12.9%. For the middle group, the future stock returns increase to 14.1%. For the highest dividend yield group, the future stock market returns average an amazing 31.5%. The difference in future stock returns for the highest and lowest dividend yield months now equals 18.6 points. Increasing the holding period does not diminish the positive relation between past market dividend yields and future stock market returns. Instead, this relation gets even stronger as we increase our holding period to 12 months.

Market dividend yields and aggregate insider trading

We next explore the interactions among market dividend yields, aggregate insider trading, and future market returns. The first question we would like to address is why the dividend yields predict future stock returns. One way to do this is to compare the predictive ability of dividend yield with that of insider trading. When we do this, one of three outcomes is possible. First, both the dividend yield and insider-trading variables may retain their predictive ability. This finding would suggest that dividend yield and insider trading are separate and independent predictors of future stock returns. In this case combining both variables would most likely result in even stronger predictors. This outcome would also tell us that both mispricing and changes in risk level do play a role in pricing of stocks.

A second possible outcome is that dividend yield may lose its predictive ability while insider trading continues to predict future stock returns. This outcome would suggest that dividend yield probably predicts some mispricing also captured by insider trading. In this case using both variables would not result in any stronger predictors than using insider trading alone.

A third outcome is that dividend yield may continue to predict future stock returns, while insider trading is no longer informative. This outcome would suggest that the predictive ability of dividend yield

Table 6.2
Returns to the 3-month-ahead equally weighted market index grouped by past aggregate insider trading and the past dividend yield for the market portfolio

Dividend level	Aggregate insider selling for past 12 months	Aggregate insider buying for past 12 months
Lowest dividend yield	1.2%	10.8%
months	(40)	(5)
Second dividend yield	2.4	2.7
months	(21)	(27)
Third dividend yield	2.6	4.7
months	(25)	(23)
Fourth dividend yield	0.4	10.4
months	(23)	(25)
Highest dividend yield	10.2	7.8
months	(27)	(21)

Note: The number of months is in parentheses.

most likely arises as a result of capturing variations in risk and that somehow insider-trading patterns are also related to changes in risk as well. In this case using dividend yields alone would do as well as using both dividend yields and insider trading.[5]

We now examine the interactions among the market dividend yields, insider trading, and the three-month-ahead stock returns (table 6.2). Aggregate insider-trading activity is measured as in chapter 4. We first classify each firm as a buyer or a seller based on the number of shares traded by insiders in that firm. If more than 50% of the firms are sellers during the past 12 months, we declare this period as a selling period. Similarly, if 50% or more of the firms are net buyers over the past 12 months, then we declare this period as a buying period.

Let's examine table 6.2 first by columns and then by rows. The rows show changing dividend yields, while the columns show insider buying and selling. The examination of the stock returns by rows indicates what happens to the predictive ability of insider trading after we control for dividend yields. The examination of the stock returns by columns indicates what happens to the predictive ability of dividend yields after we control for insider-trading activity.

Given insider selling, the positive relation between market dividend yields and three-month-ahead future stock returns weakens (table 6.2, column 1). In the lowest dividend group the three-month future stock returns average 1.2%. As dividend yields increase, the stock returns fluctuate up and down. For the fourth dividend yield group, future stock returns attain their lowest value of 0.4%. For the highest dividend yield group, the three-month-ahead stock returns rise to 10.2%. Hence there is no longer a monotonic positive relation between dividend yields and future stock returns when insiders are selling. This finding suggests that once we control for insider trading, dividend yield variable loses some of its punch.

Given insider buying, the relation between past market dividend yields and future stock returns further weakens and even turns negative (table 6.2, column 2). The highest stock returns now occur for the lowest dividend yield group, with a value equal to 10.8%. Stock returns fluctuate up and down as the dividend yield increases. For the middle group, the future stock returns average 4.7%. For the highest dividend yields and insider buying, the future stock returns average only 7.8%.

The results so far suggest that after we control for insider trading, dividend yield is no longer very informative, especially for a three-month holding period. Let's now examine the predictive ability of insider trading after we control for the level of the dividend yields. To do this, we need to examine table 6.2 by rows.

Row by row examination of table 6.2 indicates that the predictive ability of insider trading is alive and well after we control for dividend yields. In the lowest dividend yield group, aggregate insider trading maintains its predictive power (table 6.2, row 1). As we go from insider selling to insider buying, future stock returns increase from 1.2% to 10.8%. Hence insider trading adds 9.6 points after we control for the dividend yields. Continuing our examination row by row, 4 of the 5 rows show that insider buying is associated with higher returns than insider selling. The average extra returns across the five rows equal 3.9 points in favor of insider buying.[6]

Another way to judge whether insider trading loses its punch when confronted with dividend yield is to compare the extra predicted returns using insider trading with and without the dividend yield variable. From table 4.4 the unconditional predictive ability of aggregate insider trading for the three-month-ahead returns was 2.6 points. Hence controlling for the dividend yields does not reduce but in fact increases the average predictive power of the aggregate insider-trading variable by 1.3 points (3.9% versus 2.6%).[7]

Overall, our evidence suggests that when we control for the level of market dividends, aggregate insider trading still predicts future stock returns. However, when we control for the level of aggregate insider trading, the market dividend yield is no longer as informative regarding the three-month-ahead future stock returns. Hence aggregate insider trading continues as an important predictive variable while the dividend yield loses most of its punch.

Why should aggregate insider trading continue to be an important predictor while the market dividend yield weakens as a predictor? There is some additional hint of an answer in table 6.2. The numbers in parentheses show the number of observations for each cell. Using these observations, we can judge how insiders react when the market dividend yield is high or low.

Looking at the first column, we see that as the market dividend yields increase, aggregate insider selling falls. In the lowest dividend group there are 40 months with insider selling. For the highest market dividend group there are only 27 months with insider selling. Hence there are fewer months of aggregate insider selling as the dividend yields increase. This relation is not monotonic and should only be taken as suggestive. Examining the second column of table 6.2 corroborates this possibility. As the market dividend yields increase, aggregate insider buying also increases. In the lowest dividend group of the second column, there are only 5 months. In the highest dividend group of the second column, the number of months increases to 21. Hence it appears that insider buying is positively related to the level of dividends in the economy.

There is another possibility: Insiders already know and understand the implications of the changes in market dividend yields. Moreover the dividend yield has to be a noisy predictor of future stock returns. Assume that the market dividend yield is low. If insiders agree that this is a bad signal for their own stock, then they sell shares. In this case future stock returns are especially low. However, if insiders disagree with the information content of the low-dividend signal, they may buy shares. In this case the market dividend yield no longer works as a good predictor.

To flesh out this story in a little more detail, let us return to table 6.2. Assume that insiders know from past experience that sometimes when stock prices rise, there is no justification for it. Namely stock prices can sometimes overreact and be out of line from fundamentals given insiders' perspective. Assume that stock prices have overreacted to some good news and that the rise in stock price has lowered the dividend yields. In this case insiders sell stock. In table 6.2 in 40 out of 45 months, low dividend yields are associated with insider selling. Moreover after a while, as the other market participants also recognize the overpricing, stock prices fall back. Hence we see low dividend yields, insider selling, and lower future stock returns all occurring together.

At other times stock prices rise justifiably because of some good news. In this case insiders do not sell stock, and they might even buy stock. In 5 out of 45 months in table 6.2, low dividend yields are associated with insider buying. Since the rise in stock prices is justified, future stock return is not low. Hence the dividend yield variable works better if it agrees with insider trading and less well when it contradicts the insider trading. Put another way, low dividend yield is a predictor of low future stock returns because it tends to signal insider selling. We can make a similar argument for the insider buy column.[8]

Intensive insider trading and dividend yields

It is also instructive to examine the interaction between the market dividend yields and more intensive insider-trading rules. After all, our tests are somewhat biased against the insider-trading variable. We separate the dividend yield variable into five groups, which brings out a large variation in dividend yields and increases its potential predictive ability. In contrast, we sort the insider-trading variable into only buy and sell groups. Consequently we are ignoring the intensity of insider buying and selling signals. Hence, to get a better picture of how insider trading interacts with the dividend yield variable, we need to examine stronger insider-trading signals as well.

If our interpretation of the existing findings is correct, then the same interpretation should be further corroborated using more intensive insider-trading rules. Specifically more intensive rules should increase the power of the insider-trading variable while further diminishing the power of the dividend yield variable.

We now examine the interaction between intensive insider-trading signals using the 55%–45% rule (see chapter 4 or additional findings on this rule) and the market dividend yields (table 6.3). We first classify each firm as a buyer or a seller based on the number of shares traded by insiders in that firm. If more than 55% of the firms are buyers during the past 12 months, we declare this period as a buying period. Similarly, if 45% or fewer of the firms are net buyers over the past 12 months, then we declare this period as a selling period.

First, more intensive insider-trading rules increase the predictive power of the aggregate insider-trading variable. Aggregate insider buying provides an extra 8.1 point return over insider selling after controlling for the dividend yield variable.[9] Second, stronger insider-trading signals further diminish the predictive power of the market dividend yield variable. Given intensive insider selling, the three-month-ahead future market returns no longer monotonically increase with the dividend yield. In fact the lowest future returns, equal to −2.0%, coincide

Table 6.3

Returns to the 3-month-ahead equally weighted market index grouped by past aggregate insider trading and the past dividend yield for the market portfolio

Dividend level	Aggregate insider selling for past 12 months	Aggregate insider buying for past 12 months
Lowest dividend yield months	3.7% (35)	9.4% (3)
Second dividend yield months	4.1 (14)	6.4 (16)
Third dividend yield months	3.2 (18)	4.8 (7)
Fourth dividend yield months	−2.0 (12)	20.8 (4)
Highest dividend yield months	10.6 (12)	— (0)

Note: The number of months is in parentheses. The 55%–45% rule is used to determine aggregate insider buy and sell signals. If 55% or a greater proportion of the firms are buyers over the past 12 months, then that calendar month is denoted as a buying month. If 45% or a smaller proportion of the firms are buyers over the past 12 months, then that calendar month is denoted as a selling month.

with the fourth highest dividend yield month. The attenuation of the predictive power of the market dividend yield variable is similarly pronounced with increased holding periods. At 12-month holding periods, the 12-month-ahead stock returns appear to be negatively related to the dividend yields.

Our evidence suggests that aggregate insider trading and dividend signals are not independent of each other. Instead, both factors seem to pick up the same sources of mispricing. Consequently, when we include both factors as predictors of future stock returns, the information content of the dividend yield is attenuated or even overturned. Hence the dividend yield provides a noisy signal regarding occasional mispricing of stocks. In contrast, insider trading does a better job of capturing periods of stocks' mispricing. Insider trading can and does clarify the information content of the dividend yield signal. As the strength of insider trading increases, it further dominates the information content of the dividend yields.

Changes in dividend yields

As we discussed earlier, the market dividend yield variable wanders around aimlessly during the 1975 to 1994 period, without any affinity to any particular value or range of values. In such a time series the average value is not constant over time but depends on what the current dividend yield is. Consequently classifying the values of the dividend variable in such categories as significantly above the mean or significantly below the mean is inherently problematic, for its future mean value can change. However, to be consistent with previous studies of dividend yields, this is exactly what we have done in our preceding analysis. We have first looked at the entire sample of dividend yields, determined where the dividend yield has been, and decided on the cutoff levels for each of the five categories.

This procedure would have been fine as long as the future dividend yield variable would follow historical patterns. Unfortunately, given that the dividend yield variable does not show any affinity to any particular value, there is no guarantee that in the future it would stay within the same range of values as it did during the last 20 years. To address this issue, we also look at *changes* in the dividend yield variable. Since changes in dividend yields do display a stationary process, we are more comfortable that the historical patterns in dividend changes will be a good approximation for the future changes in dividend yields.

To compute changes in dividend yields, we simply subtract the dividend yield for the previous calendar month from the dividend yield for the current calendar month. Assume that the dividend yield for the last month was 3.0% and that the dividend yield for the current calendar month is 3.1%. In this case the change in dividend yield is 0.1%.

We examine the monthly *changes* in the dividend yield variable and groups each month into one of five categories based on dividend

Table 6.4

Returns to the 3-month-, 6-month-, and 12-month-ahead equally weighted market index grouped by the *changes* in past dividend yield for the market portfolio

Dividend change	Average changes in yields	Subsequent 3-month market returns	Subsequent 6-month market returns	Subsequent 12-month market returns
Largest dividend declines	−0.10%	3.6% (47)	4.3% (47)	8.2% (47)
Second largest dividend declines	−0.04	3.3 (48)	10.2 (47)	16.6 (46)
Small changes in dividend yields	−0.01	4.5 (46)	8.9 (46)	17.2 (44)
Second largest dividend increases	0.03	5.0 (48)	9.9 (46)	24.6 (45)
Largest dividend increases	0.08	6.6 (47)	12.9 (47)	30.1 (45)

changes (table 6.4). The months that exhibit the biggest declines in dividend yields are grouped into category one. The months with the second biggest declines are grouped into category two and so on. Finally the months with the biggest increases in dividend are grouped into category five. Note that a given month can be classified as a large decline in the dividend yield whether the *level* of the dividends is high or low. Hence classifying on the basis of dividend changes will produce completely different rankings than classifying on the basis of the dividend levels as we did in table 6.1.

The months with the biggest declines in dividend yields show an average decline of 0.10% (table 6.4). Hence at this rate it would take ten months for the dividend yield to decline from say 4% to 3%. The months with the biggest increases in dividends show an average increase of only 0.08%. The average month to month changes in dividends tend to be small since the dividend variable moves rather slowly.

The future 3-month-, 6-month-, and 12-month-ahead stock returns can also be predicted using changes in dividend yields. When dividends decline sharply, the 3-month-ahead stock returns average only 3.6% (table 6.4, column 2). As the dividend changes moderate and then turn positive, future stock returns increase. With sharp increases in dividend yields, the 3-month-ahead stock returns now average 6.6%.

Increases in dividend yields signal higher stock returns up to 6 months and 12 months ahead as well (table 6.4, columns 3 and 4). The strongest predictive effects are associated with the 12-month holding periods. With largest declines in dividend yields, the 12-month-ahead stock returns average 8.2%. With largest increases in dividend yields, the 12-month-ahead stock returns average 30.1%. Hence the difference in stock returns that are attributable to dividend changes is now 21.9 points (30.1% minus 8.2%). The extra returns predicted by the levels of the dividend yield variable was 18.6 points for the 12-month holding period (31.5% minus 12.9% in table 6.1). Thus looking at the predictive ability of dividend yield changes instead of the levels of the dividend yields does not appear to have diminished the predictive power of the dividend yield variable.

Next we examine the interaction between changes in dividends and aggregate insider trading. Given our earlier results, we focus on stronger insider-trading signals.[10] We also examine 12-month holding periods (table 6.5). Examining table 6.5 by rows first, aggregate insider trading maintains its predictive power when we control for the dividend yield. For all five out of five rows, the insider buy column shows higher 12-month-ahead stock returns than the insider sell column. The average extra return provided by the insider buy column is 15.9 points, which is now greater than the 14.5 points when we conditioned on dividend levels (table 6.2) and almost the same as the 15.8 point extra return that is unconditional (table 4.6). Hence the predictive power of the stronger insider-trading signals is not attenuated at all by the presence of the dividend changes variable.

Let's now examine table 6.5 by columns, which will tell us how the dividend-change variable fares after we control for the intensity of in-

Table 6.5

Returns to the 12-month-ahead equally weighted market index grouped by past aggregate insider trading using 55%–45% rule and changes in past dividend yield for the market portfolio

Dividend change	Aggregate insider selling for past 12 months	Aggregate insider buying for past 12 months
Largest dividend declines	4.5%	37.6%
	(30)	(2)
Second largest dividend declines	17.2	20.8
	(21)	(5)
Small changes in dividend yields	14.4	24.5
	(20)	(6)
Second largest dividend increases	10.7	29.5
	(7)	(6)
Largest dividend increases	8.3	22.1
	(5)	(11)

Note: The number of months is in parentheses.

sider trading. We find that dividend changes once again lose their predictive power when confronted with the intensive insider-trading signals. The first column in table 6.5 first shows an increase in future stock returns with increasing dividend yield up to the third group, and then shows a decline in future stock returns. The second column shows a large decline in future stock returns as the dividend yields increase. Hence dividend yield variable no longer predicts future stock returns after we control for the intensity of aggregate insider trading.

We can also see the reasons as to why intensive insider trading completely dominates the dividend yield variable. The numbers in parentheses in table 6.5 show the number of months in each cell. Once again there is a strong positive relation between intensive insider trading and dividend changes. As dividends increase, intensive insider selling declines from 30 months down to 5 months. Similarly, as dividend yields increase, intensive insider buying increases from 2 months up to 11 months. This strong positive relation suggests that insiders also observe the fundamental sources of mispricing that the dividend yield proxies for. Consequently intensive insider trading exploits these potential misvaluations by not only taking into account the information content of the dividend yields but also any other information that insiders know. Overall, our evidence suggests that increases in dividend yields no longer predict increases in future stock returns once we control for the intensity of insider trading.

Firm-specific dividend yields

Until now, we have examined the predictive ability of market dividend yield, both in levels and changes and their interactions with aggregate insider trading. Hence we have asked the following question: Do increases in the market dividend yields forecast increased future market returns? We now turn our attention to firm-specific dividend yields and ask the following question: At a given point in time, do stocks with higher dividend yields have higher expected future returns than do the stocks with lower dividend yields? Hence, instead of focusing on time series predictability, we now focus on cross-sectional predictability.

To examine cross-sectional predictability using dividend yields, we use a similar procedure as before. We first compute the dividend yield on each stock by summing its dividends over the past 12 months. We then group stocks into five equal-sized groups based on their dividend yield during that year. Finally we measure the net stock returns over the next calendar year. Once again, to compute net stock returns, we subtract the returns to the equally weighted market index from the returns to each stock.

We now examine the relation between dividend yields and net stock returns (table 6.6). The first column shows the number of observations. The sample size ranges from 5,124 to 13,199 for each dividend group. The second column shows the dividend yields. The dividend yields increase from 0% to 8.63% as we go from the lowest dividend group

Table 6.6
Dividend yields and subsequent 12-month net stock returns grouped by dividend yields

Cross-sectional dividends	Number of firm months	Dividend yield	Subsequent 12-month net stock returns
Lowest dividend yield stocks	13,199	0.00%	1.01%
Second dividend yield stocks	5,124	0.93	1.06
Third dividend yield stocks	9,379	2.30	−1.25
Fourth dividend yield stocks	9,321	4.20	0.29
Highest dividend yield stocks	9,176	8.63	−1.92

to the highest dividend group. Hence there is substantial variation in dividend yield.

The third column of table 6.6 shows the relative performance of stocks based on their dividend yields during the past year. Surprisingly there is no positive relation between dividend yields and relative performance vis-à-vis the equally weighted market index. If anything, low dividend stocks outperform the market index by a small amount, about 1%, while the high yield stocks underperform the market index by about 1.9%.

The apparent negative cross-sectional relation between the firm-specific dividend yields and relative stock returns is in sharp contrast to the positive time-series relations shown earlier. The negative cross-sectional results are most likely a reflection of the well-known size effect. If is well known that small stocks have on average higher returns than large firms. Moreover most small stocks pay no dividends. Hence the low dividend stocks outperform the equally weighted index by a small amount, since they tend to be smaller stocks.

Overall, our evidence demonstrates that the previously described positive time series relation between dividend yields and future performance holds only for the market dividend yield. Firm-specific dividend yields do not allow us to choose between stocks. While not shown here, we also examine the interaction between firm-specific insider trading and firm-specific dividend yields. Our results were not surprising. Firm-specific insider trading continued to be a good predictor of future stock returns without affecting the relation between dividend yields and relative stock returns.

Conclusions and investment implications

In this chapter we have analyzed the predictive ability of market dividends and the interaction between the market dividend yield and aggregate insider trading. Our main concern is to determine whether dividend yields predict future stock returns and establish the strength of this relation. We have also examined whether the predictive ability of the dividend yield is maintained when confronted with insider trading. Our analysis so far supports the following conclusions:

1. The market dividend yields predict future stock returns for the period 1975 to 1994. High levels of market dividend yields are associated with above average, positive future stock returns. Low levels of market dividend yields are associated with below average but not negative future stock returns. The predictive ability of the market dividend yield variable increases up to a one-year horizon. The highest level of dividend yields predicts additional 18-point returns over a 12-month period as compared with the lowest level of dividend yields.

2. Market dividend yields and aggregate insider trading do appear to be related. Aggregate insider buying increases when the market dividend yields increase, while aggregate insider selling declines when the market dividend yields increase. It appears that insiders in the economy as a whole already take into account the implications of the market dividend yield in their trading decisions.

3. The market dividend yield is an important predictor of future stock returns. However, when confronted with insider trading, the market dividend yield loses much of its punch. The relation between market

dividend yield and insider trading becomes flatter, nonmonotonic, and it can even turn negative.

4. More intensive insider-trading signals result in greater attenuation of the predictive ability of the market dividend yield variable.

5. Overall, the predictive ability of the aggregate insider-trading variable does not depend on the market dividend yields. It appears that the forecasting power of aggregate insider trading is derived from independent sources. However, increases in market dividend yields do not predict positive future stock returns when we control for the intensity of aggregate insider trading.

6. Since the levels of dividend yields wander around with no affinity to a particular range of values, we repeated our tests using changes in dividend yields. Changes in dividend yields provide even a stronger signal than the levels of dividend yields. However, when confronted with intensive insider-trading signals, changes in dividend yields also lose their punch. Taking into account intensive insider buying and selling signals, increases in dividend yields no longer predict positive future stock returns.

7. The evidence presented in this chapter suggests that the predictive ability of the dividend yield arises, since it captures some of the mispricing of stocks. However, this is a noisy signal. Since insider trading does a better job of capturing mispricing, it tends to dominate the dividend yield variable. Overall, investors would not be able to combine dividend yield information with aggregate insider trading to form a stronger predictor of stock returns. Instead, the insider-trading variable performs just as well as the combined variable.

8. Firm-specific dividend yields are not useful in predicting future stock returns to individual firms. Instead, there is a weak, negative relation between firm-specific dividend yields and relative stock price performance in the future.

9. Our overall advice to the typical stock market investor who follows insider trading is to ignore dividend yields.

7   *Dividend Initiations*

Why do firms pay dividends?

In chapter 6 we saw that changes in market dividend yields forecast future stock returns. In this chapter we examine the effects of dividends in more detail. Instead of looking at the predictive ability of differences in dividend yields, we now examine what happens when firms first declare a dividend. Specifically we investigate answers to questions such as what happens to a firm's stock price when firms first declare a dividend. Do stock prices go up? If so, by how much? Is the stock price reaction to dividend initiation predictable? Specifically, can an outside investor predict which firms will initiate dividends? Does the pre-announcement insider-trading predict the dividend initiation? If insiders exploit the dividend initiation information, we may be able predict dividend initiations using prior insider trading. Can we also use preannouncement insider trading to forecast the subsequent stock price performance of firms initiating dividends? If insiders use additional nonpublic information in their trading decisions, then combining both the dividend initiations and insider trading can lead to stronger signals. Our objective in this chapter is to provide a more detailed guide to outside investors who are interested in using dividend initiations as part of an investment strategy and compare it with the predictive ability of insider trading.

In perfect capital markets it should make no difference whether a firm pays dividends or not.[1] If a firm does not pay dividends, investors can always sell some of the stock and convert it to cash. Conversely, if a firm does pay a dividend and investors do not want to consume the dividend, they can always reinvest the dividends and purchase additional shares.

In real world capital markets dividends do matter, since the required buying and selling of shares will cause transactions costs. Consequently investors do care whether a firm does or does not pay dividends. For some investors who desire greater current consumption, payment of dividends can increase the attractiveness of a given stock, since it alleviates having to sell shares periodically. For investors desiring greater future consumption, payment of dividends makes a stock less attractive, since they have to pay a tax on the dividend as well as incur transactions costs when they reinvest the dividends.

There is another reason why investors do care about dividend payments and dividend initiations. Assume that managers know more about the future prospects of their firms than market participants in general. Everything we have seen so far in this book suggests that this is a reasonable assumption. When a firm pays a dividend, it disburses cash, which provides security for the managers. Less cash in the firm increases the possibility of future financial distress. Consequently payment of dividends signals that managers feel sufficiently confident about their firm's future, and they are not worried about the increased probability of future financial distress (which after all could cost them their jobs). Hence market participants interpret dividend initiations as a sign of managerial confidence. This line of logic suggests that dividend initiations should lead to stock price increases.[2]

Most small, start-up firms do not pay any dividends to their shareholders. This is because all of the funds generated by the business are needed to grow the existing business as well as to provide flexibility during tough times. Studies have shown that many small businesses often fail because they lack sufficient start-up capital. Internally generated cash is critical to fund growth, since the firm's access to debt and equity markets would be limited due to insufficient operating history and high business risk. To preserve the internally generated cash for investment and operating needs, start-up firms choose not to pay any dividends.

If the start-up firm continues to operate successfully, then at some point during its life, it matures, gains sufficient expertise in dealing with risk, and establishes a record of consistent profitability. At the same time it establishes credit worthiness as evidenced by a history of paying its taxes, its employees, and its suppliers on time. Consequently, over time, risk is better managed. After a while the firm would have a consistent record of profitability, which provides a steady source of funds, and access to capital markets, which usually involves a line of credit with a bank to deal with any unexpected contingency. The firm is now ready to finally declare its first dividend. The first dividend is also referred to as the dividend initiation.

Having mentioned that, *on average,* dividend initiations are likely to signal good news, we can also think of some situations where the dividend initiation could possibly signal bad news. Payment of dividend can signal to market participants that the start-up firm has gone beyond the rapid growth stage and that it no longer has as profitable investment opportunities. Consequently the best use of the internally generated cash is to give it back to the shareholders. If shareholders are not already aware of the reduced investment opportunities, then they can react to the dividend payment with a reduction in stock prices.

Empirical studies have shown that, on average, the stock price reaction to the dividend initiation is quite positive. Stock prices rise when the firm initiates its first dividend. The dividend initiation signals to all shareholders that the managers expect the firm to remain healthy and profitable in the long term. The board of directors in effect announces that the firm can pay a dividend yet still will be sufficiently profitable to service its existing debt commitments, honor its commitments to employees, suppliers, and customers. In addition the firm would still have sufficient internally generated cash to preserve flexibility and deal with unexpected business downturns. In short, the dividend initiation is taken as a sign of confidence in the firm's future. On average, market participants appear to be less worried about declining investment opportunities for the start-up firm.

Our objective in this chapter is to provide more detailed guidance to the typical stock market investor about the valuation consequences of dividend initiations. We will first examine the stock price reaction to dividend initiations. Do stock prices increase when dividends are initiated? If so, how much? We will also examine whether the stock price reactions continue long after the dividend initiation month. We will then attempt to predict which firms will initiate dividends using the pre-announcement insider-trading information. Do stock prices increase on announcement of dividend initiations even if insiders are net sellers of stock during the pre-announcement period? Finally, we will attempt to predict the long-run stock price reaction using the pre-announcement insider-trading information.

Dividend initiation process

Before we can begin our analysis, we need a brief summary on how dividends are paid. Each dividend payment has four dates associated with it. The first date is the dividend declaration date. The board of directors of the firm announces the dividend initiation on this date. The amount of dividends and the time they will be paid are made public on this date. The second date is the ex-dividend date. For the case of dividend initiations, the ex-dividend date follows the dividend declaration date by about a week. Anyone who buys the stock before this date is entitled to receive a dividend. Anyone who buys the stock on or following the ex-dividend date is not entitled to a dividend payment. Obviously, to compensate for this disadvantage, stock prices open lower on the ex-dividend date approximately by the amount of the dividend. The third date is the record date. Again, from an accounting perspective, to receive a dividend, one has to be shareholder on the companies' stock transfer records as of the record date. Currently the settlement period in the United States is three business days. Hence, to be a stockholder of record as of the record date, one has to buy the stock three business days earlier and pay for the stock. Therefore the record day simply follows the ex-dividend day by three business days. The final date associated with dividends is the payment date. This is the date checks are actually mailed out from the company. This date follows the record date by about three weeks.

For our purposes the important date is the dividend declaration date. This is when the board of directors announces the amount and the record date of the dividend initiation. Hence the market participants learn everything about the upcoming dividend payment on this date. In an efficient market the stock price reaction to the dividend initiations should be completed on the dividend declaration date. Consequently we focus our analysis around the dividend declaration date.

Stock price effects of dividend initiations

We begin our analysis by documenting the overall characteristics of our sample (table 7.1). We have identified 1,697 firms in 1975 to 1994 that initiated a dividend for the first time. All stock returns are computed net of market returns, which are computed by subtracting the

Table 7.1
Subsequent 12-month net stock returns for dividend initiating firms, 1975–1994

Total number of firms initiating dividends	1,697
Declaration month net return	2.1%
6-month net return	4.1%
12-month net return	7.5%

Note: Net returns are computed by subtracting the holding period returns to the equally weighted market index.

return to the equally weighted stock market index from the stock return to the dividend initiating firms.

For our total sample of 1,697 firms, the declaration month net return to the dividend-initiating firms is 2.1%. The stock market greets the announcement of the dividend initiations with significant increases in stock prices. Therefore dividend initiations are good news. The average 6-month net stock returns (including the declaration month) are 4.1% and the average 12-month net stock returns (also including the declaration month) are 7.5%.

Our evidence suggests that stock price reaction is not completed during the dividend declaration month. Instead, the stock price reaction continues for at least another year. The net additional stock price reaction during the 11 months following the declaration month is 5.4 points (7.5% minus 2.1%). This finding suggests that dividend initiations are probably followed by additional good announcements such as increased earnings in the future. This rather slow stock price reaction raises the possibility that outsiders can potentially profit by buying shares in firms initiating dividends. To develop this possibility fully, we examine stock price reaction by taking into account the dividend initiation as well as the prior insider trading.

Dividend initiations and insider trading

Our main focus is whether we can improve the potential performance of investors who wish to exploit the stock price reaction to dividend initiations. The first question we ask is whether we can predict the dividend initiations by using pre-announcement insider-trading information. If yes, then a potential investor can capture some of the announcement month's stock price increases. If not, then the investor has to wait until the dividend initiation is announced and then assess the situation.

To test whether we can predict dividend initiations using pre-announcement insider-trading information, we go through the following simple experiment. For each firm initiating dividends, we look back and examine insider trading in 12-month blocks. We then ask if the dividend initiation is more likely following insiders' purchases or following insiders' sales. If dividend initiations are more likely following insiders' purchases, our next step would be compare insiders' purchases in dividend initiating firms with insider trading in other non-dividend-paying firms.

For insider-trading information, we include all insiders. We declare a 12-month period as a buy period if the total shares bought are greater than the total shares sold by all insiders during that period. Similarly we declare a 12-month period as a sell period if the total shares sold are greater than the total shares bought by all insiders during that period. Our data do not indicate a positive relation between insider trading (purchases) and the probability of a dividend initiation (table 7.2). In fact there appears to be a slight negative relation. Dividend initiations are slightly more likely following insiders' sales rather than purchases.[3]

Our evidence suggests that pre-announcement insider trading is not motivated by a desire to exploit the announcement month net stock returns. Consequently it is not likely that the pre-announcement in-

Table 7.2
Probability of a dividend initiation based on insider trading during a 12-month preceding period

	Number of Observations	Probability of a dividend initiation over the next 1 to 6 months	Probability of a dividend initiation over the next 1 to 12 Months
Insiders buy stock during a 12-month period	8,891	4.2%	8.2%
No insider trade	8,035	4.6	8.9
Insiders sell stock during a 12-month period	4,891	5.0	9.6

sider-trading information can be used to predict the occurrence of a dividend initiation. Instead, investors have to wait until the dividend initiations are publicly announced.

A second potential strategy that investors can follow is to wait until the dividend initiation is publicly announced, look back at the pre-announcement insider trading, and then buy shares in all firms that initiate dividends based on pre-announced insider trading. Will this strategy work? Is there a profit opportunity by combining the dividend initiation information with pre-announcement insider-trading information? We explore this possibility next.

We sort the subsequent performance of firms initiating dividends by the pre-announcement insider-trading activity (table 7.3). As before, insider trading is computed by adding all the shares traded by all insiders during the past twelve months. If the total number of shares traded is positive, that firm is included in the buy group. If the total number of shares traded is negative, that firm is included in the sell group. If the total number of shares traded by all insiders sums to zero, then that firm is included in the no-trade group.

Table 7.3

Subsequent 12-month net stock returns for dividend initiating firms, 1975–1994, grouped by insider trading activity

	Number of firms	Declaration month net return	6-month net return	12-month net return
Insiders buy stock during the 12 months prior to dividend initiations	586	3.0%	8.6%	13.8%
No insider trade	715	0.8	−0.9	1.8
Insiders sell stock during the 12 months prior to dividend initiations	396	3.1	6.3	8.3

Note: Net returns are computed by subtracting the holding period returns to the equally weighted market index.

There are 586 firms in the insider-buy group, 715 firms in the no-trade group, and 396 firms in the insider-sell group (table 7.3). Hence there are more firms with insider purchases than insider sales. Buy firms outnumber the sell firms by a ratio of 1.5 to 1. This pattern is consistent with the results documented earlier that insiders in small firms tend to be heavier purchasers of their own firms' stock.

Our objective is to discover if the use of prior insider-trading information increases the profit opportunities available for outside investors following the dividend initiation month. For the insider-buy group, the declaration month returns are 3.0%, while the subsequent 12-month return equals 13.8% (table 7.3). Hence, if an outside investor invests only in firms initiating a dividend and with insider buying, the extra returns following the declaration month equal 10.8 points (13.8% minus 3.0%). For the insider-sell group, the declaration month returns are 3.1% while the subsequent 12-month return equals 8.3%. Hence, if an outside investor invests only in firms initiating a dividend and with insider selling, the extra returns following the declaration month equal 5.2 points (8.3% minus 3.1%). These results suggest that information on prior insider purchase activity allows an outside investor to more than double the extra returns available following dividend initiations. Insider-trading activity is clearly useful as an investment tool.[4]

What are insiders' motivations around dividend initiations? If insiders trade to exploit the dividend declaration month stock returns, then we would expect a positive relation between the declaration month net returns and insider trading. If insiders buy, we would expect a positive return. If insiders sell, we would expect a negative return.

Our evidence shows that the declaration month net stock returns are 3.0%, 0.8%, and 3.1% for the insider-buy, no-insider-trade, and insider-sell groups (table 7.3). Not surprisingly, based on previous results, there is little difference between insider buying and selling groups. Moreover, since the stock price reaction to firms with insider selling is not negative, this evidence is inconsistent with the view that

insider trading can help separate firms with and without good investment opportunities. Second, the insider-selling group has a higher net
return than the no-insider-trading group. This evidence is consistent
with our earlier finding that dividend initiations are slightly more
likely to follow insider selling.

Overall, our evidence is inconsistent with the view that insider selling can help identify those firms that experience a decline in investment opportunities and choose to pay dividends. Our evidence also
suggests that the pre-announcement insider trading is not motivated
due to a desire to exploit the announcement-month stock market reaction to dividend initiations. Pre-announcement insider trading clearly
fails to distinguish between presumably the high-future-earnings
group from the lack-of-investment-opportunities group. These findings should not be too surprising. All of the evidence we offered so far
in this book suggests that insiders do not attempt to exploit specific
corporate announcements. Instead, they trade on the basis of long-run
expectations of stock price performance.

There is additional evidence in support of the long-run, expectations
hypothesis. Looking at the 6-month horizon, the net stock returns are
8.6%, −0.9%, and 6.3%, for the insider-buy, no-trade, and the insider-
sell groups, respectively (table 7.3). Hence over the 6-month horizon,
the insider-buy group begins to dominate the insider-sell group. Curi-
ously, the no-trade group performs the worst of the three groups. Looking at the 12-month horizon provides further corroborating evidence.
The insider-buy group outperforms the equally weighted market index
by 13.8%. The insider-sell group outperforms the equally weighted index by 8.3%. Hence the advantage of the buy group over the sell group
widens with increasing horizon. The no-trade group still has the worst
performance of the three, outperforming the equally weighted average
by 1.8%.

We also examined the stability of our findings. To investigate this
issue, we broke up our sample into three decades, the 1970s, 1980s,

Table 7.4

Declaration month net stock returns for dividend initiating firms, 1975–1994, grouped by insider trading activity

	Declaration month net returns		
	Decade of 1970s	Decade of 1980s	Decade of 1990s
Insiders buy shares during the 12 months prior to dividend initiations	6.6% (114)	2.2% (264)	2.1% (208)
No insider trading	4.0 (98)	−0.7 (422)	2.3 (195)
Insiders sell shares during the 12 months prior to dividend initiations	6.8 (116)	1.8 (189)	1.3 (91)

Note: Net returns are computed by subtracting the holding period returns to the equally weighted market index. The numbers in parentheses are the numbers of observations in each group.

and 1990s (tables 7.4 and 7.5). The 1970s comprise a 5-year period from 1975 to 1979, the 1980s comprise a 10-year period from 1980 to 1989, and the 1990s comprise a 5-year period from 1990 to 1994. Net returns are computed by taking the difference between the actual announcement month returns to the firms announcing dividend initiations and the return for the same calendar month to the value-weight index of NYSE, AMEX, and NASDAQ stocks.

Our findings indicate that the 1970s had the most positive stock price reactions to dividend initiation declarations with an announcement month net return of 5.9%. This is followed by the 1990s, with an announcement-month net return of 2.0%. The decade of the 1980s had the smallest reaction to dividend-initiation announcements, with a net return of 0.7%. However, for all three subsamples there is not much difference between the announcement-month net returns to insider buying and selling groups. For instance, for the decade of the 1970s, the announcement-month net returns are 6.6%, 4.0%, and 6.8%, for the insider-buy, no-trade, and insider-sell groups, respec-

Table 7.5
Subsequent 12-month net stock returns for dividend initiating firms, 1975–1994, grouped by insider trading activity

	Subsequent 12-month net returns		
	Decade of 1970s	Decade of 1980s	Decade of 1990s
Insiders buy shares during the 12	34.0%	5.2%	13.5%
months prior to dividend initiations	(114)	(264)	(208)
No insider trading	26.2	−7.6	9.9
	(98)	(422)	(195)
Insider sell shares during the 12	29.8	−2.6	3.7
months prior to dividend initiations	(116)	(189)	(91)

Note: Net returns are computed by subtracting the holding period returns to the equally weighted market index. The numbers is parentheses are the number of observations in each group.

tively. For the decade of the 1980s, the announcement-month net returns are 2.2%, -0.7%, and 1.8%, for buyers, no-trade, and sellers groups, respectively. Finally, for the decade of the 1990s, the announcement-month net returns are 2.1%, 2.3%, and 1.3%, for buyers, no-trade, and sellers groups, respectively. Hence the selling group does not exhibit negative returns for any of the three subsamples.

Looking at the long-run stock price reaction for the three groups again indicates that the decade of the 1980s behaves a bit differently than the other two decades. The 12-month net returns for the decades of the 1970s, 1980s, and 1990s are 30.2%, −2.7%, and 10.3%, respectively. Hence, for both the 1970s and the 1990s, the long-run performance of dividend initiating firms is positive. In contrast, the long-run returns are negative for the decade of the 1980s. The long-run performance separated by insider trading groups and decade groups are shown in table 7.5. Looking at insider buying, no-trade, and selling groups separately for the 1980s indicate that the largest negative performance is associated with the no-trade group (−7.6%). For the insider-selling group in the 1980s, the long-run performance was −2.6%, which is still better that of the no-trade group. Hence, once again, the evidence suggests that the motivation for insider trading does not seem to come from exploiting the dividend initiation announcement-month stock price reaction.

Our examination of the decade by decade performance of the dividend initiating firms also demonstrates that the apparent slow stock price reaction to dividend initiations has not disappeared in the 1990s. As we pointed out earlier, the declaration month net stock return to insider-buying group is 2.1%. The 12-month net returns to insider buying firms is 13.5% (table 7.5). Hence, in the decade of the 1990s, an investor who buys dividend initiating stocks with insider buying earns 11.4 points (13.5% minus 2.1%) for the 11 months subsequent to the dividend declaration month.

Next we examine more selective insider-trading rules. Our objective is to see if (1) more powerful insider-trading signals create greater profit opportunities for outsiders and (2) more powerful insider-trading signals can reverse the interpretation of the dividend initiation signal. As before, we experiment with large volume of trading by all insiders as well as large volume of trading by top executives. In the interest of brevity, we do not show these results in detail.

We can summarize our results as follows: When insiders buy more than 1,000 shares during the 12 months prior to dividend initiations, the declaration month net return is 3.2%, while the 12-month net return is 14.0%. Hence large insider buying allows the outsiders to capture an additional 10.8 point return. When insiders sell more than 1,000 shares during the 12 months prior to dividend initiations, the declaration month net return is 2.5% while the 12-month net return is 7.0%. Hence large insider selling limits the outsiders' gains to only 4.5 points. Hence focusing on large insider trading increases the advantage of using insider-trading information.

Large insider selling still does not signify that the firms' investment opportunities are limited. The firms with large insider selling still experience a positive 2.5% extra return during the announcement month. Moreover this positive reaction exceeds the 1.4% positive reaction for firms with no prior insider trading. Hence our earlier conclusion that insider trading is not designed to exploit the announcement-month stock price reaction is again corroborated.

Next we examine the information content of insider trading when it exceeds 10,000 shares. When insiders buy more than 10,000 shares during the 12 months prior to dividend initiations, the declaration month net return is 4.3% while the 12-month net return is 20.0%. Hence large insider buying allows the outsiders to capture an amazing additional 15.7 point return. When insiders sell more than 10,000 shares during the 12 months prior to dividend initiations, the declaration month net return is 1.5% while the 12-month net return is 8.5%. Hence large insider selling limits the outsiders' gains to only 7.0 points. Focusing on very large insider trading further increases the advantage of using insider-trading information.

Once again, large insider selling still does not signify that the firms' investment opportunities are limited. The firms with large insider selling still experience a positive 1.5% extra return. Our earlier conclusion that insider trading is not designed to exploit the announcement month stock price reaction is again corroborated.

Finally we examine the performance of firms with large trading by top executives. These results are comparable to those for large volume of trading for all insiders. Once again, firms with large insider buying outperform firms with large insider selling, both during the declaration month as well as during the subsequent 12 month. However, there is no evidence that the large selling by top executives underperforms the market index. Consequently the combination of dividend initiation and insider selling cannot be construed as a negative signal, suggesting diminished investment opportunities.

How do we interpret these findings? The most straight forward interpretation suggests that insider trading and dividend initiations constitute independent signals. Dividend initiations usually signal good news. Insider buying signals good news, while insider selling signals bad news. Consequently dividend initiations combined with insider buying constitute unusually good circumstances. Hence these stocks outperform the market index by 20 points over the next 12 months. In contrast, dividend initiations combined with insider selling constitute offsetting signals. The evidence suggests that the positive signal provided by the dividend initiation is especially strong and dominates the negative information in insider selling. As a result firms initiating dividend with prior insider selling still outperform the market index over the next year, albeit to a smaller degree than firms with insider buying.

Conclusions and Investment Implications

In this chapter we have examined the information content of dividend initiations and the interaction between prior insider trading and dividend initiations. We are interested in providing a more detail guide to investors who use dividend initiations as an investment strategy. Our findings are as follows.

1. Dividend initiations are good news. Stock prices increase by 2.1% during the dividend initiation declaration month. Moreover stocks initiating dividends outperform the market index by 7.5% over the next 12-month period.

2. It is not possible to predict the occurrence of dividend initiations by pre-announcement insider trading. In fact dividend initiations are slightly more likely to occur following insider sales.

3. Insider trading prior to dividend initiations does not appear to be motivated by a desire to exploit the stock price response to the announcement of dividend initiations. There is no difference between

the stock price reaction to dividend initiations when we group by prior insider trading.

4. The evidence suggests that insider trading that takes place prior to dividend initiations is more likely to be motivated by the long-term performance. Consistent with this view, firms bought by insiders significantly outperform firms sold by insiders over the next 12 months.

5. There is no evidence that suggests that insider selling prior to dividend initiations signals bad news regarding the lack of investment opportunities.

8 *Earnings announcements*

Information content of earnings announcements

Earnings of a corporation is an important indicator of the fundamental value of that firm. Announcements of firms' quarterly earnings are closely studied and are anxiously awaited corporate events. Securities regulations require that at the end of each fiscal quarter, exchange-listed firms must disclose detailed accounts of their financial conditions including their revenues, costs, and earnings. Firms disclose earnings information by filing reports called 10-Q (quarterly) and 10-K (annual) to the Securities and Exchange Commission.

Prediction of firms' earnings is quite important. If for a given firm the announced earning is better than market participants' expectations, stock prices tend to go up. If the announced earnings do not live up to market participants' expectations, stock prices tend to go down. Hence a firm can announce a large increase in earnings only to have its stock price go down if the market had expected it to do even better. Similarly a firm can announce losses and have its stock price go up if the market had expected even bigger losses. Expectations are important in understanding stock price reactions to earnings announcements. Consequently an army of analysts tries to estimate and predict the earnings of large firms. Any deviations from the previous market expectations and concomitant stock price reactions receive considerable financial press coverage.

In this chapter we examine the information content of earnings announcements, subsequent stock price reactions to earnings, and the interaction between earnings announcements and insider trading. Many professional investors seek out stocks that are expected to outperform analysts' earnings predictions since these firms can experience large stock price run-ups in a fairly short time horizon. Individual investors often do not try to predict firms' future earnings. Instead, they seek out stocks in which the announced earnings are better than previously expected and sell stocks in which the announced earnings are worse than previously expected.

A puzzling finding in the finance literature is that stock prices appear to react to earnings announcements rather slowly. It is true that following positive earnings' surprises (actual earnings are better that market's expectations), stock prices go up. However, the evidence also shows that stock prices continue to go up for weeks and months following the positive surprises. Similarly stock prices continue to decline for weeks and months following negative earnings' surprises. The reasons for these drifts are not well understood. One camp believes that apparent slow stock price reaction represents a slow adjustment in stock prices. Another camp believes that apparent slow stock price reaction is due to mismeasurement of risk or selection biases.

In this chapter we take a closer look at the earnings announcements. Our first question is whether there is a significant reaction to earnings announcements. Given some level of earnings surprise, how much do stock prices react over the announcement day? Second, we would like to find out if the stock price reaction is completed swiftly or if it is slow. Do the stock prices continue to drift in the same direction as the earnings surprise for weeks and months. If so, what is the magnitude of this drift? Third, if the stock price reaction occurs slowly, is there a profit opportunity for typical stock market investors after transaction costs? Fourth, does insider trading have anything to do with the information content of earnings announcements? Specifically, do insiders buy stocks before positive earnings surprises and sell stocks before negative earnings surprises? Fifth, can we predict the sign of the earnings surprise based on the immediate prior insider trading?

Our goals in this chapter are to (1) document the stock price reactions to earnings announcements, (2) determine whether or not there are profit opportunities around earnings announcements, and (3) identify and measure the role, if any, insider-trading information can play in improving the information content of earnings announcements and lead to better trading decisions for stock market investors.

Prior literature on earnings announcements

As we stated before, a well-known finding in the finance and accounting literature is that earnings announcements matter. If earnings are higher than market's expectations, then stock prices increase on the announcement day. Similarly, if the earnings are lower than market's expectations, then the stock prices drop. Second, the stock price reaction to earnings announcements is not completed quickly. Stock prices continue to drift up or down for a period of up to six months or even longer. This apparent slow stock price reaction contradicts the efficient market hypothesis, which states that stock prices reflect all available information fully and promptly. Smart investors ought to understand that slow stock price reaction means abnormal profit opportunity for some and abnormal losses for others. In a market where the costs of obtaining, analyzing, and trading on earnings information is small relative to potential profits, the implications of earnings surprises should be incorporated into stock prices quickly.[1]

The apparently slow stock price reaction to earnings announcements is highly surprising. As a result earnings announcements have attracted the attention of both academics and investors. Investors want to know if they can earn unusual profits by following earnings announcements. Academics puzzle over the reasons for the slow stock price reaction. As usual the slow stock price reaction can be due to mispricing or lack of adequate control for the risks. If the true risk of the firm is higher than the researcher estimates, then what appears as a profit opportunity may in fact be compensation for bearing risk. Once again the issue boils down to the magnitude of the price adjustment and whether it can be accounted by risk factors.

Stock price reaction around earnings announcements

We begin our analysis by documenting the stock price behavior around earnings announcements for a recent time period. We obtained our earnings information from COMPUSTAT tapes, covering the period 1978 to 1993. These tapes provide us with the total dollar earnings, earnings announcement dates, and the quarter and year the earnings announcement pertains to.

The information content of earnings announcements depends on market expectations and the earnings surprise, which must be estimated from available data. Earnings surprise refers to the difference between actual earnings for the current quarter and market expectations of those earnings. If actual earnings come above expectations, then the surprise is positive. If actual earnings come below expectations, then the surprise is negative. Market's expectation of the earnings is formed by taking into account all relevant information that affects firm's earnings such as the past trends in firm's earnings, recent earnings announcements of other firms in the same industry, and the current economic environment.

To illustrate what we mean by earnings' surprise, an example may be helpful. Suppose that based on analysts' predictions, the market expectation of ABC firm's quarterly earnings is $1.50 a share. Also suppose that ABC firm had announced a quarterly earnings of $1.80 a share the previous quarter. Given that analysts publicize their predictions, the current stock price of ABC firm would already reflect the expectation of $1.50 per share earnings. If actual earnings for the current quarter exceed $1.50 per share, then the earnings surprise will be positive, which will constitute good news, and the stock price will likely increase. Suppose that the firm announces earnings for the current quarter to be $1.70, implying a positive earnings' surprise of $0.20 a share. In this case stock prices are likely to increase. The reader will note that stock prices would increase even though the current $1.70 represents a reduction from the previous quarter's $1.80. If the actual earnings for the current quarter come in at say $1.20 a share, this will constitute bad news, and the stock prices will likely fall.

To measure the market's expectations about the earnings, we use whatever relevant information market participants have. Some researchers have used analysts' predictions or sophisticated econometric techniques to estimate market expectations of current earnings. Research has also shown that simple methods to estimate earnings work almost as well as more sophisticated methods. The simplest way of measuring the market's expectations for the upcoming quarter is to use the earnings for the same quarter from the previous year. To give an example, suppose that we want to form an expectation about the quarterly December 1990 earnings. In this case we use the December 1989 actual earnings as our best guess. Since we match the earnings by the calendar month, this measure controls for any seasonal variation in earnings.

To be able to compare earnings surprises across firms, we compute a measure called the standardized unexpected earnings (SUE) as follows: First, we take the actual earnings per share from four quarters earlier as the market's expectation of the upcoming earnings. Earnings surprise is computed by subtracting the earnings from four quarters earlier from the current earnings. We then standardize the earnings surprise (which has units of dollars) by dividing by the time series standard deviation of quarterly earnings for that firm. These standardized earnings surprises are called the standardized unexpected earnings, or simply SUE. Finally we classify the SUE measure into five equal-sized groups based on historical distribution of SUEs. The standardized earnings surprise eliminates the differences in the dollar magnitude of the earnings and allows us to compare earnings surprises across firms.

Let's illustrate the computation of SUE for our hypothetical ABC firm. Assume that the standard deviation of the changes in earnings per share is $0.20. Given the actual quarterly earnings of $1.70 and the expectation of earnings equal to $1.50, SUE will equal 1.0 (computed as $1.70 minus 1.50 divided by 0.20). Positive SUE values indicate better-than-expected results, while negative SUE values indicate worse-than-expected results.

To measure the stock price performance following earnings announcements, we compute 12-month-ahead net stock returns with and without a 3-day announcement-period returns. Announcement period consists of the day before, the announcement day, and the day after the earnings announcement. This 3-day announcement-period window captures the fact that some firms may announce their earnings before the stock market closes at 4:00 PM or after the market closes. Allowance for another day is made to ensure that everyone can access this information. The postannouncement window extends to 12 months following the announcement in order to measure any potential stock price drifts. The 12-month-ahead net stock returns are computed by subtracting the return to the equally weighted index from each firms' return.

We sort the 12-month-ahead net returns by SUE groups (table 8.1). Firms with the most negative earnings surprises are in SUE group 1. Firms with the most positive earnings surprises are in SUE group 5. The middle SUE group represents firms whose actual earnings are close to the market's previous expectation. Hence the earnings surprise for this group is close to zero.

Each SUE group contains more than 22,000 earnings announcement. Hence our sample is quite large. For the lowest SUE group the 12-month subsequent net stock returns equal −5.9%. The lowest SUE group of stocks underperforms the market index over the next 12 months. For the middle group the 12-month subsequent net stock re-

Table 8.1

Subsequent 12-month net stock returns grouped by standardized unexpected earnings (SUE) ratios

Group	Number of observations	Subsequent 12-month net returns including announcement	Subsequent 12-month net returns excluding announcement
Lowest SUE group	22,819	−5.9%	−4.1%
Second SUE group	23,953	−3.5	−2.7
Third SUE group	24,097	−0.0	−0.00
Fourth SUE group	23,922	2.8	1.8
Highest SUE group	22,997	6.8	4.0

turns equal −0%. For the highest SUE group, subsequent net stock returns equal 6.8%. The highest SUE stocks outperform the market index over the next 12 months.

Our earnings surprise measure works pretty well. It captures the differences in stock market reaction to earnings. Low SUE stocks reveal new and disappointing information; consequently the stock market reaction is negative for the next 12 months. The firms that fall in the middle SUE group conform to market's prior expectations, and therefore they show little new stock price reaction. The firms in high SUE groups reveal new and positive information; consequently the stocks price reaction is positive over the next 12 months.

While our analysis tells us that our measure of earnings surprise is pretty good, it does not yet tell us how quickly the stock price reaction is completed. Consequently it also does not tell us whether we can use this measure of earnings surprise to buy and sell stocks profitably. To examine this issue, we examine the subsequent stock price drift after excluding the three-day announcement period. The announcement period is excluded to give an outside investor sufficient time to learn about the current earnings and formulate a trading strategy. An investor would now be able to observe the dollar earnings of the firm, compute the earnings surprise or SUE measure, and classify the firm into a SUE group based on the historical distribution of SUEs. Hence, the day after the earnings announcement, our typical investors should be able to determine whether a given firm is in the lowest or the highest SUE group and thereby make appropriate buying and selling decisions.

The subsequent 12-month net stock price reaction after excluding the 3-day announcement period returns indicates that there are profit opportunities (table 8.1, last column). For an active trader, these are potentially realizable net returns. For the lowest SUE group, postearnings net returns equal −4.1%. Hence most of the fall in stock prices occurs after the announcement period. This is called the *earnings drift* in accounting literature. Stock prices continue to drift in the same direction as the earnings surprise for about a year following the earnings announcement. Suppose that an investor observes the earnings and determines that her stock falls in the lowest group. As before let us take an estimate of the transactions costs to be about 1% for a round-trip transaction. Table 8.1 tells us that by selling the stock after the announcement, she can avoid an additional 3.1% wealth loss over the next year.

For the middle SUE group, excess returns equal 0.0%. There is no stock price adjustment during the postannouncement period. Once again this finding is consistent with our interpretation that there is no new information revealed for the middle SUE group of firms.

For the highest SUE group, the postannouncement stock price drift equals 4.0%. An investor who buys the stock after the announcement period can outperform the market index by additional three points after transaction costs. The last column of table 8.1 also tells us the difference in the postannouncement drift between the lowest SUE group to the highest SUE group equals 8.1 points, which is quite large.

Can we tell how much stock price reaction occurs during the announcement period? The difference between the second and third columns in table 8.1 is the three-day announcement-period stock price reaction. By examining the announcement-period stock price reaction, we can also tell how much of the total stock price adjustment occurs during a three-day announcement period. For the lowest SUE group, the announcement-period reaction is −1.8 points. This is the difference between 5.9% and 4.1%. For the middle group, there is no announcement-period reaction. For the most positive SUE group, the announcement-period reaction is 2.8 points. This is the difference between 6.8% and 4.0%.

Our evidence suggests that substantial price reactions occur immediately surrounding the earnings announcement day. For the most negative SUE group, 1.8 points of the 5.9% negative reaction or almost one-third of the total reaction occurs during the three-day announcement period. For the most positive SUE group, 2.8 points of the 6.8% positive reaction or two-fifths of the total reaction occurs during the three-day announcement period. This finding further corroborates that earnings announcements matter and stock prices react strongly to earnings. However, the overall evidence suggests that stock price reaction is not fully completed during the three-day announcement period.

Insider trading and earnings announcements

We next bring in the insider-trading variable to see if we can improve the information content of earnings. Specifically we would like to know whether the insider trading prior to earnings announcements anticipates the earnings surprise. Put another way, do insiders exploit the earnings announcements?[2] Do insiders buy stock prior to positive earnings surprises, and do they sell stock prior to negative earnings surprises? If the answer is yes, then we can use the insider-trading information to possibly predict the sign of the earnings surprise. This can be an important investment tactic. Second, we would like to know whether taking insider trading into consideration improves the information content of the earnings surprise over the long run. Do the stock prices continue to drift up following positive earnings surprises even if insiders sell stock? Similarly do the stock prices continue to drift down following negative earnings surprises even if insiders buy stock?

Table 8.2
Number of observations grouped by insider trading and standardized unexpected earnings (SUE) ratios

Group	Insiders sell during past 3 months	Insiders buy during past 3 months
Lowest SUE group	4,779 (55%)	3,946 (45%)
Second SUE group	6,821 (61%)	4,374 (39%)
Third SUE group	8,378 (67%)	4,056 (33%)
Fourth SUE group	7,078 (62%)	4,363 (38%)
Highest SUE group	4,692 (52%)	4,400 (48%)

We sort earnings surprises according to SUE groups and insiders' buy sell transactions over the past three months (table 8.2). If insiders buy more shares than they sell during the past three months, we classify this as a buy period. If insiders sell more shares than they buy during the past three months, we classify this as a sell period. We use a three-month period because our earnings information is quarterly and it is updated every three months.

Our evidence does not reveal a strong relation between prior insider-trading activity and quarterly earnings surprise. For the lowest SUE group, insiders sell 55% of the time over the past three months (table 8.2, column 1). As the earnings surprise becomes more positive, insiders demonstrate a greater propensity to sell. For the middle category, insiders sell 67% of the time. As the earnings surprise becomes still more positive, insider selling declines to 52% of the time. The difference in insider selling between the lowest SUE group and the highest SUE group is only 3 percentage points, which is not economically significant.

We now examine the relation between insider buying and earnings surprises (table 8.2, column 2). For the lowest SUE group, insiders buy 45% of the time over the past three months. As the earnings surprise becomes more positive, insiders in fact show a lower propensity to buy. For the middle category, insiders buy only 33% of the time. As the earnings surprise becomes still more positive, insider buying increases to 48% of the time. The difference in insider buying between the lowest SUE group and the highest SUE group is again not economically significant.[3]

Our evidence suggests that insiders' success documented in this book so far in predicting future stock returns is most likely not derived from an exploitation of the upcoming earnings announcements. The fact that insiders do not exploit earnings information should not be too surprising. As we discussed earlier, legislation enacted during the 1980s has made it very costly for insiders to exploit important corporate announcements such as dividends, earnings, and corporate takeovers. Moreover most firms have explicitly defined blackout periods that prohibit any insider trading immediately prior to earnings announcements. These blackout periods usually cover the two months prior to the earnings announcement date.

Insider trading, earnings surprise, and the stock price drift

The next question we examine is whether using insider trading as well as the earnings surprise information can help predict the long-run stock price drift better. We now examine the joint predictive power of insider trading and the earnings surprise. Table 8.3 groups the subsequent 12-month net returns by earnings surprises and whether insiders are buying or selling in the past 3 months. In this chapter, since earnings surprises are computed every 3 months using quarterly earnings, we also examine insider trading over the same 3-month period.

Our results indicate that earnings surprises retain their predictive power after controlling for insider-trading activity (table 8.3, column 1). Given insider selling and the lowest SUE, the subsequent 12-month net stock returns equal −6.7%. With increasing earnings, the subse-

Table 8.3
Subsequent 12-month net stock returns (including the 3-day announcement returns) grouped by insider trading and standardized unexpected earnings (SUE) ratios

Group	Insiders sell during past 3 months	Insiders buy during past 3 months
Lowest SUE group	−6.7%	−4.9%
Second SUE group	−4.2	−2.2
Third SUE group	−0.4	0.7
Fourth SUE group	2.5	4.0
Highest SUE group	3.7	6.1

quent net returns also rise. For the middle SUE group, subsequent returns rise to −0.4%. For the highest SUE group, the subsequent returns rise to 3.7%. Going from the lowest earnings surprise group to the highest earnings surprise group increases the subsequent 12-month net stock returns by 10.4 points.

The second column in table 8.3 shows the subsequent net stock returns when insiders are buying over the past 3 months. Given insider buying and the lowest SUE group, the subsequent 12-month net stock returns equal −4.9%. Once again, with increasing earnings surprise, the subsequent net stock returns rise. For the middle SUE group, the subsequent net stock returns equal 0.7%. For the highest SUE group, the subsequent net stock returns equal 6.1%. Going from the lowest earnings surprise group to the highest earnings surprise group increases the subsequent 12-month net stock returns by 11.0%.

Let's now examine table 8.3 by rows to see if insider-trading activity retains its predictive power when we control for the earnings surprise. This exercise will also help us determine whether insiders use the upcoming earnings announcements in their trading decisions at all. From table 8.3, for each of the five rows, insider buying is associated with higher future stock returns than the insider-selling column. Hence insider trading retains its predictive power after we control for the earnings surprise. The average difference between insider buying and selling columns equals 1.8%. To remind us of the unconditional predictive power of insider trading, we need to go back to figure 2.1. We can estimate the unconditional predictive power of the three-month insider-trading activity from figure 2.1 to be about 1.8%. Hence controlling for earnings announcements does not reduce the predictive power of the insider-trading variable at all. Once again this finding corroborates our earlier conclusion that insiders do not exploit earnings announcements.

Our evidence clearly demonstrates that when examined jointly, both the insider-trading activity and the earnings surprise continue to be good predictors of future stock returns. Examining the two columns separately shows that as earnings become more positive, subsequent net stock returns increase monotonically. Also, examining table 8.3 row by row, we see that for five out of five rows, insider buying continues to signal higher future returns than insider selling. As a result using both insider trading and earnings surprise can give an outside investor increased predictive power. For instance, in table 8.3, combining insider selling with negative earnings surprise predicts a negative net return of 6.7%. Similarly combining insider buying with positive earnings surprise predicts a positive net return of 6.1%. The difference between the worst and the best outcomes now increases to 12.8 points, compared with 8.1 points from table 8.1.

Can an outside investor exploit the apparently slow stock price reaction? Our evidence so far indicates that future stock returns are slow and monotonically increasing in earnings surprise, the 12-month returns include the 3-day announcement period. Hence these returns are not realizable for anyone who does not have advance information about the earnings surprise. To explore net profits that an outsider can achieve, we exclude the returns for the 3-day announcement window.

The potentially realizable profit opportunities are qualitatively similar while the magnitude of the excess returns are somewhat reduced

Table 8.4

Subsequent 12-month net stock returns (excluding the 3-day announcement returns) grouped by insider trading and standardized unexpected earnings (SUE) ratios

Group	Insiders sell during past 3 months	Insiders buy during past 3 months
Lowest SUE group	−5.0%	−3.6%
Second SUE group	−3.2	−1.7
Third SUE group	−0.3	0.5
Fourth SUE group	1.6	3.0
Highest SUE group	1.6	3.4

(table 8.4). Once again both the earnings surprise and insider trading continue to be good predictors of the subsequent stock returns. In each column of table 8.4, increasing earnings are monotonically associated with higher future stock returns. Looking at table 8.4 row buy row, insider buying always predicts a higher future stock returns than insider selling for each SUE group.

We can also estimate the magnitude of the profit opportunities using both insider trading and earnings' surprises. By selling stocks that exhibit insider selling and the most negative earnings' surprise, an investor can avoid a 5.0% loss over the next 12 months. Similarly, by purchasing stocks exhibiting insider buying and the most positive earnings' surprise, an outside investor can outperform the market index by 3.4% over the next 12 months. The realizable difference between the worst and best outcomes is 8.4 points.

Large insider trading

So far, the evidence shows that everyday insider trading does not rely on upcoming earnings information. What happens if we look at more selective insider-trading signals? Does the more successful insider trader use earnings information? Can we dominate the information content of earnings surprises using more informative, highly selective insider-trading signals such as large volume insider trading or transaction by top executives? We now turn to these questions.

We focus on periods when top executives bought and sold more than 10,000 shares over a quarter. We would like to find out whether top executives exploit the earnings information when they trade large volumes of stock.

When we control for large trading by top executives, we finally see some attenuation of the predictive power of the earnings surprise variable (table 8.5). When top executives sell large number of shares, excess returns range from -7.2% for the lowest SUE group to -0.8% for the SUE group (table 8.5, column 1). Going from the lowest to the highest SUE group down the first column increases the excess returns by 6.4 points. When top executives buy a large number of shares, the excess returns range from 1.6% in the lowest SUE group to 6.1% for the highest SUE group (table 8.5, column 2). Going from the lowest to the high-

Table 8.5
Subsequent 12-month net stock returns (excluding the 3-day announcement returns) grouped by trading by top executives of more than 10,000 shares bought and sold and standardized unexpected earnings (SUE) ratios

Group	Top executives sell more than 10,000 shares during past 3 months	Top executives buy more than 10,000 shares during past 3 months
Lowest SUE group	-7.2% (340)	1.6% (199)
Second SUE group	-0.4 (472)	1.3 (122)
Third SUE group	-2.9 (795)	5.2 (82)
Fourth SUE grup	1.6 (711)	13.8 (85)
Highest SUE group	-0.8 (358)	6.1 (183)

Note: In parentheses are the number of observations.

est SUE group down the second column increases the excess returns by 4.5 points.

We can compute an average predictive power of the earnings surprise following large insider trading by top executives by averaging the excess returns from columns 1 and 2. The average predictive power of the earnings surprise is about 5.5% (average of 6.4% and 4.5%). Comparing this figure with the unconditional predictive power of the earnings surprise, we see a decrease from 8.1% to 5.5% (table 8.1).

Our findings suggest that top executives do take into account the information content of earnings in their large trading decisions. Looking at both large insider trading and earnings surprises does diminish the predictive power of earnings surprise variable. Nevertheless, the earnings surprise variable retains most of its predictive ability.[4]

Predictive ability of insider trading is not affected by earnings surprises. In each of the five rows, insider buying is associated with higher stock returns than insider selling (table 8.5). The average difference between buy and sells equals 7.5 points.[5] Hence large trading volume by top executives continues to predict future stock returns after we control for earnings' surprises.

Our evidence tells us that when we use more selective insider trading, the large excess returns predicted by large trading by top executives overwhelm the direction of excess returns for the earnings' surprise. As an investment guide, insider trading becomes a more important signal than the earnings' surprise. For instance, given insider selling the excess returns for four of five rows in the first column is negative. Similarly, given insider buying, the excess returns for five of five rows in the second column are positive. These findings suggest that even with the most positive earnings' surprise, a given stock can underperform the market index by 0.8% if top executives are large sellers of the stock. Similarly, even with the most negative earnings' surprise, the stock can outperform the market index by 1.6% over the next 12 months if the top executives are large buyers of the stock.

Conclusions and investment implications

In this chapter we have examined the information content of earnings announcements and the interaction between earnings information and insider trading. Our objective is to determine whether stock prices react fully and promptly to earnings information and whether we can improve the information content of earnings by examining the preceding insider trading. Information content of earnings announcements is analyzed using a measure of earnings surprise defined as the difference between actual earnings and the earnings from four quarters earlier. Insider trading is measured during the three-month period preceding the earnings announcement. Our findings are as follows:

1. Our simple measure of earnings surprise captures the information content of earnings pretty well. When earnings surprise is positive stock prices increase. When earnings surprise is negative stock prices decline.

2. Earnings' surprises predict future stock returns for a year following the earnings announcement date. Positive earnings surprises are associated with positive drift in stock returns. Negative earnings surprises are associated with negative drift in stock returns.

3. Insiders do not appear to exploit the earnings surprise. There is no relation between insider trading during a three-month period prior to earnings announcement and the direction of the subsequent earnings surprise. The lack of a relation between insider trading and earnings surprise is robust for large transactions or even large transactions by top executives.

4. When we control for both earnings surprise and insider trading, both variables continue to predict the future stock returns.

5. Using selective insider-trading signals, such as large volume or transactions by top executives, weakens the information content of earnings surprise.

6. As an investment guide, large transactions by top executives are more important than the earnings surprise. When top executives are large-volume sellers of the stock, subsequent 12-month net stock returns are mostly negative regardless of the earnings surprise. When top executives are large-volume buyers of the stock, subsequent 12-month net stock returns are mostly positive regardless of the earnings surprise.

7. Our overall advice to the stock market investors is to combine insider-trading information with earnings surprise information. Best results are obtained when these signals reinforce each other. Firms with insider buying and positive earnings surprise do very well. Firms with insider selling and negative earnings surprise do badly. When there is a conflict between earnings surprise and insider trading, go with insider trading.

9   *Price-earnings ratio*

Value- and growth-based investing and future stock returns

Most professional investors follow one of two styles. One of these is
called the value-based investing, which tries to identify undervalued
stocks based on the balance sheet information. The other investment
style is called the growth-based approach, which tries to capitalize on
the price momentum of recent favorites. Value firms tend to be currently out of favor, characterized by recent low (or negative) growth
rates of sales, earnings, and cash flows, by low price-earnings ratios,
and by high book-to-market ratios. Growth firms tend to be currently
in favor, characterized by recent high growth rates of sales, earnings,
and cash flows, by high price-earnings ratios, and by low book-to-
market ratios.[1] In this chapter we focus on the predictive ability of
price-earnings ratios.[2] We will examine the predictive power of the
book-to-market ratios in chapter 10.

To clarify what we mean by a price-earnings (P/E) approach to investing, a numerical example may be helpful. The P/E ratio simply refers to the current stock price of the firm divided by its earnings per
share over the past year. Sometimes an estimate of the earnings per
share over the next year is also used. The P/E ratio shows the price
we must pay to purchase $1 of current earnings. Take the example of

Chrysler Corporation. In 1984 Chrysler's quarterly earnings per share were, $3.08, $3.62, $0.97, and $4.09, respectively. Around the end of 1984, Chrysler's stock price ranged in the low 30s, giving Chrysler a P/E ratio of about 2.7 ($32 divided by $11.76) for 1984. At this time investors were paying in effect $2.7 for each $1 of Chrysler's earnings. In 1992 Chrysler had earnings per share of $1.42 and was still selling for $32, giving it a P/E ratio of 21.9. [3]

In implementation, professional investors often compare the P/E ratio with the market P/E or with the P/E ratios for similar firms in the same sector. Low P/E stocks are preferred. By this logic Chrysler was cheaper in 1984 than it was in 1992.[4] Alternatively, some investors compare the P/E ratio with growth rate of earnings. A firm is said to represent good value if the P/E ratio is significantly below the growth rate of earnings. The value-based approach tends to choose low P/E stocks for a given growth rate of earnings. The growth-based approach tends to choose firms with high growth rates of sales (or earnings) which are likely to have high P/E ratios. The logic of the value-based investing is that we might be better off with stocks for which we pay less to acquire $1 in earnings per year.

Relation between P/E ratios and future stock returns

Finance literature has examined the relation between P/E ratios and future stock returns.[5] The common finding is that there is a negative relation between current P/E ratios and future stock returns. Low P/E stocks provide better than average future returns (value-based investing), while high P/E stocks provide lower than average future returns (growth-based investing). Hence P/E ratios do appear to be useful in predicting future stock returns.

Why does something as simple as a P/E ratio help predict future stock returns? Does the predictive power of the P/E ratio suggest irrational stock pricing? If so, why does anyone buy high P/E stocks, since everyone can compute the P/E ratios (in fact the *Wall Street Journal* publishes daily P/E ratios for all listed stocks). While P/E ratios do seem to predict future stocks returns, there is less of an agreement as to why. There are basically two alternative interpretations for the negative relation between P/E ratios and future stock returns.

The first interpretation is that the stock market sometimes makes mistakes in valuation. Stock prices sometimes do not fully reflect the good news or the bad news or they may overreact to some good news or bad news. A too low P/E ratio can be due to a stock price that is too low based on fundamentals. This situation can arise if market does not fully appreciate some good news or overreacts to some negative news. As informed traders recognize the situation, they will bid up the stock price. As mistakes are corrected, investors who acted early will earn unusually high profits.

Let's illustrate this interpretation with an example. Again, take the case of Chrysler Corporation in 1984. Why was Chrysler only selling at 2.7 times annual earnings in 1984? Suppose that this is because the market had not fully appreciated Chrysler's recovery. Smart investors who recognized that Chrysler had now fully recovered from its problems in the 1970s and early 1980s would have purchased Chrysler stock. As Chrysler followed its good news with additional good news in 1985, its stock price rocketed to the mid 40s, giving some investors better than 50% return in a year. Hence, if the market under appreciates some good news or overreacts to some bad news, then a low P/E ratio can signal undervalued firms.[6]

We can also tie in stock price reaction to P/E ratios, to stock price reaction to earnings announcements. In chapter 8 we already saw that stock price reaction to earnings announcements tends to be slow. Again, let's take Chrysler's example. Chrysler's earnings in 1983 were only $2.44 per share compared with $11.76 per share in 1984. Hence Chrysler's 1984 earnings represent a more than fourfold increase over 1983. Perhaps the stock price on the announcement day rose as a result, but not much as it should. Consequently the surprise rise in earnings resulted in a decline in P/E ratios. As stock prices continued to increase slowly over the next year in reaction to this surprise positive earnings news, the future stock returns were above average. In general, low P/E stocks should have above average future stock returns.[7]

An alternative interpretation of the negative relation between P/E ratios and future stock returns is based on risk considerations. Changes in firm's riskiness will be reflected as changes in its P/E ratio. As the risk of the firm increases, each dollar of future earnings should be worth less in today's dollars. Clearly in 1984 Chrysler was a risky proposition. In the late-1970s and early-1980s Chrysler came close to bankruptcy. In 1982 Chrysler stock was trading below $5.0 before rising to about $17.0. Even though Chrysler earned $2.44 in 1983, investors would have discounted these earnings heavily since Chrysler was a high risk firm. Consequently Chrysler deserved a low P/E ratio in 1983 because of its high risk.

In general, investors demand and receive greater average future returns to high-risk firms. Consequently lower P/E ratios should, on average, be associated with higher future stock returns. This line of reasoning also suggests that there should be a negative relation between P/E ratios and future stock returns. However, this negative relation represents compensation for risk, not unusual profit opportunities.[8]

The mispricing explanation is based on irrational investor behavior, while the risk-based explanation is consistent with rational investor behavior. Unfortunately, it is quite difficult to distinguish between these two stories. However, some investors may also not care why the P/E effect works as long as it really works. Either way they hope to earn higher than average returns.[9]

There are two potential tests to distinguish between mispricing and risk stories. One way to distinguish between these alternative explanations is to exploit the commonsense expectation that regardless of their risk level, investors should expect positive returns from stocks. Otherwise, why invest in stocks? Remember that the risk-based story states that high P/E stocks have low but still positive expected returns because of their low-risk levels. The mispricing story predicts that the high P/E ratio results from an unjustifiably high stock price, which is expected to decline as most investors realize the misvaluation. The higher the P/E ratio, the greater will be the probability of subsequent *negative* returns. Hence, if the subsequent returns to high P/E stocks tend to be low, yet positive, then this is consistent with the risk-based story. If the subsequent returns to high P/E stocks are negative, then this finding would be consistent with the overreaction story.

A second way to distinguish between the mispricing and risk based stories is to examine insider trading. Assume that the P/E ratios predict future stock returns because of differences in firms' risk levels. We already know that high P/E firms represent low risk, and vice versa. Given a lower risk, insiders in high P/E stocks may hold more stocks. If the risk level of a given firm rises (accompanied by a fall in the P/E ratio), insiders may reduce the level of their stock holdings by selling some stock.[10] The higher risk also implies higher future stock returns since risk-averse investors will require a higher compensation for holding riskier stocks. Hence, if the risk-based story is correct, then there should be a positive relation between insider trading and P/E ratios. Insiders should purchase stock in high P/E firms and sell stock in low P/E firm. Second, there should be a negative relation between future stock returns and insider trading.

If the mispricing story is correct, then we would expect insiders to systematically exploit the mispricing identified by the extreme P/E ratios. Hence insiders would be more likely to buy low P/E stocks and more likely to sell high P/E stocks. Second, there should be a positive relation between insider trading and future stock returns. Moreover, since both factors capture the same underlying mispricing, when we account for the forecasting power of both variables, the presence of insider trading should reduce the predictive power of the P/E ratio. Hence, by examining the interactions between insider trading and the

P/E ratios, we can attempt to separate out the underlying cause of the P/E effect.

In this chapter we first re-examine the predictive ability of absolute P/E ratios using data from 1978 to 1993. Our first objective is to determine if the predictive power of the market P/E ratio holds over a recent time period. We then examine the predictive power of relative P/E ratios to see if there are cross-sectional differences in future stock returns as a function of the differences in their relative P/E ratios. This analysis helps us establish the strength of the negative relation between P/E ratios and future stock returns.

Second, we examine the interaction between insider trading and P/E ratios. Specifically we analyze whether insiders appear to take into account P/E ratios into their trading decisions. If so, under the risk story we expect a positive relation between P/E ratios and insider trading. We would expect insiders to be more likely to buy high P/E stocks and more likely to sell low P/E stocks. Under the mispricing story we would expect a negative relation between P/E ratios and insider trading. Insiders should be more likely to sell high P/E stocks and more likely to buy low P/E stocks.

Finally we examine the joint predictive ability of aggregate insider trading and P/E ratios. Once again this analysis should also shed some light into why P/E ratios predict future stock returns. If the predictive power of the P/E ratios occur due to misvaluation and insider trading already takes into account the same misvaluation, then when we examine both factors jointly, the predictive power of the P/E ratio should disappear. This is because insiders have access a to greater set of information and they can take into account all the other conditions in their trading decisions. However, if the predictive power of the P/E ratios arise only out of risk considerations, then when we examine both factors jointly, the predictive power of the insider-trading variable should disappear. Insiders' sales should be associated with higher future stock returns than insiders' purchases. This is opposite the traditional predictive power of insider trading. Let's turn to the evidence next.

Information content of P/E ratios

We first replicate the usual P/E tests. Specifically we examine the relation between current P/E ratios and future stock returns. Unfortunately, our information on P/E ratios is restricted to a somewhat smaller set of firms and a smaller time period than our insider-trading sample. Our price-earnings data set covers a sample of 1700 firms from 1978 to 1993. P/E ratios are computed once a year on June 30 by dividing the closing stock price by the earnings per share over the past 12 months. Consequently our P/E tests will not fully utilize all of our data.

We also need to make some implementation concessions. A problem arises with negative P/E ratios. Sometimes the earnings of the firms are negative, which in turn makes the P/E ratios negative. While a very low yet positive P/E ratio is good, a negative P/E ratio is not indicative of good investment opportunities. A negative P/E ratio simply fails as an indicator of value. Investors must expect the firm to eventually survive and achieve positive earnings. Otherwise, the value of the firm would also be zero. In a way negative P/E ratios are similar to very high P/E ratios. Both of them indicate undesirable investments given the current earnings. Since it is not obvious where to classify the negative P/E ratios, we exclude all negative P/E ratios from further analysis.

We document the median P/E ratios for the period 1978 to 1993 (covering 16 years) for the sample of 1,700 firms (figure 9.1). Comparing figure 9.1 with figure 6.1, the time series pattern of the median P/E ratios inversely mirrors that of the average dividend yields. Increasing stock prices decrease the dividend yields while increasing the P/E ratios. Since both variables use the current stock price, a negative relation between dividend yields and P/E ratios is not surprising.

Year-to-year patterns in P/E ratios from 1978 to 1993 indicate small yearly changes as compared with the movements over the sixteen-year sample period.[11] The median P/E ratio starts at about 8.3 in 1978 and

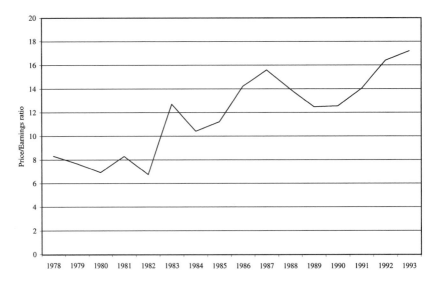

Figure 9.1
Median price-earnings ratios from 1978 to 1993

falls to about 7.7 by 1979. It fluctuates around a value of 7 until 1982. In 1982 the median P/E ratio starts a sharp climb and reaches over 14 by 1988. After 1988 it first falls to 12 and then climbs gradually to a closing value of 17.

How should we categorize P/E ratios into high and low groups? There are two possibilities, and it makes a difference how we group them. The proper approach depends to some extent why investors are interested in the predictive ability of P/E ratios.

The first method is referred to as the absolute P/E grouping. Here we use the P/E ratios without any adjustments. In 1980 the median P/E ratio was about 7, while in 1988 the median P/E ratio was about 14 (figure 9.1). If we use the entire 16 years of P/E ratios, almost all firms in 1980 would be classified as low P/E firms, while almost all firms in 1988 would be classified as high P/E firms. This method suggests that we can compare the P/E ratios for a given firm across time. For instance, we can say that ABC firm is more attractive as a candidate to be purchased if its P/E ratio is 10 in 1980 rather than 12 in 1988. Hence ABC would be a low P/E firm in 1980 and high P/E firm in 1988. We will use this classification technique to illustrate the predictive ability of the absolute P/E ratios.

If an investor is interested in timing the market, then the predictive power of the absolute P/E ratios is important. If stocks tend to do well when they have lower absolute P/E ratios, market timers can use this information to find the best time to get into the market. If stocks tend to do badly when they have higher absolute P/E ratios, again the market timers can use this information to exit the market.

An alternative method of classifying P/E ratios might be to examine P/E ratios relative to each other in each year separately. Relative P/E ratios are computed by subtracting the market P/E ratio for each year from all firms' P/E ratios for the same year. If we use this approach, the ABC firm with an absolute P/E ratio of 10 in 1980 would have a relative P/E ratio of +3.0 (10 minus 7 for all firms). By this measure it would be classified as a high relative P/E firm in 1980. The same ABC firm with an absolute P/E ratio of 12 in 1988 would have a relative P/E ratio of −2.0 (12 minus 14 for all firms). By this measure it would be classified as a low P/E firm. This approach makes sense if the P/E ratios over time are not comparable and the P/E ratios have meaning only in a relative sense. We will refer to this method as the relative P/E grouping. We will also use the relative P/E grouping approach to examine the predictive ability of P/E ratios.

If an investor is interested in stock picking, then the predictive power of the relative P/E ratios is important. If a given stock tends to do relatively well when it has a lower relative P/E ratio, stock pickers can screen on the basis of relative P/E ratios to decide which stocks to buy and sell. A low relative P/E ratio signals to the stock picker to buy the stock. A high relative P/E ratio signals to the stock picker to sell the stock.

To get an idea about our sample size and distribution of P/E ratios, we sort the P/E ratios into five equal sized groups using their 16-year

Table 9.1
Average price-earnings ratios (P/E)

Group	Number of observations	Average P/E ratio
Lowest P/E group	29,796	6.4
P/E group 2	30,516	9.3
P/E group 3	30,456	11.7
P/E group 4	30,648	15.3
Highest P/E group	30,204	66.6
All groups	151,620	21.8

distribution (table 9.1). Each firm is assigned to an absolute P/E group based on its P/E value as of last June 30 for very observation.[12] P/E values are changed only once a year. Table 9.1 shows that the lowest P/E group has an average P/E ratio of 6.4. The highest P/E group has an average P/E value of 66.6. Hence there is a large range of values for the P/Es. For the sample as a whole the average P/E ratio is 21.8.

Predictive power of absolute P/E ratios

We begin by first examining the predictive ability of P/E ratios using their absolute values. We first examine the relation between past P/E ratios based on the last 16-year distribution and future stock returns (table 9.2). Three forecasting horizons are examined: 3 months ahead, 6 months ahead, and 12 months ahead. Given that we are examining the predictive power of absolute P/E ratios, we start with raw returns for each firm. To form portfolios, we take an equally weighted average of the returns for each firm included in our sample.

For all three forecasting horizons, there is a strong *negative* relation between absolute P/E ratios and future raw returns to the stocks (table 9.2). For the 3-month horizon, raw returns start out at 6.0% for the lowest absolute P/E group. With increasing P/E ratios, raw returns fall

Table 9.2
Raw stock returns grouped by absolute price-earnings ratios (P/E)

Group	Subsequent 3-month raw returns	Subsequent 6-month raw returns	Subsequent 12-month raw returns
Lowest P/E group	6.0%	11.8%	23.2%
P/E group 2	4.6	9.4	19.9
P/E group 3	4.2	8.5	17.4
P/E group 4	3.3	6.6	14.4
Highest P/E group	2.9	5.8	11.5

monotonically. For the middle P/E group, the raw returns fall to 4.2%. For the highest P/E ratio, the raw returns fall to 2.9%. Investing in the lowest P/E stocks provides additional 3.1 percentage points, or more than double what investors could earn by investing in the highest P/E stocks over the next 3 months.

For the 6-month holding period, raw returns start out at 11.8%. Once again there is a monotonic, strongly negative relation between absolute P/E ratios and future raw returns. For the middle P/E group, the raw returns fall to 8.5%. For the highest P/E group, the raw returns fall to 5.8%. Investing in lowest P/E stocks provides additional 6.0 points, or more than double investors could earn by investing in highest P/E stocks over the next 6 months.

Finally the negative relation between absolute P/E ratios and raw returns are maintained for the 12-month horizon as well. Raw returns start out at 23.2 % for the lowest P/E group and again fall monotonically with P/E ratios. For the middle P/E group, the raw returns fall to 17.4%. For the highest P/E group, the raw returns equal 11.5%. Investing in lowest P/E stocks provides additional 11.7 points, or more than double what investors could earn by investing in highest P/E stocks over the next 12 months.

Our evidence suggests that absolute P/E ratios do predict future raw returns using stock returns from 1978 to 1993. This evidence is consistent with the results from the finance literature, which has uncovered a negative relation between P/E ratios and expected returns to stocks. Moreover the magnitude of the P/E effect is quite strong. For all three forecasting horizons the P/E effect predicts more than a doubling of the expected returns.

Our evidence also suggests that the absolute magnitude of the P/E ratio is meaningful. Hence it makes sense to compare the P/E ratios of firms over time. As P/E ratios for a given set of firms change over time, expected returns to the stocks should also change negatively with the P/E ratio.

This evidence is good news for the potential market timer. When P/E ratios are low, the future market returns tend to be high; hence this is a good time to get into the stock market. When P/E ratios are high, the future market returns tend to be low; hence this is a good time to get out of the stock market.

What does the predictability of stock returns mean? Should we only invest in low P/E stocks? If so, why does anyone ever buy high P/E stocks? Can we combine P/E ratio and insider-trading information to do even better? Low P/E stocks seem to do well. Do they continue to do well even if insiders are selling shares? Similarly high P/E stocks do not seem to do well. Do they continue to underperform even if insiders are purchasing shares? To provide some answers to these questions, we now explore the relation between insider trading and absolute P/E ratios.

Insider trading is measured as before. We sum the total shares bought or sold in a given firm and given month. If insiders in that firm buy more shares than they sell, we declare that month as a purchase month. If insiders sell more shares than they buy, we declare that month as a sale month.

We now examine the relations between absolute P/E ratios, insider trading and future raw stock returns (table 9.3). Examining the table by columns first, we see that the absolute P/E ratios continue to predict future stock returns separately for insider sales or purchases. For in-

Table 9.3

The absolute price-earnings ratios (P/E) and 12-month raw returns grouped by insider buying and selling

Group	Insider selling	Insider buying
Lowest P/E group	22.7%	25.1%
	(5,260)	(4,530)
P/E group 2	18.1	21.9
	(5,597)	(4,579)
P/E group 3	16.4	20.2
	(6,301)	(4,144)
P/E group 4	15.1	15.7
	(7,378)	(3,737)
Highest P/E group	10.7	15.9
	(7,459)	(3,458)

Note: In parentheses are the number of months.

stance, in the first column, given insider selling, average stock returns go from 22.7% monotonically down to 10.7% as the P/E ratios increase from lowest to highest. In the second column, given insider buying, the expected returns go from 25.1% monotonically down to 15.9% as the P/E ratios increase from lowest to highest. Hence P/E ratios continue to predict decreasing stock returns even after we account for the insider-trading activity.

Our evidence indicates that the absolute P/E ratios do not eliminate the predictive power of the insider-trading variable. Looking at table 9.3 row by row, we control for the P/E effect. We see that for five out of five rows, holding the absolute P/E ratio constant, insider buying predicts higher future stock returns than insider selling.

Our evidence so far suggests that (1) absolute P/E ratios predict future raw returns, (2) absolute P/E ratios continue to predict decreasing stock returns even after controlling for the insider-trading activity, and (3) the predictive power of insider-trading activity is also not attenuated after controlling for the P/E effect. While not shown here, we have also extended the evidence in table 9.3 by using only the transactions by top executives or by large volume of insider trading. These results are similar to those shown in table 9.3 and corroborate our interpretations.

What is the significance of the results so far? We have earlier argued that insider trading captures mispricing, while P/E ratios can capture both mispricing as well as risk factors. Given that both variables maintain their predictive power, the results suggest that at least some of the predictive power of the absolute P/E ratios arises because it captures risk considerations. If the absolute P/E effect was entirely due to mispricing, we would have expected one of two things to occur: Either P/E ratios to lose their predictive punch if insider trading did a better job of capturing mispricing or insider trading to lose its predictive punch if the P/E ratios did a better job of capturing mispricing.

However, there is more to the story than we have told so far. Our evidence also shows that there is a negative relation between the direction of insider trading and P/E ratios. The numbers in parentheses in table 9.3 show the number of observations. When P/E ratios are high, insiders tend to sell a lot more frequently then they buy stock. The ratio of sells to buys is better than 2 to 1. As P/E ratios fall, stocks appear to be more attractive to insiders. Insider selling falls uniformly and insider buying increases uniformly. Insiders appear to act as if they also like low absolute P/E stocks![13] Hence the evidence does not allow us to completely rule out mispricing as a potential explanation for the predictive power of the P/E ratios.

If the absolute P/E ratios capture some dimension of risk while insider trading captures mostly mispricing, then investors should be able to combine both signals to construct even more powerful predictors of future stock returns. The evidence can help us in this regard as well. If we are interested in identifying good performers, we would require low P/E ratios and insider buying. The return to these firms is 25.1% (table 9.3). If we are interested in identifying lousy performers, we require high P/E ratios and insider selling. The return to these firms is 10.7%. Using both variables helps us increase our incremental returns

14.4%. Using only the P/E variable, our incremental returns was 11.7% (table 9.2). Hence using both variables does indeed increase our predictive power over using P/E ratio alone.

What is not so clear so far is whether the P/E effect works because of a market effect or because of a firm specific effect. For instance, high P/E ratios could predict lower raw stock returns because the entire market return is going to be low or because the individual stocks with the high P/E ratios will simply have lower than average returns. Our evidence so far does not address this issue.

To investigate whether there is a market effect or a firm-specific effect, we also examine the predictive power of absolute P/E ratios for the market returns and the net stock returns. If the P/E effect is due to a market effect and not a firm-specific effect, then absolute P/E ratios would predict the market returns, but they would not predict stock returns, net of the market returns. On the other hand, if the results so far are due to a firm-specific effect but not a market effect, then the absolute P/E ratios would predict the net stock returns, but they would not predict the market returns.

To address the issue of why absolute P/E ratios predict raw stock returns, we examine the relation between absolute P/E ratios and stock returns *net* of the equally weighted market index (table 9.4). If the abso-

Table 9.4

Net stock returns (net of the market returns) grouped by *absolute* price-earnings ratios (P/E)

Group	Subsequent 3-month net returns	Subsequent 6-month net returns	Subsequent 12-month net returns
Lowest P/E group	−0.2%	−0.4%	−0.3%
P/E group 2	0.0	−0.1	−0.7
P/E group 3	0.5	0.8	1.2
P/E group 4	0.1	0.1	0.5
Highest P/E group	−0.2	−0.6	−1.9

lute P/E ratios predict a market effect, then there should be no relation between the P/E ratios and net stock returns.

The evidence shows that there is in fact little or no relation between absolute P/E ratios and future *net* returns to the stocks. For the 3-month-ahead horizon, excess returns start at −0.2% for the lowest P/E group, rise to 0.5% for the middle group, and end up at −0.2% for the highest P/E group. Hence there is no difference in the excess returns for the lowest and highest P/E groups for the 3-month holding period.

For the 6-month holding periods, the net stock returns start out at −0.4% for the lowest P/E group, rise to 0.8% for the middle group, and end up at −0.6% for the highest P/E group. Once again, the net returns appear to be independent of the P/E ratios.

For the 12-month horizon, there appears to be a weak negative relation between absolute P/E ratios and the future net returns. For the lowest P/E group, the 12-month net returns equal −0.3%. As the P/E ratios increase, the net returns first increase. For the middle group, the net returns rise to 1.2%. As P/E ratios further increase, net returns fall. For the highest P/E group, the 12-month net returns equal −1.9%.

Overall, our evidence suggests that absolute P/E ratios have either weak negative relation or no predictive power at all for future net stock returns. While not shown here, we have also examined the relation between absolute P/E ratios and market returns. As expected, there is a strong negative relation between absolute P/E ratios and future market returns.

Our interpretation of the results is as follows: (1) Absolute P/E ratios strongly predict absolute (raw) future stock returns at 3-month to 12-month horizons, (2) the predictive power of the absolute P/E ratios arise because they capture variations in future market returns, (3) the predictive power of the absolute P/E effect cannot be attributed entirely to misvaluations, since the presence of insider trading does not attenuate the predictive power of the P/E ratios, and (4) absolute P/E ratios are not useful in predicting net (relative) stock returns.

Again this evidence is good news for the potential market timer. Changes in absolute P/E ratios signal the best times to get in and out of the stock market. We now turn our attention to the concerns of the stock pickers. Can we also use P/E ratios to help pick over- and underperforming stocks relative to the stock market? To be able to predict relative stock returns, we need to examine relative P/E ratios.

Predictive power of relative P/E ratios

We now use *relative* groupings. As we stated earlier, relative P/E ratios are computed net of the market P/E for each year.[14] As the P/E ratios fluctuate over time, the highest P/E grouping can contain firms with widely different P/E ratios.

At this point it is worth re-emphasizing the difference between absolute P/E grouping and relative P/E grouping. To facilitate this discussion, take a hypothetical example of ABC firm that has a P/E ratio of 10 in 1980 and a P/E ratio of 12 in 1988. Remember that the average P/E ratio in 1980 was just about 7 in 1980 and about 14 in 1988. Using absolute P/E ratios based on table 9.1, we would classify this firm into the third P/E group in both 1980 and 1988. However, using relative P/E grouping would give us completely different rankings. Given that this firm is significantly above average in 1980, it would be classified in the fourth P/E group. Similarly, given that it is below average in 1988, it would be classified in the second P/E group. Consequently absolute and relative P/E groupings would yield different rankings for most firms.

Predictive power of the relative P/E grouping is examined in a similar fashion as the absolute P/E groups (table 9.5). This time we use net stock returns, since we are interested in relative performance of stocks based on their relative P/E ratios. Net stock returns are computed by subtracting from each stock return the return to the equally weighted market index of NYSE, AMEX, and NASDAQ stocks. Once again we look ahead 3 months, 6 months, and 12 months.

Table 9.5

Net stock returns (net of the market returns) grouped by *relative* price-earnings ratios (P/E)

Group	Subsequent 3-month net returns	Subsequent 6-month net returns	Subsequent 12-month net returns
Lowest P/E group	0.6%	0.9%	2.3%
P/E group 2	0.3	0.4	0.1
P/E group 3	−0.2	−0.5	−0.9
P/E group 4	−0.0	−0.1	−0.5
Highest P/E group	−0.4	−0.9	−2.2

For all three horizons there is again a negative relation between relative P/E ratios and future net stock returns (table 9.5). These findings are consistent with the results in the literature. For the 3-month-ahead holding period, excess stock returns are 0.6% for the lowest P/E group. Hence low P/E stocks do outperform the market index. As the relative P/E ratio rises, the future stock returns fall. For the middle P/E group, excess stock returns average −0.2%. For the highest P/E group, excess stock returns are −0.4%. Hence the highest P/E group underperforms the market index. The difference in the lowest and highest relative P/E groups equals 1.0 percentage point.

The forecasting ability of the relative P/E ratios improves with the forecasting horizon. Looking at the 6-month horizon, the net stock returns to the lowest P/E group average 0.9%. As the relative P/E ratio rises, the net stock returns fall. For the middle group, the net stock returns average −0.5%. For the highest P/E group, the net stock returns are −0.9%. The difference between the lowest and highest P/E groups now rises to 1.8 percentage points.

The 12-month forecasting horizon shows the strongest predictability. For the lowest P/E group, the net stock returns are now 2.3%. Once again net stock returns are negatively related to the relative P/E ratio. For the middle P/E group, net stock returns average −0.9%. Finally, for the highest P/E group, net stock returns fall to −2.2%. The difference between the lowest and highest P/E groups now rises to 4.5 percentage points.

Our results demonstrate that the relative P/E ratio also works. Hence the P/E effect is quite robust. We can either work with absolute P/Es or with relative P/Es. Either way, P/E ratios predict future stock returns. The evidence we have presented is also good news for the stock picker. Relative P/E ratios can help the stock picker identify which stocks will over- or underperform relative to the stock market.

Why do the P/E ratios predict future stock returns?

As we discussed earlier, the predictive power of the P/E ratio can be due to mispricing or risk. Our earlier discussion suggests that the risk story rules out negative future raw returns, since low-risk firms are expected to earn small yet still positive extra returns over the risk-free rate. If the reason is mispricing, we should also be able to identify periods when the stock is so overpriced that the expected future returns are negative. Hence the overreaction story does not rule out negative future raw returns based on extremely high P/E ratios.

To determine whether we can distinguish between our two alternative stories regarding the predictive power of the P/E ratios, we first group our sample into 20 groups based on P/E ratios. This finer partition allows us to focus on extremely high values of the relative P/E ratios, which thereby contain more information. We then examine the raw returns for 3-month, 6-month, and 12-month horizons.

We do not show our findings in full detail due to space considerations. Our evidence shows that even using a 20-group partition, the relatively highest P/E stocks still have positive raw returns for all three holding periods. For the 12-month horizon the raw returns to the highest P/E group is positive 13%. Hence examining for negative raw returns does not allow us to distinguish between the risk and overreaction explanations as the main source of the predictive power of the P/E ratios.

To understand why the relative P/E effect also works, we investigate the interaction between relative P/E ratios and insider trading. We would like to know first whether insiders take into account the relative P/E levels in their trading decisions. Specifically we examine whether insiders themselves are more likely to buy relatively low P/E stocks and more likely to sell relatively high P/E stocks. If insiders trade according to relative P/E effect, then it is quite likely that the relative P/E effect represents, to some extent, a mispricing also captured by insider trading. Second, we test whether either the P/E effect or the insider-trading effect dissipates when we control for both factors. Thus we examine what happens to the predictive ability of insider trading when we control for P/E ratios. Similarly we examine what happens to the predictive ability of the P/E ratios when we control for insider trading.

We now analyze the relation between relative P/E ratios and insider trading (table 9.6). We sort the insider-trading activity by the relative P/E groups. In the relatively lowest P/E group there are 5,265 months

Table 9.6
Insider trading months grouped by relative price-earnings ratios (P/E)

Group	Insider selling	Insider buying
Lowest P/E group	(5,265)	(4,781)
	(52%)	(48%)
P/E group 2	(5,246)	(4,750)
	(52%)	(48%)
P/E group 3	(6,348)	(4,221)
	(60%)	(40%)
P/E group 4	(7,516)	(3,530)
	(68%)	(32%)
Highest P/E group	(7,628)	(3,366)
	(69%)	(31%)

Note: In parentheses are the proportions.

with insider selling and 4,781 months with insider buying. Hence insiders sell stock 52% of the time and buy stock 48% of the time. With increasing relative P/E ratios the likelihood of insider selling increases while the likelihood of insider buying declines. In the middle P/E group, insiders sell 60% of the time and buy 40% of the time. In the relatively highest P/E group, insiders sell stock 69% of the time and buy stock 31% of the time.

Our evidence suggests that similar to the absolute P/E ratios, insiders view the differences in relative P/E ratios as if they represent profit opportunities. Insiders appear to favor relatively low P/E firms and dislike relatively high P/E firms. The differences in insider-trading proportions vary significantly across the relative P/E groups.

We next examine the predictive ability of insider trading and relative P/E ratios when we control for both variables. We use the 12-month-ahead net stock returns. There is again a negative relation. For the lowest relative P/E group, net stock returns average 2.4% (table 9.7, column 1). For the middle group, net stock returns average −0.8%. For the relatively highest P/E group, net stock returns average −2.4%. The total spread between the lowest and highest P/E groups equals 4.8 points.

The relation between relative P/E ratios and 12-month ahead net stock returns when insiders are net buyers remains also negative (table

Table 9.7
Subsequent 12-month net stock returns (net of the market returns) grouped by insider trading and relative price-earnings ratios (P/E)

Group	Insider selling	Insider buying
Lowest P/E group	2.4%	3.8%
P/E group 2	−2.1	1.8
P/E group 3	−0.8	1.0
P/E group 4	−0.3	1.6
Highest P/E group	−2.4	−0.4

9.7, column 2). For the relatively lowest P/E group, net stock returns average 3.8%. For the middle group, net stock returns average 1.0%. For the relatively highest P/E group, net stock returns average −0.4%. The total spread between the lowest and highest P/E groups reaches 4.2 points.

Our data provide two immediate observations. First, the relative P/E ratio maintains its predictive power when we control for insider trading. This is evidenced by the finding that there is a negative relation between relative P/E ratios and future net stock returns for both the insider-selling and insider-buying categories. Hence, regardless of insider trading, relatively high P/E stocks are associated with lower yet still positive future returns. Second, insider trading maintains its predictive power when we control for relative P/E ratios. For each of the five P/E rows, the net stock return to the buyer group exceeds that of the seller group. Hence it appears that both the relative P/E ratio and insider-trading variables retain their predictive power.

Overall, our evidence suggests that insiders appear to be subscribing to a relative P/E effect as well. Insiders like relatively low P/E stocks and dislike relatively high P/E stocks. Nevertheless, insiders appear to be using additional information obtained from their access to the day-to-day operations of the firm over and above the relative P/E ratios. Insider trading does not eliminate the predictive power of the relative P/E ratios. Similarly the relative P/E effect seems to reflect factors not entirely considered by insiders such as the risk factor. Hence neither effect completely subsumes each other. Both the relative P/E ratio and insider trading retain some of their predictive power.

If the P/E ratios capture risk while insider trading captures mispricing, then investors should be able to combine both signals to construct even more powerful predictors of future stock returns. Let's re-examine the evidence. If we are interested in identifying good performers, we would require relatively low P/E ratios and insider buying. The net return to these firms is 3.8% (table 9.7). If we are interested in identifying lousy performers, we require relatively high P/E ratios and insider selling. The net return to these firms is −2.4%. Using both variables helps us increase our incremental returns 6.2 points. Using only the P/E variable, our incremental returns was only 4.5 points (table 9.5). Hence, using both variables does indeed increase our predictive power over using relative P/E ratio alone.[15]

Large insider-trading volumes and P/E ratios

While everyday insider trading does not attenuate the information content of the P/E effect, we already know that everyday insider trading contains many transactions that are not information motivated. Hence an important question that arises is, What happens if we use stronger insider-trading signals? Is it possible to reduce or eliminate the information content of the P/E effect by using stronger insider-trading signals? If so, we can be more confident that the P/E ratio captures at least some of the mispricing also captured by the insider-trading variable.

We now investigate the relation between selected, stronger insider-trading signals and the relative P/E effect. The idea that we want to explore is whether the predictive ability of the relative P/E ratio arises because it proxies for intense insider-trading activity. From chapter 3 we already know that volume of insider trading and identity of insiders are important determinants of the quality of insiders' information. Hence we now focus in on months when buying and selling by top executives exceeds 10,000 shares.

When we confront relative P/E ratios with strong insider-trading signals, we find the following: (1) Insiders appear to be even more likely to sell large volumes of stock when the relative P/E ratio is high and more likely to buy large volumes of stock when the relative P/E ratio is low, (2) The information content of P/E ratio weakens after we control for large insider trading, and (3) the information content of insider trading continues to come through even after we control for P/E ratios (table 9.8).

Table 9.8
Net stock returns (net of the market returns) grouped by insider trading and by relative price-earnings ratios (P/E)

Group	Top executives selling more than 10,000 shares	Top executives buying more than 10,000 shares
Lowest P/E group	2.6%	10.2%
	(713)	(227)
P/E group 2	−3.9	2.7
	(713)	(182)
P/E group 3	−3.4	7.0
	(1,037)	(219)
P/E group 4	1.7	2.8
	(1,291)	(180)
Highest P/E group	−2.3	1.8
	(1,341)	(263)

Note: In parentheses are the number of observations.

The relation between the relative P/E ratios and future stock returns disappears after we control for large selling by top executives (table 9.8, column 1). For the lowest P/E group, the net stock returns equal 2.6%. For the second P/E group, net stock returns fall to −3.9%. This is the lowest return. As the P/E ratio increases, net stock returns increase to −3.4% and then to 1.7%. Finally net stock returns drop to −2.3% for the highest P/E group. Hence there is no longer a monotone negative relation between the relative P/E ratios and future net stock returns.

For the insider-buying group, the negative relation between the relative P/E ratio and future returns as maintained (table 9.8, column 2). The net stock returns decline from 10.2% to 1.8% (albeit erratically) as the relative P/E ratios increase.

We also find that the information content of large transactions by top executives is maintained after we control for the P/E effect. To isolate the information content of insider trading, we examine table 9.8 row by row. For five out of five rows, insider buying is associated with higher net stock returns than for insider selling. Hence insider-trading activity retains its predictive power for all five groups of P/E ratios.[16]

What does this evidence tell us? By using stronger insider-trading signals, we have been able to attenuate the predictive power of the P/E ratios. This finding tells us that at least some of the predictive ability of the P/E ratios arises because they capture the same mispricing that is also captured by insider trading. Since strong insider trading does a better job of identifying mispricing, the P/E effect loses some of its punch when confronted with the insider-trading variable.[17]

Earnings announcements and price-earnings ratios

In chapter 8 we explored the information content of the earnings surprise. Our findings indicate that a measure of standardized earnings surprise denoted as SUE provided a good description of the subsequent stock returns. Stock prices drifted up if the earnings were better than expected and stock prices drifted down if the earnings were not as good as expected. For a typical investor it is natural to ask what the relation between earnings surprise and price-earnings ratio is. After all, high earnings would affect both variables. Do these two measures capture the same variation in stock returns? When we control for both SUE and P/E, does one of them lose its forecasting power? Alternatively, can we improve our predictive power for future stock returns using both SUE and P/E ratio?

To provide some answers to these questions, we classified future one-year-ahead stock returns into one of 25 groups based on both SUE and P/E ratios. While not shown here, our evidence indicates that both SUE and P/E ratio predict future stock returns independently. Holding P/E constant, future stock returns increase uniformly across SUE groups. Similarly, holding SUE constant, future stock returns decline uniformly across P/E groups. These findings suggest that we can increase the predictive power of our tests by using both SUE and P/E ratios. As a further extension we then grouped future one-year-ahead stock returns based on insider trading, SUE ratios, and P/E ratios. These tests yielded similar results. All three variables retained some predictive ability when used together. Moreover our ability to predict future stock returns increased when all three variables were present.

Conclusions and investment implications

In this chapter we have examined the value-based and growth-based investment approaches and the predictive power of the P/E ratios. The growth-based investment approach attempts to capitalize on the price momentum and selects firms that are currently in favor as characterized by high historical and expected growth rates of earnings and sales. These firms tend to have high P/E ratios. The value-based investment approach selects firms that are currently out of favor, characterized by with low or negative recent growth rates of earnings and sales. These firms tend to have low P/E ratios. To test the effectiveness of this approach, we have examined the predictive power of the P/E ratios. Our findings are as follows:

1. Our sample contains substantial variation in absolute P/E ratios. The median P/E ratio for the sample of firms we analyze is about 12. For the sample period 1978 to 1993, P/E ratios increase from about 8 to about 17.

2. Variations in absolute P/E ratios over time do predict future raw stock returns for our sample period of 1978 to 1993. When the absolute P/E ratios are high, expected future returns to stocks are low. When the absolute P/E ratios are low, expected future returns to stocks are high. This evidence suggests that P/E ratio is an important predictor of stock returns. In addition it is meaningful to compare P/E ratios over time. Hence a particular stock might have a P/E ratio of 10 in 1980 and 15 in 1990. This means that expected returns to the stock in 1980 are higher or lower than they would be in 1990.

3. While absolute P/E ratios predict future raw stock returns, they do not predict future net stock return. Hence, when most stocks have low

absolute P/E ratios, they all tend to do well. When most stocks have high P/E ratios, they all tend to do badly. This finding suggests that the predictive power of the absolute P/E ratios arises because they predict the future market returns.

4. Insider trading is negatively related to absolute P/E levels; however, it does not attenuate the predictive power of the absolute P/E ratios. This finding suggests that movements in absolute P/E ratios mostly capture movements in risk. However, the mispricing hypotheses cannot be totally ruled out given that insiders buy low P/E stocks and they sell high P/E stocks.

5. We also use relative P/E ratios to predict relative future stock returns. For relative stock returns we compute stock returns net of the return to the equally weighted market index. Relative P/Es are computed by subtracting the market P/E from each stock's P/E ratio. The relatively high P/E ratios predict negative net stock returns, while the relatively low P/E ratios predict positive net stock returns. Specifically the relatively high P/E stocks underperform the market index by 2.2% over the next 12 months, while the relatively low P/E stocks outperform the market index by 2.3% over the next 12 months.

6. Insider trading is again related to relative P/E ratios. Insiders are more likely to buy relatively low P/E stocks. Insiders are more likely to sell relatively high P/E stocks. This finding again suggests that relative P/E ratios capture some mispricing also captured by the insider-trading variable.

7. Holding relative P/E ratios constant, insider trading still predicts the future stock returns. Hence the predictive power of insider trading is not attenuated by controlling for differences in relative P/E ratios. We can say that while insiders take relative P/E ratios into account, they base their trading decisions on additional considerations as well.

8. The relative P/E factor also retains its predictive power when we control for insider-trading activity. Whether insiders are buying or selling, relatively high P/E ratios predict lower future net stock returns.

However, the net stock returns are not monotonically decreasing in P/E ratios.

9. The predictive power of the relative P/E factor weakens significantly even when we use more selective insider-trading signals such as large volume of trading or large transactions by top executives. For large insider selling by top executives, there is no longer a negative relation between relative P/E ratios and future returns. This evidence suggests that at least some of the predictive power of the relative P/E effect is due to mispricing of stocks that is also captured by insider trading.

10. There is good news for the market timers. Potential market timers can use both the absolute P/E ratios and insider trading to decide when to get in and out of the stock market. For potential stock pickers, our evidence suggests that given insider-trading information, relative P/E ratios do not add much. Hence potential stock pickers can ignore the relative P/E signals if they follow the trading activities of insiders.

10 *Book-to-market ratio*

Value- and growth-based investment approaches

In chapter 9 we examined the value- and growth-based investment approaches and the predictive power of the price-earnings (P/E) ratios. In this chapter we focus on balance sheet information, specifically the book-to-market ratio (B/M), to examine the value- and growth-based approaches. The B/M is computed simply as the ratio of book value of equity obtained from the balance sheet to market value of equity. The value-approach holds that firms with high B/M ratios are desirable, while firms with low B/M ratios are undesirable. Hence the value-based approach selects firms using high B/M.[1]

The idea that high B/M ratio should help identify undervalued stocks goes back to the work of Graham and Dodd (1934). In their classic textbook Graham and Dodd recommend investing in high B/M firms and staying away from low B/M firms. In the view of Graham and Dodd, the market price represents the cost of the investment, while the book value represents the fundamental value of the investment. Hence the B/M approach selects firms whose true fundamental value is above the cost of the investment.

An example should clarify the logic of the value-based investment approach. Let's go back to our Chrysler example. At the end of 1984,

Chrysler's book value of equity was $3.3 billion. At the same time the market value of equity for Chrysler was about $4 billion (given a stock price $32 and 124 million shares outstanding), giving Chrysler and book-to-market ratio of 0.85. In comparison Chrysler's B/M ratio by 1985 had risen to about 1.1.

The value-based approach takes the balance sheet value of equity as a close approximation for the fundamental value for each of these firms. By this logic the market price of a firm shows the price investors have to pay to acquire $1 of the book value of these assets. The value-based approach implicitly assumes that market prices contain significant errors with respect to the true value of the underlying assets, due to fads, investor psychology, and so on. By this logic Chrysler represented a better buy in 1985 than it did in 1984. By selecting high B/M firms, investors can presumably purchase undervalued assets and avoid overvalued assets.

The preceding discussion suggests that value-based investment approach is clearly an oversimplification of reality.[2] Any changes in expectations regarding the future economic environment, interest rates, or risk factors will change the current market value of equity but will not affect the historical book value of equity. Thus there is no reason to expect that the market value of equity and the book value of equity to always equal to each other or stay in some constant proportion to each other.[3]

We can provide other examples of systematic differences in B/M ratios with no investment implications. Suppose that two stocks are identical in every respect except that one of them has higher expected earnings growth. How should these stocks be priced? Clearly the stock with the higher expected earnings growth would have a higher stock price and therefore lower B/M ratio. Should you avoid the lower B/M stock? The answer depends on just how much lower the B/M ratio is and whether differences in B/M ratios are justified by the differences in earnings growth estimates. Clearly the evidence that one stock has a lower B/M ratio by itself is not sufficient to avoid that stock. It is quite possible to imagine a situation where an investor should in fact prefer the lower B/M stock if the differences in earnings growth estimates is not fully reflected in the differences in B/M ratios.

There is another story that not only predicts differences in book-to-market ratios but also that future stock returns should be higher than average for higher B/M firms and lower than average for lower B/M firms. This story does not rely on market irrationality but simply assumes that the risk of the firm (or the economy) is not constant but varies over time. To see the logic of this story, assume that a shock to the economy increases the risk of some or all firms.[4] The increase in risk in the economy is expected to reduce the current stock prices but will have no effect on the book values of equity since these represent historical developments. Consequently the increase in risk will increase the current book-to-market ratios. Since stock market investors are risk-averse, they will also demand and receive higher future stock returns when the risk is higher. Thus changes in risk levels will not only induce varying book-to-market ratios but over time will also lead to a positive relation between book-to-market ratios and future stock returns. This risk story does not rely on market irrationality.

What do we conclude from all this? We have no reason to expect that all stocks have the same B/M ratio at a given time or for a given stock to have a constant B/M ratio over time. B/M ratios across stocks should differ because of differences in risk or expectations of growth. Similarly B/M ratios for stocks should move around over time. Moreover B/M ratios can have a predictive power for future stock returns without implying irrationality.

So, what is the basis for the value-based investment approach? The best way to view the value-based investment approach is that if the stock market occasionally makes valuation errors, then the B/M approach will help uncover these. If the differences in B/M ratios are justified due to risk and earnings growth, then the investor will who uses the B/M approach will take on more risk and get compensated for this risk. If the market occasionally makes valuation errors, then low B/M ratios will tend to point to overvalued firms, while high B/M ratios will point to undervalued firms. Hence, regardless of what else is going on, valuation errors will also induce systematic patterns into the B/M ratios as suggested by the value-based investment approach. To the extent there are other, more important reasons for the deviations in B/M ratios, the predictive power of the B/M ratio to uncover undervalued assets should be lower.

Let us now turn to the evidence. What does the evidence show? First, are the stock returns in firms with higher B/M ratios actually higher than the stock returns in firms with lower B/M ratios? If so, what is the magnitude of the differences? Is it economically significant? Second, how do we interpret the evidence of a positive relation between B/M ratios and future stock returns? Should we only invest in high B/M ratio firms? If so, why does anyone buy firms with low B/M ratios? These are all important questions an outside investors needs to understand before she can use the B/M approach effectively.

The evidence from the finance literature shows that B/M ratios do in fact predict future stock returns. High B/M stocks tend to have greater stock returns than low B/M stocks. The relation is quite strong, and it is difficult to make this positive relation go away by including other predictors of stock returns.[5]

Interpretation of the evidence is again somewhat problematic. Once again it is difficult to distinguish between the mispricing story and the risk story. First of all, these two interpretations are not mutually exclusive. The presence of risk factors does not rule out potential mispricing, and vice versa. Both stories predict a positive relation between book-to-market values and future stock returns. If mispricing is also present, this positive relation should be even stronger. Hence the difference between these two stories boils down to the strength of the relation between current book-to-market ratios and future stock returns. Since it is difficult to say precisely just how strong a relation we expect under the risk story, it has been difficult to distinguish between these alternative views.

We will nevertheless try to understand why B/M ratios predict future stock returns. We conduct two tests to try to distinguish between these two stories. When book-to-market ratio is low, the risk-based story predicts a low, yet positive expected return. This is because, on average, investors in the stock market are risk-averse, and they always require some positive compensation for bearing risk. When risk is low, this compensation will be low yet still positive. Hence the risk-based story makes it highly unlikely to predict when future stock returns will be negative based on low book-to-market ratios. In contrast, the mispricing story does not rule out predicting negative future stock returns. If positive overreaction is also present, book-to-market ratios will be very low due to very high stock prices. When everyone recognizes the situation, stock prices could drop significantly thereby producing negative stock returns. Hence one way to distinguish between these two views is to see whether very low book-to-market ratios are followed by small yet positive stock returns or negative stock returns. Finding evidence of negative stock returns would suggest that mispricing may also be present.

An alternative test to distinguish between risk and mispricing stories again relies on insider trading. If the risk story is correct, then there is no reason to expect systematic insider trading across firms according to their B/M ratios. Insiders should be just as likely to buy stock as they are likely to sell stock whether the book-to-market is high or low. Moreover, when we control for both the B/M ratio and insider trading, both should retain their predictive power since they will tend to be independent of each other. On the other hand, if mispricing is the dominant factor, then it is likely that insiders will be aware of the mispricing and exploit the opportunity systematically across B/M ratios. Consequently we would expect insiders to be more likely to buy stocks with high book-to-market ratios and more likely to sell stocks with low book-to-market ratios. Also, when we control for both factors, the presence of insider trading should attenuate the predictive power of the book-to-market ratios.

Here is our game plan. We first re-examine the predictive power of the B/M ratio from 1978 to 1993. We would like to know whether the previously published results on the positive relation between B/M ratios and future stock returns continue to hold for this time period. This analysis will also help us determine the strength of the predictive power of the B/M ratios.

Second, we examine the relation between B/M and insider trading. Specifically we would like to know whether insiders do take into account the B/M ratio when they trade their own firm's stock. Given that high B/M values predict positive future returns, it is quite likely that the insiders may be more likely to buy stocks when the B/M ratio is high. Similarly insiders may be more likely to sell stock when the B/M ratio is low. Such a finding would cause a concern that B/M ratio and insider trading may be proxying for one another.

Third, we examine the interaction between the predictive power of B/M ratios and insider trading. Specifically, does B/M ratio maintain its predictive power when we control for insider trading? Does insider trading maintain its predictive power when we control for B/M ratio? This analysis will help us better understand the marginal predictive power of B/M ratios and insider trading.

Predictive power of absolute B/M ratios

We measure book-to-market values for the same sample of 1,700 firms as we did in chapter 9. Both book values and market values are measured for equity. Once again book values are measured from last June 30 and divided by the market value of equity also computed on last June 30 to compute the book-to-market ratio for each firm. Again, for simplicity, we exclude from analysis any firm with negative book-to-market ratios that arise from negative book values of equity.

We begin with a documentation of the year-to-year variations in the book-to-market ratios, from 1978 to 1993 (figure 10.1). The median

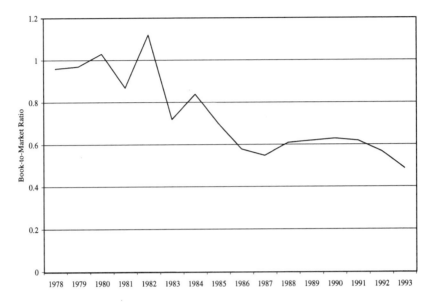

Figure 10.1
Median book-to-market ratios from 1978 to 1993

book-to-market ratios start out at about 0.96 in 1978. The median ratio increases to 1.1 in 1982, then drops down to about 0.7 by 1983 and remains there until 1985. In 1985 the average book-to-market ratio starts a gradual drop and falls to 0.57 by 1992. Its lowest value is about 0.49 in 1993. To a large degree, the movements of the median book-to-market ratios are opposite those of the movement of the median P/E ratios we have seen earlier (figure 9.1).

Once again there are alternative ways of summarizing the information in B/M ratios. We will define both absolute and relative B/M ratio groups. Absolute B/M ratio groups will be used to predict the absolute or the raw returns, while relative B/M ratio groups will be used to predict the relative or the net stock returns.

Absolute B/M ratio groups are defined by looking at the 16-year realizations of B/M ratios. To form absolute B/M groups, we put every firm in one of five equal-sized B/M groups based on their unadjusted B/M ratio. To illustrate how absolute B/M groupings are formed, let's go back to figure 10.1. In 1982 the median B/M was more than 1.0, while in 1992 the median B/M ratio was slightly below 0.6. In terms of absolute B/M ratios, most firms in 1982 would end up in a high B/M group, while most firms in 1992 would end up in a low B/M group. This approach makes sense if we are interested in using time series variation in B/M ratios to predict the future stock returns.

An alternative method of classifying B/M ratios is to examine B/M ratios relative to each other in each year separately. Relative B/M ratios are computed by subtracting the market B/M ratio in each year from all firms' B/M ratios for the same year. When we use this approach, ABC firm with an absolute B/M ratio of 0.8 in 1986 would have a relative B/M ratio of −0.2. By this measure it would be classified as a relatively low B/M firm. The same ABC firm with a B/M ratio of 0.8 in 1992 would have a relative B/M ratio of 0.2. By this measure it would be classified as a relatively high B/M firm. This approach makes sense if we are interested in predicting the relative performance of stocks based on their relative B/M ratios.

To get an idea about our sample size and the distribution of absolute B/M values, we summarize a pooled cross-sectional time series sample, which consists of observations on insider trading and book-to-market ratios (table 10.1). The overall sample consists of 151,620 firm-months. The absolute average book-to-market ratio for the overall sample equals 0.8. We also sort book-to-market ratios into five equal-sized groups. The lowest group has an average B/M ratio of 0.30 and the middle group has a B/M ratio of 0.75. The highest group has a B/M ratio of 1.51.

We begin by first examining the predictive ability of absolute B/M ratios. We would like to uncover the relation between past B/M ratios based on the 15-year distribution and future raw stock returns. Three forecasting horizons are examined: 3-months ahead, 6-months ahead, and 12-months ahead. Given that we are examining the predictive power of absolute B/M ratios, we start with raw returns for each firm. To form portfolios, we take an equally weighted average of the returns for each firm included in our sample.

Table 10.1
Average book-to-market (B/M) ratios

Group	Number of observations	Average book-to-market ratio
Lowest B/M group	30,576	0.30
B/M group 2	30,948	0.54
B/M group 3	30,852	0.75
B/M group 4	30,996	0.95
Highest B/M group	28,248	1.51
All group	151,620	0.80

Table 10.2
Raw stock returns grouped by absolute book-to-market ratios (B/M)

Group	Subsequent 3-month raw returns	Subsequent 6-month raw returns	Subsequent 12-month raw returns
Lowest B/M group	3.0%	5.9%	12.3%
B/M group 2	3.6	7.2	15.0
B/M group 3	4.0	8.0	16.6
B/M group 4	4.7	9.6	19.8
Highest B/M group	5.9	11.8	23.3

For all three forecasting horizons, there is a strong positive relation between absolute B/M ratios and future raw returns to the stocks (table 10.2). For the 3-month-ahead horizon, raw returns start out at 3.0% for the lowest absolute B/M group. With increasing B/M ratios, raw returns rise monotonically. For the middle B/M group, the raw returns rise to 4.0%. For the highest B/M ratio, the raw returns rise to 5.9%. Going from the lowest B/M group to the highest B/M group increases the 3-month-ahead raw stock returns by 2.9 points. This amounts to almost a doubling of the 3-month stock returns.

For the 6-month holding period, raw returns start out at 5.9%. Again there is a monotonic, positive relation between absolute B/M ratios and future raw returns. For the middle B/M group, the raw returns rise to 8.0%. For the highest B/M group, the raw returns rise to 11.8%. Going from the lowest B/M group to the highest B/M group provides an extra 5.9 points or again a doubling of the raw returns over the next 6 months.

The positive relation between absolute B/M ratios and raw returns are maintained for the 12-month horizon as well. Raw returns start out at 12.3% for the lowest B/M group and again rise monotonically with the B/M ratios. For the middle B/M group, the raw returns rise to 16.6%. For the highest B/M group, the raw returns equal 23.3%. Going from the lowest B/M group to the highest B/M group provides an extra return of 11.0 points over the next 12 months, or approximately a doubling of the 12-month return.

The evidence suggests that absolute B/M ratios do predict future raw returns. There is a strong positive relation between past B/M ratios and future stock returns. Moreover the magnitude of the B/M effect is quite strong. For all three forecasting horizons the B/M ratio predicts a doubling of the expected returns.

Our evidence also suggests that absolute B/M ratios would be quite useful in predicting the overall performance of stock portfolios. Hence the absolute magnitude of the B/M ratio is meaningful. A high B/M ratio for the market as a whole suggests that future stock returns to the market portfolio are likely to be greater. Similarly a low B/M ratio for the market as a whole suggests that future stock returns to the market portfolio are likely to be lower. Therefore it makes sense to compare the B/M ratios of a given firm or the market portfolio over time.

While not shown here, we have also examined the relation between absolute B/M ratios and future market returns instead of individual raw stock returns. Once again there is a strong positive relation between current absolute B/M ratios and future market returns up to 12 months ahead. This finding further corroborates our interpretation that the absolute B/M ratios capture the time series variation in the market returns.

Absolute B/M ratios and net stock returns

Next we examine if the absolute B/M ratios predict firm specific performance. To investigate whether there is a firm-specific effect in addition to a market effect, we also examine the predictive power of the absolute B/M ratios for the net stock returns. If there is a firm-specific effect as well, then we would expect the absolute B/M ratios would also predict stock returns net of the market returns.

We examine the relation between absolute B/M ratios and stock returns *net* of the equally weighted market index (table 10.3). Our evidence shows that there is little or no relation between absolute B/M ratios and future net returns to the stocks. For the 3-month-ahead horizon, net stock returns start at −0.1% for the lowest B/M group, rise to 0.4% for the middle group, and end up at −0.2% for the highest B/M group. Hence there is no difference in the net stock returns for the lowest and highest B/M groups. The results for 6-month and 12-month horizons are qualitatively the same.[6]

Our findings are as follows: Absolute B/M ratios do predict future stock returns. This evidence corroborates the findings in finance litera-

Table 10.3

Net stock returns (net of the market returns) grouped by *absolute* book-to-market ratios (B/M)

Group	Subsequent 3-month net returns	Subsequent 6-month net returns	Subsequent 12-month net returns
Highest B/M group	−0.1%	−0.6%	−1.6%
B/M group 2	0.1	−0.0	−0.1
B/M group 3	0.4	0.6	1.1
B/M group 4	0.2	0.2	−0.1
Highest B/M group	−0.2	−0.4	−0.5

ture. Second, the predictive ability of absolute B/M ratios for raw stock returns is very strong. By using absolute B/M ratios, it is possible to double expected raw future stock returns. Our findings also suggest that absolute stock returns predict only absolute (raw) returns, while absolute B/M ratios do not predict relative (net) stock returns. Absolute B/M ratios predict absolute (raw) stock returns because they capture variations in market returns. Finally absolute B/M ratios are not useful in predicting net (relative) stock returns since by definition relative stock returns are uncorrelated with the market returns.

What are the implications of our findings for the stock market investor? Our evidence strongly supports the notion that absolute B/M ratios predict future stock returns. If investors are interested in market timing or predicting the overall performance of the portfolio, they would be advised to use absolutely high B/M ratios. Finally investors should not use absolute B/M ratios to engage in stock picking. This strategy does not work. We will have more to say about stock picking using relative B/M ratios later in this chapter.

A secondary question for the stock market investors is why the absolute B/M ratios predict future stock returns so strongly? The two main explanations we have considered so far are the risk and mispricing explanations. To get an idea which explanation fits the data better, we now bring in the insider-trading variable. If insider trading can attenuate or even eliminate the predictive ability of the absolute B/M ratios, then mispricing is a strong possibility. If not, then the risk explanation would appear to contribute to the explanatory power of the absolute B/M ratios.

Relation between insider trading and absolute B/M ratios

We now explore the relation between insider trading and absolute B/M ratios. Insider trading is measured as before. We sum the total shares bought or sold in a given firm in a given month. If insiders buy more shares than they sell, we declare that month as a purchase

Table 10.4
Twelve-month raw returns grouped by insider buying and selling and the absolute book-to-market ratios (B/M)

Group	Insider selling	Insider buying
Lowest B/M group	13.0%	15.2%
	(9,420)	(3,229)
B/M group 2	15.2	16.2
	(7,617)	(4,135)
B/M group 3	15.7	18.0
	(6,087)	(4,427)
B/M group 4	19.5	22.3
	(4,889)	(4,558)
Highest B/M group	22.1	28.0
	(3,982)	(4,099)

Note: In parentheses are the number of months.

month. If insiders sell more shares than they buy, we declare that month as a sale month.

The interrelations among B/M ratios, insider trading, and future raw stock returns are examined next (table 10.4). An interesting finding is that insider trading appears to be positively related to the absolute B/M ratios. Insiders are less likely to sell stocks with increasing B/M ratios. Insider selling declines monotonically from 9,420 firm-months to 3,982 firm-months as the B/M ratios increases from the lowest to the highest group. Similarly insiders are more likely to buy stocks in general when book-to-market ratios are high. Insider buying increases from 3,229 firm-months to 4,099 firm-months with increasing B/M ratios. Hence our evidence suggests that insiders do take a positive view of the absolute B/M ratios in their trading decisions.[7]

We also examine the interaction between the predictive ability of B/M ratios and insider trading for future stock returns (table 10.4). Examining the table by columns first, we see that the absolute B/M ratios continue to predict future raw stock returns separately for insider sales or purchases. For instance, in the first column, given insider selling, expected returns go from 13.0% monotonically up to 22.1% as the B/M ratios increase. In the second column, given insider buying, the expected returns go from 15.2% monotonically up to 28.0% as the B/M ratios increase. Hence the B/M ratios continue to predict positive stock returns regardless of whether insiders are buying or selling.

Absolute B/M ratios do not attenuate the predictive power of insider-trading variable. Looking at table 10.4 row by row, we control for the B/M effect. We see that for five out of five rows, holding the absolute B/M ratio constant, insider buying predicts higher future stock returns than insider selling.

Our evidence so far suggests the following: (1) Insiders tend to view the times when stocks have a high absolute B/M ratio as a good buying opportunity. Similarly insiders view times when stocks have a low absolute B/M ratio as a good selling opportunity. (2) Absolute B/M ratios continue to predict increasing stock returns even after controlling for the insider-trading activity. High B/M ratios signal greater than average positive returns even when insiders are selling; low B/M ratios signal less than average stock returns even when insiders are buying. (3) The predictive power of insider-trading activity is also not attenuated after controlling for the B/M effect. Insider buying is always good news whether the B/M ratio is low or high. Insider selling is bad news whether the B/M ratio is low or high.[8]

What do we conclude from all this? Outsiders can use both absolute B/M ratios and insider trading in their trading decisions. In fact, by combining both variables, outsiders can significantly improve the forecasting power of their trading rules. A low B/M ratio combined with insider selling predicts an average return of 13.0% over the next year. In contrast, a high B/M ratio combined with insider buying increases the predicted returns to 28.0%, an increase of 15 points, or more than doubling of the average returns. Our advice to the outside investors is to use both insider trading and absolute B/M ratios in predicting the overall direction of the stock market.

The answer to our second question is less clear. Why does the B/M ratio predict future stock returns? The evidence we have presented so far does not allow us to choose one explanation over the other. The positive relation between insider trading and B/M ratios points to mispricing. On the other hand, the fact that insider trading does not attenuate the predictive power of the B/M ratios suggests that risk explanations is also playing a strong role. So far the evidence does not allow us to make a clear distinction between our two potential explanations.

Predictive power of relative B/M ratios

To get some further insights into the predictive power of the B/M ratios, we examine *relative* B/M ratios. This is useful for stock-picking strategy since relative ratios compare the B/M ratios of firms at a given time across firms. In contrast, our previous analysis with absolute ratios compares the B/M ratios of firms across time.

Predictive power of the relative B/M groupings to predict the relative stock returns is examined next. This time, we use net stock returns, since we are interested in stock picking or predicting the relative performance of stocks based on their relative B/M ratios. Net stock returns are computed net of the return to the equally weighted market index. Once again we look ahead 3 months, 6 months, and 12 months.

There is a positive relation between relative B/M groups and relative (net) stock returns for all three forecasting horizons (table 10.5). Looking at the first column, we see a positive relation between relative B/M ratios and 3-month-ahead net stock returns. For the lowest B/M group, the net stock returns are −0.3%. The relatively low B/M stocks slightly underperform the equally weighted market index. As the relative B/M ratios increase, the future net stock returns generally increase. For the middle B/M group, the net stock returns are also −0.3%. For the highest relative B/M group, net stock returns equal

Table 10.5
Net stock returns (net of the market returns) grouped by *relative* book-to-market
ratios (B/M)

Group	Subsequent 3-month net return	Subsequent 6-month net returns	Subsequent 12-month net returns
Lowest B/M group	−0.3%	−0.7%	−1.7%
B/M group 2	0.0	−0.2	−0.8
B/M group 3	−0.3	−0.6	−1.1
B/M group 4	0.4	0.6	0.8
Highest B/M group	0.4	0.8	1.8

0.4%. The total spread between the lowest and highest groups equals
0.7 points.

The relation between relative B/M ratios and 6-month-ahead net
stock returns remains positive (table 10.5, column 2). For the lowest
B/M group, the net stock returns equal −0.7%. For the middle group,
net stock returns rise slightly to −0.6%. For the highest group, net stock
returns rise to 0.8%. The total spread between the lowest and highest
groups equals 1.5 points.

The relation between relative B/M ratios and 12-month-ahead net
stock returns also remains positive (table 10.5, column 3). For the lowest group, net stock returns equal −1.7%. For the middle group, net
stock returns rise to −1.1%. For the highest group, net stock returns
rise further to 1.8%. The spread between the lowest and highest relative
B/M groups equals 3.5 points.

Our evidence corroborates the findings documented in the finance
literature. There is a positive relation between relative B/M ratios and
future net stock returns to the stock. Relatively higher B/M stocks have
higher average returns than the relatively lower B/M stocks. This relation appears to be strongest for the 12-month holding period.

What are the implications for stock market investing? Our findings
suggest that outsiders can use relative B/M ratios in a stock-picking
strategy. Relative B/M ratios predict the relative stock performance.

Again we turn to our second question. Why does the relative B/M ratio work? Does the predictive power of the relative B/M ratios suggest mispricing? If so, we should be able to use the relatively low B/M ratios to predict possible negative future raw returns. As we discussed earlier, the risk story predicts low, yet positive returns to low B/M ratios, while the overreaction story does not rule out negative future raw returns to low B/M ratios. To see if we can distinguish between these two explanations, we first grouped the sample into 20 subgroups based on the relative B/M ratios. This finer categorization is intended to isolate more extreme values of B/M ratios and potentially contain more information. Raw returns are examined for 3-month, 6-month, and 12-month horizons. While not shown here, the average raw returns are positive for all three horizons. For the 12-month horizon the raw returns increase from about 13% to 19%, when the B/M ratio increases from the smallest group to the highest group.

As an additional test, we also broke down the smallest relative B/M group into another 20 groups based on the relative P/E ratios. We then examined the future returns to the lowest B/M and the highest P/E stocks. Once again the 12-month-ahead raw returns are positive 8% for this group. Hence the negative return test does not allow us to distinguish between risk and overreaction as the potential source of the predictive ability of B/M ratios, since future raw returns remain positive. To distinguish between risk and overreaction stories, we one again bring in the insider-trading variable.

Insider trading and relative B/M ratios

We now analyze the interaction between insider trading and relative B/M ratios. Our purpose here is twofold. First, we would like to know if we can strengthen the predictive power of relative B/M ratios by adding insider trading as an additional forecasting variable. Second, we would like to know if the presence of insider trading attenuates the predictive power of either variable.

Table 10.6

Insider trading months grouped by relative book-to-market ratios (B/M)

Group	Insider selling	Insider buying
Lowest B/M group	9,580	3,110
	(75%)	(25%)
B/M group 2	7,915	3,766
	(68%)	(32%)
B/M group 3	5,701	4,632
	(55%)	(45%)
B/M group 4	4,896	4,732
	(51%)	(49%)
Highest B/M group	3,903	4,208
	(48%)	(52%)

Note: In parentheses are percentage of insider trading months.

All insider-trading months are sorted into sale and purchase months and five groups of relative B/M ratios. There is a strong positive relation between insider trading and relative B/M ratios (table 10.6). Insiders are more likely to be sellers and less likely to be buyers in relatively low B/M firms. For the lowest B/M group, 75% of insider transactions are sales and 25% are purchases. Hence sales are favored over purchases by a three-to-one ratio. As the relative B/M ratio increases, sell proportions fall uniformly while the buy proportions rise uniformly. For the middle B/M group, sell months constitute 55% of the total insider-trading months, while the buy months constitute 45%. For the relatively highest B/M group, the buy months in fact exceed the sell months. The sell months now constitute 48%, while the buy months constitute 52%.

Our evidence suggests that once again insiders act as if the relative differences in B/M ratios signal profit opportunities. Insiders view relatively high B/M stocks more favorably. As a result insiders are significantly more likely to buy relatively high B/M stocks as they are likely to buy relatively low B/M stocks. Similarly insiders are significantly

Table 10.7
Net stock returns (net of the market returns) grouped by insider trading and relative book-to-market ratios (B/M): Subsequent 12-month net stock returns

Group	Insider selling	Insider buying
Lowest B/M group	−1.7%	0.0%
B/M group 2	−0.5	−0.3
B/M group 3	−1.2	1.9
B/M group 4	−0.8	1.4
Highest B/M group	1.8	5.1

more likely to sell relatively low B/M stocks as they are likely to sell high B/M stocks.

To see if insider trading attenuates the predictive power of the relative B/M ratios, the interaction between insider trading, relative B/M ratios, and future net stock returns are examined next. The holding period is taken as 12 months ahead. When we control for insider trading and relative B/M ratios, both variables retain their predictive ability (table 10.7). Relative B/M ratios are still related positively to future net stock returns when we control for insiders' sales (column 1). For the relatively lowest B/M group, net stock returns equal −1.7%. For the relatively highest B/M group, net stock returns rise 1.8%. The positive relation between B/M ratios and future stock returns is also maintained after we control for insiders' purchases. For the relatively lowest B/M group, the net stock returns equal 0% (column 2). For the relatively highest B/M group, net stock returns rise to 5.1%.

Our data also show that insider trading retains its predictive power when we control for B/M ratios. Looking at table 10.7 row by row, insider buying is associated with higher net stock returns than insider selling. For five out of five rows, insider buying signals higher net stock returns than insider selling.[9]

What do we learn from examining the relative B/M ratios? Once again our evidence suggests that relative B/M ratios predict the relative performance of future stock returns. Consequently relative B/M ratios would serve as a useful variable in a stock-picking strategy. Second, adding insider trading does not attenuate the predictive power of the relative B/M variable. In fact outside investors can improve the performance of their portfolios by using both B/M ratios and insider trading. Lowest B/M ratios coupled with insider selling predicts a net stock returns of -1.7%. Highest relative B/M ratio coupled with insider buying predicts a net stock return of 5.1%, or an increase of 6.8%. This is almost double the extra returns obtainable from a relative B/M strategy alone (which was 3.5% in table 10.5).

Why does the relative B/M strategy work? The evidence is again less clear-cut with respect to our second question. The evidence we have presented so far does not allow us to choose between risk and mispricing explanations. The positive relation between insider trading and the relative B/M ratios points to some possible mispricing. On the other hand, the fact that insider trading does not attenuate the predictive power of the relative B/M ratios suggests that risk explanation is also playing a strong role. Hence there is evidence to support both explanations. Our final attempt to distinguish between our two stories brings us to stronger insider-trading signals.

Large insider trading and relative B/M ratios

The next group of analysis attempts to use more selective insider-trading signals to see that insider trading can dominate the information in B/M ratios. We use two screens to strengthen insider-trading signals. First, we examine large insider trading. Second, we examine large transactions by top executives only. If the mispricing story plays any role whatsoever, then the use of stronger insider-trading signals should begin to weaken the predictive ability of the B/M ratios.

We begin with large insider trading. We focus in months when insiders trade more than 1,000 shares. As before, we examine 12-month-ahead holding periods. More selective insider trading indeed begins to weaken the information content of B/M ratios. Holding large insider

Table 10.8

Net stock returns (net of the market returns) grouped by insider trading and relative book-to-market ratios (B/M)

Group	Insider selling more than 1,000 shares	Insider buying more than 1,000 shares
Lowest B/M group	−2.0%	−0.4%
	(7,611)	(1,392)
B/M group 2	−1.5	−0.9
	(5,936)	(1,724)
B/M group 3	−0.9	3.1
	(3,945)	(2,044)
B/M group 4	−1.0	1.9
	(3,213)	(1,889)
Highest B/M group	−3.0	5.7
	(2,614)	(2,115)

Note: In parentheses are the number of observations.

selling constant, there is no longer a positive relation between B/M ratios and future net stock returns (table 10.8, column 1). Instead, future net stock returns seem to be declining with higher B/M ratios. As the B/M ratio increases from the lowest to highest group, the net stock returns in fact decline from −2.0% to −3.0%. This is the first evidence that strong insider trading attenuates the predictive power of the B/M ratios. For large insider purchases the positive relation between B/M ratios and future returns remains intact (table 10.8, column 2). As the relative B/M increases from the lowest group to highest group, net stock returns increase from −0.4% to 5.7%. Overall, table 10.8 suggests that when the strength of the insider-trading signal increases, it weakens but does not eliminate the information content of the relative B/M ratio.

Our data also tell us why large insider trading appears to weaken the information content of the relative B/M signal. It appears that large insider trading is even more strongly related to the relative B/M ratio.

The numbers in parentheses in table 10.8 show the number of insider-trading months. Looking at the first row, for the smallest B/M group, there are 7,611 insider sales and 1,392 insider buys. Hence insider selling accounts for 85%, while insider buying accounts for only 15% of the sample. For comparison purposes, all insider selling accounted for 75% of the transactions for the relatively lowest B/M group (table 10.6). As the relative B/M ratio increases, the probability of large insider selling falls sharply, while the probability of large insider purchases increases sharply. For the relatively highest B/M group, the proportions are 55% for sales and 45% for purchases. This finding suggests that when insiders trade large amounts, they pay even closer attention to the factors that also affect the relative B/M ratio.

Finally we restrict our attention to the large transactions of top executives. Once again more selective insider-trading signals weakens the information content of the relative B/M ratios. Conditioning on large sales by top executives, the relation between B/M and future net stock returns once again turns negative (table 10.9, column 1). For large purchases by top executives, the positive relation between the relative B/M ratios and future net stock returns are maintained (column 2).[10]

Conclusions and investment implications

In this chapter we have examined the information content of the book-to-market (B/M) ratios to select stocks. Value-based investment approach regards the book value of equity as a measure of the fundamental value of the stock, while the market value of equity is viewed as the cost of acquisition. Hence value-based investment approach favors high B/M stocks whose fundamental value is presumed to be above the cost of acquisition. Our findings are as follows:

1. Our sample displays significant variation in B/M ratios. The average B/M ratio for the sample of firms we analyze is about 0.8. For the sample period 1978 to 1993, B/M ratios range from 0.3 to 1.5. Given this variation, the differences in B/M ratios should be informative.

Table 10.9

Net stock returns (net of the market returns) grouped by insider trading and relative book-to-market ratios (B/M)

Group	Top executives selling more than 1,000 shares	Top executives buying more than 1,000 shares
Lowest B/M group	−0.7%	−2.6%
	(1,794)	(189)
B/M group 2	−2.0	0.6
	(1,434)	(176)
B/M group 3	−0.5	5.5
	(764)	(196)
B/M group 4	−0.2	6.3
	(593)	(224)
Highest B/M group	−1.7	11.1
	(510)	(286)

Note: In parentheses are the number of observations.

2. Absolute B/M ratios predict the future raw returns to stocks. As book-to-market ratio increases from the lowest to the highest groups, the raw returns approximately double for 3-month, 6-month, and 12-month horizons. Hence the value-based investment approach works.

3. Absolute B/M ratios also predict market returns, while they do not predict the relative performance of stocks. This finding suggests that differences in absolute B/M ratios are meaningful. Also some of the predictive power of the B/M ratios appears to come from predicting the time variation in market returns. These findings suggest that absolute B/M ratios would be most useful in a market-timing strategy.

4. The presence of insider trading does not attenuate the predictive power of the absolute B/M ratios. This finding suggests that the predictive power of the absolute B/M ratios cannot be attributed completely to mispricing of stocks. Hence, by using both variables, outsiders can do better in predicting future stock returns.

5. Relative B/M ratios are used to predict relative future stock performance. *Relative* B/M ratios do predict the *relative* future stock returns.

There is a strong positive relation between past relative B/M ratios and future net stock returns. The lowest group of the relative B/M ratio stocks underperforms the market index by 1.7% over the next 12 months. The middle relative B/M stocks underperform the market index by 1.1%. The relative highest group of B/M stocks outperforms the market index by 1.8%. These findings suggest that relative B/M ratios must be useful in a stock-picking strategy.

6. Insiders appear to view the variations in both absolute B/M ratios and relative B/M ratios as if they represent some potential profit opportunities. Insiders are more likely to sell both absolutely and relatively low B/M stocks. Similarly insiders are more likely to buy both absolutely and relatively high B/M stocks.

7. Holding relative B/M ratios constant, insider trading still predicts future stock returns. Hence the predictive power of insider trading is not attenuated by controlling for differences in relative B/M ratios.

8. The relative B/M variable retains its predictive power when we control for everyday insider-trading activity. Whether insiders are buying or selling, high B/M ratios predict higher future net stock returns. Again, by using both variables, outsiders can do better in predicting future stock returns.

9. The predictive power of the relative B/M variable only begins to weaken when we use more selective insider-trading signals. Conditioning on large insider selling, the relative B/M ratio is in fact negatively related to future stock returns. Similarly we also examine the predictive ability of B/M ratios when we control for large trading by top executives. Once again, conditioning on large selling by top executives, we see that the relative B/M ratio is negatively related to future net stock returns.

10. Overall, our evidence suggests that the B/M approach works quite well in practice in predicting future stock returns. Unfortunately, the evidence is less clear on *why* it works. There is some evidence to support both the risk and mispricing explanations.

11   *Insider trading in target firms*

What is the information content of takeover announcements?

Corporate takeovers represent a change in the management of public companies, often through a change in the ownership of the firm. In corporate takeovers various management teams including the incumbent management compete for the right to control the decision-making rights within the target firm. Takeover announcements also generate great investor enthusiasm because they usually lead to large increases in stock prices of the selling firms. A typical premium offered to the shareholders of the selling firms ranges between 20% and 30%.

Corporate takeovers can be through mergers, tenders offers, or through proxy contests. Mergers and tender offers involve change in ownership of the target firms, while proxy contests attempt to replace the board of directors. In a friendly merger the management of the buying firm (called the bidder) negotiates all terms of the takeover agreement with the management of the selling firm (called the target). After both sides agree on all the terms, a merger is announced. If the merger is not challenged on anticompetitive grounds by the Federal Trade Commission, the Justice Department, or any other party, then it becomes effective after a certain date. The target firm then becomes part of the bidder firm.

In tender offers, the bidder firm's managers directly appeal to the shareholders of the target firm by offering a premium price to buy their shares. The management of the target firm is bypassed. A tender offer is usually considered hostile by the target management, since it attempts to replace them without their acquiescence. In fact some tender offers follow failed merger negotiations. By buying sufficient number of the shares of the target firms, the bidder firm acquires the right to name their board of directors and replace the incumbent management of the target firm with a new team. The average premium offered to the shareholders of the target firms tends to be around 30%, which is 10% higher than in mergers.

A third method of corporate takeovers occurs through proxy fights. In a proxy fight, competing teams attempt to get their slate of candidates elected to the board of directors by appealing to shareholders' votes. Usually a dissident group of shareholders challenges the incumbent management and proposes a competing set of candidates. Each side attempts to win votes at a shareholders' meeting by explaining how they can increase the value of the firm through reorganization or changes in the operating strategy of the firm. Evidence shows that win or lose, proxy fights result in an increase of about 8% in the value of target firm's shares.

As the discussion above makes clear, corporate takeovers often create significant new wealth for the shareholders of the target firms. Some have questioned whether the shareholders' gains have been achieved at the expense of other stakeholders of the target firms such as bondholders, taxpayers, employees, suppliers, customers, competitors, or the communities in which the firms operate. While a full airing of all the issues involved is beyond the scope of this book, the evidence suggests most shareholder gains come from eliminating inefficiencies. On average, corporate takeovers enable the more efficient management team to control the decision rights at the target firm.[1]

Our concern in this book is from the perspective of a potential investor in the stock market. The interesting questions from such an investor's perspective include the following: (1) How large are the stock price changes in target firms as a result of the takeover announcement? (2) Is it possible to make money following the public announcements of the takeovers? (3) Is there a leakage of takeover information prior to the public announcement? (4) Is there a possibility of predicting which firms are more likely to be takeover targets? (5) Do corporate insiders trade for their personal accounts exploiting the upcoming takeover announcements?

Given that the top management of the target firms would be involved in either direct negotiations or be informed about an upcoming offer, it is natural to expect that they might use this information in some way. If so, can outsider investors observe insider trading in target firms and deduce the likelihood of a takeover attempt? If insiders buy large amounts of stocks prior to takeover announcements, this can signal to outsiders that something important is likely to happen soon. Finally a related issue is whether outsider investors can use publicly available insider-trading information to trade profitably on the basis of the upcoming takeover announcement. In this chapter we attempt to answer all of these questions. In the next chapter we will analyze corporate takeovers from the bidder firms' perspective.

Price effects of corporate takeovers

We start our analysis with a review of the characteristics of our takeover sample (table 11.1). Our sample consists of 1,913 target firms during 1975 to 1992 period. Of this total, 89% of the firms are eventually taken

Table 11.1
Target firms, 1975–1992

Total number of target firms	1,913
Proportion successfully taken over	89%
Announcement month net return	21.2%
Six-month net return	21.5%

over. We call these firms successful targets. If a target firm is not eventually taken over, then it is called an unsuccessful target. In our sample only 11% of the takeover targets have remained as independent firms. The takeover attempt can fail for many reasons, including lack of shareholder enthusiasm for the offer price, tenacious takeover defenses by an entrenched target management, antitrust challenges by the Federal Trade Commission or the Department of Justice, a lawsuit by any other firm, or a change of mind by the management of the bidder firm.[2] Any one of these factors can lead to a failure of the takeover attempt.

As a result of the takeover attempt, target firms' shareholders experience large increases in wealth. Announcement month net stock returns to target firms equal 21.2%. Contrary to some critics' claim, target shareholders do not lose their wealth in takeovers. In fact the finance literature has not uncovered any evidence of losses by the target shareholders as a result of the attacks by so called raiders. Target firms do not retain the large stock price increase in the long run. The six-month net stock returns including the announcement month equal 21.5%. These results confirm that virtually all of the abnormal returns to target firms occur during the announcement month and there is no discernible upward or downward drift in stock prices following the announcement month.

Finance studies using daily stock returns also corroborate the finding that the stock price reaction to takeover announcements is completed quickly.[3] These studies show that while stock prices tend to drift up prior to the takeover announcement due to possible insider trading, leakage of information, or public dissemination of the rumors regarding the possibility of a takeover, there is no stock price drift following the takeover announcement. Hence the stock price reaction in target firms is completed on the announcement day.

The evidence already answers two of the questions we posed in the introduction. Stock price reactions to takeover announcements are large. They vary between 20% and 30%. This evidence strongly confirms that takeovers benefit target firms shareholders. Second, there is

Table 11.2
Insider trading and 6-month net stock returns in target firms grouped by the success of the takeover attempt

	Number of firms	Announcement month net returns	6-month net return	Insider trading during the past 12 months
Takeover attempt is successful	1,703	22.0%	24.4%	4,329
Takeover attempt is unsuccessful	210	14.8	−0.5	−2,608

no delayed reaction to takeover announcements. The drift for the six months following the announcement month is only 0.3 points. This evidence suggests that it is not possible for an investor to buy the target stock after the takeover announcement month and make money.

To gain further insights into the stock price behavior of target firms, we examine success of the target firms. For the 1,703 firms for which the takeover attempt is successful, the net stock price reaction during the announcement month is 22.0% (table 11.2). For the 210 unsuccessful target firms, the announcement-month net stock price reaction is 14.8%. Shareholders gain more during the announcement month if the takeover is eventually successful. Also the market participants appear to distinguish between successful and unsuccessful firms to some extent even during the announcement month.

In the long run successful targets keep and add to their gains, while unsuccessful targets lose all of their gains (table 11.2). For the successful target firms, the six-month abnormal returns equal 24.4%. There is only a 2.4 point drift for the six months following the announcement month. For the unsuccessful target firms, the six-month abnormal returns (including the announcement month return) equal −0.5%. Hence all of the initial returns are lost during the six months following the announcement month for the unsuccessful takeover targets.

Our evidence allows us to distinguish between two alternative explanations for the source of gains in takeovers: (1) synergy between bidder and target firms and (2) undervaluation of the target firm in the stock market. If the synergy story is correct, then a successful combination between the bidder and the target is essential to maintain the initial price gains. In contrast, if the combination does not take place, then we would expect the price of the target firm's stock to go back to pre-announcement levels. If the undervaluation story is correct, then the most important factor is the release of information about the true value of the target's assets. Once everyone realizes that the target firm possesses much more valuable assets then investors realized previously, then the value of the target firm will remain high whether or not the combination is successful.[4]

Our evidence also suggests that synergy plays an important role in the creation of value in corporate takeovers. When the corporate takeover is successful, the combination of the bidder and target firms generates synergy, and the bidder firm is forced to share some of these gains with the shareholders of the target firms. As a result the value of the target firm increases permanently. In contrast, when the attempted corporate takeover is unsuccessful, there can be no synergy, and the value of the target firm goes back to its original value prior to the takeover announcement. Consequently there is no real increase in the value of the target firm.

What do insiders do prior to takeover announcements? Do they buy shares in large numbers? In successful takeovers, insiders average a net purchase of 4,329 shares (table 11.2). In unsuccessful takeover, insiders average a net sale of 2,608 shares. On average, insiders buy more shares in firms that eventually become successful targets than firms that become unsuccessful targets. This finding suggests that insiders in target firms may be aware of the possibility of a takeover attempt. Insiders take advantage of this information by buying shares in the successful firms but not in the unsuccessful firms. The difference in successful and unsuccessful firms may be attributed to the short-swing profits rule. Insiders cannot sell any shares they buy for at least a six-month period.

Short-swing profits rule may discourage insider buying in the unsuccessful firms since the positive returns dissipate within six months.

While greater insider buying in successful targets than in unsuccessful targets is interesting, we should not get too excited. Remember how table 11.2 is constructed. We know which firms are takeover targets already. We also know which firms have been successfully taken over. Unfortunately, we cannot construct the table 11.2 before the takeover is announced. Instead, we have to wait not only until the takeover is announced but also until after the outcome of the takeover attempt is resolved. Hence, after the fact, insiders do appear to be buying more in successful targets; however, this kind of knowledge about insider trading is not useful to outside investors as an investment tool. What we need to know is whether insider trading *before* the takeover announcement predicts the eventual success of the takeover attempt. We will address this issue fully later in this chapter.

Pre-announcement stock price drift

We have already seen that takeover attempts are not a complete surprise to everyone. There is some evidence to suggest that insiders in target firms may be aware of the potential takeover attempts on their own firms. A direct way of examining market expectations regarding the takeover attempts is to examine the pre-announcement stock prices. If there is no drift in pre-announcement stock prices, then we can safely say that most market participants are not aware of the takeover attempt. If, however, stock prices drift up during the pre-announcement period, we can be confident that a significant number of market participants expect an upcoming takeover attempt.[5]

Let us first examine the evidence. Our sample contains 1,913 target firms during the six months prior to the takeover announcement month. The contemporaneous return to the equally weighted market index is subtracted in computing net returns. The cumulative net returns for the six-month pre-announcement period is 6.3% (table 11.3).

Table 11.3

Pre-announcement stock price drift in takeover targets

	Net returns	Cumulative net returns
Month −6	0.2%	0.2%
Month −5	−0.3	−0.1
Month −4	0.6	0.5
Month −3	1.0	1.5
Month −2	1.1	2.6
Month −1	3.7	6.3

Note: Month 0 represents the takeover announcement month. Month −6 is six months prior to the takeover announcement month.

Table 11.4

Cumulative pre-announcement stock price drift in takeover targets grouped by the success of the takeover attempt

	Unsuccessful takeovers	Successful takeovers
Month −6	−0.4%	0.3%
Month −5	−1.4	−0.1
Month −4	−0.4	0.9
Month −3	0.5	1.9
Month −2	1.2	3.2
Month −1	2.5	7.2

Note: Month 0 represents the takeover announcement month. Month −6 is six months prior to the takeover announcement month.

Hence more than a fifth of the total returns to target firms occurs before the takeover is even announced. Almost all of this drift occurs during the three months prior to the takeover announcement month. The largest monthly drift of 3.7% occurs immediately prior to the announcement month.[6]

To shed further light on the pre-announcement stock price drifts, we sort the pre-announcement drift by the success of the takeover attempt. In unsuccessful targets, the drift averages only 2.5% (table 11.4).

In successful targets the drift averages 7.2%. Most of the drift in successful targets occurs during the three months immediately preceding the
takeover announcement.

This evidence suggests that market participants are more likely to
anticipate the takeover attempt if it is eventually successful. This finding makes sense. If the takeover is friendly, it is announced after a period of negotiations with the target management. This increases the
possibility of leaks. If the takeover is hostile, it may be launched without target management knowledge. This makes the possibility of leaks
less likely.

Clearly takeovers do not appear to be the best kept secrets. There is
pre-announcement insider buying. Stock prices drift up prior to takeover announcements. The pre-announcement drift is higher for successful targets. What is the source of these stock price drifts? Is it
because of insider trading? What other explanations can there be? Why
do the stock price drifts depend on the success of the takeover attempt?

If insiders do in fact exploit the takeover information for their personal accounts and inform their friends and family members, we can
certainly get a lot of people start buying large volume of shares based
on confidential information. In this case both the trading volume
and stock prices would rise prior to the takeover announcement. To
help answer this question, we bring back pre-announcement insider
trading.

Is there a relation between pre-announcement insider buying and
pre-announcement price leaks? If the pre-announcement stock price
drift is caused by pre-announcement insider trading, then we would
certainly expect a greater stock price drift to occur when insiders are
buying. Since takeovers are most likely to be known to top management, we restrict our attention to the transactions of top executives
only. We first compute the number of shares traded by top executives
during the six months prior to the takeover announcement. If in a
given target firm the shares sold exceed the shares bought, we classify
this firm as a seller. If the shares bought exceed the shares sold, we

Table 11.5
Cumulative pre-announcement stock price drift in takeover targets grouped by pre-announcement trading by top executives

	Top executives sell	No trade	Top executives buy
Month −6	1.3%	−0.1%	0.4%
Month −5	2.1	−0.8	0.8
Month −4	1.7	0.0	1.5
Month −3	2.7	0.7	3.8
Month −2	3.6	1.6	6.2
Month −1	7.9	5.2	9.4

Note: Month 0 represents the takeover announcement month. Month −6 is six months prior to the takeover announcement month.

classify this firm as a buyer. If the shares sold equal to the shares bought, or if there is no insider trading, we classify this firm as a no-trade group.

There is significant pre-announcement drift whether insiders are buying or selling (table 11.5). For sellers, the six-month drift equals 7.9%. For buyers, the six-month drift equals 9.4%. The difference is small. Firms with no insider trading have the smallest drift at 5.2%. The extra drift for insider-buying group over the selling group is only 1.5 percentage points. Hence our evidence suggests that the link between pre-announcement trading by top executives and the pre-announcement stock price drifts is weak at best.

The evidence presented so far suggests that pre-announcement trading by top executives is not the likely cause of the pre-announcement stock price drifts. If so, what else can account for the pre-announcement stock price drifts? Once again, why do successful targets have much greater pre-announcement stock price drifts? We can think of at least three alternative explanations, which do not rely on illegal insider trading.

First, takeovers do not occur randomly across all firms. Instead, they occur in waves and there is a strong industry effect. When a firm in the oil industry is taken over, the probability that additional industry consolidations will occur jumps dramatically. This is usually because the prevailing conditions apply to all oil firms. For instance, if the oil industry is characterized by oversupply due to a sudden decline in demand, usually no firm wants to be the first to leave the industry voluntarily. Takeovers can facilitate this necessary reduction in output and elimination of wasteful exploration and development expenses. Hence, when one oil firm is taken over, the stock prices of other potential takeover targets will also rise. This anticipation can result in pre-announcement drifts without implying any illegal insider trading.

Another possible explanation is that the probability of a takeover for a given firm depends on its industry affiliation or its financial characteristics. As firms disclose their earnings, debt levels, and other financial information, investors constantly update these takeover probabilities. As the probability of a takeover increases, the pre-announcement stock price ought to increase. Since the probability of a takeover should be higher in those eventually successful targets, the higher drift is consistent with this explanation.

Finally, disclosure requirements alert investors to changing takeover probabilities. When an investor accumulates a 5% or higher equity position in another firm, he/she has to file a 13-D statement within ten days with the Securities and Exchange Commission. These statements disclose the investor's intent and the reasons for the investment. A 13-D filing certainly increases the possibility that a firm will end up "in-play." Once again an increasing probability of a takeover based on publicly available information will result in pre-announcement drifts without implying any illegal insider trading.

Insider trading in target firms

We are now ready to bring in insider trading evidence directly. First, do insiders in target firms exploit their knowledge about the upcoming takeover attempt? Second, can outside investors profitably use the insider-trading information to predict the probability of takeovers, the eventual success of the takeover attempt, or the profitability of the takeover for the target firms' shareholders? To answer these questions, we must examine insider trading prior to takeover announcements.[7] Since the knowledge about a takeover attempt would be restricted to top executives only, we focus our attention on top executives.

Our first concern is whether top executives buy more shares in target firms than they do in nontarget firms. If so, then it is possible to use the insider-trading information to predict the probability of a takeover attempt for a given firm. To help address this issue, we compare the transactions of the top executives in target and nontarget firms both 3 months and 12 months prior to takeover attempt. A control group of nontarget firms is chosen to provide a benchmark for the top executives' transactions in target firms. One nontarget firm is randomly chosen and matched in size with each of the target firms. For both groups, insiders' transactions are examined during the same calendar time.

Our evidence suggests that top executives do not exploit their information about the takeover. Looking at a 3-month period prior to takeover announcements, the top executives in target firms are buyers in 4.3% of the sample and sellers in 7.3% of the sample (table 11.6). Hence, on average, sellers exceed buyers by 3.0 points. In nontarget firms, top executives are buyers in 2.1% of the sample and sellers in 3.3% of the sample. Hence sellers exceed buyers by 1.2 points. Therefore comparing net trading in target and nontarget firms corroborates our previous interpretation that managers in target firms do not exploit their knowledge about upcoming takeover announcements.

Looking at the 12-month period prior to the takeover announcement corroborates the same type of behavior as the 3-month period. In target firms top executives are buyers in 11.8% and sellers in 17.7% of the firms. On net, top executives are sellers in 5.9% of the firms. In contrast, in nontakeover firms, sellers exceed buyers only by 2.6 points. Hence once again top executives in target firms do not buy stock prior to takeover announcements.

Table 11.6
Cumulative pre-announcement stock price drift in takeover targets grouped by the success of the takeover attempt

	Target firms	Nontarget firms
Proportion of firms where top executives buy shares during the 3 months prior to takeover attempt	4.3%	2.1%
Proportion of firms where top executives sell shares during the 3 months prior to takeover attempt	7.3	3.3
Proportion of firms where top executives buy shares during the 12 months prior to takeover attempt	11.8	5.0
Proportion of firms where top executives sell shares during the 12 months prior to takeover attempt	17.7	7.6

Note: Month 0 represents the takeover announcement month. Month −6 is six months prior to the takeover announcement month.

Our evidence indicates that the top executives in target firms do not exploit their knowledge about the upcoming takeover announcements. Top executives in target firms appear to have higher sales and purchases that the top executives in nontarget firms. Alternatively, even if they do exploit this information, they either do not trade in their own names or do not report these transactions. Consequently we can state confidently that the predictive ability of insiders documented in this book does not arise because of insider trading prior to takeover announcements.[8]

How do we interpret these findings? Overall, our evidence suggests that top executives do not exploit proprietary information preceding takeover announcements. As we discussed earlier in this book, the U.S. Congress has passed two important pieces of legislation that have significantly increased the penalties for insider trading. There are (1) the Insider Trading Sanctions Act of 1984 and (2) the Insider Trading and

Securities Fraud Enforcement Act of 1988. Together these two pieces of legislation have increased the maximum prison sentences upon conviction for insider trading to ten years, increased criminal fines to $1 million, authorized the SEC to impose treble damages, introduced bounty payments to third parties who report insider trading, and enabled third parties who lose to insiders to bring civil suits against insiders. In addition improvements in market surveillance have made it easier for the Securities and Exchange Commission to detect illegal insider trading. Consequently it would be highly unusual if top executives were trading prior to takeover announcements or earnings announcements. Trading prior to these important corporate events would simply invite costly legal problems, if not heavy fines and possibly lengthy prison sentences.

So far the evidence suggests that insider trading cannot be used to predict the probability of a takeover attempt for a given firm.[9] How about after the takeover is announced? Using insider trading, can we predict the *success* of the target firms following the announcement. The evidence we have seen so far suggests that the answer to this second question is probably also negative. Nevertheless, it is helpful to directly examine this issue.

To gain additional insights into insider-trading behavior prior to takeover announcements, we sort the probability of success of the target firms by the prior insider-trading activity. We sort the overall sample into three groups, insider-buying, no-insider-trading, and insider-selling groups. To place a firm in a given category, we add all shares traded by insiders during a 12-month period preceding the takeover attempt. If the sum of all shares traded is positive, we place the firm in buy category. If the sum of all shares traded is negative, we place the firm in the sell category. If the sum is zero, we place the firm in no-trade category.

Our sample contains more firms with insider selling than insider buying (table 11.7). Of the total sample, 636 firms show a net insider

Table 11.7
Probability of success of the target firms grouped by prior insider trading

	Number of firms	Probability of success
Insiders buy shares during the 12 months prior to takeover attempt	636	89%
No insider trading	429	86
Insiders sell shares during the 12 months prior to takeover attempt	848	91

buying during the 12 months preceding the takeover attempt. In contrast, 848 firms show insider selling during the 12 months preceding the takeover announcement. A total of 429 firms show no insider-trading activity or where insider purchases exactly equal insider sales.

The probability of success of the target firms is not related to prior insider trading. For the insider-buying group, the probability of success is 89%. For the no-trade group, the probability of success falls to 86%. Finally, for the insider-sell group, the probability of success rises to 91%. Hence there appears to be no relation between prior insider trading and the subsequent probability of the success of the takeover attempt.[10]

If we cannot predict the probability of a takeover attempt or the probability that an announced takeover attempt will be successful, how about the profitability of an announced takeover attempt? Are insiders more likely to buy shares in takeover targets that increase more in price? To address this third question, we next examine whether prior insider trading helps predict the relative performance of the target firms.

The evidence suggests that the target firms purchased by insiders during the preceding 12 months do not outperform the target firms sold by insiders (table 11.8). The average announcement-month net returns to takeover targets with prior insider purchases is 20.4%, while the average announcement-month net returns to takeover targets with prior

Table 11.8
Six-month net stock returns in target firms grouped by prior insider trading

	Number of firms	Announcement month net return	6-month net return
Insiders buy shares during the 12 months prior to takeover attempt	636	20.4%	22.6%
No insider trading	429	19.5	18.0
Insiders sell shares during the 12 months prior to takeover attempt	848	22.7	23.1

insider selling is 22.7%. The slightly better performance by the sellers holds up over the next six months as well.

Our evidence so far has shown that insiders refrain from exploiting their special information around corporate takeovers. Three findings support this conclusion. First, insiders are not more likely to buy shares in target firms than in nontarget firms. Consequently it is not possible to use insider-trading information to predict the probability of a takeover attempt. Second, prior insider trading does not predict the probability of success for the target firms. Third, prior insider trading does not predict the relative subsequent performance of the target firms.

While we have examined the trading behavior of all insiders, the most informed group of insiders are likely to be the top executives group. Do top executives exploit their knowledge about the take-over attempt? To help answer this question, we also restrict our attention to top executives only. Once again the number of sellers exceeds the number of buyers. On average, top executives are not buying the stock of their firms (table 11.9). Second, there is hardly any difference in either announcement month returns or the six-month returns based on top executive trading activity. Hence top executives also restrain themselves from exploiting the takeover information.[11]

Table 11.9
Six-month net stock returns in target firms grouped by prior trading by top executives

	Number of Firms	Announcement month net return	6-month net return
Top executives buy shares during the 12 months prior to takeover attempt	226	20.2%	21.4%
No trading by top executives	1,344	21.5	22.4
Top executives sell shares during the 12 months prior to takeover attempt	343	21.0	19.9

Conclusions and investment implications

In this chapter we have examined the stock price reactions to corporate takeover announcements. We have also examined for potential signals to predict the probability of takeover attempts using prior stock price drifts. In addition we have explored the possibility of whether prior insider trading can predict the likelihood of a takeover, the probability of a success of an announced takeover, or the profitability of an announced takeover event. Our findings are as follows:

1. Targets of corporate takeover experience large increases in stock price. On average, stock prices of takeover targets increase between 20% and 30%. In successful targets the price increases are permanent. In unsuccessful targets prices drop back to pre-takeover levels. Shareholders win if the takeover attempt is successful. Shareholders do not lose if the takeover attempt is unsuccessful.

2. Stock prices of target firms drift up prior to takeover announcements. Approximately one-fifth of the total stock price reaction occurs before the takeover announcement. Stock prices of successful targets show greater drifts than the stock prices of unsuccessful targets.

3. The evidence suggests that the pre-announcement drifts are not due to insider trading. Whether insiders are buying or selling, the pre-announcement stock price drifts seem to be about the same. Instead, evidence suggests that investors update takeover probabilities using publicly available information such as developments in the industry, newspaper reports, disclosure of the firms' financial conditions, and 13-D filings.

4. Insiders in target firms do not systematically exploit the takeover announcement. Insiders do not buy shares of the takeover targets compared to a nontarget sample.

5. Pre-announcement insider trading cannot be used to predict the probability of the takeover attempt.

6. Following an announcement of a takeover attempt, prior insider trading cannot be used to predict the probability that the attempt will be successful.

7. Insider trading prior to the takeover announcement is not useful in predicting the relative performance of the target firms following the announcement. In fact target firms sold by insiders during the pre-announcement period have slightly higher announcement and post-announcement excess returns.

8. Overall evidence suggests that insiders refrain from using their special information to exploit stock price changes around corporate takeovers. Consequently it is quite difficult to use insider-trading information to outperform other market participants around corporate takeovers. This finding is most likely due to stiff sanctions insiders face as well as the relative ease of detection.

12 *Insider trading in bidder firms*

How do bidder firms fare in takeovers?

In the previous chapter we examined the stock price performance of the target firms and whether insider trading helps predict the likelihood of a takeover attempt and the profitability of investing in target firms' stock. In this chapter we focus our attention on bidder firms. Once again we are interested in similar issues regarding the bidder firms. How well do the bidder firms fare in corporate takeovers? Do insiders in bidder firms exploit the information about the takeover attempt? Can insider trading in bidder firms be used to help predict the probability of success and the subsequent stock price performance of the bidder firms? These are the issues we turn to next.

The finance literature has produced evidence that shows that bidder firms do not perform terribly well in corporate takeovers.[1] On average, the bidder firms neither gain nor lose as a result of making a takeover attempt. The stock prices of the bidder firms do not change very much as compared with the pre-announcement stock price.

There are several reasons why bidder firms do not perform as well as the target firms. First, bidder firms are much bigger than target firms. In a typical takeover, especially during the 1970s and the early 1980s, the bidder firm could be ten times the size of the target firm. Consequently, even if the bidder and target firms share the dollar gains evenly, the net benefit to the bidder firms would still be much smaller as a proportion of the size of the bidder firm.

Second, it seems that bidder firms are forced through competition to offer most of the benefits of synergy, through a higher offer price to the shareholders of the target firms. Often the special resource lies with the target firm and any number of potential bidder firms can unlock the synergy. In hostile takeovers potential bidder firms compete with each to acquire the target firm by driving the bid price successively higher. If, as a result of competition, bidder managers end up overpaying for the target firm, then bidder shareholders can experience a wealth loss as a result of the takeover. In some cases bidder firms have experienced stock price declines on announcement of the takeover bids, which suggests that at least some market participants believe that the bidder managers are paying too much. As more hostile takeover attempts have occurred in the 1980s, the average returns to the bidder firms on takeover announcement days has declined and even turned negative.

Third, the Williams Act of 1968 requires that bidder firms file a 13-D statement with the Securities and Exchange Commission within ten days of acquiring 5% of the target firms stock. These 13-D statements must disclose the identity and the intent of the buyer. Once 13-D statements become public, potential competitors are alerted to the possibility of a takeover. Consequently the stock price of the target firm increases between 3% to 8%.[2] The upper end of this range occurs when the 13-D statement indicates some possibility of change of control as the intent of the acquirer. The mandatory public disclosure makes it more difficult for bidder firms to hide their true intentions and acquire the target's firms stock at pre-acquisition prices, further increasing their acquisition costs. Evidence also suggests that that the takeover markup is unrelated to pre-announcement stock price increases, indicating that leakage causes additional acquisition costs on bidders.[3]

Finally bidder firms frequently announce that they are in the market looking for an acquisition target prior to making one or a series of acquisitions. Alternatively, some bidder firms may raise new funds by arranging for increased lines of credit, selling assets or divisions, raising new debt, or otherwise accumulating large amounts of cash necessary to launch a takeover bid. These activities alert the investing public to the increased probability that the firm may be interested in making an acquisition. Consequently some of the stock price effects for the bidder firms may be incorporated in the bidder firm's stock price prior to the public announcement of the takeover attempt.

In addition to differences in size, increased competition, and changing securities laws that require greater disclosures by the bidder firms, target firms have been developing new and more effective takeover defenses. These defenses include super majority amendments, fair price amendments, dual class recapitalizations, changes in the state of incorporation, targeted share repurchases and poison pills.[4] These new defenses give target firm managers greater leverage to fend off unwanted takeover attempts and increase the costs of acquisitions by bidder firms. As a result bidder firms are forced spend more on legal battles or give up more of the premium to the target firms.

Stock price performance of bidder firms

We begin our analysis by examining the overall characteristics of our sample. Our sample consists of 815 bidders from 1975 to 1992 period (table 12.1). A bidder firm is considered successful if it succeeds in tak-

Table 12.1
Bidder firms, 1975–1992

Total number of bidder firms	815
Proportion successful	79%
Announcement month net return	0.4%
Six-month net return	2.3%

Note: Net stock returns are computed by subtracting the contemporaneous holding period returns to the equally weighted market index.

ing over the target firm whether or not it initiated the takeover process. Of the total of 815 bidders, 644 or 79% are successful.

Announcement month net stock returns for bidder firms as well as the six-month net stock returns are much smaller than those for target firms. The announcement month net stock price reaction is 0.4%, while the six-month net stock returns are 2.3%. Our sample corroborates the results from the finance literature that the bidder firms neither gain much nor lose much from takeovers. Consistent with our earlier interpretations, most if not all of the gains from the takeover goes to the target firms' shareholders.

Next we examine the performance of the bidder firms grouped by the success of the takeover attempt. The reader should keep in mind that the success or failure of the takeover attempt usually takes months to be resolved. There are 642 successful and 173 unsuccessful attempts in our sample. There are small yet detectable differences in the initial stock prices for these two groups. For the eventually successful group, the announcement month net return is 0.7% (table 12.2). For the eventually unsuccessful group, the announcement month net returns are −0.7%. Hence it appears that to some extent, the market participants can tell the differences between successful and unsuccessful takeover

Table 12.2
Insider trading and 6-month net stock returns in bidder firms grouped by the success of the takeover attempt

	Number of firms	Announcement month net return	6-month net return	Insider trading during the past 12 months
Takeover attempt is successful	642	0.7%	2.9%	−1,597
Takeover attempt is unsuccessful	173	−0.7	1.1	−41,168

Note: Net returns are computed by subtracting the holding period returns to the equally weighted market index.

attempts. Looking at the six-month net returns strengthens this interpretation. The six-month net returns for the successful bidders is 2.9%, while the six-month net returns for the unsuccessful bidders is only 1.1%.

It is important to note that the stock price reaction for the successful bidders is greater than the stock price reaction for the unsuccessful bidders. These differences become measurable during the announcement month and they are maintained over a six-month period following the takeover announcement. This evidence suggests that (1) the bidding process is costly and (2) bidder firms can also benefit from the takeovers, especially if the takeover is successful and the combination can achieve synergy.

Do bidder insiders trade prior to the announcement of the takeover attempts? If yes, do they buy or sell shares? Can we use insider trading to predict either the announcement or the success of the takeover attempt?

To shed some light on these issues, we sort the total shares traded by insiders during the 12 months prior to the announcement of the takeover attempt by the success of the takeover. For the successful bidders, insiders sell 1,597 shares. For the unsuccessful bidders, insiders sell 41,168 shares.[5] Hence there is some indication that insiders in unsuccessful takeovers are more pessimistic than the insiders in successful takeovers.

Unfortunately, we cannot conclude on the basis of this evidence that insider trading predicts the success of the bidder firms. This is because table 12.2 is again constructed after the fact. After the takeover is announced and the success of the takeover attempt has been determined, we look back to see how the insiders have traded. To be a useful investment guide, we need to examine the predictive ability of insider trading before the fact. We first need to measure the insider trading, decide if insiders are buying or selling, and then examine the subsequent performance of the bidder firm.

Table 12.3
Pre-announcement stock price drift in takeover bidders

	Net returns	Cumulative net returns
Month −6	0.5%	0.5%
Month −5	0.9	1.4
Month −4	0.9	2.3
Month −3	0.7	3.0
Month −2	0.5	3.5
Month −1	1.4	4.9

Note: Month 0 represents the takeover announcement month. Month −6 is six months prior to the takeover announcement month.

As we discussed earlier, the announcement period and the subsequent six months may not capture all of the stock price changes in the bidder firms. If the market participants anticipate that the bidder firm is about to engage in an acquisition either because of an announcement or cash accumulation by the bidder firms, then some of the price effects may take place prior to public announcements. To get a true picture of the wealth changes for bidder firms, we need to include the pre-announcement period as well.

What are the stock price reactions around takeover announcements? For the six-month-period prior to the announcement of their takeover attempts, the total stock price drift is 4.9% (table 12.3). Hence, most of the stock price effects for the bidder firms appears to occur before the announcement of the takeover attempt. In fact at this time neither the forthcoming announcement nor the identity of the target firm is known by market participants. A second observation is that the pre-announcement stock price drift is pretty evenly distributed over the six-month period. Almost half of the drift occurs during the first half of the six-month period. This finding corroborates our earlier interpretation that the market participants expect an acquisition attempt long before the company actually announces the details.[6]

Once again we take the perspective of a potential stock market investor. The issues that the potential investor would be concerned with relate to the investment opportunities associated with takeovers. What are the wealth effects for the bidder firms? Do the shareholders of the bidder firms benefit or are they hurt by the takeover process?

We have already answered the last question. Evidence presented so far tells us that corporate acquisitions increase the wealth of bidder firms' shareholders. Unlike the target firms, the wealth effects for bidder firms are spread out over a six-month period. Given that there are costs involved, successful bidders have greater wealth increases than unsuccessful bidders. Unsuccessful bidders only pay the costs, and they do not enjoy the synergistic benefits.

Other issues of concern to the potential stock market investor are the following: Given that successful bidders do better, is it possible to predict which bidder firms will be successful? Do insiders exploit their knowledge about the upcoming takeovers? Is it possible to predict the subsequent performance of the bidder firms using the prior insider trading and other publicly available information. We now turn to these issues.

Insider trading in bidder firms

Does prior insider trading in bidder firms help predict the eventual probability of success in bidder firms? If it does, then an outside investor can be more selective in choosing which bidder firms to bet on. Since success is related to better stock price performance, such a strategy would increase the outside investor's return.[7]

The pre-announcement period is taken as the 12 months preceding the takeover announcement month. We have also experimented with a 6-month period as well. There are 220 bidders in which insiders buy stock, 248 bidders with no insider trading, and 360 bidders in which insiders sell stock before the announcement of the takeover attempt (table 12.4).

Table 12.4
Probability of success of the bidder firms grouped by prior inside trading

	Number of firms	Probability of success
Insiders buy shares during the 12 months prior to takeover attempt	220	79%
No insider trading	248	79
Insiders sell shares during the 12 months prior to takeover attempt	360	79

Success of the takeover attempt is not related to the pre-announcement insider trading in bidder firms. Regardless of whether insiders buy, sell, or do not trade, the probability of success is 79%. Hence there is no relation between prior insider trading and the eventual success of the takeover attempt. As an additional test we have also examined the relation between pre-announcement stock price drifts and the probability of success. Once again there is no relation. Bidder firms with no prior drift have a 78% chance of success, while bidder firms with pre-announcement drift have a 79% chance of success.[8]

We next examine whether we can directly predict the subsequent performance of the bidder firms. This is the central question an outside investor would be concerned with. Once again we use prior insider trading and prior stock price drifts as predictor variables.

There is a positive relation between subsequent six-month performance of the bidder firms and pre-announcement insider trading (table 12.5). For the insider-buying group, the announcement month net returns are 0.1% and the 6-month net returns are 6.1%. For the no-insider-trading group, the net returns are 1.1% and 1.2%, respectively. For the insider-selling group, the net returns are 0.2% and 0.8%, respectively.

Insider buying in bidder firms predicts a moderate, subsequent good performance, while insider selling does not predict subsequent nega-

Table 12.5
Six-month net stock returns in bidder firms grouped by prior insider trading

	Number of firms	Announcement month net return	6-month net return
Insiders buy shares during the 12 months prior to takeover attempt	220	0.1%	6.1%
No insider trading	248	1.1	1.2
Insiders sell shares during the 12 months prior to takeover attempt	360	0.2	0.8

Note: Net returns are computed by subtracting the holding period returns to the equally weighted market index.

tive performance. The no-insider-trading group is approximately the same as the overall sample. Overall, the evidence suggests that there is some value to insiders' transactions prior to the takeover announcement. Insider buying is more likely to indicate subsequent good performance by the bidder firm.[9]

Many finance studies have shown that the form of payment for the acquisition can also serve as a signal for the value of the bidder firms. Bidder firms can pay either in cash or in stock. Cash payments subject the target firms' shareholders to an immediate capital gains tax while a stock swap postpones these capital gains. Holding all else constant, cash payments therefore are more costly and would not be used unless they have a countervailing benefit.

To see the benefits of cash payments, assume that bidder managers are better informed about the value of their firm as well as the synergistic benefits of the combination with the target firm than the typical market participants. If bidder managers expect that the stock market is undervaluing the bidder firm, they will have incentives to pay cash for the target firm. By paying cash, the bidder firm avoids sharing the eventual benefits of the synergistic gains with target shareholders. Alternatively, assume that bidder managers believe that the stock price of the bidder firm overvalues its true prospects. In this case the bidder managers have an incentive to pay for the target firm using their own stock. By paying with stock, the bidder firm passes some of the over-valuation costs to shareholders of the target firms.[10]

Obviously target firms' shareholders also understand these arguments. Consequently they will tend to value the cash offers more highly than the stock offers. Moreover market participants will also revise their valuation of the bidder firms based on the type of payment. Cash payments imply higher-valued bidder firms than stock payments.[11]

We have examined the relation between the form of payment and the bidder firms' performance in takeovers. The evidence shows that the firms that pay cash for the target firm tend to do better than those that pay in stock. The 6-month net stock returns are 5.6% and -1.5% for the cash and stock groups, respectively. The 12-month net stock returns are 10.6% and -2.8%, respectively. Hence the evidence supports our conjecture that the form of payment serves as a signal of the value of the bidder firms.

Next we attempt to improve the predictive ability of the insider-trading variable by focusing on more selective insider-trading months. If the insider-trading variable is truly capturing the long-term performance of the bidder firms, then we ought to be able to do better by requiring large transactions by all insiders or large transactions by top executives.

To be considered in the buy or sell category, we now require that insiders buy or sell more than 10,000 share during the previous 12 months. Bidder firms with large insider purchases tend to have a more positive long-term performance than those with large insider selling (table 12.6). Hence, large volume of insider buying does appear to be a good signal regarding the eventual performance of the bidder firm.

We also examine the performance of the bidder firms sorted by large transactions by the top executives. If top executives buy more than

Table 12.6
Six-month net stock returns in bidder firms grouped by prior insider trading

	Number of firms	Announcement month net return	6-month net return
Insiders buy more than 10,000 shares during the 12 months prior to takeover attempt	81	−0.2%	6.3%
Other bidder firms	545	0.7	2.6
Insiders sell more than 10,000 shares during the 12 months prior to takeover attempt	202	−0.2	0.6

Note: Net returns are computed by subtracting the holding period returns to the equally weighted market index.

10,000 shares during the previous 12 months, the bidder firm is classified as a buy firm. If the top executives sell more than 10,000 shares
during the past 12 months, then the bidder firms is classified as a sell
firm. Our first observation from this analysis is that there are not a lot
of firms with large trading by top executives. There are only 13 firms
in the buy category and 68 firms in the sell category (table 12.7). Once
again, top executives do not appear to exploit their information aggressively.

The subsequent performance of bidder firms based on large trading
by top executives is quite similar to the previous results. Bidder firms
in the buy category outperform the market index by about 13.5% over
the six months. Bidder firms in the sell category do not experience
unusual performance. Overall, these finding confirm the earlier conclusion that pre-announcement insider buying constitutes a good signal regarding the eventual stock price performance of the bidder firms.

As a final test we combined our predictive variables. These results
are consistent with our previous findings. Both variables retain their
predictive ability. In addition the subsequent six-month performance
of the bidder can be further improved to 24.5% by requiring both large
buying by top executives and positive pre-announcement run-ups

Table 12.7

Six-month net stock returns in bidder firms grouped by prior trading by top executives

	Number of firms	Announcement month net return	6-month net return
Top executives buy more than 10,000 shares during the 12 months prior to takeover attempt	13	1.1%	13.5%
Other bidder firms	747	0.4	2.3
Top executives sell more than 10,000 shares during the 12 months prior to takeover attempt	68	0.2	0.7

Note: Net returns are computed by subtracting the holding period returns to the equally weighted market index.

(table 12.8). We also included the form of payment as an additional explanatory variable. These tests show that the all three predictors retain their forecasting ability. Moreover the bidder returns can be improved by additional three points by requiring that the form of payment be in cash.

Conclusions and investment implications

In this chapter we have examined the stock price performance of bidder firms. Our tests focus on whether or not an outside investor can predict which firms are likely to be bidder firms, the success of the takeover attempt by the bidder firm, and the relative subsequent performance of the bidder firms. We have used the pre-announcement insider trading, pre-announcement stock price run-ups, and the method of payment as predictor variables to predict the probability of success of the takeover attempt and the eventual stock price performance of the bidders firms. Our findings are as follows:

Table 12.8

Announcement month and the subsequent 6-month net stock returns in bidder firms grouped by prior trading by top executives and whether there is pre-announcement run-up in bidder's stock price

	Without pre-announcement drift	With pre-announcement drift
Top executives buy more than 10,000 shares during the 12 months prior to takeover attempt	−3.1%, +4.1%	6.1%, 24.5%
Other bidder firms	0.6%, 2.9%	0.1%, 2.0%
Top executives sell more than 10,000 shares during the 12 months prior to takeover attempt	−1.2%, −2.2%	1.5%, 3.4%

Note: Net returns are computed by subtracting the holding period returns to the equally weighted market index. If the 6-month pre-announcement net stock returns are positive, then a bidder is classified as a firm with run-up.

1. Bidder firms do not experience large stock price changes when the takeover is announced. During the announcement month, the stock price of the bidder firms outperforms the market index only by 0.4% which is not significant. During a six-month period including the announcement month, bidder firms outperform the market index only by 2.4%.

2. The identity of many bidder firms is most likely to be known by market participants prior to the announcement of the takeover attempt. As a result most of the stock price movement occurs prior to public announcement of the takeover. Bidder firms experience a run-up of almost 5.0% during the six-months prior to the takeover announcement.

3. Successful bidders appear to do better than the unsuccessful bidders. During the announcement month, successful bidders show a gain of

0.7%, while unsuccessful bidders experience a loss of 0.7%. This finding suggests that there are costs to making an acquisition. If the bidder firms do not succeed, they are stuck with the costs and do not enjoy the synergistic benefits of the takeover.

4. It is very difficult to predict which bidder firms are likely to succeed in their takeover attempts. Insider buying prior to the announcement of the takeover does not predict the eventual success of the takeover attempt. Pre-announcement stock price run-ups also do not predict the relative success of the bidder firms.

5. Insider buying prior to the announcement of the takeover attempt does predict the subsequent stock price performance of the bidder firms. Firms purchased by insiders outperform the market index by about 6%.

6. Large insider buying prior to the takeover attempt provides an especially good signal regarding the eventual performance of the bidder firms. Bidder firms whose top executives buy 10,000 shares or more during the 12-months prior to the announcement of the takeover outperform the market index by 13%.

7. Other predictors of the subsequent performance of the bidder firms include the pre-announcement stock price run-ups and the method of payment. The best performing bidder firms are those with large insider buying especially by top executives before the announcement, firms with a pre-announcement stock price run-ups, and firms that pay cash to their targets.

13   *Momentum and mean reversion*

Trend investing

We have already analyzed the performance of the price-earnings ratios and book-to-market ratios in chapters 9 and 10. These strategies involve identifying undervalued assets whose current stock prices are below their true fundamental values. In value-based investing it is assumed that firm's underappreciated earning capacity or its underappreciated assets on the balance sheet will exert a dominant influence on the future stock price. We have already seen that both of these approaches are successful in predicting the direction of future stock price changes.

In this chapter we will examine two more investment styles. These are based not on estimating the fundamental value of the stock, but on stock price trends.[1] Consequently we call these *trend-based investment styles*. We will analyze two trend-based investment styles. The first investment style is called momentum investing, which simply states that stock prices continue to change in the same direction. If stock prices have been increasing in the recent past, they will keep increasing for a while. If stock prices have been decreasing, they will keep decreasing for a while.

The logic of the momentum investing approach is that the market participants cannot instantaneously analyze, digest, and cope with all the information available about the stocks. Because of differences in costs of accessing and analyzing information, some investors catch on early, others catch on late. The consequent slow progression of information gives rise to a momentum in stock prices. The usual time frame for momentum investing is one year or less. For instance, if a firm suddenly reports sharply higher earnings, it takes different market participants different amounts of time to sort out whether this is a temporary or a permanent increase, whether it is genuinely due to improving business conditions or window dressing due to sale of assets or reduction in research and development. This slow progression of information then gives rise to a slowly increasing stock prices.[2] This strategy maintains that investors should buy stocks that have recently increased in price and hold them for about a year. Similarly investors should sell stocks that have recently decreased in price and avoid them for about a year.

Another investment style is mean-reversion or contrarian investing. This investment style states that investors sometimes get carried away with their emotions and bid stock prices up or down more than justified. Consequently stocks with extreme performances tend to revert back to normal over a longer time period. Extreme winners tend to lose some of their luster. Extreme losers bounce back to some extent. The usual time frame for mean reversion investing is between one to five years. This strategy maintains that investors should buy stocks that have posted extreme losses over the past one to five years and be prepared to hold them over the next one to five years. Similarly investors should sell stocks that have posted extreme gains over the past one to five years and be prepared to avoid them over the next one to five years.[3]

In this chapter we will analyze in detail the performance of both of these investment approaches. Is it possible for recent stock price trends to predict future movements in stock prices? If so, what is the magnitude of the predicted future returns? We will also examine some alternative explanations for the stock price predictability based on trends.

Finally we will bring in insider-trading information and examine the interaction between insider-trading information and trend investment styles.

Alternative explanation for stock price trends

An alternative scenario maintains that the predictability of the future stock prices arises from variations in risk premiums over time. These variations can be due to changes in the risk level of the economy or due to changes in demand for funds.[4] When the level of risk is high, the required compensation for holding risky assets will also be high. Alternatively, when the economy is strong and the demand for funds is high, the required risk premium will also be high to induce investors to save and invest in risky ventures rather than consume immediately. These stories suggest that the required compensation for bearing risk is not constant but varies slowly over time. Consequently periods of higher expected returns tend to be followed by similarly high expected returns. During these times, both stocks and bonds will earn higher-than-historical-average returns. The stock return patterns produced under this scenario will also have trends, that is, periods of persistent high or low returns.

An example should make our point clearer. For instance, during the early part of 1980, short-term interest rates rose over 20% due to high inflation and stayed high for a while. Most investors would probably not regard this high interest rate as a great bond buying opportunity. Interest rates on corporate and government bonds were high because the expected inflation rate was high. Similarly expected stock returns must also be high due to the high expected inflation. Therefore this second scenario argues that high expected stock returns can represent compensation for bearing higher risk. Moreover periods of high stock returns are followed by future periods of high stock returns, not because of mispricing of stocks but because the required compensation for bearing risk tends to change slowly.

While these two stories present sharply contrasting alternative views, there are not necessarily mutually exclusive. It is possible that both factors contribute to predictability of stock returns. For instance, when a supply shock increases the risks in the economy, expected stock and bond returns must rise due to the higher risks. In addition, if investors overreact to bad news and drive the security prices below fundamental values, then expected stock returns would be even higher as some of the mispricing is corrected in the future. Hence both stories predict higher expected stock returns followed by higher average stock returns. To be fair to both camps, it is difficult to distinguish between these two stories. They have similar predictions and thus the evidence that the stock returns are predictable does not help us decide why they are predictable.

A second problem in distinguishing between these alternative scenarios is that we cannot even be sure that there is genuine predictability. To measure the predictability of stock returns accurately, we need a lot of independent data, which we don't have. For instance, even if we use 70 years of data, it still does not give us sufficient sample of independent returns. If we are interested in five-year predictability, then 70 years of data provide us with only 14 nonoverlapping five-year periods which is not enough to make accurate statements about predictability. A single unusual event such as the stock market crash of 1929, followed by additional negative returns during the Great Depression years can give the appearance of significant predictability even if this was a chance event.

A third measurement problem is the survival bias. By necessity we tend to work with stock market data, which has to survive wars, revolutions, and severe crashes. It is true that the U.S. stock market has survived the Civil War, two World Wars, and the Great Depression. The fact that the U.S. market has survived these potentially catastrophic events itself creates the mean reversions in the data. If the U.S. market had not survived, we would have simply observed the stock price declines and the closing of the market without the bounce-backs. Hence mean reversion occurs because the market has survived. If we were to examine the returns to the markets that did not survive, the mean reversion would not be as strong.[5] Hence we need to be cautious in interpreting the stock return patterns in the light of these caveats.[6]

The previous discussion suggests that it is difficult to settle the question of predictability with logical arguments or even with empirical evidence. Nevertheless, let's look at the data. By bringing insider trading into the picture, we can get a clearer view of whether insiders regard these patterns in the return data as profit opportunities. We also promise not to overinterpret our findings. What do the data show? Do past price patterns predict future movements in stock prices? What is the predictability for holding periods less than one year? What is the predictability for holding periods up to five or ten years?

The evidence from finance literature shows that over short horizons up to one year, stock prices exhibit positive momentum. High stock returns tend to be followed by high stock returns and low stock returns tend to be followed by low stock returns for this horizon. Looking at longer-term horizons, the patterns reverse and stock returns tend to exhibit mean reversion. These reversals tend to be strongest over a five-year horizon. During these long horizons, periods of high stock returns tend to be followed by periods of low stock returns and vice versa.

Our objective in this chapter is first to re-examine the predictability of future stock returns using past stock returns. We will analyze the stock returns from the last 20 years from 1975 to 1994 for evidence of predictability. Using a recent time period is also intended to separate out the influence of earlier data. We will examine both short-horizon (one-year-ahead stock returns) and long-horizon returns up to three years ahead.

Second, we will examine the relation between insider trading and past stock returns. We would like to know whether insiders think about past movements in stock prices as a profit opportunity or as a risk factor. In addition we would like to find out whether both past returns and insider trading remain as a predictor of future stock returns when we control for both variables.

Short-horizon predictability

We begin by examining predictability of stock returns for holding periods up to one year. Given the intuitive approach this book takes, we will investigate the predictability of stock returns using a winners and losers approach. We can restate the evidence from the finance literature in terms of winners and losers as follows: The short-term predictability results suggest that winners during the past year continue to enjoy higher than average stock returns over the next year. Losers during the past year continue to suffer from below average stock returns over the next year. First, let's find out if this pattern is still present in a recent time period from 1975 to 1994. Next, we will establish the strength of this relation.

To begin, we define winners and losers as follows: First, every month, we compute the holding period returns for the last 3, 6, and 12 months for each stock as well as the equally weighted market index. We subtract the holding period return for the equally weighted market index of NYSE, AMEX, and NASDAQ stocks from the holding period return for the stock, to compute a net return. If the stock outperforms the market index by 20% or more, we consider it a winner. If the stock underperforms the market index by 20% or more, we consider it a loser. We move ahead one month at a time, and repeat this procedure.[7]

We investigate the subsequent performance of winners and losers using the 20% cutoff over 3-month, 6-month, and 12-month holding periods. When we examine 3-month predictability, we define winners and losers from the immediately preceding 3-month period. Similarly, when we examine 6-month or the 12-month predictability, we define winners and losers from the immediately preceding 6-month and 12-month periods, respectively.

Table 13.1
Subsequent net stock returns grouped by winners and losers

Last year's	Subsequent 3-month net return	Subsequent 6-month net return	Subsequent 12-month net return
Winners	0.3%	2.5%	3.2%
	(159,757)	(218,533)	(257,716)
Losers	−1.1	−2.5	−0.9
	(184,966)	(291,437)	(383,131)

Note: Net returns are computed by subtracting the holding period returns to the equally weighted market index. Winners are those firms that outperform the market index by at least 20% during the prior 3, 6, or 12 months. Losers are outperformed by the market by at least 20% during the prior 3, 6, or 12 months. The numbers in parentheses are the number of observations in each group.

Our data set contains 184,966 losers and 159,757 winners over the past three months (table 13.1). The losers outnumber the winners given our definition. Moreover, as we increase our holding period, the losers outnumber the winners by even a larger margin. For the 6-month holding period, losers outnumber the winners by 291,437 to 218,533. For the 12-month holding period, losers outnumber the winners by 383,131 to 257,716. In addition the total observations increase as we increase our holding periods. This is because as the holding period increases, there is a greater chance that a given stock return will deviate from the market return by more than 20%, therefore qualifying to be on the winners and losers list.

The fact that losers outnumber the winners is an outcome of a statistical artifact rather than an economic phenomenon. Individual stock returns exhibit what is called right-skewness, which is a statistical term to describe the fact that biggest negative stock returns are bounded by −100%, while there is no upper limit for the biggest positive stock returns. By definition, the most an investor can lose in stocks is all of the investment, giving a return of −100%. However, there is no upper limit to positive returns. Investors can enjoy returns of 200%, 1,000%, or even more. Hence extremely large stock returns must by definition be positive returns rather than negative returns. A necessary implication of this phenomenon is that a few very large, positive returns to some stocks increase the average return for the benchmark equally weighted market index above the return for a typical firm. Hence the average holding period return to the index will be greater than the holding period return than most of the stocks.[8]

Our evidence corroborates what most finance studies have found. Stock prices do exhibit positive momentum over the short term. Past winners continue to outperform the market index, while past losers continue to lag the market index. Looking at the 3-month horizon, the net returns to winners over the past 3-months are 0.3%. Thus the past winners continue to outperform the market index by a small amount. For the losers the net returns over the past 3 months are −1.1%. Thus losers continue to underperform the market index. Hence both winners and losers exhibit positive momentum over a 3-month period. The difference between the winners and losers equals 1.4 points.

Let's examine the longer holding periods. Remember that the 6-month-ahead net returns to winners and losers classified on the basis of the previous 6-month returns. These winners experience a net return of 2.5% while these losers experience a net return of −2.5% (table 13.1, column 2). Hence a 6-month momentum is even stronger than the 3-month momentum for both winners and losers. The difference between the winners and losers grows to 5.0 points.

At the 12-month horizon, momentum is still present, albeit weaker than before. The 12-month-ahead net return to winners is now 3.2%, while the 12-month-ahead net return to losers is −0.9% (table 13.1, column 3). Hence over a 12-month horizon the momentum for winners gets stronger while the momentum for losers begins to weaken. The difference between the winners and losers declines to 4.1 points.

To summarize our findings so far, using 3-month, 6-month, and 12-month horizons, both past winners and losers exhibit positive momentum. Our results indicate that the positive momentum starts fairly modestly at 3-month horizon. The positive momentum is strongest at about 6 months and once again begins to show some signs of weakness over the 12-month horizon.

Earlier in this chapter we discussed a couple of potential stories for the predictability of stock returns. The evidence presented so far is consistent with both the mispricing and risk stories and does not help us distinguish between them. It would be interesting to find out corporate insiders' reaction to this predictability. If past winners continue to outperform the market index because they are underpriced, then we would expect the corporate insiders to buy these stocks. Similarly, if past losers continue to lag behind the market index because they are overpriced, then we would expect the corporate insiders to sell these stocks. On the other hand, if the positive momentum is being driven due to risk factors, we would not expect insiders to be trading on the basis of these patterns.

We examine the relation between insider trading, past winners and losers, and the subsequent 12-month stock price performance next. For these tests we focus on the 12-month horizons. Once again we replicated our analysis using 3-month and 6-month periods as well. The results are similar and therefore are not shown separately. Insider trading is measured over the same 12 months during which net returns are computed. If the total number of shares traded by insiders over the past 12 months is positive, then that firm is grouped into buy category. If the total number of shares traded by insiders over the past 12 months is negative, then that firm is grouped into sell category.

The evidence does not suggest that insiders view the predictability of returns over a 12-month horizon as a profit opportunity. If they did, we would have expected insiders to buy past winners and sell past losers. Instead, insiders do the opposite. In the winner group, there are 23,864 purchases against 45,742 sales (table 13.2). Hence sales outnumber purchases by 2 to 1. In the loser group, there are 39,498 purchases and 37,630 sales. Hence purchases slightly exceed the sales. This

Table 13.2
Subsequent net stock returns grouped by winners and losers and insider trading

Last year's	Insiders buy	No insider trades	Insiders sell
Winners	8.4%	3.2%	0.4%
	(23,864)	(188,110)	(45,742)
Losers	2.4	−0.6	−6.7
	(39,498)	(306,003)	(37,630)

Note: Net returns are computed by subtracting the holding period returns to the equally weighted market index. Winners are those firms that outperform the market index by at least 20% during the prior 12 months. Losers are outperformed by the market by at least 20% during the prior 12 months. The numbers in parentheses are the number of observations in each group.

evidence suggests that insider trading is *not* motivated by the expectations of positive momentum carrying into the next year.

We also examine the subsequent 12-month-ahead performance of winners and losers sorted by insider-trading activity. The evidence indicates that insider trading and past winners and losers exert independent influences on future stock returns. Moreover using both insider trading and past winner-loser status improves the predictability of stock returns.

Let's first examine table 13.2 by columns, which helps us focus on the predictive ability of winner-loser status holding insider trading constant. Holding insider purchases constant, for winners, stock prices outperform the equally weighted market index by 8.4% over the next year. When insiders buy past losers, losers outperform the market index by 2.4%. The difference between the winners and losers now grows to 6.0 points from 4.1 points (table 13.1, column 3). Hence, after taking into account the insider-trading status, the predictive ability of past winners and losers increases.

Holding insiders' sales constant, for winners, stock prices outperform the equally weighted market index by 0.4% over the next year (table

13.2, column 3). When insiders sell past losers, they underperform the market index by 6.7%. The difference between the winners and losers now grows to 7.1 points from 4.1 points. Once again, taking into account the insider-trading status, the predictive ability of past winners and losers almost doubles.

Finally the middle column shows the predictive ability of past winners and losers when there is no insider trading. These results are very similar to unconditional results. Winner-loser status predicts future stock returns and the magnitude is 3.8 points, comparable to the 4.1 points (table 13.1).

Let us now examine table 13.2 by rows. Looking at table 13.2 separately by rows can help clarify the information content of insider trading after controlling for the past winners and loser status. Looking at the table 13.2 by rows shows that insider buying always produces higher net returns than insider selling. For the first row, holding past winner status constant, insider buying gives 8.4% compared with 0.4% for insider selling. This is a difference of 8.0 points. For the second row, holding the past loser status constant, insider buying gives 2.4% compared with −6.7% for insider selling. This is a difference of 9.1 points. Hence the insider-trading variable retains its predictive power after we control for past winners and losers.

This evidence corroborates our findings from earlier chapters in this book. As usual, insider trading provides a strong, independent signal of value. For instance, the positive signal from insider buying dominates the negative signal from past loser status. When combined, the past losers bought by insiders outperform the market index by 2.4% over the next 12 months instead of lagging the market index.

We next examine whether we can further outweigh the information content of the past winners and losers by focusing on more selective insider-trading months. This will also help us determine whether momentum or mean reversions reflect a profit opportunity for outsiders. To this end we examine large volume of insider trading as well as the

Table 13.3
Subsequent net stock returns grouped by winners and losers and insider trading

Last year's	Insiders buy 1,000 shares or more	Insiders sell 1,000 shares or more
Winners	9.5%	−0.3%
	(11,253)	(36,761)
Losers	3.4	−7.8
	(22,177)	(28,303)

Note: Net returns are computed by subtracting the holding period returns to the equally weighted market index. Winners are those firms that outperform the market index by at least 20% during the prior 12 months. Losers are outperformed by the market by at least 20% during the prior 12 months. The numbers in parentheses are the number of observations in each group.

trading by top executives. Our purpose is to establish whether we can increase the predictive ability of both past winner-loser status as well insider trading by taking both factors into account.

To qualify as a purchase period, we now require that insiders to have purchased 1,000 or greater shares over the past 12 months. To qualify as a sale period, we also require that insider sell 1,000 or a greater number of shares over the past 12 months. Our evidence suggests that insider act as if the profit opportunities are associated with mean reversions. Evidence indicates that insiders are heavy sellers of past winners rather than past losers (table 13.3). Once again insiders do not appear to be exploiting short-term positive momentum in stock prices. Instead, both insider trading and past winner-loser status provide independent signals. Focusing only on large volume transactions further corroborates this conclusion. Large volume insider trading increases the information content of insider trading. In addition the information content of past winners and losers is also increased when we control for insider trading.

To isolate the information content of insider trading, let's first examine table 13.3 row by row. Looking at the winners' row, insider buys are associated with significantly higher future returns than insider sales. The difference between net returns to insider buying and selling reaches 9.8 points. Looking at the losers' row, insider buys are again associated with significantly higher future returns than insider sales. The difference between net returns to insider buying and selling now equal 11.2 points. Hence, after we control for past winner and loser status, the information content of insider trading is maintained.

To isolate the information content of past winners and losers, we examine table 13.3 column by column. Looking at the first column controls for insider buying. Holding insider buying constant, we see that winners outperform losers by 6.1 points. While both winners and losers outperform the market, winners do so by 6.1 points over the losers. Hence there is still positive momentum. Looking at the second column controls for insiders selling. Holding insider selling constant, winners outperform losers by about 7.5%. This time both winners and losers lag the market index. However, winners lag the market index to a lesser degree than the losers, thereby again exhibiting positive momentum. Hence once again the information content of winners and losers is maintained after we control for insider trading.

Both insider trading and past winner-loser status provide useful signals, while insider trading provides stronger predictive ability. With large insider trading an outside investor cannot simply rely on past winner and loser status to buy or sell stocks. If there is large insider buying, past losers in fact outperform the market index instead of trailing the market. Hence a past loser status is not sufficient to sell the stock if there is large insider buying. Similarly past winners underperform the market index if there is large insider selling. Hence a past winner status is not sufficient to buy the stock if there is large insider selling.

Finally we use top executives' transactions to provide even stronger insider-trading signals. Here we attempt to see if using stronger insider-trading signals can further influence the information content of winners and losers. These results are qualitatively similar to those by all insiders. There is an important difference, however. As the strength of

Table 13.4
Subsequent net stock returns grouped by winners and losers and trading by top executives

Last year's	Top executives buy	No trades by top executives	Top executives sell
Winners	9.9%	3.3%	−0.3%
	(4,772)	(238,598)	(14,346)
Losers	6.9	−1.0	−7.3
	(9,264)	(364,924)	(8,943)

Note: Net returns are computed by subtracting the holding period returns to the equally weighted market index. Winners are those firms that outperform the market index by at least 20% during the prior 12 months. Losers are outperformed by the market by at least 20% during the prior 12 months. The numbers in parentheses are the number of observations in each group.

the insider trading signal increases, it begins to attenuate the predictive ability of past winner-loser status.

Let's first examine all transactions by top executives. Once again, top executives tend to sell winners relatively more heavily than they sell the losers (table 13.4). Trading by top executives strongly predicts future stock returns. For instance, for winners, the predictive ability of insider trading equals 10.2 points (9.9% minus −0.3%). For losers, the predictive ability of insider trading increases to 14.2 points (6.9% minus −7.3%). A second observation is that stronger insider-trading signals from top executives' transactions do begin to attenuate the predictive ability of past winner-loser status. For instance, for the insider-buying group, the past returns predict only a 3.0 point differential between winners and losers (9.9% minus 6.9%). For the insider-selling group, the past returns predict 7.0-point differential between winners and losers (−0.3% minus −7.3%).

Our strongest evidence is obtained by looking at large transactions by top executives. These results further strengthen and corroborate earlier results. Once again, trading by top executives strongly predicts future stock returns (table 13.5). For instance, for winners, the predictive

Table 13.5

Subsequent 12-month net stock returns grouped by winners and losers and insider trading

Last year's	Top executives buy 1,000 shares or more	Top executives sell 1,000 shares or more
Winners	12.2%	−0.7%
	(1,963)	(12,546)
Losers	10.9	−8.0
	(5,004)	(7,356)

Note: Net returns are computed by subtracting the holding period returns to the equally weighted market index. Winners are those firms that outperform the market index by at least 20% during the prior 12 months. Losers are outperformed by the market by at least 20% during the prior 12 months. The numbers in parentheses are the number of observations in each group.

ability of insider trading equals 12.9 points (12.2% minus −0.7%). For losers, the predictive ability of insider trading increases to 18.9 points (10.9% minus −8.0%). For past winner-loser status, the predictive ability further declines. For insider-buying group, the past returns predict only a 1.3 point differential between winners and losers (12.2% minus 10.9%). For insider-selling group, the past returns predict 7.3-point differential between winners and losers (−0.7% minus −8.0%).

What do these results mean? One interpretation of the results presented so far is that most of the predictive ability of past winners and losers is due to movements in the required compensation for risk bearing. As a result both everyday insider trading and past winner-loser status maintain their predictive ability when we control for both variables. However, the results also do not rule out the possibility that there may also be some overreactions present. Our evidence for the top executives' transactions suggest that when there is significant mispricing, top executives take this mispricing into account when they trade large volumes of stock. Hence both past winner-loser status and top executive trading captures the same mispricing. Consequently, when we take both factors into account, the predictive ability of the past stock returns is attenuated.

Long-horizon predictability

So far we have been concerned with predictability of stock returns up to one year. We now examine the long-horizon stock price patterns for our sample period of January 1975 to December 1994. Previous studies in finance have found that stock returns exhibit mean reversion over a three- to ten-year horizon. Mean reversion simply means that stock returns revert back to historical means. Past winners underperform the market index. Hence winners revert down to market average over the next three to ten years. Past losers outperform the market index. Hence once again losers revert up to market averages over the next three to ten years.

There is some evidence that suggests that mean reversion is especially strong if we look back to the last 70 years, including the decade of 1920s. However, this long period includes the strong bull markets of the 1920s, which are immediately followed by the crash of 1929 and the lean years of the Great Depression. Hence any finding of mean reversion over this long period would be strongly influenced with this historical pattern of strongly positive returns followed by strongly negative returns. Whether mean reversion holds during more recent periods is a topic we will examine here specifically.

The finding of long-horizon mean-reverting stock returns is again consistent with two opposing interpretations: One story suggests that over the long run, stock prices overreact to some good and bad news. Moreover these overreactions are corrected over long horizons as most market participants realize the fundamental values of the stocks. For instance, suppose that a given firm is going through some financial difficulties. If the market participants overreact to such a bad news, then the stock price of this firm will decline by more that it is justified by the fundamentals. In this situation the firm fundamental earning capacity would be better than suggested by the current low stock price. Over the next five years or so, we would expect this firm to perform better than expected. Given a long track record of better than expected earnings, the stock prices should rebound. This pattern of large stock price declines followed by large stock price increases gives rise to mean reversion.

A similar scenario can be constructed with good news: Suppose that most market participants are overly enthusiastic about the commercial prospects of the Internet, which is a global computer network linking universities, businesses and individuals. In this case market participants could bid up the prices of firms such as Netscape, which sells software to help navigate the Internet. Let us presume that this overenthusiasm pushed up Netscape's stock price to levels unjustified by the fundamentals. For instance, after going public on August 9, 1995, at an adjusted price of \$14, Netscape stock was selling at \$72 on February 7, 1996. Following the initial listing, Netscape price soared more than 500% to \$85.50 (on December 5, 1995), before falling to \$72, which still translated to a price-earnings multiple of more than 20,000. Clearly market participants expect an absolutely great performance from Netscape over the next few years.[9] Otherwise, they would not have bid up the stock price of Netscape to such lofty levels. If Netscape does not perform in line with these great expectations over the next five years or so, then its stock prices should significantly underperform the market index. Hence large positive stock returns would be followed by large negative stock returns, once again giving rise to mean reversion.

The second story of mean reversion is based on changes in risk. This story suggests that the shocks to risk, and therefore the risk premium itself, are mean reverting. An unanticipated increase in the risk of a given stock lowers its current stock price and increases its expected future stock returns. Over the next five years or so, this additional risk dissipates and the stock returns will revert down to normal levels. Hence this story also predicts that large negative returns will be followed by above-average positive returns, and vice versa. However, in this case, it is the slow movements in firm-specific risk premium that gives rise to the mean-reverting behavior of stock returns. Once again it is difficult to separate these two alternative views. We need to examine the reaction of the insiders to large past stock price movements in an attempt to distinguish between these alternative views.

We begin by documenting the magnitude of the long-horizon mean reversion behavior in stock returns. Starting in January 1975, we look at the past five years of holding period returns for each stock. To classify firms into winners and losers, we chose a benchmark performance level of 50%. We chose a higher benchmark rate for long-horizon tests, since the longer holding period will show many more firms with large positive and negative returns. We have also experimented with a 100% cutoff level. These results are similar, and therefore they are not shown separately.

Given our definition above, we classify a firm as a winner if its stock price outperforms the equally weighted market index by 50% or more. If its stock price underperforms the equally weighted market index by 50% or more, we classify it as a loser. We repeat this procedure for all stocks in our sample. We then look forward to subsequent one-year, two-year, and three-year horizons to see how past winners and losers fare over the long run. We move forward one month and repeat this analysis.

Our sample contains 128,625 instances of winners and 243,335 instances of losers (table 13.6). Once again, as we explained earlier, the fact that losers outnumber the winners is an outcome of a statistical artifact known as right skewness rather than an economic phenomenon. Over longer holding periods, right skewness becomes more important, thereby increasing the frequency of losers over winners.

Our evidence corroborates the findings of previous studies in finance that stock prices exhibit mean reversion over the long run. Past winners seem to be doing worse than the equally weighted market index, while the past losers do significantly better than the equally weighted

Table 13.6
Subsequent net stock returns grouped by winners and losers

Last 5 years	Number of observations	Subsequent 1-year net return	Subsequent 2-year net return	Subsequent 3-year net return
Winners	128,625	1.2%	−0.2%	−1.1%
Losers	243,335	1.9	8.7	17.1

Note: Net returns are computed by subtracting the holding period returns to the equally weighted market index. Winners are those firms that outperform the market index by at least 50% during the prior 5 years. Losers are outperformed by the market by at least 50% during the prior 5 years.

market index. Over the one-year horizon, there is not much difference in the performance of winners and losers. However, over the subsequent three-year horizons, the winners underperform the equally weighted index by 1.1%, while the losers outperform the equally weighted index by an amazing 17.1%. The evidence suggests that the short-horizon positive momentum dissipates at about the one year mark and turns into mean reversion. Moreover the magnitude of the mean reversion gets stronger with the increasing holding period.[10]

Next we bring in the insider-trading variable. Once again, similar to the short-horizon winners and losers, insiders are more likely to sell past winners and buy past losers (table 13.7). Insiders are more than twice as likely to sell long-term winners as they are likely to buy long-term winners. In contrast, selling exceeds buying only by a small margin for the long-term losers.

Examining table 13.7 by columns shows that after we control for insider trading, long-horizon mean reversion still holds. Looking at the first column, holding insider buying constant, long-term losers outperform long-term winners by 22.1 points over the next three years. For the second column, given no insider trading, long-term losers outperform the long-term winners by 20.9 points over the next three years. Finally, looking at the third column, holding insider selling constant, long-term losers outperform long-term winners by 12.2 points over the

Table 13.7
Subsequent 3-year net stock returns grouped by winners and losers and insider trading

Last 5 years	Insiders buy	No insider trades	Insiders sell	All firms
Winners	3.0%	−3.7%	−1.9%	−1.1%
	(31,740)	(27,780)	(69,105)	(128,625)
Losers	25.1	17.2	10.3	17.1
	(73,702)	(84,740)	(84,893)	(243,335)
All firms	18.0	11.5	4.6	—
	(105,442)	(112,520)	(153,998)	

Note: Net returns are computed by subtracting the holding period returns to the equally weighted market index. Winners are those firms that outperform the market index by at least 50% during the prior 5 years. Losers are outperformed by the market by at least 50% during the prior 5 years. the numbers in parentheses are the number of observations in each group.

next three years. Hence Table 13.7 suggests that after we control for insider trading, long-run mean reversion still holds.

After we control for past long-term winners and losers, insider-trading activity also predicts future performance. Past long-term winners purchased by insiders outperform the market index by 3.0% over the next three years. Past long-term winners sold by insiders underperform the market index by −1.9% over the next three years. The difference between the performance of stocks bought and sold by insiders is 4.9 points over three years. Given the long horizons involved, the effects of insider trading on past long-term winners seem to be somewhat small.

The predictive power of insider trading holds after we control for past winners and losers. Past long-term losers bought by insiders outperform the market index by 25.1% over the next three years. Past long-term losers sold by insiders outperform the market index by 10.3% over the next three years. The difference in the future performance of losers bought and sold by insiders is now 14.8 points.

Our evidence suggests that after controlling for insider trading and past winners and losers, neither effect dominates the other in the long run. Both variables continue to predict future performance of the stocks. This finding suggests that long-run past winner and loser status does not suggest mispricing. If the past winner and loser status indicated strong mispricing component, we would have expected insider-trading variable to attenuate and even eliminate the predictive content of the past winner-loser factor. We next explore whether stronger insider-trading signals can affect the predictive power of past winners and losers. To this end we examine large insider trading by all insiders as well as large insider trading by top executives.

First, we confront past winners and losers with all insider buying and selling that exceeds 10,000 shares (table 13.8). Examining table 13.8 first by rows then by columns indicates that both insider trading and past winners and losers maintain their information content when we control for both variables. Looking at the first row, insider buys outperform insider sells by 1.3 points for past winners. In the second row, insider buys outperform insider sells by 20.4 points for past losers. Hence the direction of future stock price movements agrees with insider-trading signals for both past winners and losers.

Table 13.8
Subsequent 3-year net stock returns grouped by winners and losers and insider trading

Last 5 years	Insiders buy 10,000 shares or more	Insiders sell 10,000 shares or more	All firms
Winners	−4.7%	−6.0%	−5.8%
	(11,011)	(45,024)	(56,035)
Losers	26.0	5.6	13.9
	(30,826)	(44,394)	(75,220)
All firms	17.5	−0.6	—
	(41,837)	(89,418)	

Note: Net returns are computed by subtracting the holding period returns to the equally weighted market index. Winners are those firms that outperform the market index by at least 50% during the prior 5 years. Losers are outperformed by the market by at least 50% during the prior 5 years. The numbers in parentheses are the number of observations in each group.

Past winners and losers also continue to signal future stock returns. Looking at the first column, losers outperform winners by 30.7 points holding insider buying constant. Looking at the second column, losers outperform winners by 11.6 points, holding insider selling constant. Hence neither the insider-trading variable nor the past winner-loser status is dominated when we examine stronger insider-trading signals.

Our results suggest that instead of weakening the mean reversion, conditioning on large insider trading appears to strengthen the mean reversion. Previously the differences in the three-year performance of winners and losers is 18.2 points, resulting from a 1.1% negative performance for winners and 17.1% positive performance for losers (table 13.6). Winners now underperform the market index by more than 5.8%, while losers outperform the market index by 13.9%, resulting in a net difference of 19.7 points. Not surprisingly, conditioning on large insider trading also increases the information content of insider buy and sell signals. The difference between buyers and sellers grows to 18.1 points in table 13.8, up from 13.4 points (table 13.6).

A bit of a reflection reveals why using stronger insider-trading signals also strengthens the hold-horizon mean reversion. As we pointed out earlier, insiders are more likely to sell past winners than they are likely to sell past losers. Mean reversion implies that past winners will do worse than the market index. Hence, as we use stronger insider-trading signals, both signals reinforce each other. Greater insider selling combined with the past winner status means that future returns are likely to be more negative. A similar argument applies for past losers.

Finally we examine the large transactions of top executives to construct the strongest insider-trading signals. Once again conditioning on strongest insider-trading signals strengthens the mean reversion instead of weakening it. Winners now underperform the market index by 13.1%, while losers outperform the market index by 15.6%, resulting in a net difference of 28.7% (table 13.9), up from 19.7% before (table 13.8). The information content of insider trading is also strengthened by focusing only on the large transactions of top executives. The buy

Table 13.9
Subsequent 3-year net stock returns grouped by winners and losers and insider trading

Last 5 years	Top executives buy 10,000 shares or more	Top executives sell 10,000 shares or more	All firms
Winners	−8.4%	−13.6%	−13.1%
	(1,540)	(18,525)	(20,065)
Losers	40.5	2.6	15.6
	(6,952)	(13,699)	(20,651)
All firms	31.1	−7.1	—
	(8,492)	(32,224)	

Note: Net returns are computed by subtracting the holding period returns to the equally weighted market index. Winners are those firms that outperform the market index by at least 50% during the prior 5 years. Losers are outperformed by the market by at least 50% during the prior 5 years. The numbers in parentheses are the number of observations in each group.

group outperforms the market index by 31.1%, while the sell group underperforms the market index by 7.1%. The difference between insider buy and sell groups increases to 38.2 points, up from 18.1 points. Hence neither insider trading nor past winners and losers are dominated when we control for both variables.

Conclusions and investment implications

In this chapter we have examined the predictable patterns in stock returns using past winners and losers. We also examined insiders' reaction to large stock price movements in the past to determine if insiders view these price changes as a potential profit opportunity. Our findings are as follows:

1. Stock prices exhibit positive momentum at horizons up to one year. Past winners continue to outperform the market index, while past losers continue to underperform the market index.

2. Insiders tend to sell past winners and buy past losers. This finding holds for both short horizons up to one year as well as long horizons up to five years.

3. The information content of insider trading as well as past winners and losers remains intact when we control for both variables. Hence this evidence suggests that the predictable returns based on short-horizon momentum are not likely to represent market inefficiency.

4. Stock prices exhibit mean reversion over long horizons up to five years. Past winners tend to underperform the market index, while the past losers outperform the market index.

5. Both insider trading and long horizon past winners and losers maintain their predictive ability when we control for both variables.

14   *Implementation and conclusions*

Outsiders' profits

In this chapter we attempt to put into practice the knowledge that we have gained about insider trading so far. Can a potential stock market investor mimic insiders and make profits? If so, what is the magnitude of the profits? What kinds of risks does a mimicking strategy impose on outside investors? Given the risks, is it still worth it? After all, for many of you, the reason you are interested in this book is to find out whether or not mimicking insiders is profitable. We left these issues to the end since our earlier evidence has already provided ample guidance as to what to do and what not to do.[1] Hence we now turn to this important question. Following the discussion of the implementation issues, we reflect on our findings and offer overall conclusions.

So far we have examined the profits insiders make for themselves. Our results show that insiders do earn substantial profits from trading the securities of their own firms. While this is good news for outsiders, it is still difficult to assess the full implications of this finding for outside investors. As we stated earlier, outside investors care about whether or not they can make profits if they imitate insiders. An important question that needs to be addressed is whether the stock price reactions are completed by the time insider-trading information be-

comes publicly disseminated or whether the stock price reactions continue after the publication of insider-trading information? If for
important insider transactions the stock price reaction occurs within
one month and insiders take two months to report these transactions
to the public, then insider-trading information will be useless regardless of how much profits insiders earn for themselves.

There are basically three factors that determine whether or not outsiders can successfully imitate insiders. First, insider-trading information must become publicly available fairly soon after insiders trade.
Second, potential stock price movements after insiders report their
transactions must exceed outside investors' transaction costs. Third,
the risk from imitating insiders must be small enough to be acceptable
to outsiders. We now examine each of these factors in detail and determine the extent to which outsiders can make profits by imitating
insiders.

Reporting delays

As we mentioned earlier in this book, securities laws require insiders
to report their transactions both to the exchange where the transaction
took place and to the Securities and Exchange Commission (SEC)
within ten days of the end of the month in which they trade. Hence
insiders who trade at the beginning of the month have about 40 calendar days to report and still comply with the law. In contrast, insiders
who trade at the end of the month have only 10 calendar days to report
and still comply with the law.

Our data base contains not only the date insiders trade but also the
date they report their transactions to the SEC and the exchange where
the security is listed. Consequently we can examine reporting delays
(the difference between the trading date and the reporting date) using
our data base. A critical issue for outsiders is not what the law says
insiders must do, but just how tardy insiders report their transactions

in practice. The longer the delay between when insiders trade and when they actually report their transactions, the greater will be the stock price adjustment before outsiders find out, thereby leaving less of a profit opportunity for outsiders who imitate insiders.

Examination of reporting delays shows that the typical (median) reporting delay is 26 calendar days. This finding implies that outsiders can find out about half of all insiders' transactions within a month of the trade day. The reporting delays for 25% of trades exceed 36 calendar days. Approximately 75% of the insider trading becomes publicly available within 36 calendar days. This finding implies that outsiders will have access to a majority of insiders' transactions within a month or so.[2]

On average, the reporting delays do not appear to be substantial. While there are some reporting delays on average, the problem appears to be manageable. However, the average reporting delays may understate outsiders' problems. There is some reason to suspect that the reporting delays and profitability may be related. In fact, if insiders are worried that information-based transactions can attract unwanted regulatory attention, they may report these transactions with a greater delay. On the other, there is no reason to delay reporting a transaction that is strictly liquidity motivated. Consequently the average reporting delay could understate the difficulties of imitating insiders.

To help shed some light in insiders' motivations from late reporting of their transactions, we examined the relation between trade size, insiders' identity, and firm size and reporting delays. Contrary to what one might expect, larger transactions are not reported with greater delays. Instead, insiders report their smallest transactions with most delays. The median reporting delay for transactions of 100 shares or less is 28 days. The reporting delays decline monotonically with trade size. The median reporting delay for transactions of more than 10,000 shares equals 24 days. Hence it seems that insiders do not attempt to hide their large transactions by tardy reporting. In fact they report larger transactions more promptly even if it subjects them to more effective regulatory scrutiny. Once again insiders feel that from a regulatory compliance perspective, it is most important to report their large transactions more promptly. Additional delays in reporting their small transactions are not expected to be costly from a regulatory perspective.

We also examined the relation between insiders' identity and reporting delays. The evidence suggests that there is no relation between the identity of insiders and reporting delays. Whether insiders are officers, top executives, directors, or large shareholders, the median reporting delay is 26 days. Hence outsiders have an opportunity to follow top executives' transactions without any additional reporting delays.

Finally we also examined reporting delays in different size firms. Insiders in small firms (market value of equity is $25 million or less) report with greatest delays. The median reporting delay in small firms equals 27 days. The reporting delay falls with firm size. In large firms (market value of equity exceeds $1 billion) the median reporting delay falls to 24 days. Since insider trading in smallest firms is most profitable, longer reporting delays are undesirable for the outside stock market investor. However, the differences in reporting delays are small and should not present a serious obstacle to imitating insiders' transactions.

The only way to determine whether outsiders can profitably imitate insiders is to examine insiders' transactions following the reporting dates instead of the original trading dates. Given improvements in communication technology, outside investors can have access to insider-trading information as soon as insiders report their transactions to the SEC by subscribing to on-line electronic insider trading services. For those insiders who subscribe to nonelectronic publications such as *Official Summary*, *Insiders*, or *Insiders' Chronicle*, there would be an additional publication delay in addition to reporting delay. While reporting dates are not available for every transaction in the data set, they are available for the vast majority of the transactions.

Transaction costs

The second factor that outsiders have to consider in imitating insiders is transaction costs. Active trading strategies are more costly than buy and hold strategies. Traders have to pay additional commission fees and implicit or explicit bid-ask spreads. Moreover a large transaction can cause a price impact, which will further reduce outsiders' profits. While it is not possible to establish exact trading costs for all situations, we can guestimate the magnitude of these costs. The commission fees for many discount brokers is in the neighborhood of about 0.5% for round trip transactions and typically decline with trade size. For large transactions such as a 5,000-share trade, commission fees can be even lower. For instance, Brown and Co., a discount broker, currently charges a commission fee of $19 for up to 5,000 shares traded.[3] Assuming a stock price of $20, this works out to 0.02%. Hence, for this discount broker, the round trip commission fee would average 5 basis points.

The bid-ask spread is another cost of active trading. The bid and ask prices represent prices at which investors can immediately buy and sell stocks. The ask price is the price investors have to pay for immediate purchase, while the bid price is the price investors receive for immediate sale. The ask price typically exceeds the bid price anywhere from 1% to 10%, depending on which exchange the stock is listed, the stock price, number of shares to be traded, and the liquidity in the market. The bid-ask spread (defined as the difference between ask and bid prices) will generally be higher for larger volumes of trading, for lower priced stocks, and for stocks without a lot of trading activity. The bid-ask spread also tends to be higher in proportionate terms for NASDAQ stocks than for NYSE stocks.

If investors do not demand immediacy, they can submit limit orders at say the middle of the bid and ask prices and avoid paying the bid-ask spread. The cost of submitting a limit order is that the transaction may take days to execute and in some cases, it may not execute at all, thereby requiring a revision of the limit price. In chapters 2 and 3 we have seen that the stock price reactions following insider trading tend to take place over a period of months, there is no reason to demand immediacy. Hence it is assumed that outsiders will submit limit orders and will not lose much by waiting for a day or a few days for their transactions to execute.

The third cost of active trading is the price impact. A large buy order will move the price up while a large sell order will move the price down against the trader. The price impact of a transaction generally increases with size of the trade. While difficult to estimate precisely, the price impact depends on such factors as the usual trading volume and the time of day.[4] For a typical transaction by a small investor, the price impact is likely to be negligible.

In this book we use an average transaction cost of 1% for a round-trip transaction. While this may be conservative for some transactions and not conservative enough for others, it is sufficient to cover the commission fee and make some allowance for the bid-ask spread and price impact costs. Ultimately transactions costs for outsiders will depend on what the underlying firm is, how many shares they trade, the immediacy with which they want to execute their transactions, and the price and trading volume in that firm. Of course, if the investor had decided to trade for other reasons, then the marginal cost of using the insider information would be zero.

Potential profits from mimicking insiders

To discover whether profits are available to outsiders from mimicking insiders, we now examine the stock price movements in firms with reported insider trading. Hence we examine reported insider-trading activity and decide whether insiders are buying and selling by looking at all the reported transactions in that month; at the beginning of the next month, we are ready to imitate insiders. This is a realistic and implementable strategy for outsiders.

Table 14.1
One-year returns net of the market returns (defined as the equally weighted index) following all insider reporting months

	Number of reporting months	Subsequent 12-month net return
Buy	123,066	2.0%
Sell	142,284	−3.3

To evaluate the feasibility of imitating insiders' transactions, the following approach is adopted: We assign a buy signal if the *reported* transactions in a given calendar month involve more shares bought than sold by insiders. Similarly we assign a sell signal if the *reported* transactions in a given calendar month involve more shares sold than bought by insiders. Later in this section we will improve this rule by insisting that insider-trading month be relatively recent as well. Clearly insider-trading information is most useful if it pertains to relatively recent insider-trading activity.

We examine the average profitability to outsiders' mimicking transactions next. Our sample contains 123,066 months in which the reported insider-trading activity shows net purchases (table 14.1). Similarly our sample contains 142,284 months in which the reported insider-trading activity shows net sales. Hence our total sample size is 265,350. We lose a total of 43,843 trading months (14% of the overall sample), since the reporting date is not available for all transactions.

During the 12 months following insider purchases, stock prices outperform the market index by 2.0% (table 14.1). For the 12 months following the sales, stock prices underperform the market index by 3.3%. The average for both buys and sells is 2.7%. Compared with the results in chapter 2, the profitability of insider purchases seems to be hurt more than the profitability of insider sales from the reporting delays. While there is some stock price adjustment from the trade date to report date, most of the profitability still remains following the reporting of insiders' transactions. Hence the reporting delays do not completely

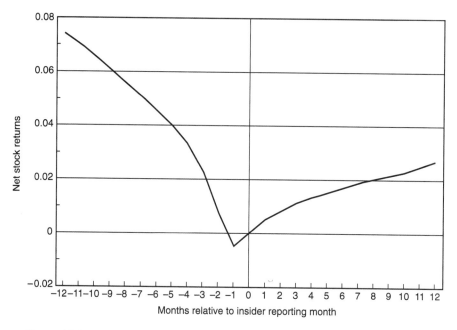

Figure 14.1
All insiders' profits around insider reporting month

eliminate the profit opportunities for outsiders who are interested in imitating the insiders. Again this is good news for the outsiders.

To get a complete picture of the stock price movements around the reporting month, figure 14.1 shows net stock returns from 12 months before the insider reporting month to 12 months following the reporting month. To make insider sales comparable with purchases, the net stock returns for sales are multiplied by minus one and then averaged with the net stock returns for insider purchases.

There is a V-shaped stock price reactions around insider trading (figure 14.1). Stock prices decline before the insider-trading month and rise afterward for insider purchases (and rise before and fall after insiders' sales). The minimum point occurs before the insider-reporting month since insider-trading month precedes the reporting month by one to two months. Data also show that outsiders do not lose much by having to wait until after the reporting date to imitate insiders. The stock price adjustment from the trade month to the report month is about 0.5%. Figure 14.1 indicates that for an outsider who pays 1% in transactions costs, it takes about three months to attain profitability net of the assumed 1% in transactions costs. Hence outsiders interested in imitating insiders must be willing to hold on to their positions for at least three months.

Stock prices decline before the reporting month for purchases and prices rise before the reporting month for sales (figure 14.1). These patterns suggest that outsiders can also use the stock price movements prior to the insider-reporting month to separate out active and passive transactions.

Determinants of outsiders' profits

In chapter 2 we discussed the determinants of the profitability of insiders' transactions. We now revisit this issue using only publicly available information. Specifically we would like to find out whether firm size, trading volume, and identity of insiders can be used to identify profitable situations for outsiders using only publicly available information.

We first examine the profitability in different size firms following the reporting month. The average profits for a 12-month period following insider reporting month in the smallest firm group is 5.0%. With increasing firm size, profitability declines to 2.0%, 1.7%, and 1.5%, respectively (figure 14.2). Overall, firm size still provides a good guide to the potential profitability of outsiders' mimicking transactions after the reporting date.

Our evidence suggests the following conclusions: First, profitability continues to vary negatively by firm size. Profitability is highest in smallest size firms and lowest in largest size firms. Second, outsiders would lose about 1% of the profits in small firms by having to delay their transactions by a month. Third, for an outsider who pays 1% in

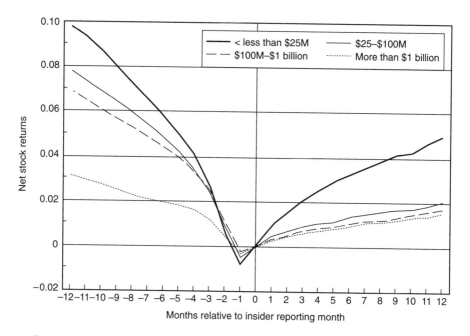

Figure 14.2
All insiders' profits around insider reporting month grouped by firm size

costs for a round-trip transaction and who imitates every insider transaction, potential profits net of transactions costs exist in all firms.
Fourth, outsiders must be able to hold on to these shares for about one
to five months in order to recover the transaction costs. In smallest
size firms, it takes only about one month to recover the transaction
costs. In large size firms, it takes about five months to recover the transaction costs. Fifth, price reversals prior to insider trading are also ordered by firm size. Prices show the largest reversals in smallest size
firms.

We next examine the volume of trading as another signal for the
profitability of insiders' transactions using publicly available data. The
profitability of insider trading around the reporting month grouped
by the number of shares traded is shown in figure 14.3. Profitability is
again ordered by increasing volume of trade. Only those transactions

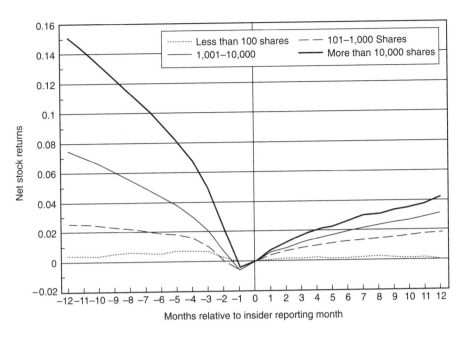

Figure 14.3
All insiders' profits around insider reporting month grouped by volume of trade

exceeding 100 shares attain a postreporting profitability of 1% or more. Transactions between 100 and 1,000 shares reach a profitability of about 2%, those between 1,000 and 10,000 share reach a profitability of 3.2%, while transactions more than 10,000 shares reach a profitability of 4.2%. It takes between one and two months for transactions exceeding 10,000 shares to pay for the 1% transactions costs, while it takes two months for transactions between 1,000 and 10,000 shares to pay for the 1% transactions costs.

We now analyze the information content of the identity of insiders using publicly available data. Our results earlier indicated that large shareholders do not have any information. Moreover the profitability of the transactions by the members of the board of directors is quite similar to the profitability of officers' transactions, both of which are dominated by the profitability of top executives' transaction. Conse-

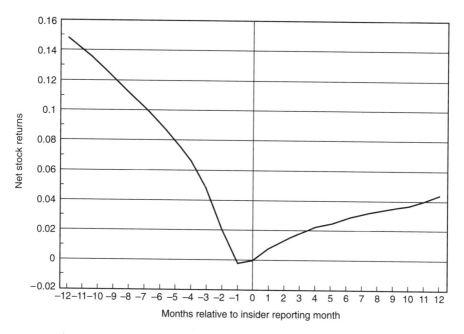

Figure 14.4
Top executives' profits around insider reporting month

quently we will focus only on the most profitable group, namely the top executives' transactions.

We first look at the profitability of top executives' transactions using publicly available data. The average profits reach 4.4%, 12 months after the reporting month (figure 14.4). There is hardly any loss of profits from having to delay the transactions between the trading month and the reporting month. Moreover an outsider must be willing to hold on to the stock for about one month in order to offset a transaction cost of 1%.

We also combine the predictor variables. First, we examine the profitability of top executives' transactions grouped by firm size (figure 14.5). Once again profitability of top executives' transactions depends on firm size. Profitability in the smallest firm size reaches 7.4%, and it takes about one month to reach the 1% threshold level. For larger firm

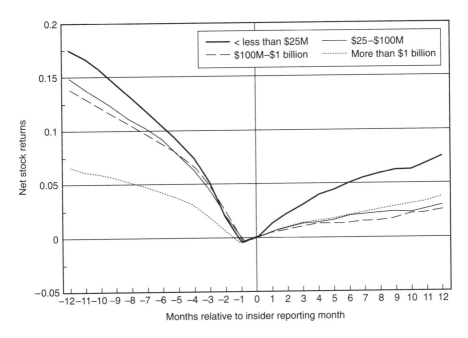

Figure 14.5
Top executives' profits around insider reporting month grouped by firm size

size groups, profitability varies between 2% to 3%, and it takes about three months to reach the 1% level.

Finally we examine top executives' transactions grouped by the number of shares traded. Large volume of trading continues to signal more valuable insider information using publicly available data. Very small transactions do not attain any profitability whatsoever. For transactions involving between 1,000 and 10,000 shares, profitability averages 5.0%, and it takes about one to two months to reach the 1% level (figure 14.6). For transactions involving 10,000 or a greater number of shares, profitability averages 6.7%, and it takes about one month to reach the 1% level.

Examining top executives' transactions following the reporting month shows that once again most of the price adjustments continue to occur past the reporting month. This is good news for outsiders.

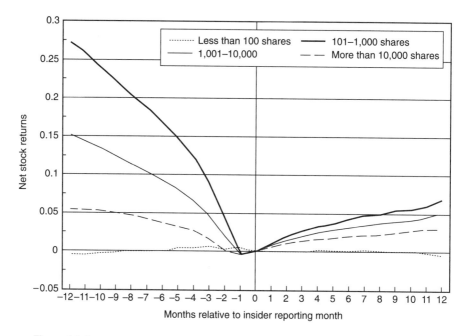

Figure 14.6
Top executives' profits around insider reporting month grouped by volume of trade

Outsiders who imitate top executives' transactions are also advised to
focus on small firms and transactions that exceed 1,000 shares. Outsiders must also be able to hold on to shares purchased between one to
three months in order to pay for an assumed 1% in transaction costs.

A potential source of noise for the results presented so far is that
reported transactions include some very stale transactions which no
one would try to imitate. As pointed out earlier, some 5% of the transactions are reported with almost five months of delay. Clearly it will
not be a good idea to imitate these transactions. To address this issue,
all reported transactions that are older than 90 days are eliminated.
This filter reduced the number of reporting months by an additional
10,044 months. For the remaining 255,306 reporting months, the 12-
month net return following purchases is 2.2%, while the net return

following sales is 3.3%. Hence the profitability of purchases improves 0.2% with timely purchases, and there is no change in the profitability of sales. While an interesting consideration, focusing on timely reported transactions does not make a big difference.

Comparing the overall profitability of insiders' transactions following the trade month versus the reporting month shows that the reporting delays are on average *not* very costly. As discussed in chapter 2, stock price reactions do continue albeit at a slower rate after 12 months following the insider-trading month. Hence losing one or two months of price movements immediately following insiders' transactions due to reporting delays is made up to some extent by the price adjustments after 12 months following the insider-trading month. For instance, the 12-month profit following the insider-trading month is 3.5% (table 2.2). In contrast, the 12-month average profit following the reporting month is 2.7% (figure 14.1). Outsiders do lose something by having to wait to obtain the insider trading reports; however, most of the stock price adjustment still takes place following the reporting month.[5]

Summarizing the above findings, firm size, identity of insiders, and trading volume continue to predict outsiders' profits following the reporting of insider trades. Outsiders who imitate insiders' transactions are best advised to focus on top executives, small firms, as well as those transactions that exceed 1,000 shares in all firms. In addition outsiders must also be able to hold on to shares purchased usually between one to three months in order to pay for an assumed 1% in transaction costs.

Risks of mimicking insiders

Our third factor is the risk of losses while imitating insiders. Until now we have focused solely on average profitability. However, individual investors care not only about the average profits but also the probability of making losses as a result of mimicking insiders. Most individual investors would require additional compensation from active trading strategies if the risk of losses is higher. We now address this issue of risk.

Our results so far show that on average some profit opportunities do remain past the reporting month. However, when we consider whether or not risk-averse investors would want to mimic insiders using publicly available information, looking solely at average profits is not sufficient. Risk-averse individual investors will also care about the *probability* that they will actually lose money while trying to imitate insiders. If this probability is large, risk-averse investors will limit themselves only to the most profitable transactions or they will not chase after some modest insider-trading profits at all. Hence we need to first ascertain exactly how large the risks of mimicking insiders are.

Let us begin with a definition of risk. We define risk as the probability of a loss, which is the probability that a passive investment in the market portfolio will outperform an active strategy of imitating insiders. Suppose that an outsider imitates insider buying and the stock price underperforms the market index (increases less than the market increase or falls more than the market fall). Then such a transaction is considered a loss, since it causes the insider to be beaten by the market index. Similarly, suppose that an outsider imitates insider selling and the stock price outperforms the market index (increases by more than the market rise, or declines less than the market fall). Then the sale is considered a loss, since it causes the insider to perform worse than a passive investment in the market portfolio. Probability of loss is computed by dividing the number of losing transactions by the total transactions attempted.[6]

Risk-averse investors can deal with the probability of loss in three ways. First, if the risk is too high, individuals will simply prefer to make buy and hold investments in say an indexed portfolio. This way investors guarantee themselves that they will always perform as well as the index. Moreover they avoid the additional information gathering and transactions costs associated with an active trading strategy. Second, risk-averse investors can simply limit their active transactions to the most profitable transactions. This way they receive additional compensation for taking on additional risk. Third, risk-averse investors can attempt to reduce the probability of a loss by engaging in multiple mimicking transactions. To the extent the returns from separate mimicking transactions are not perfectly correlated, the probability of a loss on the entire portfolio is thereby reduced. In this chapter we will examine the latter two strategies separately.

We begin by measuring the probability of a loss on a single mimicking transaction. To ensure that outsiders can actually perform our calculations, we work with only the reported insider transactions. We also stratify the probability of loss by firm size, by number of shares traded, and by the identity of insiders. We then examine what happens to the probability of a loss as the outsider engages in increasing number of mimicking transactions. This analysis will establish how many mimicking transactions are necessary if the outsider would like to reduce the probability of a loss below a threshold level such as 10% or 5%. If the number of mimicking transactions necessary to reduce the probability of losses below the threshold level is small, then this is good news for the outside investor. If an extremely large number of mimicking transactions is necessary to obtain an acceptable probability of a loss, then outsiders would not want to imitate such insider transactions.

We examine the probability of a loss following all *reported* insider trading sorted by firm size. Probability of a loss is computed assuming no trading costs as well as 1% round-trip trading costs. These two outcomes provide information about the distribution of the stock returns as well as the effect of trading costs on the final outcome.

The probability of a loss from imitating insiders even with no trading costs is right around 50% (table 14.2). Moreover, when 1% trading costs are also taken into account, the probability of loss on a given transaction rises to 51.7% for the overall sample. Hence, for those investors who have to pay 1% trading costs, trying to beat the market by imitating a single insider trading is worse than a fair coin toss.

Table 14.2
Probability of a loss incurred in imitating insiders grouped by firm size

Firm size	Number of reporting months	Probability of loss (no commission)	Probability of loss 1% trading costs
All firms	255,306	49.5%	51.7%
Less than $25 million	72,484	51.6	53.3
$25–$100 million	67,814	49.6	51.5
$100 million–$1 billion	84,151	48.5	50.9
More than $1 billion	30,857	47.4	50.3

How can the probability of a loss equal 50% while, on average, there are 2% to 3% profits from imitating insiders? The answer is that while, on average, success is no more than a fair coin toss, outsiders earn more from their successful transactions than they would lose from their unsuccessful transactions. Put alternatively, most of outsiders' profits would accrue from some very successful transactions. This reasoning suggests that outsider who plan to imitate insider trading must imitate a fair number of transactions to ensure success.

Trade-off between profitability and risk of losses

As we discussed earlier, investors can also deal with risk by limiting their transactions only to the most profitable transactions. To examine this issue, we also stratify our sample by firm size, number of shares traded, and by identity of insiders. If risk levels do not vary by profitability, then outsiders can simply choose more profitable transactions for a given level of risk.

Table 14.2 also shows the probability of loss on a given transaction grouped by firm size. Remember from our earlier findings that profitability is negatively related to firm size. Similar to the average profitability figures shown in chapters 2 and 3, probability of a loss is also decreasing in firm size. In the smallest firms the probability of a loss is the greatest. The probability of a loss on a mimicking transaction in the smallest firms after paying the trading costs is 53.3%. This probability of loss uniformly declines to 50.3% in the largest firm size category. Hence, for all firm size groups, the probability of loss remains over 50%.

Once again, as the results in table 14.2 suggest, we have a contradiction. Earlier we found that the profitability of outsiders' transactions is the greatest in smallest firms. Table 14.2 indicates that the probability of a loss is also the greatest in smallest firms. How is this possible? Is there a contradiction?

The answer to this puzzle once again lies in the distribution of the returns. The trading profits in small firms appear to be even more right skewed. The higher profitability in smaller firms comes from even fewer successful transactions as compared to the larger firms. In addition the profitability in large firms shows less of dispersion. These two factors can explain the apparent contradiction between the profitability and the probability of loss results.

Our findings so far suggest that while insider trading is on average most profitable in the smallest firms, imitating insiders in the smallest firms also subjects outsiders to the greatest risk. Viewed alternatively, there is a good reason why seeming profit opportunities remain available for months after the reporting date in the smallest firms. Most outsiders are probably unwilling to mimic insider trading in the smallest firms due to the higher risks involved. This finding makes the availability of greater profit opportunities in small firms perhaps less surprising.

When we examine risk versus profitability of top executives' transactions by firm size, we again find similar results. The risk is highest in small firms, which also contain the most profitable transactions. Hence once again there is a positive relation between risk and profitability.

Overall, imitating insiders is in no way a sure thing for a risk-averse outsider. The probability of a loss in a randomly chosen transaction is about 50%. Especially for those insiders who pay a 1% round-trip transactions costs, the probability of loss on a given mimicking trans-action remains above 50%.

Multiple mimicking transactions

A third option available to outsiders to manage risk is to engage in multiple mimicking transactions. Holding all else constant, as the probability of loss on a given transaction increases, outsiders have to rely on a greater number of successful transactions in order to keep the loss on their portfolio to an acceptable level. For instance, let us assume that the expected profitability of mimicking a particular insider trade is 7%. There is also a 50% chance of making losses on any single mim-icking transaction of this type. One way for the outsider to reduce this 50% probability of loss is to engage in many mimicking transactions. As the outsider mimics 5, 10, or even 100 insider transactions of this type, he/she will be more confident of earning 7% on the portfolio. Put another way, as the outsider mimics an increasing number of inde-pendently drawn insider transactions, the probability of loss on his portfolio will diminish gradually. However, a higher probability of loss will require a greater number of mimicking transactions.

What happens to the probability of a loss as the number of mimick-ing transactions increase to 5, 10, 100, or more? As we discussed earlier, one way to outsiders to reduce the probability of a loss in imitating insider trading is to mimic a lot of transactions. The critical issue here is how fast the probability of a loss falls with the increasing number of mimicking transactions. We now investigate the number of mimicking transactions necessary to reduce the probability of a loss on the entire portfolio below some acceptable levels of risk.

We analyze the probability of incurring a loss from mimicking a se-ries of top executives' transactions, stratified by firm size. Our evidence from chapters 2 and 3 suggests additional variables that signal the value of insiders' information such as active-passive transactions, con-sensus among insiders, lack of a conflicting signal over the past six months or so, and buy-sell transactions, as well as all the interactions between these seven variables. To provide additional insights into the risks of mimicking transactions, we eliminate all passive transactions as well as any transactions with a conflicting signal during the past three months.

To ensure that the outsiders can actually perform these mimicking transactions, we once again charge a 1% transaction cost and use only publicly available data following the reporting month of insiders' transactions. To determine how many mimicking transactions are necessary to reduce the loss probabilities, we experiment with 10, 50, 100, 250, and 1000 transactions.[7] For an individual investor, 100 to 250 mimicking transactions would be at the upper end of an imitation strategy. Clearly the 1,000 mimicking transactions are only appropriate for large institutional investors.[8]

The loss probabilities fall fairly rapidly for 50 or 100 mimicking transactions (table 14.3). In small firms, which have the most profitable insider trading, the probability of a loss (after 1% transaction costs) falls most rapidly with increasing mimicking transactions.

Table 14.3
Probability of loss after 1% transactions costs from imitating top executives' transactions after reporting month grouped by the number of mimicking transactions

Firm size	Number of transactions 10	Number of transactions 50	Number of transactions 100	Number of transactions 250	Number of transactions 1,000
Less than $25 million	33.5%	20.1%	12.2%	3.2%	0.0%
$25–$100 million	34.4	31.1	24.8	17.6	3.7
$100 million–$1 billion	39.4	31.9	26.0	20.1	4.6
More than $1 billion	36.6	30.3	24.6	15.4	2.0

Table 14.4
Probability of loss after 1% transactions costs from imitating top executives' transactions after reporting month grouped by the number of mimicking transactions

Firm size	Number of transactions 10	Number of transactions 50	Number of transactions 100	Number of transactions 250	Number of transactions 1,000
1-100 shares	59.4%	80.6%	88.2%	96.7%	97.0%
101–1,000	53.6	53.2	49.9	51.7	7.3
1,001–10,000	41.3	32.1	23.1	14.5	1.6
More than 10,000 shares	37.2	10.5	6.0	0.3	0.0

For 50 mimicking transactions, the probability of loss is 20.1%. The probability of loss falls to about 12.2% for 100 mimicking transactions. As the number of mimicking transactions increases further, the probability of loss falls further to 3.2% (250 trades), and then to 0% (1,000 trades).

With increasing firm size, the probability of loss is somewhat more complex. The probability of loss first increases slightly with increasing firm size as the average profits fall, and later falls with very large size firms as the volatility of returns fall. In the largest firm size group, which exhibits less volatility of returns than small firms, the probability of loss for 1,000 mimicking transactions falls to about 2%.

We also segment implementation strategy by the number of shares traded by top executives (table 14.4). Outsiders can reduce their risk of loss by limiting their mimicking activity only to those transactions involving more than 1,000 shares. Risks fall even faster for trades that are greater than 10,000 shares. Mimicking only those transactions involving more than 10,000 shares, outsiders can limit their risk of loss to 10.5% (50 trades), or down to 6% (100 trades). Risk is virtually eliminated for 250 to 1,000 mimicking trade strategies.

Our evidence suggests that outsiders must be prepared to mimic at least 50 to 100 insider transactions to reduce the risks to about

10% to 20% range. Alternatively, outsiders must be prepared to accept a somewhat higher risk of loss (20%–30% range) for a smaller number of mimicking transactions. Outsiders can also reduce the risks by trading in the smallest firms and or mimicking large volume of trades only.

In summary, there are some risks in mimicking insiders' transactions. It takes about 50 mimicking trades to reduce the probability of loss to acceptable levels. However, we have not examined all the possible signaling variables. In particular, by using additional combinations of the seven signaling variables we have identified in chapter 3, outsiders can further reduce the risks of imitating insiders. For instance, by using combinations of trading volume and firm size, outsiders can reduce risks below levels presented already. In addition, outsiders can introduce price-earnings ratios, book-to-market ratios, or dividend yields to further fine tune a trading strategy.

Recommendations to investors

Our objective in this chapter was to take a simple insider-trading strategy and examine the risks and profits available to outsiders after taking into account the availability of the information, trading costs, and risks of mimicking. Our evidence shows that most of the profits described in this book are still available after the reporting of insider trades. Transaction costs do reduce outsiders' profits but do not eliminate them. Finally some risks remain. Outsiders must be ready to imitate at least 50 trades.

Our evidence in this chapter shows that the strategies described in this book are for the most part implementable strategies. Using a realistic approach, we have shown that investors can take advantage of the insider-trading information in their trading decisions. However, it is important to keep in mind that the past stock price behavior does not guarantee future performance. Realistically speaking, some future event such as changes in insider-trading regulations can reduce or eliminate the information content of future insider trading. Outside investors need to exercise caution and take care in monitoring their own performance. Hence outside investors need to limit the size of bets they make, diversify their bets across a large number of mimicking transactions, and monitor their performance.

On the positive side, we have not exhausted all possible ways of exploiting insiders' information. Results presented in earlier chapters in this book suggest that investors can improve the performance of their portfolios by using earnings surprises, book-to-market ratios, and price-earnings ratios in addition to the insider-trading information. Keeping track of aggregate insider trading and industry-specific insider-trading patterns should also be useful. Our overall recommendation to outside investors is that they should simply incorporate insider-trading information as an additional tool into their day-to-day investment decisions. Hence insider trading works best as part of an overall investment strategy rather than as a substitute for security analysis.

Conclusions

We have examined the availability of profits to outsiders who mimic insiders' transactions. Outsiders interested in mimicking insider trading have to deal with three additional concerns: reporting delays, transaction costs, and the risk of incurring losses from imitating a small number of transactions. Given delays in reporting and publication of insiders' information, outsiders must wait until insider information becomes publicly disseminated. Any delays in obtaining insider-trading information will reduce the available profits to outsiders, since some of the stock price reaction is likely to occur immediately following insider trading and before insiders report their transactions. Moreover outsiders have to pay a transactions cost to mimic insider-trading activity. Finally risk-averse outsiders need to consider the probability of losses arising from mimicking insiders. Our conclusions are as follows:

1. There are some delays in reporting of insider-trading information; however, these are not excessive. Insiders take a mean of 47 days and a median of 26 days to report their transactions. Approximately 25% of insider trades are reported with more than a 36-day delay, 10% of insider trades are reported with a 67-day delay. Put another way, outsiders can have access to 90% of insiders' transactions approximately within two months of insider-trading day.

2. Delays in reporting do not appear to be systematic. For instance, larger trades are not reported with greater delays. Similarly there is no difference in reporting delays among the different classes of insiders.

3. For the 12-month period following the reporting of insiders' transactions, buys outperform the market index by 2.0%, while sells underperform the market index by 3.3%. Hence significant price movements occur following the reporting of insiders' trades. Delays in obtaining insider-trading information do not eliminate the possibility of successfully imitating insiders.

4. Given price adjustments that take place prior to the insider re-porting month and the effect of transactions costs, outsiders must hold on to their shares between two to three months in order to reach a profitability level of 1%, which is sufficient to just offset the transactions costs.

5. There are some risks in imitating insiders. The probability of loss for imitating a given insider trade usually exceeds 50%. Consequently, to increase the chances of success, outsiders must be able to mimic multiple transactions by insiders.

6. Outsiders can reduce the probability of a loss from imitating insiders by mimicking multiple insider transactions. Outsiders must be ready to mimic approximately 50 insider transactions to reduce the loss probabilities to low levels. Alternatively, outsiders must be willing to accept a risk of loss of approximately 20% to 30% for a smaller number of mimicking transactions.

Notes

Introduction

1. If information acquisition and processing were costless and everyone agreed on the interpretation of the information, then publicly available information could not be used to beat a buy-and-hold strategy. This is referred to as the efficient markets hypothesis; see Fama (1970, 1991). DeLong, Shleifer, Summers, and Waldmann (1990), Grossman and Stiglitz (1980) and Shiller (1981) provide some opposing views.

2. Insiders take about a month to report their transactions to the Securities and Exchange Commission. There are additional delays in publication.

3. One does not have to be an insider to profitably manipulate stock prices. Allen and Gale (1992) show that if uninformed traders simply think that the manipulator is informed, then manipulation will be profitable.

4. Despite unprecedented recent coverage of insider-trading activity, there are no direct ways the average stock market investor can turn abundant insider-trading information into promising investment opportunities. This distinction between information and knowledge is especially important in this context. Information about what insiders are doing does not really tell us why they did it and how the stock price is likely to move. A string of recent insider purchases may be due to some soon-to-be-announced good news, or because the insider received her cash bonuses and there is moral pressure to buy shares of her own firm. Alternatively, increased insider selling activity may signal bad news or that the executive needs cash to make University of Michigan Business School tuition payments. Can we tell why some executives trade their own firms' stock? For most of us, there is no way to separate information-based insider trading from liquidity-based trading.

5. See *The Hulbert Guide to Financial Newsletters* by Mark Hulbert (5th ed., Dearborn Financial Publishing, pp. 197 and 239).

6. See the books by Peter Lynch and John Rothchild, *Beating the Street* (Fireside, 1994) and *One Up on Wall Street* (Penguin, 1990).

7. Material information is somewhat vague. It is defined as information that would affect the trading decision of a typical investor.

8. There are additional individuals who are not subject to reporting requirements, yet who are legally considered insiders and must refrain from trading under special circumstances. These are the individuals who come into contact with insider information as a result of their occupation. Examples of these individuals include, but are not limited to, bankers, investment advisors, and partners in a law firm or an investment banking firm. These individuals work on important corporate financial transactions such as loan arrangements, mergers and acquisitions, and issuance of securities that provide them with important, nonpublic, proprietary information about their clients. These individuals can neither exploit this information for their benefit nor pass this information to others. Failure to abstain would be a violation of securities laws.

Another group of informed individuals include journalists and other media reporters. These individuals possess advance information about the news stories they will publish, which can move the stock prices of the firms they feature. Selling, bartering, or using this advance information for their personal benefit can be considered a form of insider trading. In addition these individuals are also prohibited from passing this information to others. Since these individuals are not allowed to trade at all, there are no transactions to report. Consequently our data base contains no reported transactions by any of these insiders.

9. This is required by Section 16(a) of the Securities and Exchange Act of 1934. See Fishman and Haggerty (1995) for a model of insider trading with mandatory disclosure requirement.

10. The omission of straight debt from insider-trading regulations is a clear oversight on the part of the U.S. Congress and the SEC, since trading in straight debt can present just as profitable trading opportunities for insiders. To demonstrate how insiders can get around insider-trading regulations by using straight debt securities, assume that a firm gets in financial distress after it loses a substantial amount of money for a few years. Let's also assume that the firm has trouble making principal or interest payments on its public debt. Given this negative outlook, both the stock price and the price of its public debt will be substantially depressed. In fact in this case the price of its public debt will act just like the stock price. If the prospects of the firm improve, then the price of straight debt will increase substantially toward its par value. If the prospects of the firm worsen or if the managers file for bankruptcy, then

the price of the straight debt will decline even more. When the firm is in financial distress, its straight, public debt will in effect replace its common stock. In this case insiders can buy or sell straight debt securities without having to worry about reporting or complying with insider trading restrictions. Clearly insiders can make just as much profit by buying and selling straight debt. Insider trading in financially distressed firms is examined by Gosnell, Keown, and Pinkerton (1992), Loderer and Sheehan (1989), and Seyhun and Bradley (1997).

The logic of omitting straight debt has to do with the fact that small investors do not tend to be active in this market. Instead, bond trading is dominated by sophisticated institutional traders. Since the stated purpose of insider-trading restrictions is to create a fair and liquid *stock* market, the omission of bond trading does not appear to be a major concern for small individual traders.

11. The Securities and Exchange Commission has a rule making authority to augment and clarify legislation.

12. Theoretically, insiders can avoid Section 16(b) by colluding. One insider could sell to start the stock price reaction; another could buy a larger amount after the prices have declined.

13. Apparently, prior to the passage of the Securities and Exchange Act, some managers manipulated the stock price and profited by short-selling. For instance, in 1901, managers of the American Steel and Wire Company shorted their firm's stock, then closed their steel mills, and caused a price drop from $60 to $40. The managers then purchased the stock at $40 for a $20 profit and reopened the mills. See Wycoff (1968).

14. Call and put options on the stock are also included in the definition of insider trading. Hence insiders cannot buy put options on more shares than they own, since this would be tantamount to short-selling.

15. A sale could signal positive information if insiders manipulate stock prices. Potential stock price manipulation by insiders will be explored in more detail later.

16. Each transaction reported by insiders is checked against other sources of public information. For instance, if insiders report trading more shares than the total trading volume recorded for that day, then this insider transaction is eliminated from the data base. Cleaning up the data base in this manner resulted in elimination of about 1% of the reported transactions.

Chapter 1

1. We will see later that anonymity is quite important to insiders. Fishman and Haggerty (1995) analyze a model where insiders are required to disclose their transactions *after* trading. They show that with mandatory disclosure, insiders' expected

trading profits increases because it allows insiders to trade even then they have no information.

2. Insiders can also acquire or dispose of shares by exercising stock options, warrants, and convertible securities. Gifts, private transactions, redemptions, stock splits, employee benefit plans, tender offers, dividend reinvestment plans, and inheritance represent just some of the other ways insiders can acquire and dispose of shares. These other types of stock acquisitions and dispositions are either involuntary or are not likely to be motivated by information. For instance, shares acquired through stock splits or stock dividends are clearly involuntary. Moreover every shareholder receives the same proportion of shares. Receiving additional shares through stock splits or stock dividends does not provide insiders with an advantage over other shareholders. Other acquisitions such as through gifts or private purchases are not likely to be motivated by insiders' information, since the traders on the other side would know the identity of the insiders by definition of a private trade. Since it is less likely that the insiders would attempt to take advantage of their friends and acquaintances, we exclude private transactions wherever possible.

Insiders can also acquire and dispose of shares through option exercises. A stock option allows the insiders to acquire the shares by paying a fixed price, called the exercise price. When insiders hold stock options, they benefit from price increases, and they are hurt from price decreases. Similarly, when insiders exercise their stock options and acquire the underlying stock, they give up their option and replace it with common stock. Hence their basic long position in the stock is not changed. What is different is the leverage associated with their position. Holding common shares rather than options involves greater equity investment and less leverage. Hence, there is no clear change in insiders' incentives. For this reason shares acquired or disposed of through option exercises are also excluded from most of the analysis. In view of the above, we concentrate our analysis to insiders' open market sales and purchases.

3. Unanimity can also be defined in terms of number of insiders, number of shares, or net number of transactions and so on.

4. We have also computed the number of firms with open market insider-trading activity from 1975 to 1995. For each year during the last 20 years, there are more than 2,000 firms in which insiders buy and sell the stock of their own firms in the open market. Again, for those who would like to imitate insiders, this is good news. It is possible to gauge potential future stock price movements in most firms based on the recent insider-trading activity.

5. Insider buying in Ford could be good news if it signals improved prospects for auto stocks in general. Alternatively, it could be bad news if it signals that Ford is

increasing its profitability at the expense of GM and Chrysler. Finally both effects can be present. Sometimes the signal can be complementary and sometimes detrimental.

6. A word of caution is appropriate here. Our definition of insiders includes only those who have a legal obligation to report their transactions. However, typical investors would worry about losing to all informed traders whether they have to report their transactions or not. Hence the probability of losing to legal insiders understates the true probability of losing to all informed investors. Holderness and Sheehan (1985) and Larcker and Lys (1987) examine the profitability of trades by so-called raiders.

7. Our evidence also makes it clear why the small investors are often most opposed to insider trading. The small investors are often most active in small stocks where the probability of trading against insiders is also the largest.

8. This is similar to the reasoning that a person can drown in a river that is "on average" one foot deep. And, I don't mean a short person here. What matters in crossing a river is not the average depth but the maximum depth.

9. Insiders have acquired about 880 million shares through option exercises during the period 1975 to 1994. On net, insiders appear to be disinvesting in their own firms.

10. See Seyhun (1993) for evidence on seasonal stock returns.

11. Manipulation works best if there is only one insider or if insiders collude. Hart (1977), Vila (1989), Bagnoli and Lipman (1991), Allen and Gale (1992), Jarrow (1992), and John and Narayanan (1997) explore the implications of price manipulation by insiders. Flynn (1935) reports that such a manipulation occurred on the London Stock Exchange by some traders around England's victory at Waterloo over the French. As early news of the hostilities came in, most investors expected England to win the battle. However, some manipulators apparently began to sell British shares on the London Stock Exchange quite publicly. This led to a large sell-off, following which manipulators purchased even a bigger number of shares privately. Some individuals were prosecuted for price manipulations after the war. Also see Sobel (1965, pp. 11–12).

12. Positive correlation of insider trading does not necessarily imply slow stock price reaction to insider trading. If outsiders understand the time series properties of insider trading, then they will take this into account when pricing stocks.

13. Specifically, Section 16(b) of the SEC Act requires that all profits made within six months must be returned to the corporation. To keep their profits, insiders must wait more than six months. Section 16(b) is enforced by private lawyers who track

insider-trading activity, uncover potential violations, and earn litigation fees in the process.

14. There is a very large literature on insider-trading regulations. For a sample of studies, see Arshadi and Eyssell (1991), Brodsky and Swanson (1988), Carlton and Fischel (1983), Carney (1987), Cleeton and Reeder (1987), Cox (1986), Dooley (1980), Estrada (1994, 1995), Gaillard (1992), Haddock and Macey (1987), Heller (1982), Jaffe (1974), Janvey (1986, 1987), Karjala (1982), Macey (1991), and Seyhun (1992). Seyhun empirically examines the effectiveness of the increases in insider-trading sanctions in the 1980s.

15. As we mentioned before, a group of insiders could theoretically evade Section 16(b) by colluding. One insider may do the buying while another insider may do the selling, thereby evading the 16(b) rule.

16. Part of this increased detection is also due to increased insider trading. However, as shown earlier, the total number of insider-trading months increased from about 14,000 in 1975 to about 24,000 in 1995. This is less than twofold increase while enforcement has increased by fifteenfold. For detection statistics, see *Business Week,* "A Bigger Stick against the Insiders," May 27, 1996, p. 34.

17. Apparently the SEC prefers it this way. Ambiguity about what is illegal is supposed to prevent risk-averse executives from crossing over into gray territory.

18. In addition the defendant has a right to a jury trial.

19. See Seyhun (1992b) for this evidence.

20. Insider-trading regulations are examined by Ratner (1988), Silver (1985), Scott (1980), Gaillard (1992) and Langevoort (1992). Gaillard (1992) compares the insider-trading regulations in the United States with those in Europe and Japan.

21. See studies by Schotland (1967), Brudney (1979), and Seligman (1985).

22. The relation between insider information and corporate financial management is studied by Myers and Majluf (1984), Seyhun (1990a), John and Lang (1991), Karpoff and Lee (1991), and Bebchuck and Fershtman (1994).

23. Diamond and Verrecchia (1981), Dye (1984), Fishman and Haggerty (1989), Glosten (1989), Manove (1989), Ausubel (1990), Kyle (1985), Leland (1992), Khanna, Slezak, and Bradley (1994), and Bernhardt, Hollifield, and Hughson (1995) examine the information effects of insider trading. Leland (1992) concludes that insider trading from officers is more detrimental than the insider trading from large shareholders. Bernhardt, Hollifield, and Hughson (1995) show that if investment is information elastic, then insider trading is welfare increasing.

24. Greater information efficiency increases stock prices by leading to better investment decisions. For instance, stock prices provide useful signals for capital issuance, managerial compensation, and business expansion and contraction decisions. In the case of capital issuance, more accurate stock prices allocate capital where it is most productive. See, for example, Bernhardt, Hollifield, and Hughson (1995).

25. Henry Manne (1966a, b) is the first to articulate this view. Also see Carlton and Fischel (1983), Haddock and Macey (1986), Carney (1987), and Bhide (1993).

26. Herzel and Katz (1987) examine this issue.

Chapter 2

1. For studies that have empirically examined the profitability of insider trading using U.S. data, see Baesel and Stein (1979), Benesh and Pari (1987), Brick, Statman and Weaver (1989), Cornell and Sirri (1992), Finnerty (1976a,b), Jaffe (1974a), Karpoff and Lee (1991), Keown and Pinkerton (1981), Kerr (1980), Larcker and Lys (1987), Lin and Howe (1990), Penman (1982), Rozeff and Zaman (1988), Seyhun (1986, 1988a, b, 1992a, b), and Trivoli (1980). Some authors have examined the profitability of insider trading outside the United States: Golder (1983), Lee and Bishara (1989), and Pope, Morris, and Peel (1990). Stewart (1991) and Winans (1986) provide entertaining accounts of of recent insider trading scandals. Meulbroek (1992) analyzes illegal insider trading.

2. Bagehot (1989), Black (1986), Copeland and Galai (1983), Glosten and Milgrom (1989), Hasbrouck (1988), and Klein (1980) discuss the trading costs of active strategies.

3. The bid-ask spread can vary anywhere from less than 1% to 10% depending on the market capitalization of the firm, where the stock is listed, and number of shares traded. Of course investors can also submit limit orders which specifies the price at which the investor is willing to buy or sell stock and avoid paying the bid-ask spread. In this case they will not be certain that the transaction will be executed immediately. A limit order can execute one of two ways. First, the current market price may move to the limit price. For a limit *buy* order to execute, the market price must fall to the limit price. Alternatively, another matching limit order at the same price must materialize. Otherwise, the limit order remains unexecuted. Finally any attempt to buy shares, especially if we are trying to buy a large number of shares, will impact the prices. Prices will increase on us if we are trying to buy stock and decline on us if we are trying to sell stock. Moreover the price impact increases with increasing trade size. These price movements are costly. All of these costs reduce the potential profitability of actively imitating insiders.

4. The difference between the returns to buying and selling portfolios is highly significant due to the huge sample size. There is less than one in 10,000 chance that such a difference in returns can arise due to chance. For those readers who are familiar with statistics, the difference has an autocorrelation-adjusted t-statistic of 5.8. We will report statistical significance of selected findings throughout the book.

5. As we discussed in chapter 1, we did examine the profitability of additional classification schemes. When we use unanimity principle, the profitability of insiders' sales does not change, while the profitability of insiders' purchases improves to 5.1%. Requiring unanimity also reduces the number of insider trading events by about 12%. Because of the reduction in sample size, we use net number of shares traded even if there is disagreement among insiders. We also examined the net number of transactions to classify insider-trading months. The profitability of insider trading is not monotonic in net number of transactions. As the net number of transactions increases to 3 or 4, the profitability increases. As the net number of transactions increase beyond that point, profitability decline though it is still positive. The decline in insider profitability with increasing net number of transactions suggests the possibility of attempted stock price manipulation by a group of insiders who act in concert. We do not examine this conjecture in detail.

6. See, for instance, Lorie and Niederhoffer (1968), Scholes (1972), Jaffe (1974), Finnerty (1976), and Seyhun (1986, 1988).

7. Short-selling refers to borrowing shares, selling at the current market price with the hope of replacing them at a lower cost later on. Hence short-sellers hope to make money from price declines.

8. Clearly stock market reaction to insider trading is not instantaneous. Instead, there appears to be a slow adjustment process over the course of a year.

9. The method by which we measure the abnormal returns is called an event study, pioneered by Fama, Fisher, Jensen, and Roll (1969). Brown and Warner (1980, 1985) examine robustness of various methods used to estimate abnormal performance in event studies.

10. We use additional benchmarks such as size-adjusted returns and mean-returns adjusted portfolios. Our results are not sensitive to the choice of the benchmark.

11. Once again the difference between the market adjusted returns to buying and selling portfolios is highly significant due to the huge sample size. The probability is less than two out of 10,000 that such a difference in net returns can arise due to chance. The difference in net returns has an autocorrelation-adjusted t-statistic of 4.5. We also experimented with putting equal weight on each firm as opposed to each firm-month. These tests once again improved insiders' performance. Abnor-

mal profits for sales now average 5.2% while abnormal profits for purchases average 5.1%.

We can compute insiders' abnormal performance by using additional benchmarks. We experimented with two additional approaches. First, we used size-based portfolios instead of the equally weighted average. This approach produced profit estimates of 4.5% for sales and 1.5% for purchases over a holding period of 12 months. Second, we used mean returns to each firm as the measure of normal returns. Mean returns are computed from 60 months to 31 month before the insider-trading month and 61 months to 90 months after the insider-trading month. If there are less than 24 valid returns to estimate the mean return, such an observation was excluded. This approach produced profit estimates of 6.1% for sales and 2.2% for purchases. Hence all three approaches corroborate the information content of insiders' transactions.

12. A separate estimate of the corresponding market return is made for each insider transaction. For instance, suppose that for a given firm there is an insider purchase in February 1975. The insider purchase column records the net return for this firm from March 1975 through February 1976. The market return column records the market return for this event also from March 1975 through February 1976.

13. The finding that profitability of insider trading continues in the 1990s despite stricter enforcement of insider trading regulations is consistent with our observation in chapter 1 that some regulations *improve* the information content of insider trading.

14. The last column of table 2.3 shows the performance of the market index following insiders' transactions in that calendar year. This column is provided to get some idea whether the performance or the mistakes made by insiders are related to the overall market performance. The best showing of insiders' purchases occurs in 1992 when the market index was up sharply by 21.5%. Similarly the second-best performance of insider sales occurred in 1975 when the market was up even higher by 40.8%. Similarly there are three years when the market index was down. These years are 1987, 1989, and 1994. In two out of three of these years, insiders' purchases outperformed the market index and insiders' sales underperformed the index. Insiders can predict whether their firms will do better or worse than the market index in up or down markets. Hence firm-specific performance does not seem to be affected by market performance.

15. Even if insider information pertains to events one or two years in the future, in an information efficient market stock price reaction ought to occur immediately after insider trade becomes public.

16. In figure 2.1 net stock returns for month 0 pass through the origin (zero-profit point) by construction. Our objective is to measure insider-trading profits relative to the insider-trading month. Consequently insider-trading profit at the origin is zero

by *construction*. The construction of the graph also requires care in interpreting the profitability of insider trading before the insider-trading month. From figure 2.1 net returns decline from +2.5% a year before insider-trading month to 0% for the insider-trading month. This means that the net stock returns actually declined by 2.5% before insider purchases. Similarly the net stock returns increased from −16.0% to 0% during the year before insiders' sales. This means that the net stock returns actually increased by 16.0% before insider sales.

17. Using market-adjusted returns approach similar to table 2.2 and equal firm-weights, estimates of insiders' abnormal profits are 5.2%, 6.7%, 7.5%, 7.8%, and 7.1% after 1, 2, 3, 4, and 5 years, respectively. Hence there is minimal price adjustment after two years. Using size-based portfolio returns adjustment and equal firm weights, estimates of insiders' abnormal profits are 5.7%, 7.8%, 8.2%, 8.2%, and 7.6% after 1, 2, 3, 4, and 5 years, respectively. Finally, using mean-adjusted returns and equal firm weights, estimates of insiders' abnormal profits are 5.4%, 7.5%, 8.2%, 8.2%, and 8.4% after 1, 2, 3, 4, and 5 years, respectively. The fact that all three approaches produce similar estimates and the lack of continuing drift after two years suggests that estimates of insiders' profits cannot be attributed to potential biases. Since most investors like to evaluate their performance over one-year holding period, the rest of this book mostly focuses on one-year holding periods.

18. For a potential stock market investor, the distinction between active and passive transactions is critically important. If a given insider sale represents an active transaction, then imitating insiders and selling shares in that firms should be a good bet. After all, insiders are selling in anticipation of future stock price declines. However, if a given insider sale represents a passive transaction, then doing nothing is the appropriate strategy. In this case insiders are simply closing a previously established purchase position.

19. See Brealey and Myers, *Principles of Corporate Finance* (3rd ed., McGraw Hill, p. 126).

20. Why limit ourselves to a three-month horizon? As we discussed before, there are no shortages of possible improvements. Alternatively, we can require that no conflicting signals be present during the past 4 months, 6 months, or even 12 months. If there are any conflicts, we can exclude such observations from further consideration. These filters ensure that insider trading provide a clear buy or sell signal over a longer time period. Obviously, as we go back longer periods and require no conflicting signals, we will be excluding more and more observations.

Other strategies might involve requiring that trading in the same direction must indeed be present during the past three months or the past six months. For instance, to consider that a positive signal is present, we may require that insiders purchase net shares not only for one month, but for three consecutive months or six consecutive months. If insiders tend to break up their information-related transactions into smaller volumes and spread these transactions over a long time horizon, then these more restrictive filters may work even better to isolate times when insiders may be camouflaging their intent. We are free to formulate whatever additional information we may require to determine that a positive or a negative signal has been received. However, more restrictive formulations such as requiring that there be six consecutive months of buying will result in a significant reduction in potential trading situations. Hence we need to trade off the reduction in the number of trading opportunities against our desire to maximize the profitability of any one transaction. Moreover, since there are large numbers of possibilities, any consideration of an optimal trading rule would have to evaluate a large number of alternatives. Since such an exercise is beyond the scope of this book, we will experiment with a couple of ways of strengthening the insider-trading signals.

21. We did experiment with other rules to strengthen the quality of insider-trading signals. Instead of requiring no conflicting signals over the past 3 months, we also required no conflicting signals over the past 6 months. Since this is a more restrictive requirement, the number of trading months that pass this hurdle now decreases to 61,961. The 12-month holding period returns following purchases increases to 30.4% while the 12-month holding period returns following sales declines to 10.1%. The difference is now 20.3 percentage points. This finding implies that (1) by eliminating conflicting signals, we improve the predictive power of the insider-trading signals and (2) the magnitude of the improvements declines with increasing horizons. In other words, avoiding conflicting signals at extremely long horizons is not likely to be fruitful. Instead, it is important to avoid recent conflicting signals. The net stock returns for this strategy following insider purchases now rises to 7.6%. The net return following insider sales declines to -6.8%. The difference in net returns also grows to 14.4 percentage points. This represents an additional 0.8 point improvement over the 3-month horizon results.

Comparing the results of 6-month horizon with those of 3-month horizon gives us increased confidence that by eliminating weak and conflicting signals, we are indeed improving the quality of the insider-trading information. We have been able to devise some simple yet logical restrictions that have significantly increased the information content of insider trading.

As a final comparison we have also required no conflicting signals in the last 12 months. This most restrictive rule resulted in the smallest sample size and best performance of all. The sample size has now decreased to 39,115. Compared with the original sample, we have now excluded almost 90% of the sample. However, the 12-month holding period returns following purchases has now risen to 30.5%, while the 12-month holding period returns following sales has declined to 9.5%. The difference is now a full 21.0 percentage points. Clearly, eliminating conflicting signals unambiguously improves the information content of insider trading.

Chapter 3

1. There are three categories of active/passive, sales/purchases, and conflict/no-conflict classifications. In addition there are four categories of identity of insiders, firm size, consensus, and volume of trade. Overall, there are 2,048 combinations of these seven variables.

2. Golder and Ambachtsheer (1983), Nunn, Madden, and Gombola (1983), and Seyhun (1986) examine the relations between the identity of insiders and average profitability.

3. The operations executives are directly in touch with the implementation of new production technologies, delays or reductions in production time, or even inventory build-ups or run-downs. These are useful signals regarding changes in the health of their firm, and they will affect the valuation of the firm. Financial executives are familiar with changes in firm's cash flows, profitability, sales levels, gross margins, major financial transactions such as acquisitions and spin-offs, negotiations with the banks, changes in bond ratings, credit approval and rejection decisions, and so on. All of these signals directly affect the valuation of the firm in the capital markets. Accounting executives are familiar with all changes in the financial statements of the firm. Marketing executives are involved in all planning and execution of product design, pricing, and promotional issues. Human resource executives are familiar with changes in compensation of top executives, major layoffs and hiring, and personnel departures and arrivals. Finally executives in strategic planning are familiar with planning and execution of major new initiatives of the firm.

4. The profitability of insider trading for officers and directors is statistically significant. The probability that the measured profitability can arise due to chance is less than one in 10,000 for top executives. In contrast, the profitability of large shareholders' transactions is less clear-cut. The likelihood that the measured profitability can arise due to chance is about than one in 20 for large shareholders.

5. These findings corroborate the findings in the finance literature. See Scholes (1972), Nunn, Madden, and Gombola (1983), and Seyhun (1986).

6. Table 3.1 also provides a clear answer to the question, "Where does insider-trading information come from?" The answer provided by our evidence is that insider-trading information clearly comes from being associated with the day to day operations of the firm. Top executives who are closest to the operation of the firm are the best informed. Officers follow the top executives. The information possessed by officers is probably more limited in scope and importance than the information possessed by top executives. Moreover officers probably come into contact with important information at a somewhat later date than the top executives. The delay in obtaining

the information will result in attenuation of the value of the information as some stock price reaction will occur during the interim time period. Directors follow officers. Once again this finding suggests that directors learn of important initiatives even later than the officers. While important, directors' knowledge about major initiatives and changes in overall strategic direction of the firm probably lag both top executives and officers. Finally the least-informed group is the large shareholders. These insiders are most removed from day-to-day operations of the firm. Given our designation, large shareholders have no executive function within the firm. Many of the large shareholders are other corporations, employee stock ownership plans, pension plans, and so on. To call these groups insiders is something of a misnomer. However, insider-trading regulations classify them as insiders. Our evidence suggests that their knowledge about potential order flows that they themselves initiate does not appear to be an important factor in predicting future stock price movements.

7. There is a large literature on volume and insider information. Milgrom and Stokey (1982), Kyle (1985), Easley and O'Hara (1987), Admati and Pfleiderer (1988), Grundy and McNichols (1989), Campbell and Kyle (1993), Foster and Viswanathan (1993), Shalen (1993), and Wang (1994) analyze the relation between volume and special information.

8. Once again these choices are arbitrary and we will examine additional cutoffs. Nevertheless, this simplification should suffice in providing a basic relation between volume and profitability.

9. We have also estimated insiders' abnormal profits using comparison period abnormal returns instead of the market-adjusted returns. To compute comparison period abnormal profits, we first excluded 30 months of return data before and after the insider-trading month. We then estimated the average realized returns to each stock from months -60 to -31 and $+31$ to $+60$ around the insider-trading month. If less than 24 months of returns were available to estimate the comparison period returns, we excluded these observations. Abnormal profit is estimated by subtracting the mean return for the comparison period from the actual return to insiders' firm. Net returns for insiders' sales are multiplied by minus one. This procedure produced estimates of abnormal returns in 304,195 months. The overall abnormal profitability was 4.0%. Moreover abnormal profitability averaged -0.8%, 2.3%, 4.9%, and 6.3% for the four trading volume groups, respectively. This finding suggests that inadequate control for risks of each firm does not lead to biased estimates of insiders' profits. Finally we estimated the statistical significance of insiders' abnormal profits. For each of higher trading volume groups, the estimate of insiders' profits is statistically significant at the 1% level. Also there is less than 1% probability that the differences in profitability between large and small volume of trading can be attributed to chance.

10. It is also important to remember how we define trading months. Existence of at least one trade by a large shareholder allows us to classify that calendar month as a large shareholder month. When we examine large shareholders' trades, we do not constrain what other insiders may be doing. Hence there may be additional purchases and sales by officers at the same time that large shareholders trade.

11. What seems to be surprising is the potential regulatory cost of these large transactions. Why don't top executives worry about the potential regulatory costs of their extremely large transactions? There is some evidence that suggests that they in fact do. The data show that the stock price reaction to the very large transactions by top executives does not take place for two to three months following the month they trade. This evidence suggests that top executives trade extremely large volumes only to exploit information that is more distant in the future. By separating their trading activity from the stock price reaction, top executives may be able to avoid regulatory scrutiny.

12. Further separating top executives' extra large transactions into buying and selling months provides additional lessons. Evidence shows that top executives in large firms have very few months in which they purchase over 100,000 shares. There are only 44 such months in the entire data base. While it is difficult to make precise statements about such few observations, these purchases are profitable. One potential explanation for this finding is that the top executives may prefer to break up large purchases into smaller pieces and execute them over a period of time. Such a change in behavior may explain the paucity of these transactions. In contrast, the data base contains 535 months in which top executives in large firms sell over 100,000 shares. However, the profitability following these extra large sales is a paltry 0.8%. This finding suggests that top executives may be especially worrying about potential shareholder lawsuits if they sell huge number of shares prior to large stock price declines. Consequently, while more common, these large sales are most likely due to liquidity reasons. Once again potential stock market investors should feel more comfortable imitating insiders' purchases than imitating insiders' sales.

13. A related question is whether insiders in large firms are able to trade profitably at all. It is possible that too many factors that are beyond insiders' control affect the stock prices of most large firms, thereby making it very difficult for insiders to trade profitably. For instance, most large firms have many divisions and subsidiaries. It is possible that most insiders in very large organizations have more limited responsibilities that cover a particular division or part of the entire organization. In this case most insiders may observe only a limited amount of information that affects the entire organization in a small way.

14. We measure firm size as the market value of equity at the beginning of the year. Hence changes in the market value of equity during our measurement period do not

affect our classification. Also a firm can appear in more then one group depending what happens to the market value of equity over time. Hence a given firm can be classified as a small firm in 1975, and because of its growth, it may then be classified as one of the medium size firms by the 1980s.

15. We again re-estimated insiders' abnormal profit using the comparison period approach. (See notes 11 and 17 of chapter 2 for details.) Estimates of insiders' abnormal profits for the four firm size groups were 5.4%, 3.7%, 3.6%, and 3.1%, respectively. For all firm size groups, profitability of insider trading is statistically significant. The probability that the positive insider profitability is due to chance varies between less than one in 10,000 in small firms, to about 5% in large firms. Moreover the probability that the differences in profitability between the small and large firms is due to chance is again less than one in 10,000.

16. Once again we experimented with different ways of measuring abnormal returns to be sure that our findings are not specific to the particular methods employed here. First, we examined raw returns for purchases and sales for each size groups separately. The difference in 12-month raw returns between purchases and sales (higher for purchases) using equal weights on firms for the four firm size groups are 11.5%, 6.4%, 3.7%, and 1.9%, respectively. Hence raw returns exhibit the same negative relation between firm size and profitability of insider trading. This finding suggests that the particular method to adjust returns does not cause the differences in insiders' profits across firm size groups. Using size-based portfolio returns adjustment, the difference in 12-month abnormal returns between purchases and sales (higher for purchases) for the four firm size groups are 7.6%, 5.2%, 4.1%, and 2.9%, respectively. Finally using mean-adjusted returns, the difference in 12-month abnormal returns between purchases and sales (higher for purchases) for the four firm size groups are 7.3%, 4.9%, 4.7%, and 2.5%, respectively. All approaches produce the same negative relation between profitability and firm size.

17. While not shown here, we have examined officers' and top executives' profits grouped according to consensus. The results show that consensus has even a stronger influence for officers and top executives. Our evidence shows that the average profitability for officers equals 0.0% with zero consensus. With a selling consensus of −1, profitability equals 1.8%. As selling consensus increases to −3 or more, officers' average profits increase uniformly to 4.9%. Hence an increase in selling consensus from −1 to −3 increases profitability by 2.1 percentage points. Table 3.15 also indicates that buying consensus also increases the profitability of officers' transactions. When buying consensus equals +1, profitability equals 4.7%. When buying consensus equals +3 or more, profitability rises to 6.8%, again a 2.1 percentage point increase. The consensus analysis for top executives is somewhat stronger than it is for officers. With zero consensus, top executives' profits average 1.0%. When selling consensus

equals −1, profitability equals 2.4%. When selling consensus equals −3 or more, top executives' profits rise uniformly to 6.7%, a 4.3 point rise. On the buying side, consensus seems to make a difference although less strongly than for the selling side. When buying consensus equals +1, top executives' profit equals 6.2%. When buying consensus increases to +3 or more, top executives' profits rise uniformly to 8.7%, a 2.5 percentage point rise.

18. Once again we have not analyzed the interaction between consensus and other quality variables. In particular, we have not kept constant the number of shares traded with increasing consensus levels. We would expect that at least some of the information content of consensus variable is due to higher number of shares traded as consensus increases.

19. Back (1993) analyzes the pricing of options in the presence of insider information.

20. Short-swing profits rule declares that all profits arising from a buy and sell orders within six months are recoverable by the corporation.

21. To get a better sense of whether insiders time their option exercises, we also examine top executives' transactions. For top executives, net stock returns following call option exercises equals 2.3% for the 14,703 trading months. For exercises for put options, stock returns remain high at 8.4%. These results suggest that the option exercise decisions of top executives are quite similar to those for the overall sample.

22. We can further extend our analysis of option exercises by combining with the seven indicators of the quality of insiders' information we have discussed earlier. For instance, insiders' put option exercises are a bullish signal. By requiring open market stock purchases at the same time put option exercises take place, the information content of put option exercises is likely to increase. Also call option exercises are a bearish signal (after 1991). Similarly we can require open market stock sales at the same time call option exercises take place. Once again these more selective rules are likely to increase the information content of option exercises. We leave these exercises to a future project.

We have examined other types of acquisitions and dispositions by insiders. This is a catchall category that covers a whole spectrum of stock acquisitions and dispositions. Following other stock acquisitions, stock prices rise, but only 1.0% more than the market. Hence there is a small signal value to these transactions. Following other stock dispositions, stock prices rise 1.1% rather than falling more than the market. Hence other stock dispositions are not informative. The lack of information content for insiders' other acquisitions and dispositions underline the importance of anonymity and open market transactions. Consequently potential stock market investors are advised to stay away from insiders' non-open-market stock acquisitions and dispositions.

Chapter 4

1. The relation between aggregate insider trading and future stock market returns is examined by Seyhun (1988b, 1992b).

2. As a second example, consider a change in foreign exchange rates. Assume that the U.S. dollar has strengthened against the Japanese yen over the past three months. Holding all else constant, such a change would help firms who import from Japan and hurt firms who export to Japan. However, only the corporate insiders have the specific hedging information to accurately estimate the effects of such a change on their own firm's profitability. For instance, consider the specific situation of a prefabricated housing materials manufacturer. The biggest market for these firms is in Japan. Consequently the revenues tend to be denominated in Japanese yen, while the labor and manufacturing costs are in U.S. dollars. For some firms the materials costs may be denominated in Canadian dollars if they import lumber from Canada. However, in order to ensure that the firm does not suffer from an unexpected decline in the value of Japanese yen or a strengthening of the Canadian dollar, most manufacturers will hedge their currency exposure by selling yen futures and buying Canadian dollar futures. Let us suppose that our manufacturer has also sold yen futures and fully hedged its currency exposure. In this case the exporter would not be hurt from the decline in the value of the yen. A decline in yen would translate the firm's Japanese earnings into fewer dollars; however, the firm now has an offsetting gain in the Japanese yen futures. The decline in the value of the yen would have no net effects for this firm. Once again an outsider and an insider can observe the same publicly available information about changes in exchange rates, yet the insider will understand what this means for her firm while the outsider will again be at a disadvantage.

3. To be considered statistically significant, correlations must exceed 13% in absolute value, indicated by thin dashed lines in figure 4.1.

4. In fact insiders in GM sold a net of 2,246 shares in January 1976. Hence GM would get a weight of −1 for this month.

5. The way we defined the buy and sell signals using aggregate insider-trading activity is not the only possible procedure. Alternatively, we could have added up all the shares traded in all firms in a given calendar month and based on this number we could have determined a buy or a sell signal. This procedure implicitly assigns higher weights to larger firms since the number of shares traded increases with firm size. The procedure would be preferred over our procedure if larger firms are more sensitive to macroeconomic conditions and/or insiders in larger firms are more likely to observe the effects of macroeconomic changes. On the other hand, a weakness of this alternative approach is that a single trade involving extremely large number of shares traded would outweigh insider-trading activity in a large number of firms with

smaller volumes. As a result this approach would not capture a general tendency across a large number of firms. Moreover this measure would depend on how many firms exist. Since there are more firms toward the end of the sample period than at the beginning of the sample period, net-trading volumes would be larger at the end of the sample period. Consequently the relation between future stock returns and this insider trading measure could be affected mostly by what happened at the end of the sample period.

6. Seyhun (1992b) performs this refinement. Alternatively, we could have worked with the number of insiders or the net number of transactions by insiders. Both of these other approaches are good candidates as well. However, they are subject to the same kinds of advantages and disadvantages as the aggregate number of shares traded. Most problematically these measures are not completely insensitive to the number of firms outstanding. Since there are a large number of potential ways of measuring aggregate insider-trading activity, we have not experimented with all possibilities.

7. One objection to the above conclusion might be that the results in tables 4.1 and 5.4 are not directly comparable. The tests in table 4.1 contain 79 holding periods, while the tests in table 4.4 contain only 76 holding periods. The reason for this difference is that we only lose the first three months of 1975 in table 4.1, while we lose all twelve months of 1975 in table 4.4 to compute the first aggregate insider-trading signal. To control for this issue, the predictive ability of the 3-month aggregate insider trading has also been examined as of 1976. This adjustment still leaves the 12-month aggregate insider-trading signal as a better predictor of the 3-month-ahead returns to the equally weighted index. Hence aggregation of insider-trading signals over a 12-month window provides a better signal for short-term market returns than aggregation over the three months.

8. For the readers who are familiar with regression analysis, we conducted the following tests. We regressed nonoverlapping future stock returns using the equally weighted market index against the past 12-month aggregate proportion of firms with insider buying. All regression coefficients were positive with t-statistics of 1.43, 1.64, 1.68, and 2.94 at 3-month, 6-month, 9-month, and 12-month future holding periods, respectively. For the 12-month holding period the probability that the positive relation between insider trading and future stock returns can be attributed to chance is less than 1%. Also aggregate insider trading explains 29% of the variation in one-year-ahead returns to the equally weighted market index.

9. We also examine the characteristics of the excluded sample. When the proportion of net buying firms remains between 45% and 55%, there is only a weak insider sentiment signal. When the proportion is between 50% and 55% (a weak buy signal) using the past 12-month aggregate insider trading, the 3-month-ahead returns to the equally weighted index averages only 3.8% with 77.8% positive. When the propor-

tion of buying firms remains between 45% and 50% (a weak sell signal), the 3-month-ahead returns to the equally weighted index averages 2.9%, with 55.6% positive. Hence, while still informative, the weak buy and sell signals provide only a minimal distinction between future market returns. The difference between buy and sell signals averages only 0.9%.

10. As we discussed previously, the cutoff proportions to determine insider buy and sell signals are arbitrary. To shed some additional light on the forecasting ability of aggregate insider-trading activity, we briefly illustrate the results of some additional cutoff rules. We did examine 60%–60% proportions. A given period is considered a buy period if 60% or a greater proportion of firms exhibit insider buying. Similarly a given period is considered a sell period if lower than 60% of the firms exhibit insider buying. The higher cutoff proportions reduce the number of buy signals and increase the number of sell signals. Using the 60%–60% cutoff rule, there is now only one three-month period that is preceded by an insider buy signal. The return for this period is 31.7%. There are a total of 75 three-month periods preceded by a negative insider-trading signal. The average return for these periods is 4.2%. Higher cutoff proportions improve the information content of the insider buy signal to a great extent, while reducing the information content of the insider sell signal by a small amount. Hence extreme insider buying is associated with extremely good news for the stock market. We also examined the strongest 60%–35% rule, which focuses on only a few of the most extreme insider-trading signals on either side. A buy signal is obtained if the proportion of buying firms exceeds 60%. A sell signal is obtained if the proportion of buying firms remains at 35% or below. The drawback of using such extreme insider-trading signals is that such restrictions eliminate most of the insider-trading months from consideration. In fact there are only four 3-month periods that pass this screen, with one buy and three sell signals. Once again the return to the buy period equals 31.7%. The average return for the three strong sell periods is −2.2%. Moreover the market return is negative for all three 3-month periods. Hence the most restrictive negative signals do succeed in predicting an actual market downturn over a 3-month period.

11. The probability that such a difference in returns can occur due to chance is less than 1 percent.

12. Damodaran and Liu (1993) provide industry specific application to real estate investment trusts (REITs).

13. There is less than one in a thousand chance that the agreements among the sign of insider trading can be attributed to chance. For readers who are familiar with statistics, the bivariate correlation coefficients are 23% between Ford and GM, 29% between Ford and Chrysler, and 11% between GM and Chrysler. The likelihood that the correlation coefficients are due to chance are 0.0003, 0.0001, and 0.08, respectively.

14. An example should clarify our procedure. Method 1 is the usual approach of using Ford insider trading to forecast Ford stock returns. In method 2 we use insider trading in Chrysler and GM to buy and sell Ford stock. Similarly we use insider trading in Chrysler and Ford to buy and sell GM stock. Finally in method 3 we look at the aggregated insider trading in Ford, GM, and Chrysler to buy and sell all three stocks.

15. This finding suggests another reason why enforcing insider trading regulations may be so difficult. If stock returns across firms in a given industry are highly positively correlated, insiders can always trade in the stocks of competitor firms, without having to disclose their transactions.

16. Since we cannot establish a priori whether these cross-correlations are positive, zero, or negative, industrywide predictions are likely to be more difficult.

Chapter 5

1. For various potential explanations of the crash, see Miller et al. (1988), Metz (1988), Barrow et al. (1989), Kleidon (1992), and Seyhun (1990b).

2. See Miller et al. (1988), Mitchell and Netter (1989), Roll (1989), and Amihud, Mendelson, and Wood (1990).

3. Portfolio insurance refers to the practice of selling shares when the market declines and buying shares when the market increases. The proceeds of the sales are invested in short-term Treasury securities. Idea is to reduce one's exposure to stock prices as prices fall. If the portfolio is invested entirely in Treasury securities, then it is completely "insured" against further stock price declines. The portfolio insurance as described above was initially pioneered by the firm of LOR Associates in 1981. By 1987 the estimated value of assets covered by portfolio insurance was $100 billion, $50 billion of which was managed directly or indirectly by LOR Associates. This represented about 13% of all pension fund assets at the time. See Tufano (1994). Jacklin, Kleidon, and Pfleiderer (1992) present a model where underestimation of the portfolio insurance can serve as a trigger for the cash. Also see Grossman (1988), Genotte and Leland (1990), and Brennan and Schwartz (1989).

4. See Black (1989) and Jacklin, Kleidon, and Pfleiderer (1992).

5. For a discussion of the settlement process during the crash, see Bernanke (1992). Schwert (1992) analyzes the volatility during and after the crash. He concludes that the volatility increased during and after the crash and returned to normal levels by March of 1988.

6. Shiller (1987, 1988) makes this point.

7. Obviously everyone cannot sell at the same time. For each seller there must be a buyer. The point is that *at the current prices* there were more investors who wanted to sell than those who wanted to buy.

8. Portfolio insurance strategies also did not work very well during the crash since large sell orders could not executed quickly enough. Since popular press blamed portfolio insurance for the crash, the demand for portfolio insurance declined. Following the crash, assets under management at LOR Associates shrank to $10 billion from $50 billion.

9. Obviously the bounce-back occurred from a lower base than the crash. Hence stock returns cannot be simply added to compute the total returns.

10. Seyhun (1990b) conducts a similar analysis as this chapter.

11. In addition to the personal insider purchases, some corporations also announcement corporate buy-back programs immediately following the crash. However, not many of these announcement were actually followed through with purchases (Netter and Mitchell 1989).

Chapter 6

1. See studies by Ball (1968), Rozeff (1984), Keim and Stambaugh (1986), Fama and French (1988), and Poterba and Summers (1988), Campbell and Shiller (1989), Shiller (1989), Kothari and Shanken (1992), Hodrick (1992), and Nelson and Kim (1993). Goetzman and Jorion (1995) argue that long-term predictive ability of dividend yields may be affected by the survival bias.

2. Another possibility is that higher dividends cause greater tax burden, since the tax rate on dividends is higher than the tax rate on capital gains. This can also potentially increase the expected returns when dividend yields are higher.

3. Remember that the yield is simply the dollar dividend paid over the past year divided by the current stock price.

4. Such a behavior is called a nonstationary time series. A formal statistical test confirms that the dividend yield is nonstationary during 1975 to 1994. The first differences of the dividend yield are stationary, and they can be represented by a third-order autoregressive time series. A characteristic of nonstationary time series is that the future behavior of the variable can be quite different than its historical behavior. Consequently we need to be careful in projecting future distribution of the dividend variable from its past distribution. Analysis of non-stationary time series requires special attention, to which we will return later in this chapter.

5. Another possibility is that some insiders only use the dividend levels in their trading decisions, while other insiders trade for liquidity reasons. This explanation does not seem plausible, however.

6. To clarify how the 3.9-point advantage of insider buying over insider selling after controlling for the dividend yield is computed, let us examine each row separately. In rows 1 through 5, the extra returns provided by insider buying over insider selling are 9.6 points, 0.3 points, 2.1 points, 10.0 points, and −2.4 points, respectively. The 3.9 points is the arithmetic average of these five values.

7. In a multiple regression of stock returns against aggregate insider trading and dividend yields, aggregate insider trading retains its significant predictive ability while the dividend yield is no longer statistically significant.

8. We have also explored the relation between dividend yields, insider trading, and longer horizon stock returns. The 6-month holding horizon corroborates the findings from table 6.2. After controlling for aggregate insider trading, the predictive ability of the market dividend yield is once again weak. Given insider selling, in the lowest market dividend group, the future stock returns average 3.7%. As the market dividend yields increase, the future stock returns bounce around. The lowest stock returns occur once again for the fourth highest dividend group. However, with the highest level of the market dividend yields, the future stock returns now average 19.4%. With insider buying and low dividends, the future stock returns average 15.8%. The returns once again bounce around with increasing dividend yields. For the middle group stock returns fall to 9.1%. For the highest dividend yield groups, the stock returns rise to about 16.7%. In contrast, aggregate insider-trading variable continues to maintain its predictive power after we control for the level of dividends. For four of the five rows, insider buying is associated with higher stock returns than insider selling. The average extra return predicted by insider buying is now equal to 6.2 points. This value compares well with the unconditional extra return from table 4.5 which was 7.9 points. Finally we have also explored the 12-month holding periods. Increasing the holding period, appears to increase the predictive power of both the market dividend yield and aggregate insider trading. Given aggregate insider selling, first there is a negative and then a positive relation between dividend yield and 12-month-ahead future stock returns. In the lowest dividend group, the stock returns average 11.9%, falling to −0.2% for the second row, before increasing to 26.1% for the highest dividend group. Given aggregate insider buying, future stock returns also first decline and then sharply increase with dividend yields. In the lowest dividend group, the future stock returns average 19.2%, declining to 15.6% for the middle dividend yield group. In the highest dividend group, future stock returns now rise to 38.4%. Examining the predictor power of insider-trading, holding the market dividend yields constant shows that aggregate insider trading continues to be a strong predictor of future stock returns. All five out of five rows show higher stock returns for

insiders' purchases than for insiders' sales. The average magnitude of the extra returns predicted by insider buying over insider selling equals 11.6 points (compared with an unconditional value of 15.8 points from table 4.6). Hence controlling for dividend yields once again does not significantly reduce the predictive power of insider trading.

9. The extra returns provided by intensive insider buying over intensive insider selling increases to 12.7 points for the 6-month holding period after controlling for the dividend yield. For the 12-month holding period, intensive insider buying is associated with an additional 14.5 percentage point return over intensive insider selling months, holding the market dividend yield constant. This result is not surprising, and it is consistent with our findings from chapter 4.

10. Using the 50%–50% rule instead of the 55%–45% provides similar results. For all five out of five rows, the insider-buy column shows higher 12-month ahead stock returns than the insider sell column. The average extra return provided by the insider buy column is 6.6 points, which is less than the 11.6 points when we conditioned on dividend levels (table 6.4) or the 15.8 points unconditional extra returns (table 4.6). Hence changes in dividend yields somewhat reduces but does not eliminate the information content of aggregate insider trading. We find that dividend changes also maintain some of their predictive power after we control for aggregate insider-trading activity.

Chapter 7

1. Perfect capital markets refer to situations where the taxes, trading costs, and information costs are zero, and they can therefore be ignored. Irrelevancy of the dividends to shareholders' wealth in perfect capital markets is due to Miller and Modigliani (1961).

2. Miller and Rock (1985) explore the dividend policy under asymmetric information. Evidence is consistent with this reasoning. See Asquith and Mullins (1983) and John and Lang (1991).

3. We replicated our analysis by using large transactions by all insiders, total transactions by top executives, as well as large transactions by top executives. These results are all the same. Dividend initiations are not predictable using prior insider purchase activity.

4. These results understate the profit opportunities available to outsiders, since we force outsiders to wait until the beginning of the next month to purchase stock. If insiders purchase stock immediately following dividend initiations, they can further increase their profits.

Chapter 8

1. See Joy, Litzenberger, and McEnnally (1977), Ball (1968), Jones and Litzenberger (1970), Penman (1985), Rendleman, Jones, and Latane (1982), Bamber (1986), Bernard (1990, 1992), Bernard and Thomas (1989) for stock price reaction to earnings announcements.

2. Penman (1985) and Seyhun (1992) examine the relation between earnings announcements and insider trading.

3. As an additional test we have directly examined the relation between immediate 3-month past insider trading and the earnings surprises. Prior to each earnings announcement date, we have examined the total shares traded by all insiders as well as top executives and recorded the subsequent earnings surprise. If insiders were to exploit the earnings surprise, we would expect a positive relation between these two. We would expect insiders to buy a large number of shares immediately before a big positive earnings surprise and sell a large volume of shares immediately before a big negative earnings surprise. Instead, our evidence suggest that there is no relation between past insider trading and the earnings surprise. Insiders do not appear to exploit the upcoming earnings announcements.

4. We also replicated these tests for all insiders and 1,000-share transactions. These tests yield corroborating results. Using selective insider-trading signals increases the information content of insider trading and decreases the information content of earnings surprises. Similar to the results shown earlier, there does not appear to be a systematic relation between insider trading and the earnings surprise. Hence both insider trading and earnings surprise continue to provide independent signals about the future stock price performance. Given insider selling of more than 1,000 shares, the excess returns range from −5.2% for the lowest SUE group to 1.1% for the highest SUE group. Given large insider selling, earning surprises continue to predict future stock returns. The difference between the lowest and highest SUE groups equal 6.3%. Given insider buying of 1,000 shares or more, the excess returns range from −3.5% for the lowest SUE group to 4.0% for the highest SUE group. Once again, given large insider buying, earnings surprises continue to predict future stock returns. The difference between the lowest and highest SUE groups now equals 7.5%. Overall, this test does not indicate any attenuation of the predictive power of earnings surprises after we control for large insider-trading activity. After controlling for the earnings surprise, insider buying indicates higher future stock returns than the insider selling columns. Hence controlling for earnings surprises again does not diminish the predictive power of the insider-trading variable.

5. Looking at each row separately, the excess returns for insider buying over insider selling equal 8.8%, 1.7%, 8.1%, 12.2%, and 6.9%, respectively. The 7.5% is the average of these figures.

Chapter 9

1. Some investors combine these two approaches. This can be characterized as growth at a good price or value with some prospects for growth. In general, growth-based approach seeks out firms with high growth rates of earnings or high growth rates of sales. The idea is to discover future IBMs and Microsofts before everyone else does. To ensure that these firms represent good value, some investors also require that the price-earnings ratio (P/E) be small. After everyone else discovers these high-growth firms, the P/E ratios often skyrocket, and they no longer represent a good buying opportunity.

2. Studies by Basu (1977), Jaffe, Keim, and Westerfield (1989), Chan, Hamao, and Lakonishok (1991), Fama and French (1992), and Lakonishok, Shleifer, and Vishny (1994) examine the predictive ability of P/E ratios. The general finding is that low P/E stocks outperform high P/E stocks.

3. We can compare Chrysler with Ford. In 1984 Ford's earnings were $15.79 per share. Ford closed the year about $45 giving it a P/E ratio of $2.9. In 1992 Ford's earnings were negative giving it a negative P/E ratio.

4. Using the same P/E logic, Chrysler was cheaper than Ford in 1984.

5. See Basu (1977), Chan (1988), Fama and French (1992, 1993), and Lakonishok, Shleifer, and Vishny (1994).

6. Lakonishok, Shleifer, and Vishny (1994) show that glamour stocks (high P/E ratios) tend to be characterized by high rates of recent growth rates of sales and earnings which reverts down to average over a two to five year horizon. Similarly value stocks (low P/E ratios) have low and negative growth rates of earnings which revert up the average over a two- to five-year horizon. This finding is consistent with the overreaction story.

7. As this example illustrates, overreaction to good news can produce similar effects as underreaction to bad news.

8. There is another camp. Some authors claim that the relation between P/E ratios and future stock returns is due to look ahead bias. If a firm has low P/E ratio and fails, it is removed from the data set. Hence the surviving low P/E ratio firms will have a high future return. See Kothari, Shanken, and Sloan (1994). This criticism can be minimized by examining the predictive ability of large firms only.

9. We need to qualify this conclusion. If investors have a short investment horizon, then they may not care. However, if they plan to stay with the stock for a long time, then only fundamentals should matter. If rational pricing is true, then stock price changes should be permanent. If irrational pricing occurs, then subsequent returns may prove to be temporary after fundamental information is released. Hence inves-

tors *may* care whether mispricing or risk story is correct if they have a long investment horizon.

10. This argument assumes that insiders are trading with a risk neutral party such as institutions.

11. Similar to the dividend yields, this pattern is indicative of a nonstationary series.

12. For instance, for an observation in May 1987, we take the P/E ratio from June 30, 1986. For July 1987, the P/E ratio is obtained from June 1987.

13. This evidence is consistent with the story that most market participants tend to extrapolate the most recent performance thereby leading to overreaction. Insiders are aware of the true fundamental value of the firm and therefore act like informed contrarians. Also see Lakonishok, Shleifer, and Vishny (1994).

14. To form relative P/E groupings, we examine each year separately. For instance, we group all stocks in 1978 into one of five groups based on the distributions of their relative P/E ratios in 1978. We then continue in this fashion separately for each year until 1993. Consequently the highest relative P/E group contained firms with P/E ratios that were 11 and above in 1980, while the minimum cutoff for the highest P/E grouping in 1988 was 28.

15. We also replicated the results for 3-month and 6-month holding periods. These results are similar to those for the 12-month holding periods. Once again net stock returns are negatively related to the relative P/E ratio for both insider selling and insider-buying groups for both 3-month and 6-month holding periods. In addition insider trading retains its predictive power for ten out of ten P/E groups. Hence the results for 3-month and 6-month holding periods further corroborate the results for 12-month holding periods.

16. We also replicated our tests using large transactions (more than 1,000 shares traded) for all insiders. These results corroborate our evidence from top executives. Given large insider selling, for the relatively lowest P/E group and large insider selling, net stock returns average 2.3% over the next 12 months. For the second P/E group, net stock returns drop to −2.5%. For the next two groups, net stock returns rise to −0.4%. Finally net stock returns fall to −3.0% for the relatively highest P/E category. Hence the relation between P/E ratios and future net stock returns become quite murky when we control for large insider selling. As for large insider-buying group, the negative relation between P/E ratio and future returns is also weakened. The net stock returns average 3.9% for the lowest P/E group. As the P/E ratio rises, net stock returns fall to a minimum value of 0.8% for the middle group. Net stock returns then rise to 2.9% for the fourth highest P/E group and settle to 1.2% for the highest P/E group. In contrast with the behavior of the relative P/E effect, insider trading does not lose its predictive ability after we control for the relative P/E ra-

tios. After we control for the level of P/E ratio, we see that insider buying always signals a higher average return than insider selling. For five out of five rows, insider trading provides the correct signal. Hence insider trading retains its predictive power when it is confronted with P/E effect. These results agree with those in table 9.8.

17. Additional extensions of this line of inquiry are possible. For instance, in chapter 3 we have identified additional determinants of the quality of insider' information such as lack of a conflicting transactions, unanimity, and active versus passive transactions. The information content of the insider-trading signals can be further strengthened by using these additional observable characteristics. Using even stronger insider-trading signals is likely to further erode the information content of the relative P/E effect.

Chapter 10

1. See Stattman (1980), Rosenberg, Reid, and Lanstein (1985), Chan, Hamao, and Lakonishok (1991), Fama and French (1992, 1993, 1995), and Kothari, Shanken, and Sloan (1995).

2. Some investors believe that in equilibrium, the market value of equity must exceed the book value of equity by a constant fraction. This premium is necessary to induce investors to form corporations.

3. We can provide some simple examples to illustrate this point. Suppose that interest rates fell suddenly. The fall in interest rates will raise stock prices, which in turn will raise the market values above the book values. In this case all stocks will tend to have lower B/M ratios than before. Should investors sell their stock holdings now? The answer is obviously no, unless investors conclude that it was irrational for interest rates to fall in the first place. The problem with irrationality is that if stock prices are set irrationally now, there is no reason to expect that rationality will prevail in the future.

4. This can be because of a supply shock such as an increase in oil prices, a technological shock such as a new development overseas that renders some of the industrial assets in the U.S. obsolete, a political shock such as a revolution in Mexico or the sudden popularity of a fringe movement in the United States, or a monetary shock.

5. See Fama and French (1992, 1993, 1995). Book-to-market ratio and size attenuate the predictive power of beta and price-earnings ratios, while they remain as significant predictors of future stock returns. Fama and French argue that B/M is a risk factor, since high B/M ratios signals persistent poor earnings while low B/M ratios signal strong earnings.

6. For the 6-month horizon in table 10.3, the net stock returns start out at −0.6% for the lowest B/M group, rise to 0.6% for the middle group, and end up at −0.4% for the highest B/M group. Once again the net stock returns appear to be independent of the B/M ratios. For the 12-month horizon, again there appears to be no relation between absolute B/M ratios and the net future stock returns. For the lowest B/M group, the 12-month net stock returns equal −1.6%. As B/M ratios increase, the net stock returns first increase and then fall. For the middle B/M group, the net stock returns rise to 1.1%. For the highest B/M group, the 12-month net stock returns fall back to −0.5%. Overall, the evidence in table 10.3 suggests that absolute B/M ratios have no predictive power at all for the net future stock returns.

7. The relation between insider trading and relative B/M ratios will be examined later.

8. We have also extended the evidence by using only the transactions by top executives or by large volume of insider trading. These results are similar to those shown in table 10.3.

9. We have repeated the analysis using both 3-month-ahead and 6-month-ahead holding periods. These results are similar to those for the 12-month-ahead holding period. In every case after we control for B/M ratios, insider buying predicts higher future returns than insider selling. Moreover B/M ratios retain their predictive ability for 3 months ahead as well as 6 months ahead when we control for insider-trading activity. Hence the evidence from 3-month and 6-month holding periods strengthen our conclusions using the 12-month holding periods.

10. One fruitful extension would be to examine the interaction between P/E ratios discussed in chapter 7 and the book-to-market approach discussed in this chapter. It would be interesting to control for both factors at the same time and examine whether both factors matter. Another extension would be to confront both P/E ratios as well as B/M ratios with yet other determinants of the quality of insiders' information that we uncovered in chapter 3.

Chapter 11

1. See Jensen and Ruback (1983) and Jarrell, Brickley, and Netter (1988) for a review of the evidence on the wealth effects of corporate takeovers. Gilson (1986) discusses legal issues regarding takeovers.

2. For discussion of takeover defenses, see Smiley (1981), Bradley and Wakeman (1983), Dann and DeAngelo (1983), DeAngelo and Rice (1983), Linn and McConnell (1983), Wier (1983), Ryngaert and Netter (1987), and Agrawal and Mandelker (1990).

3. The literature on takeover announcements is quite large. For a sample of studies, see Auerbach and Reishus (1988), Asquith and Kim (1982), Dodd and Ruback (1977),

Bradley (1980), Bradley, Desai, and Kim (1983), Brown and Medoff (1988), DeAngelo and DeAngelo (1989), Dennis and McConnell (1986), Jarrell and Bradley (1980), Franks and Harris (1989), Nathan and O'Keefe (1989), Sanders and Zhanowicz (1992), and Shleifer and Summers (1988).

4. Bradley, Desai, and Kim (1982) make this point.

5. Eyssell (1990), Gupta and Mishra (1988), Jarrell and Poulsen (1989), Pound and Zeckhauser (1990), and Schwert (1996) examine pre-announcement is stock prices to see if this is due to insider trading.

6. We have also examined the relation between pre-announcement drifts and the announcement month net returns. The evidence suggests that the pre-announcement drift comes at the expense of the announcement month returns rather than signaling a more profitable takeover. When there is positive pre-announcement drift, the announcement month net returns equal 18.5%. When there is no pre-announcement drift, the announcement month net returns equal 24.5%. The difference of 6% is almost equal to the average pre-announcement drift.

7. Studies by Elliott, Morse, and Richardson (1984), Eyssell (1990), Eyssell and Arshadi (1993), Jarrell and Poulsen (1989), Keown and Pinkerton (1981) and Keown et al. (1985) examine insider trading in target firms.

8. We have also examined the number of shares traded by top executives. This evidence corroborates the evidence in table 11.6. Top executives are, on net, no more likely to buy shares in target firms than they do in nontarget firms prior to takeover announcements. Specifically, top executives in target firms on net sell 3,988 shares during the 12-month period prior to takeover announcement. During the same time period, top executives in nontarget firms sell 4,577. The difference is small and insignificant. We replicated the evidence in table 11.6 using all insiders instead of top executives only. These results were also quite similar to those of the top executives. Overall, our evidence suggests that target managers do not exploit their knowledge about the upcoming takeover announcements.

9. Brown and Raymond (1986) and Palepu (1986) investigate whether the identity of takeover targets can be predicted.

10. We have also replicated our analysis using large transactions by all insiders. These are almost identical to those in table 11.7. In addition we looked at all transactions by top executives as well as large transactions by top executives. For top executives the probability of success was 89% regardless of insider buying, selling, or no trade. Finally large transactions by top executives also produced results quite similar to those in table 11.7. Overall, these findings corroborate the conclusion that insider trading in target firms does not help predict the success of the target firms.

11. We have restricted the sample to those firms where the top executives buy or sell more than 10,000 shares. Using the large transactions of top executives is designed to measure the intensity of insider-trading activity. These results once again corroborate the earlier interpretations. Looking at large transactions eliminates more of the buy sample. There are now only 30 firms in which top executives reported buying 10,000 or more during a 12-month period prior to the takeover announcement. Moreover both the announcement month returns and the 6-month returns are lower for the buy group than they are for the sell group. The announcement month returns for the buy group average 13.8% compared with 20.3% for the sell group. Similarly the 6-month net returns for the buy group average 12.3% compared with 15.9% for the sell group. Once again our results show that insiders do not appear to be exploiting the takeover announcements in their own firms.

Chapter 12

1. Jarrell and Poulsen (1989b), Magenheim and Mueller (1988), Mitchell and Lehn (1990), and Morck, Shleifer and Vishny (1990) examine the price effects of takeovers on bidder firms.

2. Mikkelson and Ruback (1985) and Holderness and Sheehan (1985).

3. Schwert (1996).

4. For a review of takeover defenses, see Jarrell and Poulsen (1987), Lease, McConnell, and Mikkelson (1983), DeAngelo and DeAngelo (1985), Partch (1987), Dodd and Leftwich (1980), Netter (1987), and Mikkelson and Ruback (1985).

5. Bidder firms tend to be large firms. Seyhun (1986) shows that the insiders in large firms are, on average, net sellers of stock. Hence the fact that there is net insider selling in both successful and unsuccessful targets is to be expected to some extent.

6. Another possible explanation for this finding is that only those potential bidders who experience positive stock price reaction proceed with the takeover plans. Those firms who experience stock price drops say because of negative earnings announcements abandon or postpone takeover plans. This reasoning can also result in pre-announcement positive drift for bidder firms.

7. See Seyhun (1990a) for an analysis of insider trading in bidder firms.

8. We have replicated our analysis using large transactions by all insiders, all transactions of top executives, and the large transactions by top executives. All of these produced similar results as those in table 12.4. For instance, for top executives, the probabilities of success are 76%, 79%, and 79% for the buy, no trade, and sell groups, respectively. The buy group is associated with slightly lower probability of success

than the sell group. Hence our conclusion appears to be robust. It is difficult to predict which bidder firms are more likely to be successful.

9. We have also examined other predictors of future stock returns in bidder firms. There is no difference in the subsequent performance of the bidder firms based on the pre-announcement stock price drifts up to 6 months. For both groups, the 6-month net stock returns equal exactly 2.5%. However, over a 12-month period, bidder firms with positive pre-announcement drifts do somewhat better than those with no pre-announcement drift. The 12-month net stock returns for the two groups are 5.2% and 4.2%, respectively.

10. See, for instance, Asquith, Bruner, and Mullins (1987), Franks, Harris, and Mayer (1988), Fishman (1989), and Eckbo, Giammarino, and Heinkel (1990) for these arguments.

11. For evidence, see Travlos (1987), Asquith, Bruner, and Mullins (1987), Wansley, Lane, and Yang (1987), Servaes (1991), Aggrawal, Jaffe, and Mandelker (1992), and Martin (1996).

Chapter 13

1. Keim and Stambaugh (1986), Summers (1986), Lo and McKinlay (1988), Fama and French (1988), Poterba and Summers (1988), Breen, Glosten, and Jagannathan (1989), Conrad and Kaul (1989), and Lo and McKinlay (1995) examine stock return predictability. Kandel and Stambaugh (1996) investigate the asset allocation decision of an investor in the presence of predictability.

2. So called technical analysis is also based on the premise that the future stock returns are predictable from past stock returns. The underlying concept is that stock prices exhibit positive momentum in the short term. If stock prices have fallen recently, they will continue to fall in the near term. If stock prices have risen recently, they will continue to rise in the near term. In practice, technical analysts use charts to map the recent stock price patterns and identify potential future movements. The actual practice of technical analysis is too subjective to be of much scientific value, and hence we will not be concerned with it per se.

3. Brennan and Cao (1996) present a model where uninformed traders behave as rational trend followers while the informed traders follow a contrarian strategy. DeBondt and Thaler (1985, 1987), Chan (1988), Chopra, Lakonishok and Ritter (1992), Jegadeesh and Titman (1993), and Lakonishok, Shleifer, and Vishny (1994) examine the profitability of contrarian strategies.

4. See, for instance, Fama and French (1988, 1993, 1995, 1996). For a counterview, see Lo and McKinlay (1995).

5. Of the large stock markets, German and Japanese stock markets were shut down during wars. Portugal's stock market was closed by the Salazar government. The Bolshevik government renounced the foreign currency denominated debt obligations of the previous Czarist regime in 1917.

6. Brown, Goetzmann, and Ross (1995) argue that survival bias induces the stock return patterns.

7. Clearly the methods we use to define winners and losers are somewhat arbitrary. We could have used another benchmark market index such as the value-weighted market index, or the Standards and Poor's 500 index as a benchmark or we could have used another cutoff rate instead of the 20%. We did experiment with these other measures as well. For instance, we used the value-weighted index, as well as a 50% cutoff rate, for winners and losers. These results are similar and therefore they are not reported separately. Nevertheless, if the phenomenon we are investigating is a genuine relation, it should show up consistently regardless of the particular implementation choices we make.

8. We can illustrate this concept with an example. Suppose that we have ten stocks, 9 of which have a return of exactly 10%, while one firm has a return of 200% (exhibiting right skewness). In this case the average return for the index of these ten stocks will be 29%, which beats out 9 of the 10 firms. Alternatively, the net returns for 9 of the 10 firms will be negative. In our example losers outnumber the winners simply due to a statistical artifact called right skewness. Moreover our evidence above demonstrates that right skewness becomes more important with longer holding periods.

9. At the time of this writing, Netscape announced a quarterly earnings loss due to intense competition from Microsoft for internet browser business. Netscape's stock price is currently in the teens.

10. We also replicated the analysis in table 13.6 using subsequent five-year horizons as well. These were similar qualitatively and somewhat stronger in magnitude. Specifically the winners performed very similar to the equally weighted market index while the losers outperformed the market by over 30% in five years. Since looking forward to the subsequent five years results in greater loss of data, we focus on the three-year horizon numbers.

Chapter 14

1. Second, some of these issues involve statistical considerations that are best left for the end.

2. We have also examined more tardy reporting. The reporting delays for the most tardy 10% of all trades exceed 67 days. Put alternatively, outsiders can find out about

90% of insider trading within about two months of the trade. Finally, the most tardy 5% of insider trading is reported with more than 143 days (almost five months) of delay. Given some very late reported transactions, the average reporting delay comes out to 47 days.

3. See *Wall Street Journal*, Wednesday January 7, 1998, p. c5.

4. To explain the price impact better, a bit of a digression may be in order. Investors can submit two kinds of orders, a market order or a limit order. A market order must be executed immediately. Hence there is no question about the quantity of shares to be bought or sold, however, the execution price is uncertain. A large buy order can only be executed immediately if concession is given in terms of a (temporary) higher price. This temporary change in stock price to facilitate the order execution is called the price impact. In contrast, traders can also submit a limit order. A limit order will only execute if the market price reaches the limit price specified by the trader. Here the price is fixed but the quantity is uncertain. By definition, the limit order has no price impact; however, the order may never execute. Which is better depends on why the investor is trading.

5. We also conducted similar analyses for officers, directors and large shareholders as well. Our conclusions for these groups are similar in nature. For instance, for officers' transactions, the overall profitability for the 12 months following the reporting month reached about 3%. Following officers' transactions in small firms, the post reporting profitability approached almost 7%, which is more than sufficient for profitable imitation by the outsiders. Finally, for large transactions by officers (more than 10,000 shares), profitability during the 12 months following the reporting month exceeded 5%.

6. An example should clarify our definition of risk. Suppose that an outsider imitated 100 insider transactions, 50 purchases, and 50 sales. Following 50 purchases, stock prices outperformed the market index 30 times. Hence 20 transactions led to losses. Following the 50 sales, stock prices underperformed the market index by 25 times. Hence 25 transactions led to losses. In this example the risk of loss is 45% (20 plus 25 divided by 100).

7. To estimate loss probabilities, we randomly pick with replacement a given size portfolio 1,000 times. For instance, for the 250-mimicking transaction strategy, we estimate outsiders' profits 1,000 times using 250 randomly chosen insider trades. Statistically savvy readers will recognize that this simulation exercise is equivalent to statistical significance tests using a bootstrapping approach to modeling the distribution of outsiders' profits.

8. Loss probabilities are set equal to the sample fractions of losing transactions in 1,000 replications.

References

Admati, A., and P. Pfleiderer. 1988. A theory of intraday patterns: Volume and price variability. *Review of Financial Studies* 1:3–40.

Agrawal, and G. Mandelker. 1990. Large shareholders and the monitoring of managers: The case of antitakeover charter amendments. *Journal of Financial and Quantitative Analysis* 25:143–61.

Allen, F., and D. Gale. 1992. Stock price manipulation. *Review of Financial Studies* 5: 503–29.

Amihud, Y., H. Mendelson, and R. W. Wood. 1990. Liquidity and the 1987 stock market crash. *Journal of Portfolio Management* 16:65–69.

Arshadi, N., and T. H. Eyssell. 1991. Regulatory deterrence and registered insider trading: The case of tender offers. *Financial Management* 20:30–39.

Asquith, P., and E. H. Kim. 1982. The impact of merger bids on the participating firms' security holders. *Journal of Finance* 37:1209–28.

Asquith, P., and D. Mullins. 1983. The impact of initiating dividend payments on shareholder's wealth. *Journal of Business* 56:77–96.

Auerbach, A., and D. Reishus. 1988. The effects of taxation on merger decision. In *Corporate Takeovers: Causes and Consequences,* A. Auerbach, ed. Chicago: University of Chicago Press, pp. 157–83.

Back, K. 1993. Asymmetric information and options. *Review of Financial Studies* 6: 435–72.

Barrow. R. J., E. F. Fama, D. R. Fischel, A. H. Meltzer, R. W. Roll, and L. G. Tesler. 1989. In *Black Monday and the Future of Financial Markets*, R. W. Kampuis, R. C. Kormendi, and J. W. H. Watson, eds. Mid-America Institute for Public Policy Research. Homewood, IL: Irwin.

Baesel, J. B., and G. R. Stein. 1979. The value of information: Inferences from the profitability of insider trading. *Journal of Financial and Quantitative Analysis* 14:553–71.

Bagehot, W. 1989. The only game in town. *Financial Analysts Journal* 22:12–14.

Bagnoli, M., and B. L. Lipman. 1991. Stock price manipulation through takeover bids. Working paper. Indiana University.

Baker, G., M. Jensen, and K. Murphy. 1988. Compensation and incentives: Prospective vs. theory. *Journal of Finance* 43:593–616.

Bamber, L. S. 1986. The information content of annual earning releases: A trading volume approach. *Journal of Accounting Research* 24:40–56.

Basu, S. 1977. Investment performance of common stocks in relation to their price earnings ratios: A test of the efficient market hypothesis. *Journal of Finance* 32:663–82.

Benesh, G. A., and R. A. Pari. 1987. Performance of stocks recommended on the basis of insider trading activity. *The Financial Review* 22:145–58.

Bernanke, B. 1990. Clearing and settlement during the crash. *Review of Financial Studies* 3:133–51.

Bernhardt, D., B. Hollifield, and E. Hughson. 1995. Investment and insider trading. *Review of Financial Studies* 8:501–43.

Black, F. 1986. Noise. *Journal of Finance* 41:529–43.

Black, F. 1988. An equilibrium model of the crash. In *NBER Macroeconomics Annual 1988*. S. Fisher, ed. Cambridge: MIT Press, pp. 269–75.

Bradley, M., and L. Wakeman. 1983. The wealth effects of targeted share repurchases. *Jornal of Financial Economics* 11:301–28.

Breen, W., L. R. Glosten, and R. Jagannathan. 1989. Economic significance of predictable variations in stock index returns. *Journal of Finance* 44:1177–89.

Brick, I. E., M. Statman, and D. G. Weaver. 1989. Event studies and model misspecification: Another look at the benefits of outsiders from public information about insider trading. *Journal of Business, Finance, and Accounting* 16:401–20.

Brickley, J., R. Lease, and C. Smith. 1988. Ownership structure and voting on anti-takeover amendments. *Journal of Financial Economics* 17:267–91.

Brodsky, E., and R. P. Swanson. 1988. Insider trading litigation: The obstacles to recovery. *Securities Regulation Law Journal* 16:31–53.

Brown, S., and J. Warner. 1980. Measuring security price information. *Journal of Financial Economics* 8:205–58.

Brown, S., and J. Warner. 1985. Using daily stocks returns: The case and event studies. *Journal of Financial Economics* 14:1–31.

Brown, K. C., and M. V. Raymond. 1986. Risk arbitrage and the prediction of successful corporate takeovers. *Financial Management* 15:54–63.

Brown, C., and J. Medoff. 1988. The impact of firm acquisitions on labor. In *Corporate Takeovers: Causes and Consequences*, A. Auerbach, ed. Chicago: University of Chicago Press, pp. 9–28.

Brudney, V. 1979. Insiders, outsiders and informational advantages under the federal securities laws. *Harvard Law Review* 93:322–76.

Campbell, J., and A. S. Kyle. 1993. Smart money, noise trading, and stock price behavior. *Review of Economic Studies* 60:1–34.

Carlton, D. W., and D. R. Fischel. 1983. The regulation of insider trading. *Stanford Law Review* 35:857–95.

Carney, W. J. 1987. Signalling and causation in insider trading. *Catholic University Law Review* 36:863–98.

Chalk, A., and J. Peavy, III. 1985. Understanding the pricing of initial public offerings. *Research in Finance* 8:203–40.

Chan, K. C. 1988. On the contrarian investment strategy. *Journal of Business* 61: 147–63.

Chan, L. K. C., Y. Hamao, and J. Lakonishok. 1991. Fundamentals and stock returns in Japan. *Journal of Finance* 46:1739–64.

Chopra, N., J. Lakonishok, and J. Ritter. 1992. Measuring abnormal performance: Do stocks overreact? *Journal of Financial Economics* 40:793–805.

Chopra, N., J. Lakonishok, and J. Ritter. 1992. Measuring abnormal performance: Does the stock market overreact? *Journal of Financial Economics* 31:235–68.

Cleeton, D. L., and P. A. Reeder. 1987. Stock and option markets: Are insider trading regulations effective? *Quarterly Review of Economics and Business* 27:63–76.

Coase, R. 1937. The nature of the firm. *Econometrica* 4:386–405.

Coase, R. H. 1960. The problem of social cost. *Journal of Law and Economics* 3:1–44.

Coase, R. 1988. *The Firm, the Market, and the Law.* Chicago: University of Chicago Press.

Copeland, T., and D. Galai. 1983. Information effects on bid-ask spread. *Journal of Finance* 38:1457–69.

Cornell, B., and E. R. Sirri. 1992. The reaction of investors and stock prices to insider trading. *Journal of Finance* 47:1031–59.

Cox, J. D. 1986. Insider trading and contracting: A critical response to the Chicago School. *Duke Law Journal* 1986:628–59.

Dahlman, C. 1979. The problem of externality. *Journal of Law and Economics* 23:148.

Damodaran, A., and C. Liu. 1993. Insider trading as a signal of private information. *Review of Financial Studies* 6:79–120.

Dann, L., and L. DeAngelo. 1983. Standstill agreements, privately negotiated stock repurchases, and the market for corporate control. *Journal of Financial Economics* 11:275–300.

DeAngelo, H., and L. DeAngelo. 1989. Proxy contests and the governance of publicly held corporations. *Journal of Financial Economics* 18:29–59.

DeAngelo, H., and E. Rice. 1983. Antitakeover charter amendments and stockholder wealth. *Journal of Financial Economics* 11:329–60.

DeLong, J. B., A. Shleifer, L. H. Summers, and R. J. Waldmann. 1990. Noise trader risk in financial markets. *Journal of Political Economy* 98:703–38.

Demsetz, H. 1967. Towards a theory of property rights. *American Economic Review* 57:347–59.

Dennis, D., and J. McConnell. 1986. Corporate mergers and security returns. *Journal of Financial Economics* 15:143–87.

Diamond, D. W., and R. E. Verrecchia. 1981. Information aggregation in a noisy rational expectations economy. *Journal of Financial Economics* 9:221–35.

Dodd, P., and R. S. Ruback. 1977. Tender offers and stockholder returns: An empirical analysis. *Journal of Financial Economics* 5:351–73.

Dooley, M. P. 1980. Enforcement of insider trading restrictions. *Virginia Law Review* 66:1–83.

Dye, R. A. 1984. Insider trading and incentives. *Journal of Business* 57:295–312.

Easley, D., and M. O'Hara. 1987. Price, trade size, and information in securities markets. *Journal of Financial Economics* 19:69–90.

Eckbo, B. E., R. M. Ciammarino, and R. L. Heinkel. 1990. Asymmetric information and the medium of exchange in takeovers: Theory and tests. *Review of Financial Studies* 3:651–75.

Elliot, J., D. Morse, and G. Richardson. 1984. The association between insider trading and information announcements. *Rand Journal of Economics* 15:521–36.

Estrada, J. 1994. Insider trading: Regulation, deregulation, and taxation. *Swiss Review of Business Law* 5:209.

Estrada, J. 1995. Insider trading: Regulation, securities markets, and welfare under risk aversion. *Quarterly Review of Economics and Finance* 35:421.

Eyssell, T. H. 1990. Corporate insiders, toehold acquisitions, and information leakage: Do insiders tip their hands? *Akron Business and Economic Review* 21:90–103.

Eyssell, T. H., and N. Arshadi. 1993. Insiders, outsiders, or trend-chasers? An investigation of pre-takeover transactions in the share of target firms. *Journal of Financial Research* 16:49–59.

Fama, E. F. 1970. Efficient capital markets: A review of theory and empirical work. *Journal of Finance* 23:383–417.

Fama, E. F. 1991. Efficient capital markets: II. *Journal of Finance* 46:1575–1617.

Fama, E. F., L. Fisher, M. Jensen, and R. Roll. 1969. The adjustment of stock prices to new information. *International Economic Review* 10:1–21.

Fama, E. F., and K. R. French. 1988a. Dividend yields and expected stock returns. *Journal of Financial Economics* 22:3–25.

Fama, E. F., and K. R. French. 1988b. Permanent and temporary components of stock prices. *Journal of Political Economy* 96:246–73.

Fama, E. F., and K. R. French. 1992. The cross-section of expected returns. *Journal of Finance* 47:427–66.

Fama, E. F., and K. R. French. 1993. Common risk factors in the returns on bonds and stocks. *Journal of Financial Economics* 33:3–56.

Fama, E. F., and K. R. French. 1995. Size and book-to-market factors in earnings and returns. *Journal of Finance* 50:131–55.

Finnerty, J. E. (1976a). Insiders and market efficiency. *Journal of Finance* 31:1141–48.

Finnerty, J. E. 1976b. Insiders' activity and inside information: A multivariate analysis. *Journal of Financial and Quantitative Analysis* 11:205–16.

Fishman, M. J. 1989. Preemptive bidding and the role of the medium of exchange in acquisitions. *Journal of Finance* 44:41–57.

Flynn, J. T. 1934. *Security Speculation and Its Economic Effects*. New York: Harcourt, Brace.

Foster, F. D., and S. Viswanathan. 1993. Strategic trading with asymmetrically informed traders and long-lived information. Working paper. Duke University.

Franks, J., and R. Harris. 1989. Shareholder wealth effects of corporate takeovers: The U.K. experience 1955–1985. *Journal of Financial Economics* 18:225–49.

Gaillard, E. 1992. *Insider Trading, the Laws of Europe, the United States and Japan*. Boston: Kluwer Law and Taxation.

Gennotte, G., and H. Leland. 1990. Market liquidity, hedging and crashes. *American Economic Review* 80:999–1021.

Gilson, R. 1986. The law and finance of corporate acquisitions. New York: Foundation Press.

Glosten, L. R., and P. R. Milgrom. 1985. Bid, ask and transaction prices in a specialist market with heterogeneously informed traders. *Journal of Financial Economics* 14:71–100.

Glosten, L. R. 1989. Insider trading, liquidity, and the role of the monopolist specialist. *Journal of Business* 62:211–35.

Goetzmann, W. N., and P. Jorion. 1995. A longer look at dividend yields. *Journal of Business* 68:483–508.

Golder, R. 1983. The inside edge: A study of insider trading in Canada. *Business Review*: 67–72.

Golder, R., and K. Ambachtsheer. 1983. Are some insiders more "inside" than others? Comment. *Journal of Portfolio Management* 10:75.

Gosnell, T., A. J. Keown, and J. M. Pinkerton. 1992. Bankruptcy and insider trading: Differences between exchange-listed on OTC firms. *Journal of Finance* 47:349–62.

Grossman, S. J. 1988. Analysis of the implications for stock and futures price volatility of program trading and dynamic hedging strategies. *Journal of Business* 61:275–98.

Grossman, S. J., and J. E. Stiglitz. 1980. On the impossibility of informationally efficient markets. *American Economic Review* 70:393–408.

Grundy, B., and M. McNichols. 1989. Trade and revelation of information through prices and direct disclosure. *Review of Financial Studies* 2:495–526.

Gupta, A., and L. Misra. 1988. Illegal insider trading: Is it rampant before corporate takeovers? *Financial Review* 23:453–64.

Haddock, D. D., and J. R. Macey. 1987. Regulation on demand: A private interest model, with an application to insider trading regulation. *Journal of Law and Economics* 30:311–52.

Hart, O. D. 1977. On the profitability of speculation. *Quarterly Journal of Economics* 90:579–96.

Hasbrouck, J. 1988. Trades, quotes, inventories and information. *Journal of Financial Economics* 22:229–52.

Heller, H. 1982. Chiarella, SEC rule 14e-3 and Dirks: "Fairness" versus economic theory. *Business Lawyer* 37:517–58.

Herzel, L., and L. Katz. 1987. Insider trading: Who loses? *Lloyds Bank Review*: 15–26.

Hodrick, R. 1992. Dividend yields and expected stock returns: Alternative procedures for inference and measurement. *Review of Financial Studies* 5:357–86.

Jacklin, C. J., A. W. Kleidon, and P. Pfleiderer. 1992. Underestimation of portfolio insurance and the crash of October 1987. *Review of Financial Studies* 5:35–63.

Jaffe, J. 1974a. Special information and insider trading. *Journal of Business* 47: 410–28.

Jaffe, J. 1974b. The effect of regulation changes on insider trading. *Bell Journal of Economics and Management Science* 5:93–121.

Janvey, R. S. 1986. SEC investigation of insider trading. *Securities Regulation Law Journal* 13:299–331.

Janvey, R. S. 1987. Criminal prosecution of insider trading. *Securities Regulation Law Journal* 15:136–53.

Jarrell, G., and M. Bradley. 1980. The economic effects of federal and state regulation of cash tender offers. *Journal of Law and Economics* 23:371–88.

Jarrell, G., J. Brickley, and G. Netter. 1988. The market for corporate control: The empirical evidence since 1980. *Journal of Economic Perspectives* 2:49–68.

Jarrell, G. A., and A. B. Poulsen. 1989a. Stock trading before the announcement of tender offers: Insider trading or market anticipation? *Journal of Law, Economics, and Organization* 5:225–48.

Jarrell, G. A., and A. B. Poulsen. 1988b. The returns to acquiring firms in tender offers: Evidence from three decades. *Financial Management* 18:12–19.

Jarrow, R. A. 1992. Market manipulation, bubbles, corners, and short squeezes. *Journal of Financial and Quantitative Analysis* 27:311–36.

Jegadeesh, N. 1990. Evidence on the predictable behavior of stock returns. *Journal of Finance* 45:881–98.

Jegadeesh, N., and S. Titman. 1993. Returns to buying winners and selling losers: Implications for stock market efficiency. *Journal of Finance* 43:65–91.

Jegadeesh, N., and S. Titman. 1995. Overreaction, delayed reaction, and contrarian profits. *Review of Financial Studies* 8:973–93.

Jensen, M., and R. Ruback. 1983. The market for corporate control: The scientific evidence. *Journal of Financial Economics* 12:5–50.

John, K., and L. H. P. Lang. 1991. Insider trading around dividend announcements: Theory and evidence. *Journal of Finance* 46:1361–89.

John, K., and R. Narayanan. 1997. Market manipulation and the role of insider trading regulations. *Journal of Business* 70:217–47.

Kandel, S., and R. F. Stambaugh. 1996. On the predictability of stock returns: An asset-allocation perspective. *Journal of Finance* 51:385–424.

Karjala, D. S. 1982. Statutory regulation of insider trading in impersonal markets. *Duke Law Journal* 1982 (September): 637–49.

Karpoff, J. M., and D. Lee. 1991. Insider trading before new issue announcements. *Financial Management* 20:18–26.

Keim, D., and R. Stambaugh. 1986. Predicting returns in stock and bond markets. *Journal of Financial Economics* 17:357–90.

Keown, A. J., and J. M. Pinkerton. 1981. Merger announcements and insider trading activity: An empirical investigation. *Journal of Finance* 36:855–69.

Keown, A. J., and J. M. Pinkerton, L. Young, and R. S. Hansen. 1985. Recent SEC prosecution and insider trading on forthcoming merger announcements. *Journal of Business Research* 13:329–37.

Kerr, H. S. 1980. The battle of insider trading vs. market efficiency. *Journal of Portfolio Management* 6:47–50.

Kleidon, A. W. 1992. Arbitrage, nontrading, and stale prices: October 1987. *Journal of Business* 65:483–507.

Kothari, S., and Shanken, J. 1992. Stock return variation and expected dividends: A time-series and cross-sectional analysis. *Journal of Financial Economics* 31:177–210.

Kothari S. P., J. Shanken, and R. G. Sloan. 1995. Another look at the cross-section of expected stock returns. *Journal of Finance* 50:185–224.

Kyle, A. S. 1985. Continuous auctions and insider trading. *Econometrica* 53:1315–35.

Kyle, A. S. 1989. Informed speculation with monopolistic competition. *Review of Financial Studies* 56:317–55.

Lakonishok, J., A. Shleifer, and R. W. Vishny. 1994. Contrarian investment, extrapolation, and risk. *Journal of Finance* 49:1541–78.

Lang, L. H. P., R. H. Litzenberger, and V. Madrigal. 1992. Testing financial market equilibrium under asymmetric information. *Journal of Political Economy* 100:317–48.

Langevoort, D. C. 1992. Theories, assumptions, and securities regulation: Market efficiency revisited. *University of Pennsylvania Law Review* 140:851–920.

Larcker, D. F., and Lys, T. 1987. An empirical analysis of the incentives to engage in costly information acquisitions: The case of risk arbitrage. *Journal of Financial Economics* 18:111–26.

Lee, M. H., and H. Bishara. 1989. Recent Canadian experience on the profitability of insider trades. *Financial Review* 24:235–49.

Leland, H. E. 1992. Insider trading: Should it be prohibited? *Journal of Political Economy* 100:859–87.

Leland, H. E., and D. H. Pyle. 1977. Informational asymmetries, financial structure, and financial intermediation. *Journal of Finance* 32:371–87.

Linn, S., and J. McConnell. 1983. An empirical investigation of the impact of "Antitakeover" amendments on common stock prices. *Journal of Financial Economics* 11: 361–400.

Lin, J., and J. S. Howe. 1990. Insider trading in the OTC market. *Journal of Finance* 45:1273–84.

Lo, A. W., and A. C. MacKinlay. 1990. When are contrarian profits due to overreaction. *Review of Financial Studies* 3:175–205.

Lo, A. W., and A. C. MacKinlay. 1995. Maximizing predictability in the stock and bond markets. Working paper. MIT and University of Pennsylvania.

Loderer, C., and D. P. Sheehan. 1989. Corporate bankruptcy and managers' self-serving behavior. *Journal of Finance* 44:1059–75.

Macey, J. 1991. Insider trading, economics, politics, and policy. American Enterprise Institute for Public Policy Research.

MacKinlay, A. C. 1995. Multifactor models do not explain deviations from the CAPM. *Journal of Financial Economics* 38:3–28.

Magenheim, E., and D. Mueller. 1988. Are acquiring firm shareholders better off after an acquisition? *Corporate Takeovers: Causes and Consequences*, A. Auerbach, ed. Chicago: University of Chicago Press, pp. 171–93.

Malkiel, B. 1987. Efficient market hypothesis. In *The New Palgrave: A Dictionary of Economics*, vol. 2, J. Eatwell, M. Milgate, and P. Newman, eds. London: Macmillan, pp. 120–23.

Mankiw, N., D. Romer, and M. Shapiro. 1991. Stock market forecastability and volatility: A statistical appraisal. *Review of Financial Studies*, 4, 455–478.

Manne, H. 1966. Insider trading and the stock market. New York: Free Press.

Manne, H. 1966. In defense of insider trading. *Harvard Business Review* 44:113–22.

Manove, M. 1989. The harm from insider trading and informed speculation. *Quarterly Journal of Economics* 104:823–46.

Martin, K. J. 1996. The method of payment in corporate acquisitions, investment opportunities, and management ownership. *Journal of Finance* 51:1227–46.

Metz, T. 1988. *Black Monday: The Catastrophe of October 19, 1987 and Beyond.* New York: William Morrow.

Meulbroek, L. 1992. An empirical analysis of illegal insider trading. *Journal of Finance* 47:1661–1700.

Mikkelson, W., and M. Partch, 1986. Valuation effects of security offerings and the issuance process. *Journal of Financial Economics* 15:31–60.

Milgrom, P., and N. Stokey. 1982. Information, trade and common knowledge. *Journal of Economic Theory* 26:17–27.

Miller, M. H., J. D. Hawke, B. Malkiel, and M. Scholes. 1988. *Final Report of the Committee of Inquiry Appointed by the Chicago Mercantile Exchange to Examine the Events Surrounding October 19, 1987.* Chicago: Committee of Inquiry.

Miller, M. H., and F. Modigliani. 1961. Dividend policy, growth and the valuation of shares. *Journal of Business* 34:411–33.

Miller, M. H., and K. Rock. 1985. Dividend policy under asymmetric information. *Journal of Finance* 40:1031–51.

Mitchell, M., and K. Lehn. 1990. Do bad bidders make good targets? *Journal of Applied Corporate Fianance* 3:60–69.

Morck, R., A. Shleifer, and R. Vishny. 1988. Management ownership and market valuation. *Journal of Financial Economics* 17:293–315.

Morck, R., A. Shleifer, and R. Vishny. 1990. Do managerial objectives drive bad acquisitions? *Journal of Finance* 17:31–48.

Morse, D. 1981. Price and trading volume reaction surrounding earning announcements: A closer examination. *Journal of Accounting Research* 19:374–83.

Myers, S., and N. Majluf. 1984. Corporate financing and investment decisions when firms have information that investors do not have. *Journal of Financial Economics* 13: 187–221.

Nathan, K., and T. O'Keefe. 1989. The rise of takeover premiums. *Journal of Financial Economics* 18:101–19.

Netter, J. M., and M. L. Mitchell. 1989. Stock-repurchase announcements and insider transactions after the October 1987 stock market crash. *Financial Management* 18:84–96.

Nunn, K. P., G. P. Madden, and M. J. Gombola. 1983. Are some insiders more "inside" than others? *Journal of Portfolio Management* 9:18–22.

Palepu, K. G. 1986. Predictive takeover targets: A methodological and empirical analysis. *Journal of Accounting and Economics* 8:3–37.

Penman, S. H. 1982. Insider trading and the dissemination of firms' forecast information. *Journal of Business* 55:479–503.

Penman, S. H. 1985. A comparison of the information content of insider trading and management earnings forecasts. *Journal of Financial and Quantitative Analysis* 20:1–17.

Pope, P. F., F. C. Morris, and D. A. Peel. 1990. Insider trading: Some evidence of market efficiency and directors' share dealings in Great Britain. *Journal of Business, Finance, and Accounting* 17:359–80.

Pratt, S. P., and C. W. DeVere. 1978. Relationship between insider trading and rates of return for NYSE common stocks, 1960–66. In *Modern Developments in Investment Management*, James Lorie and Richard Brealey, eds. Hinsdale, IL: Dryden Press.

Ratner, D. 1988. *Securities Regulations*, St. Paul, MN: West Publishing.

Roll, R. W. 1989. The international crash of October 1987. In *Black Monday and the Future of Financial Markets*, R. W. Kamphuis Jr., R. C. Kormendi, and J. W.

Watson, eds. Mid-America Institute for Public Policy Research Inc. Homewood, IL: Irwin.

Rosenberg, B., K. Reid, and R. Lanstein. 1985. Persuasive evidence of market inefficiency. *Journal of Portfolio Management* 11:9–17.

Rozeff, M. S. 1987. Insider trading: What we know and what we don't know. In *The Effects of Organizational Transformation.* New York: Quorum Books.

Rozeff, M., and M. Zaman. 1988. Market efficiency and insider trading: New Evidence. *Journal of Business* 61:25–44.

Ryngaert, M., and J. Netter. 1988. Shareholder wealth effects of the Ohio antitakeover law. *Journal of Law, Economics and Organizations* 6:253–62.

Sanders, R. W., and J. S. Zhanowicz. 1992. Target firm abnormal returns and trading volume around the initiation of change-in-control transactions. *Journal of Financial and Quantitative Analysis* 27:109–29.

Scott, K. E. 1980. Insider trading, rule 10b-5, disclosure and corporate privacy. *Journal of Legal Studies* 9:801–18.

Seyhun, H. N. 1986. Insiders' profits, costs of trading, and market efficiency. *Journal of Financial Economics* 16:189–212.

Seyhun, H. N. 1988a. The January effect and aggregate insider trading. *Journal of Finance* 43:129–41.

Seyhun, H. N. 1988b. The information content of aggregate insider trading. *Journal of Business* 61:1–24.

Seyhun, H. N. 1990a. Do bidder managers knowingly pay too much for target firms? *Journal of Business* 63:439–64.

Seyhun, H. N. 1990b. Overreaction or fundamentals: Some lessons from insiders' responses to the market crash of 1987. *Journal of Finance* 45:1363–88.

Seyhun, H. N. 1992a. The effectiveness of the insider trading sanctions. *Journal of Law and Economics* 35:149–82.

Seyhun, H. N. 1992b. Why does aggregate insider trading predict future stock returns. *Quarterly Journal of Economics* 107:1303–31.

Seyhun, H. N., and M. Bradley. 1997. Corporate bankruptcy and insider trading. *Journal of Business* 70:189–216.

Schwert, W. 1990. Stock volatility and the crash of '87. *Review of Financial Studies* 3:77–102.

Schwert, W. 1996. Mark-up pricing in mergers and acquisitions. *Journal of Financial Economics* 41:153–92.

Shalen, C. 1993. Volume, volatility, and dispersion of beliefs. *Review of Financial Studies* 6:405–34.

Shiller, R. J. 1989. Comovements in stock prices and comovements in dividends. *Journal of Finance* 44:719–29.

Shiller, R. 1981. "Do Stock Prices Move Too Much to be Justified by Subsequent Changes in Dividends?" *American Economic Review* 71:421–36.

Shleifer, A., and L. Summers. 1988. Breach of trust in hostile takeovers. In *Corporate Takeovers: Causes and Consequences*, A. Auerbach, ed. Chicago: University of Chicago Press, pp. 33–56.

Shleifer, A., and R. Vishny. 1986. Large shareholders and corporate control. *Journal of Political Economy* 94:461–88.

Silver, C. B. 1985. Penalizing insider trading: A critical assessment of the insider trading sanctions act of 1984. *Duke Law Journal* 1985:960–1025.

Simon, C. 1989. The effect of the 1933 securities markets. *Journal of Business* 37:117–42.

Smiley, R. 1981. The effects of state securities statutes on tender offer activity. *Economic Inquiry* 19:426–35.

Sobel, R. 1965. *The Big Board: A History of the New York Stock Exchange*. New York: Free Press.

Stattman, D. 1980. Book values and stock returns. *Chicago MBA: A Journal of Selected Papers* 4:25–45.

Stewart, J. 1991. *Den of Thieves*. New York: Simon and Schuster.

Summers, L. H. 1986. Does the Stock Market Rationally Reflect Fundamental Values? *Journal of Finance* 41:591–600.

Travlos, N. G. 1987. Corporate takeover bids, methods of payment, and bidding firms' stock returns. *Journal of Finance* 42:943–63.

Trivoli, G. W. 1980. How to profit from insider trading information. *Journal of Portfolio Management* 6:51–56.

Vila, J. L. 1989. Simple games of market manipulation. *Economic Letters* 29:21–26.

Wang, J. 1993. A model of intertemporal asset prices under asymmetric information. *Review of Economic Studies* 60:249–82.

Wansley, J. W., W. R. Lane, and H. C. Yang. 1987. Gains to bidder firms in cash and securities transactions. *Financial Review* 22:403–14.

Weinberger, A. M. 1990. Preventing insider trading violations: A survey of corporate compliance programs. *Securities Regulation Law Journal* 18:180–93.

Wier, P. 1983. The costs of antimerger lawsuits: Evidence from the stock market. *Journal of Financial Economics* 11:207–24.

Winans, R. F. 1986. *Trading Secrets*. New York: St. Martin's Press.

Wycoff, R. D. 1968. *Wall Street Ventures and Adventures*. New York: Greenwood.

Index

Insider trading (cont.)
information efficiency and, 29
intensity, 11–12, 33
intensive, dividend yields and, 164–66
investment styles and, xxiii–xxv
large, 204–206 (*see also* Large transactions, by top executives)
learning from, xxxiii–xxxvii
long-term winner-loser status and, 310–15
measuring, 3–4, 248–49
3-month-ahead stock returns, dividend yields and, 160–63
normal patterns, 14–17
past-future correlations, 22, 33–34
patterns, 1–2
pre-announcement, 278
predictive ability, 206, 145–46
prior to dividend initiations, 189–90
relative B/M ratios and, 253–58
seasonal patterns, 17–18
short-term winner-loser status and, 301–304
signals (*see* Signals)
in target firms, 271–76
time series properties of, 20
transactions. *See* Transactions
volume, profitability and, 74–80
Insider Trading and Securities Fraud Enforcement Act of 1988 (ITSFEA), 26, 27, 274
Insider trading predictive power, absolute P/E ratio and, 221–22
Insider Trading Sanctions Act of 1984 (ITSA), 26, 27, 273–74
Intensity of trading, 52–53
Interest rates, short-term, 110
Investors
inside (*see* Insiders)
insider-trading regulations and, 31
outside (*see* Outsiders)

recommendations for, 339–40
regulations and, 34
risk-averse, 332–33
ITSA (Insider Trading Sanctions Act of 1984), 26, 27, 273–74
ITSFEA (Insider Trading and Securities Fraud Enforcement Act of 1988), 26, 27, 274

January effect, 33

Large transactions, by top executives, 204–206, 208
in bidder firms, 288–89, 292, 304, 306–308
dividend initiation and, 188–89
long-term horizon predictability and, 314–15
outsider profitability and, 329
reporting, 319–20
Legal issues. *See* Regulations; *specific laws*
Liability, for insider-trading, 26–27
Liquidity, 19, 30–31
Long-term horizon predictability, of corporate takeovers, 308–15
Loss probability. *See* Risk

Macroeconomic developments, signals and, 110
Managers, dividends and, 176
Market dividend yield. *See* Dividend yield
Market performance, total *vs.* relative, 41–43
Market returns
distribution following insider trading, 43–44
following aggregate insider trading signals, 119, 126–28, 135
future, 118–24, 158

future net stock, absolute P/E ratios
and, 223–24
future raw stock, 218–20, 249
year-by-year, 43–45
Market timing
absolute P/E ratio, insider trading
and, 236
aggregate insider trading-based, 128–
31
defined, 108
strategies, 107–109
Mean reversion
defined, 294
of stock prices over long horizon,
308–14
Mergers, 261
Misappropriation theory, 29
Mispricing of stock
large transactions by top executives in
bidder firms and, 307–308
vs. risk, 212–13, 240–41
Momentum, 21–22
Momentum investing, 293–94
Mutual fund investors, 107–108
active, 108
aggregate inside trading and, 124–25
choices, 108
passive, 108

NASDAQ, 5
Net stock returns
absolute book-to-market ratio and,
247–48
after option exercises, 102–103
dividend yields and, 170–72
preceeding insider sales, 55
profitability and, 77
for purchases, 47–48
relative, 60–61
for sales, 47–48
New York Stock Exchange, 5

Officers
defined, 70
firm size, profitability and, 93
information possessed by, 68–69, 72
profitability of transactions, 71, 83–
84, 93
volume of trading and, 83–84
On-line reporting services, xx
Option exercises, 100–103
timing, 102, 105
types, 101
Outsiders
active insider trading and, 58
imitating insider trading in large
firms, 95
insider trading in small firms and, 92
profit determinants, 325–31
profits, 217–318
replication of most profitable trading,
97–98
reporting delays and, 318–20
signal of quality of insider information, 78
trading costs for, 36

Passive trading
defined, 40, 50
elimination, 64
firm size and, 91
future stock prices and, 51
future stock returns and, 51–52
mutual fund investors and, 108
profitability, 54–58
purchases, 55
for risk-aversion, 53
strategies, 64
by top executives, 53–54
Payment date, in dividend initiation
process, 179
Payment forms, for corporate takeovers, 287–88